Pitfalls of Trained Incapacity

American Society of Missiology Monograph Series

Series Editor, James R. Krabill

The ASM Monograph Series provides a forum for publishing quality dissertations and studies in the field of missiology. Collaborating with Pickwick Publications—a division of Wipf and Stock Publishers of Eugene, Oregon—the American Society of Missiology selects high quality dissertations and other monographic studies that offer research materials in mission studies for scholars, mission and church leaders, and the academic community at large. The ASM seeks scholarly work for publication in the series that throws light on issues confronting Christian world mission in its cultural, social, historical, biblical, and theological dimensions.

Missiology is an academic field that brings together scholars whose professional training ranges from doctoral-level preparation in areas such as Scripture, history and sociology of religions, anthropology, theology, international relations, interreligious interchange, mission history, inculturation, and church law. The American Society of Missiology, which sponsors this series, is an ecumenical body drawing members from Independent and Ecumenical Protestant, Catholic, Orthodox, and other traditions. Members of the ASM are united by their commitment to reflect on and do scholarly work relating to both mission history and the present-day mission of the church. The ASM Monograph Series aims to publish works of exceptional merit on specialized topics, with particular attention given to work by younger scholars, the dissemination and publication of which is difficult under the economic pressures of standard publishing models.

Persons seeking information about the ASM or the guidelines for having their dissertations considered for publication in the ASM Monograph Series should consult the Society's website—www.asmweb.org.

Members of the ASM Monograph Committe who approved this book are:

Paul V. Kollman, University of Notre Dame
Roger Schroeder, Catholic Theological Union
Bonnie Sue Lewis, University of Dubuque Theological Seminary

RECENTLY PUBLISHED IN THE ASM MONOGRAPH SERIES

J. Scott Bridger, *Christian Exegesis of the Qur'an: A Critical Analysis of the Apologetic Use of the Qur'an in Select Medieval and Contemporary Arabic Texts*

Byungohk Lee, *Listening to the Neighbor: From A Missional Perspective of the Other*

Keon-Sang An, *An Ethiopian Reading of the Bible: Biblical Interpretation of the Ethiopian Orthodox Tewahido Church*

Pitfalls of Trained Incapacity
The Unintended Effects of Integral Missionary Training in the Basel Mission on Its Early Work in Ghana (1828–1840)

BIRGIT HERPPICH

Foreword by Wilbert R. Shenk

American Society of Missiology Monograph Series vol. 26

☙PICKWICK *Publications* · Eugene, Oregon

PITFALLS OF TRAINED INCAPACITY
The Unintended Effects of Integral Missionary Training in the Basel Mission on Its Early Work in Ghana (1828–1840)

Copyright © 2016 Birgit Herppich. All rights reserved. Except for brief quotations in critical publications or reviews, no part of this book may be reproduced in any manner without prior written permission from the publisher. Write: Permissions, Wipf and Stock Publishers, 199 W. 8th Ave., Suite 3, Eugene, OR 97401.

Pickwick Publications
An Imprint of Wipf and Stock Publishers
199 W. 8th Ave., Suite 3
Eugene, OR 97401

www.wipfandstock.com

PAPERBACK ISBN 13: 978-1-4982-2952-4
HARDCOVER ISBN 13: 978-1-4982-2954-8

Cataloguing-in-Publication Data

Herppich, Birgit

Pitfalls of trained incapacity : the unintended effects of integral missionary training in the Basel Mission on its early work in Ghana (1828–1840) / Birgit Herppich.

xii + 372 p. ; 23 cm. Includes bibliographical references.

ISBN 13: 978-1-4982-2952-4

1. Missionaries, Training of. 2. Evangelische Missionsgesellschaft in Basel History 19th century. 3. Missions Ghana History 19th century. I. Title. II. Series.

BV2063 H43 2016

Manufactured in the U.S.A.   01/14/2016

This book is dedicated to Käte and Erich
who first believed in me and brought me up to "stand my (wo)man."
I wish you had lived to see this completed.

Contents

Tables and Figures | viii
Foreword by Wilbert R. Shenk | ix
Acknowledgments | xi
List of Abbreviations | xii

Introduction: Integral Missionary Training and the Basel Mission | 1

Part I: The Community of Practice of the Basel Mission Training Institute

1   A Learning Community Shaped by German Pietism | 31

2   A Shared Vision of Christian Foreign Mission | 69

3   Diverse Participants with a Shared Practice | 117

Part II: Indications for Trained Incapacity in the Beginnings of the Basel Mission in Ghana

4   The African Context and the Early Basel Mission (1828–1831) | 185

5   Andreas Riis's Pioneering (1832–1840) | 235

6   Early Failures at Mission Work (1836–1840) | 293

Conclusion: Pitfalls of Trained Incapacity in Integral Missionary Training | 336

Bibliography | 351

Tables and Figures

Table 1: Geographical Origin of BMTI Students until 1881
Table 2: Geographical Origin of Basel Missionaries in Ghana 1828–1854
Table 3: Vocations of BMTI Applicants until 1881
Table 4: Vocations of Basel Missionaries in Ghana 1828–1854

Figure 1: "Mission House in Basel" Leonhardsgraben
Figure 2: Room Plan of the Mission House Leonhardsgraben
Figure 3: The First Three Directors of the Basel Mission: Blumhardt, Hoffmann, Josenhans
Figure 4: "The First Gold Coast Missionaries" of the Basel Mission
Figure 5: Andreas Riis in 1831
Figure 6: Illustrating Replication: The Mission House in Basel and the "Secondary School Akropong"

Foreword

THE FIELD OF INTERCULTURAL studies remains a fertile and inexhaustible source of insight. The vast archives of trading companies, colonial governments, and voluntary agencies, including missionary societies, in Europe, the British Isles, and North America provide the enterprising scholar with a wealth of material to pursue fresh lines of research. This study based on the experience of the Basel Mission throws light on several important dimensions of early European efforts to engage with an African culture effectively.

Using the sociological concept of *trained incapacity*, Dr. Birgit Herppich examines how the training missionary candidates received in the early 1800s interfaced with Ghanaian culture. The study is limited to the first contingent of missionaries sent to Ghana by the Basel Mission during the years 1828–1840.

In 1800 the academic study of sociology, anthropology, linguistics, and the religions had not yet been established. Oxford and Cambridge only admitted students from the Anglican Church. The initiatives of the British Methodists in 1786 and Baptists in 1792 set the course for the modern mission movement. It was Evangelical Anglicans and Nonconformists in Great Britain and Pietists on the Continent who furnished the people and financial support for this initiative. The typical missionary candidate had only a rudimentary education. Mission societies recognized that candidates needed basic preparation for service in foreign lands. For this purpose missionary training schools were set up. The curriculum was decidedly practical. No courses were offered in culture, language study, or theology of mission. Medical science was still rudimentary and missionary candidates were encouraged to acquire basic training in treating various common illnesses. There was no known cure for malaria and other tropical diseases. The mortality rate among missionaries was appallingly high. Effective treatment of these dread diseases lay decades in the future.

The Basel Mission, founded in 1815, became the leading Pietist-sponsored missionary agency in German-speaking Europe. Initially, it saw its role to be the training of people for missionary service. For this purpose it set up the Basel Mission Training Institute. BMTI graduates served with the Anglican Church Missionary Society and various European societies. For several decades the Basel Mission and the Church Missionary Society had a formal agreement whereby CMS accepted BMTI-trained workers for appointment to their missions in Africa and Asia. Early in the 1820s the Basel Mission began establishing missions and sending missionaries.

The BMTI curriculum was shaped by the values promoted by the Pietist movement: emphasis on cultivating personal piety, conservative personal ethics, and a defensive posture toward the world. Missionary candidates who completed the BMTI course were shaped by the Basel Mission ethos. Graduates were not trained to think in terms of missionary adaptation to the host culture. Indeed, the Euro-American attitude in the early nineteenth century toward other cultures was to regard them as inferior. The author shows that this training regime resulted in missionary practices that erected barriers between the Ghanaians and the missionaries. While a few missionaries succeeded in surmounting these obstacles, most did not.

With all the resources available to us in the twenty-first century—linguistic tools, cultural studies, a global world system—one would like to believe we have progressed in our capacity for respectful and effective intercultural communication and collaboration. But the evidence compels caution. Every generation is faced with the challenge of learning how to engage appropriately and respectfully with people of other cultures. Our cultures remain biased toward "trained incapacity."

Wilbert R. Shenk
Senior Professor of Mission History
Fuller Graduate School of Intercultural Studies
Pasadena, California

Acknowledgments

RESEARCH ALWAYS IS A journey. The report reflects only a fraction of what the researcher explored, considered, and contemplated along the way. There were many helpful companions, guides, and faithful supporters that made this journey possible. Their names are too many to all be mentioned here, but a few need special recognition.

During the doctoral research at Fuller School of Intercultural Studies that enabled this project my mentors became friends as well as academic guides. Thanks go to Dr. Elizabeth "Betsy" Glanville for starting me off on this journey and being my cheerleader to the end; to Dr. Jehu J. Hanciles, now at Emory University, for guidance and challenges to grow as a scholar; to Dr. Wilbert R. Shenk for encouragement, support, and leading me across the finishing line; to Drs. Judy and Sherwood Lingenfelter for good times, timely advice, and hospitality beyond the proverbial second mile. I also greatly appreciate the staff at the Basel Mission Archive of *mission 21* who granted every access and assistance a researcher could wish for.

The academic work would have been impossible without a host of supportive friends. I so appreciate all the encouragement, hospitality, and generosity from my friends at HOPE Christian Fellowship, fellow students at Fuller, colleagues in WEC International, and friends in Germany and around the world. I am so grateful to you for keeping me grounded, believing with me through the journey to its completion, and for your practical support and faithful prayers. Finally, above all, praise and thanks belong to God. Only by His enabling grace this project was possible. My prayer is that it will glorify Him and contribute to the expansion of His purposes in the world.

Abbreviations

BMA	Basel Mission Archive; in references followed by the signature of the cited document
BMTI	Basel Missionary Training Institute (in the documents often *Missions-Schule*, i.e., Mission-School)
BV	*Brüderverzeichnis* (Brothers Register), the register of missionary applicants of the BMTI
CMS	Church Missionary Society
HB	*Heidenbote* (Heathen Messenger), a popular publication of the Basel Mission
JB	*Jahresbericht* (Annual Report of the Basel Mission)
KP	*Komittee-Protokoll* (Minutes of the governing Board—*Committee*—of the Basel Mission)
LMS	London Missionary Society
MM	*Missions-Magazin* (Basel Mission journal published from 1816, in 1853 renamed *Evangelisches Missions-Magazin*, EMM)
NMG	*Norddeutsche Missions-Gesellschaft* (North German Mission)
PF	Personnel File (of individual Basel missionaries)
SPCK	Society for the Propagation of Christian Knowledge

Introduction

Integral Missionary Training and the Basel Mission

MY INTEREST IN THE preparation of missionaries for intercultural work originates in my own experience of the challenges of cross-cultural ministry and appreciation for the missiological training I had received prior to working in Ghana. As a trained teacher my interest was initially in educational questions, particularly in how to improve curriculum and teaching methods to prepare men and women more effectively for cross-cultural engagement. Experiential educational approaches like the concept of *Communities of Practice* stood out for their engagement of the whole person in the learning process and their effectiveness in facilitating learning. However, the analysis of such integral training in the Basel Mission from sociological perspectives revealed a more foundational issue that impacts all kinds of missionary preparation, regardless of curriculum or educational methodology.

Research that explores effectiveness of training is often based on self-assessment by the educators or directors of programs.[1] However, the true outcomes of preparation for foreign missions are revealed in the cross-cultural context and in long-term results of intercultural engagement. Moreover, persons not directly involved in the organization are more likely to present a balanced evaluation. While I am as a German who worked in Ghana for eight years quite familiar with the general context in Germany as well as in Ghana, I have no direct involvement with the Basel Mission, its successor organization *mission 21*, or the church

---

1. For example, Whiteman's survey asked leaders to rate their missionary preparation with the result that all reported their programs as effective or highly effective, and the assessments of training schools in Brynjolfson and Lewis's volume are invariably presented by the program leaders. See Brynjolfson and Lewis, *Integral Ministry Training*; Whiteman, "Integral Training."

that resulted from their work in Ghana. Thus, I offer my evaluation as a relative outsider to the study objects.

Furthermore, evidence for the proposed links between preparation processes and intercultural praxis is best produced by the in-depth analysis of specific contexts and organizations which case studies permit. They allow for identification of particular influences that shaped an educational approach and how these in turn are reflected in intercultural ministry. However, thoroughly assessing a contemporary context would necessitate extensive observation and long term qualitative research which require considerable resources. By contrast, a historical study is more accessible and enables the necessary depth and critical analysis because the perceptions and actions of the missionaries can be elicited from the sources, long-term outcomes can be traced, and possible organizational interests are less likely to interfere directly with the findings. Historical study reveals how peoples' thinking and emphases, what they regard as important, and the value judgments they make are shaped by their individual and corporate past. On the other hand, history allows inferences of the effects of human attitudes, decisions, and actions on events and other people in the immediate context and in the long run. For these reasons I focused on a historical case study in which the long-term outcomes of training and characteristics of cross-cultural engagement are readily available. However, the methodological approach had to consider the likely biases, problems of accessibility, and limitations of historical sources.

The Basel Mission suggested itself for a number of reasons. My German background enables me to read with comparative ease the old German script of the primary sources and contributes to my interest in this society. I was also highly attracted by learning more about their earliest ministry in Ghana—one of the first in the country by European missionaries—because of my own experience in this country which today is over 70 percent Christian.[2]

More importantly, the Basel Mission was the most significant German mission in the nineteenth century having far reaching influence across central Europe and beyond through its extended networks of

---

2. The 2010 Ghana census showed "that 71.2 percent of the population profess the Christian faith, followed by Islam (17.6 percent). Only a small proportion of the population either adhere to traditional religion (5.2 percent) or are not affiliated to any religion (5.3 percent)." See Ghana Statistical Service, "2010 Population and Housing Census Summary," 6.

communication, collaboration, and publication. The Basel Missionary Training Institute (BMTI) was the first of its kind and British mission societies developed their institutions looking to it as a model.

With the founding of agencies for the purpose of advancing Christian mission in non-European lands at the end of the eighteenth century, Protestant leaders felt for the first time the need for specialized preparation of missionaries. Early ideas on missionary training had been advanced by David Bogue (1750–1825) of the London Missionary Society (LMS) from 1795 onwards.[3] The Lutheran Pastor Johannes Jänicke (1748–1827) led a small seminary in Berlin from 1800 to 1827 which provided the first missionaries for the British London and Church Missionary Societies.[4] But it was the Basel Mission that developed a systematic approach to the training of Christian foreign missionaries. The BMTI was declared by its founders as German contribution to the foreign missionary movement already under way elsewhere in Europe. It was established in 1815 and the first course commenced in August 1816.

The Basel Mission was the first and largest continental mission and became the main motivator and channel of German missionary passion in the nineteenth century. It was enormously influential beyond German-speaking Europe through the numerous German missionaries it supplied for other societies, foremost the Church Missionary Society (CMS). Moreover, Walls and Piggin point out that the BMTI provided the model for the training institutes those societies established later on.[5]

In spite of this significance, very few studies exist on the Basel Mission, or German missions in general, especially in Anglophone scholarship—a neglected area of study.[6] No previous study focuses explicitly on

3. Bogue's educational ideas and practice is described by Terpstra, "David Bogue." Terpstra's dissertation is the most comprehensive study on this important mission thinker and educator.

4. Information on Jänicke's school is sparse. The most detailed account is provided by Schick, *Vorboten und Bahnbrecher*.

5. Andrew Walls highlights the fact that German Pietist circles both provided the first missionaries for the Protestant missionary societies and developed seminaries and systems for training of missionaries in Walls, "Missionary Vocation." The point that British training institutes reflect the BMTI is made in the detailed analysis of approaches to training missionaries by British societies by Piggin, *Making Evangelical Missionaries*.

6. If German missions are considered at all, the focus is typically on the earlier efforts of the Danish-Halle mission in India and the Moravian missions. The significant engagement of other European missionaries in the nineteenth century is generally overlooked in Anglophone preoccupation with British and American ventures.

the impact of the Basel missionary preparation processes on intercultural engagement. The analysis of the influences and emphases of the BMTI presented here therefore furthers understanding of the development and impact of foreign missionary training in the nineteenth century, as well as appreciation of the contribution of BMTI trained missionaries to the work of dominant Anglophone organizations.

Beyond its historical significance, this study contributes to a more profound assessment of the breadth of influences which impact on the preparatory processes of missionaries and in turn on their engagement in an environment vastly different from their own cultural and religious background. The findings expose aspects of missionary preparation which can result in many of the maladjustments and difficulties missionaries face in cross-cultural contexts. The historical case of the Basel Mission reveals among other things the common presumption of universality of Christian values and practices which are, in fact, culturally and locally determined and their imposition on the people being served. Hence, it identifies causes which are not usually paid attention to for the frequent struggles and lack of contextual adjustment in cross-cultural Christian mission.

THESIS AND KEY CONCEPTS

This study examines the ways in which context of origin and deliberate preparation processes correlate with the engagement of missionaries in a cross-cultural environment. Specifically, it investigates how the cultural, socio-economic, and religious background and the intentional preparatory processes of Basel Missionaries affected their work in Ghana (former Gold Coast)[7] in the beginning years (1828–1840).

Using the educational concept of *Communities of Practice* and the sociological notion of *trained incapacity* as conceptual tools to explicate missionary training and engagement, I advance the thesis that the Basel Missionary Training Institute constituted a "community of practice" which produced various levels of "trained incapacity" in the missionaries it sent to foreign lands. This poses a crucial influence of the background

---

7. The modern nation of Ghana is not identical with Danish Guinea or the later British Colony Gold Coast. The areas of the Basel Mission work were in the South of today's Ghana, in the regions of former Danish Guinea which in 1850 became part of the British Gold Coast. For this reason I use these names interchangeably in this study, except where the identification of the Danish or British claimed area is relevant to the argument.

and context of missionaries and their constituencies on the goals and designs of deliberate preparation processes affecting missionary attitudes and practices. Especially when groups engaging in cross-cultural Christian ministry are essentially homogeneous in terms of their religious and socio-ethical emphases (like the Basel Mission and its participants) their training processes have a strong propensity to establish inflexible mental frameworks of theological assumptions and social ideals that are potentially detrimental to intercultural engagement; thus illustrating *trained incapacity*.

Speaking of training or preparation processes indicates the wide range of factors that influence people. Participants of any educational effort are shaped by dynamics of informal socialization before and during formally designed training. The term *hidden curriculum* was coined by Philip Jackson to highlight the influence of latent values and assumptions built into the social expectations and procedures of the school environment which are at least as powerful, if not more so, as the stated curriculum pursued in the classroom.[8] Preparatory processes include the whole range of educational means which are employed intentionally and implicitly by an organization, the criteria and procedures for selection of candidates and the goals, content, teaching methods, and general design of the training provided for missionaries. However, the accumulative effect of previous experience and intentional intervention together determines the attitudes, ideas, values, and practical approaches people take to new situations. Therefore, it is paramount to include the various influences on missionaries beyond formal education in assessing their preparation for ministry in a foreign environment. Consequently, this study offers a thorough investigation of the historical context and life experience of the missionary candidates as well as the intentional preparation provided by their organization.

Both theoretical frameworks enable such a comprehensive analysis of preparatory processes because of their sociological definitions of "proficiency" in a *community of practice* and "training" in *trained incapacity*.

Communities of Practice

According to Etienne Wenger "Communities of practice are formed by people who engage in a process of collective learning in a shared domain of human endeavor," they are "groups of people who share a concern or

---

8. Jackson, *Life in Classrooms*.

a passion for something they do and learn how to do it better as they interact regularly."⁹ *Communities of practice* have three crucial characteristics: (1) Members are committed to a *shared domain of interest*, they have common goals, visions, or problems, (2) *the community* in which members interact and learn together, and (3) *the practice*—members "develop a shared repertoire of resources to improve what they do: experiences, stories, tools, ways of addressing recurring problems—in short a shared practice." Only all three elements working together constitute a *community of practice*. For example, teachers may share the common interest to ensure that their students learn better. When a group of teachers regularly share their experience and learn from each other how to improve a particular approach to help their students learn, it becomes a *community of practice*.

This theoretical framework was first articulated by Jean Lave and Etienne Wenger in 1991. They pose that learning does not just take place in specifically designed experiential contexts but social participation itself is a learning process. Learning is "a process of participation in communities of practice, participation that is at first legitimately peripheral but that increases gradually in engagement and complexity."¹⁰ Traditional apprenticeships were a chief illustration for this "situated learning" which stressed "the process by which newcomers become part of a community of practice." "Legitimacy" described the ways of belonging to the community and the idea of "peripherality" the location in the community as newcomers move towards full participation.¹¹ A novice enters at the periphery and moves towards the center which represents proficiency in the practice of the community. However, the authors emphasized that they were not promoting apprenticeships per se but a new theory of learning which identifies it as a social process in contrast to the mere acquisition of impersonal knowledge.

Wenger developed the concept further and—in part in response to critique on the earlier book—revised the idea of "legitimate peripheral participation" so far that he has all but dropped the term in favor of "a process of negotiation between reification and interaction." By this he means that tangible and non-tangible representations of the practice of a community are constantly revised in the interaction processes of the

---

9. Wenger, "Introduction."
10. Lave and Wenger, *Situated Learning*, 7.
11. Ibid., 34–35.

community.¹² However, a "common ground" of basic knowledge and skills that are taken for granted as basis for the interactions of a group is still regarded as necessary and does create varying levels of participation. Together with other factors like motivation to be involved, Wenger, Dermott and Snyder identify three levels of participation, the core group, the active group and those on the periphery.¹³ Wenger and others apply these concepts to organizational and knowledge development in contemporary Western contexts which in part explains the emphasis on a more egalitarian understanding of the participants in communities of practice.

This experiential theory of learning highlights the situational context and the social character of learning and emphasizes the importance of patterns of joint activities. It provides critical insights into the Basel Mission's preparatory processes. The leaders articulated intentions for the BMTI that indicate a perception of social participation as a learning process and they intentionally employed community life and patterns of joint activities to foster a particular practice. Finally, a common vision (*domain of interest*) of foreign Christian mission motivated and guided all participants in the enterprise. Therefore *community of practice* provides a fitting analytical framework for explicating the dynamics and influences at the BMTI.

Trained Incapacity

The term *trained incapacity* was coined in sociological studies to indicate a situation in which education, training, and experience establish mental frameworks and practices so thoroughly in people that they are unable to adjust appropriately to changed circumstances. Thorstein Veblen (1857–1929) first used the term in 1914 to describe the proclivity of businessmen and workers to evaluate their actions solely from the perspective of pecuniary gain. He posed that this proclivity originated in the experience and education of the business world of his time and saw this as particularly problematic in the case of businessmen who hold power to affect their workers, organizations, and society at large. The tendency—induced by training and experience—to measure actions only by the money that can be made leads to incapacity to see the negative social outcomes and wider repercussions of business behavior. Veblen continued to explore how the perception of success purely in pecuniary

---

12. Wenger, *Communities of Practice*, 51–71.
13. Wenger et al., *Managing Knowledge*, 55–58.

parameters leads to seeing those as successful in society who deceive many people into paying them more than their services and goods are worth, thereby taking advantage of society.[14]

In 1935, Kenneth Burke (1897–1993) in his deliberations on "Permanence and Change" contemplated how Veblen's concept of *trained incapacity* and John Dewey's *occupational psychosis* can help to identify mental patterns that may have become obsolete.[15] Burke used the concepts to propose the need for changed thinking and possibly very different approaches to life during the Great Depression. He claimed that attitudes, behaviors and ways of thinking that people have been trained in by previous experience and education, and that served them well in the past, may lead to serious maladjustments under the new and changed conditions and cause actions which ultimately are detrimental to people's wellbeing and survival.

Over a decade later Robert Merton (1910–2003) used Burke's discussion and defined *trained incapacity* as

> that state of affairs in which one's abilities function as inadequacies or blind spots. Actions based upon training and skills that have been successfully applied in the past may result in inappropriate responses *under changed conditions*. An inadequate flexibility in the application of skills, will, in a changing milieu, result in more or less serious maladjustments.[16]

Applying the concept to the "Dysfunctions of Bureaucracy," Merton sketches the importance of discipline in highly streamlined processes that demand exactness and consistency in the application of rules and regulations. People working in this context are trained to follow processes with rigidity, so much so that it can lead to *trained incapacity*, the inability to flexibly adjust to changed conditions and different circumstances. Discipline becomes so engrained that exact application of regulations becomes a goal in itself to be "followed to the letter" thereby creating what is

---

14. Veblen, *Instinct of Workmanship*, 343–50; Wais, "Trained Incapacity." Wais refutes the claim that the phrase does not appear in the works of Thorstein Veblen and provides a helpful discussion of Veblen's original use of the term and Kenneth Burke's adaptation and expansion of its meaning.

15. Dewey, "Understanding the Savage Mind." Burke, *Permanence and Change*, 7–11, 38–47. Interestingly, Dewey proposed the notion of *occupational psychosis* to "understand the savage mind" as a more positive and comprehensive framework to understand the workings of non-western cultures.

16. Merton, *Social Theory*, 197–200. Emphasis in original.

experienced as "red tape" which has the potential to defeat the purposes of the organization the bureaucratic apparatus was set up to serve. Thus, *trained incapacity* describes a condition where training, education, and experience produce mental predispositions, attitudes, values, and behaviors in people in such a way that their capacities become potential impediments; they lack flexibility to adjust attitudes and actions under changed conditions or in different circumstances.

In this book I posit that the preparatory processes of the Basel Mission shaped the missionary agents in such a way that their intercultural engagement illustrates trained incapacity, i.e., an "inadequate flexibility" in the application of learned judgments and practices which resulted in the vastly different circumstances "in more or less serious maladjustments." While both theoretical constructs I employ were articulated in the twentieth century, they describe educational and sociological dynamics which are timeless aspects of the human experience. Therefore, their application to the Basel Mission is not anachronistic but sheds light on this particular historical experience from new angles. In this way *trained incapacity* provides an explanatory framework for the struggles, difficulties, and tensions encountered by Basel missionaries in the cross-cultural context of Ghana.

In order to assess the character of the Basel Mission as an essentially homogeneous *community of practice* I investigated the ways in which the general historical context and the social, economic, religious and intellectual background of the Basel Mission leaders, supporters, and missionaries shaped their motivations and approaches towards cross-cultural mission and Africa. Furthermore, I examined the extent to which the deliberate preparatory processes of the BMTI reflected the theological convictions and practical emphases of its participants and shaped the missionaries' attitudes and approaches. The findings show that the BMTI closely reflected and functioned largely to deepen the German cultural and Pietist religious values, practices and emphases of the participants' background.

Trained incapacity of Basel missionaries in the intercultural encounter with the African context is assessed through an investigation of the attitudes, practices, and experience of the Basel missionaries in Ghana. I understand intercultural capacity or effective intercultural engagement in Christian mission as the ability to adjust to life, build relationships, and communicate the gospel of Jesus Christ meaningfully with people of another culture in order to initiate and foster the development of culturally relevant and missionally engaged communities of indigenous believers. While such communities are ultimately dependent on indigenous agency and appropriation of the Christian message, cross-cultural missionaries play an important initial catalyzing role that can foster or hinder their development. Thus, the assessment of prevalent characteristics of the initial Basel Mission engagement in Guinea was guided by three criteria: adjustment to the cross-cultural situation, the mission's declared objectives, and African responses. The study shows that BMTI training established religious convictions and practical emphases which were applied inflexibly in the intercultural encounter. This impeded adjustment to different contexts, the realization of organizational goals, and the emergence of an African appropriation of Christianity, and constituted a major factor in the mission's initial failure.

The examination of Basel missionaries' intercultural engagement is confined to the first twelve years of their work in Ghana (1828–1840). This earlier period represents the organization's initial engagement and sets the precedence for their basic approaches to ministry in Africa. However, there was little success towards organizational goals which raises the question of causes of such failure that this study addresses. Because of this failure most scholars brush over the first years of the mission. But while there is ample evidence for the trained incapacity proposed here in the later years—as the brief analysis of the replication model shows that became fairly standard in nineteenth century Protestant missions in Africa—direct correlations between preparation processes and intercultural engagement are clearer in the pre-colonial period.

I am conscious that this delimitation affords only a limited sample, but not only does it offer a detailed analysis of a period that is typically neglected in accounts of the Basel Mission in Ghana, it enables an evaluation of the missionaries' cross-cultural ministry, their actions and experience in Africa before European governments—and in the case of the Basel Mission organizational intervention—interfered with policies and practices in Ghana. From the 1840s colonial governments sponsored missionary "civilization" work in Africa. In Ghana, the last Danish governor envisioned the Basel Mission in this vein.[17] In 1850 Britain became the sole colonial power in the area where Basel missionaries worked and enforced stronger colonial control. Furthermore, within the organization,

---

17. Carstensen letter October 20, 1843; "Remarks concerning the Danish-Guinean possessions" June 30, 1844 and letter July 25, 1844 in Carstensen, *Closing the Books*, 58–60, 78, 84.

from 1844 detailed rules for the relationships of missionaries to the Basel leadership were introduced and from 1850 the new Director Joseph Josenhans (1812–1884) began to implement ideas of stricter organization of the mission fields which obscure the dynamics this study analyses.[18]

PIETISM AND THE BASEL MISSION

The roots of the Basel Mission in German Pietism are undeniable. I present a brief analysis of the missional impetus of common characteristics of this movement across its various streams and their presence in the Basel Mission. However, I do not engage the discussions on the definition and scope of German Pietism, nor the copious analyses of variations of the movement that typically focus on the late seventeenth and eighteenth century and tend to sideline the ongoing importance of German Pietism, especially in missionary engagement outside Europe.[19]

The chronological and geographical scope of what constitutes "Pietism" has been hotly discussed in recent decades.[20] Strom and Lehmann provide helpful summaries and represent scholarship that emphasizes the heterogeneity and international significance of Pietist movements.[21] Both identify the activism of German Pietists in the global expansion of Protestantism as needing further research.[22] Lehmann poses "the historical phenomenon we call Pietism" should be studied as "part of a series of religious revivals in Central Europe, which were, from the seventeenth century to the nineteenth century and beyond, part of a series of religious revivals in many European countries and in the Atlantic world." He repeatedly advocated for sociological-political investigations and a wider definition of Pietism than the typical church histories' limitation to

---

18. Schlatter, *Heimatgeschichte*, 228–45. Schlatter commends Josenhans's new regulations as "a system of consequently exercised typical German order" and cites at length the newly introduced rules.

19. Strom provides a good summary of the issues related to Pietism studies and Lehmann an overview of how definitions changed in the past century: Lehmann, "Pietism"; Strom, "Problems and Promises." However, the still prevalent foci are clear in the majority of articles in the representative yearbook Brecht and others, *Pietismus und Neuzeit*.

20. Representative is the conversation between Brecht and Wallmann: Brecht, "Einleitung"; Brecht, "Zur Konzeption der Geschichte des Pietismus"; Wallmann. "Fehlstart."

21. Lehmann, "Pietism"; Strom, "Problems and Promises."

22. Lehmann, "Aufgaben der Pietismusforschung," 12–13; Strom, "Problems and Promises," 554.

"an epoch . . . which lasted about from 1675 to 1725."[23] A clear endpoint of Pietism is difficult to define. The comprehensive four-volume multi-authored German work representative of recent scholarship, for example, takes the *History of Pietism* into the nineteenth and twentieth century.[24] My study embraces the inclusion of later developments and activities by individuals and groups of Pietist convictions, identifies the Basel Mission and their networks as dominant among them, and constitutes such a sociological-political investigation. It highlights the ongoing significance of the Pietist movement and proffers its foundational importance in the development of missionary thinking and engagement in German-speaking Europe.

In contrast to prevalent discussions of differences between various Pietist strands, I focus here on shared emphases of European pious circles and the missional impulse they entailed which led to the founding of the Basel Mission and shaped its priorities and practices. Common characteristics of Pietism are defined by various authors whose work I use in my analysis. Ernest Stoeffler has been critiqued for his "inclusion of a pietistic Puritanism within Pietism" and his definition of Pietism which he derived primarily from theological criteria.[25] However, as Strom rightly observes, in English, Stoeffler "remains the most comprehensive work on early Pietism" and his second volume outlines the five main strands of German Pietism.[26] Reginald Ward places Pietism within the wider context of Protestant revival movements in Europe and America.[27] Dale Brown's short account presents a defense of Pietism that emphasizes the intentions of its early representatives, but he shows the religious and social background German Pietism arose from and its multi-faceted legacy.[28]

---

23. Lehmann, *Pietismus und weltliche Ordnung*, 14. See his various articles on the subject: Lehmann. "Grenzüberschreitungen"; Lehmann, "Pietism"; Lehmann, "Einführung"; Lehmann, "Aufgaben der Pietismusforschung."

24. Brecht and others, *Geschichte des Pietismus*.

25. Lehmann, *Pietismus und weltliche Ordnung*, 14; Stoeffler, *Rise of Evangelical Pietism*, 13; Strom, "Problems and Promises," 547.

26. Stoeffler, *German Pietism*. The five strands typically identified are the Spener-Francke-Halle Axis, Zinzendorf and the Moravians, and Reformed, Württemberg, and "radical" Pietism.

27. Ward, *Evangelical Awakening*. Lehmann astutely observes: "While Stoeffler expanded the notion of Pietism to include large portions of Puritanism, Ward reduced the role of Pietism to an episode within early modern religious awakenings that originated in England." See Lehmann, "Pietism," 15.

28. Brown, *Understanding Pietism*.

Most recently, Shantz provides a fresh *Introduction to German Pietism* which highlights its antecedents in earlier movements, religious and cultural significance, and continuing legacy in inspiring Evangelicalism.[29]

Most literature on German Pietism focuses on controversies within and with its critics. Despite recognition of the Danish-Halle and Moravian missions, often little is being said about the impulse to Christian mission generated by this movement.[30] Indicative for this tendency is the brevity of the chapter on *Mission* in Brecht's extensive study.[31] However, in the final volume Wellenreuther compares the Moravian and Halle missions and briefly mentions that the BMTI as "the largest of its kind in the German speaking area contributed much to the professionalization of the training of missionaries."[32] A smaller specific study is Peter Zimmerling's exploration of the missionary ideas of Francke and Zinzendorf.[33] More recently, Mason and Vogt highlight the influence of Moravian missionary experience and ideas on Protestant missionary societies in Britain and Germany.[34] Quite incomprehensibly, Vogt excludes the prominent German outcome of missionary passion, the Basel Mission. However, he offers insightful "explanations of the relationships between Pietism and

---

29. Shantz, *Introduction to German Pietism*.

30. Both, the Halle and the Moravian missions have attracted recent research. See, for example, Jensz, *German Moravian Missionaries*; Mettele, *Weltbürgertum*; Liebau, *Tranquebarmission*; Gross, Kumaradoss, and Liebau, *Halle*. An older detailed study is Lehmann, *It Began at Tranquebar*.

31. Rennstich, "Mission." The first two volumes also include brief descriptions of the Halle and Moravian missions respectively: Brecht, "August Hermann Francke," 514–40; Meyer, "Zinzendorf und Herrnhut," 68–74.

32. Wellenreuther, "Pietismus und Mission." However, his statements regarding the Basel Mission are in part incorrect. For example, he claims that, leaning on the example of the Moravians, the BMTI initially did not make educational demands on its applicants. This contradicts the extensive curriculum that was pursued from the beginning. Also, the statement that the first German mission societies initially only supported other missions financially is incorrect regarding the Basel Mission. This claim does not differentiate between support associations and mission societies in the proper sense. The Basel Mission depended on the financial support they received from English and German supporters.

33. Zimmerling, *Pioniere*.

34. Mason, *Moravian Church*; Vogt. "Mission der Brüdergemeine." Vogt cites Mason extensively for Moravian influences in Britain and shows similar influence on the continent for the Dutch Mission Society (founded 1797), the Senfkorn Mission Society (founded 1798 as support society for other ventures), and Jänicke's Missionary training school in Berlin (founded 1800). He delimits his study to the period from 1792 to 1802.

mission."[35] In my study I focus on the Basel Mission and its preparation processes for missionaries. While I recognize the influences of the Danish-Halle mission and the Moravian missions, in particular in relation to ideas of preparing missionaries, I do not offer a comparison of the Basel Mission with these earlier Pietist missionary efforts.

Many influences of the various strands of Pietism are visible in the Basel Mission but most of its participants originated from Württemberg. Therefore, studies on the specific character of Pietism in this German region inform my analysis. Lehmann contributes a careful investigation of the relationships between Württemberg politics and Pietist church leaders from the seventeenth to the twentieth century and an important analysis of two key values—community and work.[36] Significant for the cultural influences on the religious emphases reflected in the BMTI is Martin Scharfe's analysis of Pietism in the life and practice of common people.[37] Paul Jenkins points to the influence of Württemberg Pietism on the Basel Mission in two articles which curiously have not received much attention.[38] Finally, Dieter Ising's detailed biography of Johann Christoph Blumhardt (1805–1880)—a friend of the organization's second director and teacher in Basel for seven years (1830–1837)—provides important insights into the background of BMTI teachers.[39]

HISTORICAL RESEARCH OF THE BASEL MISSION

As a study of so-called "mission history" this research has to engage with the prevalent one-sided approaches and presumptions both from proponents and opponents of the modern Western missionary venture. I approach the subject as a Christian convinced of divine action in the processes of history but not with the assumption that all actions by Christian players are intrinsically positive and necessarily leading to positive results. I acknowledge the complexities of relationships between Christian engagement and the circumstances of the social, economic, religious, and political historical context and assume the embeddedness of the missionary experience in the forces of general history, both in Europe

---

35. Vogt, "Mission der Brüdergemeine," 211–13.

36. Lehmann, *Pietismus und weltliche Ordnung*; Lehmann, "Community and Work."

37. Scharfe, *Die Religion des Volkes*.

38. Jenkins, "Towards a Definition"; Jenkins. "Villagers as Missionaries."

39. Ising, *Johann Christoph Blumhardt*.

and Africa. In this I build on Max Warren's *Social History and Christian Mission* which first drew attention to the inextricable links between the missionary narrative and general social history.[40] Furthermore, I will not discuss the validity of engagement in cross-cultural Christian mission. It is my assumption that the Christian faith is implicitly missional and the community of believers is called to partake in the mission of God to draw men and women from all peoples to himself with the goal of establishing new communities of believers in diverse cultural contexts. Therefore, the actors are presented with the assumption that their intentions represent this missional call without negative intent toward the people they engaged.

Historiography of the European missionary movement and its impact on the non-Western world has undergone major reorientations since the first missionary reports of the kind we find in the Basel Mission archive. In reaction to missionaries' and mission societies' hagiographic accounts of their achievements, twentieth century scholarship has tended to condemn the enterprise as collaboration with imperial colonialism.[41]

A recent example of many studies that investigate the role of missionaries within British (and other European) imperialism are Stanley, Porter, and Etherington who see their work as more balanced presentation and a response to earlier criticism that assumed a close collaboration between empires and missionaries of the same nationality.[42] While they offer some evaluations that also apply to the Basel Mission in Ghana, much of the critique is directed to the dynamics of imperial colonial rule and obscures the issues this project highlights.

European missionary approaches in Africa did not originate in colonial overlordship but in the Evangelical-Pietist mindset of Protestant missions and their cultural background in Europe. The Basel Mission was the specifically German version of this. Consequently, studies on their specific background and involvement in Ghana are the most pertinent. Two in particular, provide interesting insights. Thorsten Altena's survey of six case studies that include the Basel Mission in Cameroon and the

---

40. Warren, *Social History*.

41. A relatively recent and one of the most influential critiques of missionary motivations and actions is Comaroff and Comaroff, *Of Revelation and Revolution*. The five volume *History of the Basel Mission* by Schlatter is an example for the Euro-centric perspective of mission history writing: Schlatter, *Geschichte der Basler Mission*.

42. Etherington, *Missions and Empire*; Porter, *Religion versus Empire*; Stanley, *Bible and Flag*.

North German Mission (NMG) in Togo offers incisive analyses of the missionaries' background, their images of the African context, and their role in Africa.[43] However, like many scholars he draws direct correlations between the missionaries' context of origin and their cross-cultural engagement without giving much consideration to their training as a crucial period between. In addition, the political dynamics were different in the former Gold Coast because here the Basel Mission began work much earlier and they did not operate under German colonial government but under Danish and later British rule. The Ewe tribal area to the east where the NMG worked eventually became "German Togoland" (1884–1914). A link exists nevertheless because the NMG missionaries were trained in the BMTI. Consequently, Birgit Meyer's study of the implications of Pietist spiritual worldview on the engagement with Ewe religion offers important insights to evaluations and dynamics also prevalent in the Basel Mission encounter with African beliefs.[44]

Both of these represent the polycentric approach to mission history that I also take in this study by investigating both, the European and the African side of the story and interrelations between them. This methodology reflects the call for a global Christian history that represents a significant shift in approach to research and writing the whole history of Christianity. In part, this is a response to the unprecedented growth of Christianity in the non-Western world since the middle of the twentieth century.

Towards a Global Christian History

Traditionally, the tendency has been to talk about "Church History" when the subject of study is the development of the church in Europe and North America and "Mission History" to refer to the beginnings and growth of the church in other parts of the world, especially Africa, Latin America, and Asia. Hanciles critiques this "bifurcation of historical study" within the Western theological curriculum and rightly points out that in both "the Western experience provides the central interpretative lens."[45] *Church history* is typically confined to carefully selected "themes and developments that are deemed relevant to the Western experience"

---

43. Altena, *Ein Häuflein Christen*.
44. Meyer, *Translating the Devil*.
45. Hanciles, "New Wine in Old Wineskins."

and *mission history* focuses on the impact of Western missionary initiatives, agents, and strategies on non-Western societies.

From the middle of the twentieth century the first Western scholars with extended experience in Africa began to write accounts that did not outright condemn African traditions and gave more attention to African contributions and perspectives.[46] Foster and Kimble are examples for the Ghanaian context of studies that focused on religious, social and political change induced by the missionary encounter and colonial policies.[47] Interestingly, at the same time various denominational accounts were published, while Hans Debrunner's *History of Christianity in Ghana* explicitly countered such parochialism with his ecumenical work.[48] However, these Europeans for the most part maintained the traditional focus on European agency.

Since the 1960s African scholars offered new perspectives on "mission history" that emphasized "the role and contribution of indigenous agency, . . . the rich heritage of pre-Christian past and encounters with the Christian Gospel outside the direct influence of European missionary action."[49] They also pointed out that Western authored mission histories did not constitute African Church History and called for Africans to write their own accounts.[50] Sanneh and Kalu's edited volume are examples for such histories written by Africans from African perspectives.[51] They emphasize that the history of Christian presence in Africa is a study of religious change that needs to begin with the character of the societies that engaged the new faith and focus on African agents in the process.

In the 1990s Western scholars began to add their voices in critique of the traditional historiography and called for a "global church history" in light of the "southward shift" of global Christianity.[52] The collection of

---

46. Most significantly: Oliver, *Missionary Factor*; Beyerhaus, *Die Selbständigkeit*; Taylor, *Growth of the Church in Buganda*; Sundkler, *Bantu Prophets*; Welbourn, *East African Rebels*. See also the evaluation of these early studies by Shenk. "Toward a Global Church History," 52–53.

47. Foster, *Education and Social Change*; Kimble, *Political History*.

48. Debrunner, *Christianity in Ghana*. For the Methodist and Presbyterian churches respectively: Bartels, *Ghana Methodism*; Smith, *The Presbyterian Church of Ghana*.

49. Hanciles. "Missionaries and Revolutionaries," 146. He cites as examples Nigerian accounts: Ajayi, *Christian Missions in Nigeria*; Ayandele, *The Missionary Impact on Modern Nigeria*.

50. Ajayi and Ayandele, "Writing African Church History," 90.

51. Kalu, *African Christianity*; Sanneh, *West African Christianity*.

52. Robert, "Shifting Southward"; Shenk, "Global Church History"; Shenk, "A

articles that came out of a symposium of historians from all continents in 1998 still represents the most comprehensive treatment of the complex challenges involved.[53] Hanciles suggests that a "global Christian history" would include a thorough exploration of local experience and expressions of the faith, the development of new conceptual models, and new historiographical methods that allow a full view of Christian history as a whole and do not restrict it to traditional Western categories.[54] In recent publications the term "global" is used in various ways.[55] First, it depicts the effort to present a fuller retrieval of the past that includes perspectives and actors often overlooked like local agents, women, the poor, and those declared heretics. Second, new historical relationships based on new themes and insights are posited, and finally, a new presentation of the entire history of Christianity from a global perspective. The first attempt at the latter is Irvin and Sunquist's three volume work which is still in the making.[56]

African Perspectives

African critiques are most significant for this study because they address many of the attitudes and practices of Europeans and highlight African responses to the missionary encounter and African contributions to Christianity in Africa. Within the Basel Mission outstanding African individuals have attracted research; most importantly the pastor and missionary David Asante (c. 1834–1892) and the pastor and teacher Carl Christian Reindorf (1834–1817).[57] Reindorf's *History of the Gold Coast and Asante* is the "first substantial and systematic history of a region of Africa written by an African."[58] Contrary to Mobley's dismissal of it as "literature of tutelage" I agree with Hauser-Renner that it "clearly displays his intellectual independence" and selective adoption of missionary

---

Global Church"; Walls, "Eusebius Tries Again."

    53. Shenk, *Enlarging the Story*.

    54. Hanciles, "New Wine in Old Wineskins," 377–78.

    55. I follow Kollman's insightful evaluation here, in Kollman. "After Church History."

    56. Irvin and Sunquist, *Earliest Christianity*; Irvin and Sunquist, *Modern Christianity*. Volume three is still forthcoming.

    57. Abun-Nasr, *Afrikaner und Missionar*; Jenkins, *Recovery of the West African Past*; Hauser-Renner, "'Obstinate' Pastor."

    58. Reindorf, *History*; Jenkins, *Recovery of the West African Past*, 13.

ideas.⁵⁹ Therefore Reindorf provides valuable insight into the context the Basel Missionaries entered in Ghana. Nevertheless, Mobley is a crucial study of "published critiques of Christian missionaries" by Ghanaian "intelligentsia" from 1897 to post-independence.⁶⁰

Various collections from conferences of African Theologians beginning in 1955 reveal African responses to the missionary encounter that emphasize the continuity of African religious tradition in African Christianity, focus on a "theological and Christocentric understanding of the church," and show a "shift from missionary and nationalist genre to ecumenical historiography . . . and the emergence of a theology of political engagement."⁶¹ An outstanding Ghanaian contribution to the development of African theology is Kwame Bediako's.⁶² He generally evaluates the Basel Mission contribution positively, as does Addo-Fenning, which is in contrast to the wholesale condemnation of missionaries in Africa by other Ghanaian authors like Awoonor.⁶³

Tufuoh's article on the *Relations between Christian Missions, European Administrators, and Traders in the Gold Coast* draws an interesting contrast between Methodist engagement with British government and the Basel Mission's representatives, especially Riis's hostile relationship with the Danish authorities.⁶⁴ Investigating this missionary's relationships with both colonial authorities and local African leaders more closely the articles by Daniel Antwi and Paul Jenkins provide critical insights.⁶⁵

---

59. Hauser-Renner, "'Obstinate' Pastor," 65; Mobley, *Ghanaian's Image*, 7.

60. Among the Ghanaian authors he cites, Joseph Kwame Boakye Danquah (1895–1964) is most significant because of his upbringing in the Basel Mission founded church. He was the son of Emmanuel Yaw Boakye who was a pastor in the Basel Mission church until his death in 1914. See Addo-Fenning. "From Traditionalist to Christian Evangelist and Teacher"; Mobley, *Ghanaian's Image*, 50–53. Danquah's most significant works are: Danquah, *Gold Coast*; Danquah, *Akan Doctrine of God*.

61. Kalu, *African Christianity*, 2. Examples of collections of conference papers are: Christian Council of the Gold Coast, *Christianity and African Culture*; Baëta, *Christianity in Tropical Africa*; Appiah-Kubi and Torres, *African Theology en Route*; Fyfe and Walls, *Christianity in Africa*.

62. Bediako, *Theology and Identity*; Bediako, *Christianity in Africa*.

63. Addo-Fenning, "Christian Missions"; Awoonor, *Ghana*.

64. Tufuoh, "Relations."

65. Antwi, "African Factor"; Antwi and Jenkins, "Moravians"; Paul Jenkins, "Scandal."

Missionaries as Participants in Two Social Histories

Like many Westerners writing on Christian history in Africa, I come to this study with the experience of extensive exposure to an African society and with a sympathetic predisposition to African perspectives.[66] I hope to counteract potential biases by employing previous studies from various fields, where possible by African scholars, in a multi-disciplinary approach. My assessment is informed by the framework of a global Christian history and both, the local and global aspects of the new historiography. While the primary focus is not on African actors, this study investigates new perspectives on foreign missionaries including African perceptions and evaluations of their practices. African environment, responses, and actions are taken into account as well as the long-term outcomes in their context.

At the same time this study pays attention to the origin of the missionaries who came to Africa, the influences upon them, and the ways their background and training affected interactions with the African context. The roots of the Basel Mission in German Pietism, especially in its Württemberg expression, are considered. This approach acknowledges the fact that cross-cultural missionaries are shaped by and contribute to (at least) two social histories, their context of origin and the ministry context.[67] Therefore I examine both, the missionaries' place in the social and religious history in Europe that influenced their ideas and actions as well as the context of the African community that received and responded to these change agents. The focus is on the interaction between the two sets

---

66. See Gundani's evaluation of five Western authors: Gundani. "Teaching." The more recent works he reviews are: Baur, *2000 Years*; Hastings, *Church in Africa*; Isichei, *Christianity in Africa*; Shaw, *Kingdom of God*; Sundkler and Reed, *Church in Africa*.

67. Paul Jenkins, the Basel Mission archivist for many years with nine years teaching experience in Ghana prior, stated as much when he wrote that mission history is "... a branch of social history—indeed, of two social histories ..., the history of two movements. There is the movement here, made up of the people linked to a missionary society through its organization, communication network and supporters. What have been the changing social dimensions of this movement? ... What have been the main interactions between the movement and its surrounding society ... and how has it impacted the environing society? Parallel questions have to be asked about the movement there, in the Third World, which has developed from the contact of missionaries with a specific area or cultural group and the people who have to some degree taken on a Christian identity or have been influenced by Christian social or cultural forms." While he employed old nomenclature, his point that missionaries are influenced by and influence two social histories is important for the dynamics this research highlights. See Jenkins, "Manifesto," 199–200.

of worldview and privileged practices. What the missionaries intended and thought they were doing on the one hand, and how their actions and message were perceived and appropriated by Africans. The resonances and dissonances between these two aspects of the encounter are the clues to the intercultural competence or incapacity this study identifies.

With Dana Robert, I believe that every movement in Christianity "should be studied from within its own internal logic."[68] She relates it to the application of the label "Pentecostal" to a variety of non-Western movements, but this is just as important in relation to the Basel Mission with its roots in German Pietism and the missionary movement it spawned. This European development as well as the movement to Christianity initiated by the Basel Missionaries in Ghana need to be considered on their own terms in their specific context. Therefore it is for example not helpful or even legitimate to apply indiscriminately to Basel missionaries in Ghana categories and judgments from studies of British missionaries at a later time under the colonial control of their own government—an approach frequently taken.[69] At the very least such applications need to be made with great caution.

By contrast, to avoid Euro-centric analysis, in African historiography "the story begins among African communities that had viable structures for existence. It then delineates the permeation of Christian influence . . . attentive to the varieties of the reactions, however ambiguous, of the communities to the Christian change agent. . . . Attention shifts from the process of insertion to the process of appropriation."[70] I follow this approach by beginning with a description of the environment in Southern Ghana which the Basel Missionaries entered and through attentiveness to responses by Ghanaians to the missionary encounter.

Historical Sources and Data

The historical sources available for this enquiry are quite substantial and more comprehensive than for most contexts of comparable historical distance.

---

68. Robert, "Shifting Southward," 57.

69. Most recently such indiscriminate application is offered in Quartey, *Missionary Practices*.

70. Kalu, *African Christianity*, 21.

Archival Material

The Basel Mission Archive (BMA)—located in the former Mission-House—is one of the most complete and well catalogued in existence. I spent two months in the archive from October to December 2008, took digital photographs of all the material I identified as relevant to this project, kept a detailed log, and recorded my observations.

The materials are of primary and secondary nature. First, there are letters, official documents and reports in the personnel files (PF) of individual missionaries pertaining to their application to the training institute, times spent in Europe, and correspondence regarding their children's education and after they left the mission. The "Brothers-Register" (*Brüderverzeichnis*), a directory of all missionaries, recorded basic information about places of origin, dates of entry into the BMTI, and ministry assignments. Bound books collected correspondence from the stations in Ghana (D-1 signature) and the *Komitee Protokolle* (KP) are the minutes of Board meetings. The BMA has complete copies of the published magazines; especially the *Missions-Magazin* (MM) and the *Heidenbote* (HB) contain many reports by and articles about the missionaries in Ghana and official annual reports. Furthermore, the archive holds manuscripts and publications by people involved with the mission. Most relevant for this research are writings by the mission's directors,[71] by long term missionaries in Ghana,[72] by Africans related to the mission,[73] and the in-house historical accounts of the organization.[74] Of the latter Wilhelm Schlatter's five volume work is the most thorough overview. These sources display a strongly favorable and uncritical evaluation of the mission, its personnel and proceedings. They belong to the categories of "missionary historiography" Kalu identifies[75] and are clearly representative of the Eurocentric bias described above.

This nature of the sources presents a challenge as it is no longer acceptable to restrict description and evaluation to their uncritical Eurocentric perspective. Letters and reports reflect the viewpoint of the

---

71. See, for example, Blumhardt, "Geographischer Überblick"; Hoffmann, *Missionsgesellschaft*; Hoffmann, *Eilf Jahre*.

72. For example Dieterle, "30 Jahre"; Joseph Mohr, "Tagebuch."

73. For example Opoku, *Riis, the Builder*.

74. Eppler, *Geschichte der Basler Mission*; Ostertag, *Entstehungsgeschichte*; Schick, *Vorboten und Bahnbrecher*; Schlatter, *Geschichte der Basler Mission*.

75. Kalu, "African Church Historiography," 15–16.

missionaries and publications are directed to their European audience. However, confidential sources like minutes of Board meetings and letters also reveal difficulties, disagreements, setbacks, doubts, and even occasional self-critique. Their existence allows for different evaluations. Eiselen, Miller, and Prodolliet are examples for judicious analyses, but they also reveal "the politics of discourse."[76] In contrast to official publications that served to justify mission policies and decisions, contemporary studies are often characterized by their own historical context that calls for a more critical approach, sometimes overly critical. Typically, this is an expression of Western postcolonial embarrassment—especially of late twentieth century secular scholarship—with previous confident Christian missionary expansion and thus constitutes again a Euro-centric perspective. In the final analysis, any historical writing is a "meaningful story of the past," meaningful for the constituency it is addressed to in the present.

My approach to the available sources is guided by missiological and educational questions of the effects of missionary training on cross-cultural engagement. Consequently, I employ particular theoretical concepts to reveal specific insights into the dynamics of the preparation processes of the Basel missionaries and their encounter with the African context. The frameworks of *communities of practice* and *trained incapacity* drive an examination which attempts to transcend the overly positive evaluations of older histories as well as the overly critical assessments of more recent studies, looks for the issues revealed in letters, reports and minutes, and seeks where accessible African perspectives of the events and missionary actions. In this I rely considerably on previous in-depth studies of specific aspects or part of the history.

Data from Other Sources

In cross-cultural contexts missionaries faced challenges they expected and many situations they were not prepared for, their activities led to outcomes they did not anticipate, and Africans often perceived things and responded differently than anticipated. The missionaries' accounts reflect their understanding of these challenges, including tensions of opinion and between personalities that arose. However, African perspectives are harder to identify because much of the evidence is either hidden in oral traditions or between the lines of European descriptions and evaluations.

76. Eiselen, "Erziehung"; Miller, *Missionary Zeal*; Prodolliet, *Schamlosigkeit*.

A praiseworthy effort at reconstructing a piece of African history from such limited sources is Kwamena-Poh's account of Akuapem state politics in 1730–1850.[77] He is of particular interest because he covers in detail the period of this study and focuses on the region where the Basel Mission first established a church, including an evaluation of the most prominent missionary of this early engagement, Andreas Riis. From the first European contacts the Asante Empire and the Akan people attracted a number of reports by diverse travelers to the region.[78] While the various biases of these authors need to be taken into account, they offer contemporary descriptions of the politics, culture, and religion of the main African society the Basel missionaries engaged in the Gold Coast. More recent anthropological studies of Akuapem by Gilbert and Middleton provide important background and Rattray's extensive research is still the most comprehensive source for religious and socio-economic traditions of the Asante.[79]

I adopted a multi-disciplinary polycentric approach that employs these and other previous studies to reconstruct a more comprehensive account of the Basel missionaries, both their background in Europe and their encounter with the African context. Like most recent discourse in the study of nineteenth-century missions, I explore specific aspects of interrelations between this movement and the general historical environment and do not attempt a comprehensive description or evaluation of the Basel Mission or its work. This study is also not a judgment of their actions by later insights, which would be anachronistic, but a description of observable sociological dynamics related to missionary training and practice, in order to gain insights for present day intercultural preparation and engagement.

Effects of Missionary Training in the Nineteenth Century

Very few scholars explore the preparation processes of nineteenth century missionaries. The most comprehensive is Stuart Piggin's analysis of training provided by the various British societies for missionaries to

---

77. Kwamena-Poh, *Akuapem State*.

78. Beecham, *Ashantee*; Bowdich, *Mission*; Freeman, *Journals*; Meredith, *Gold Coast*.

79. Gilbert, "Aesthetic Strategies"; Gilbert, " Executioner"; Gilbert, "Ethnic Construction"; Middleton, "Home-Town"; Middleton, "One Hundred and Fifty Years"; Rattray, *Ashanti*; Rattray, *Religion and Art*; Rattray, *Ashanti Law*.

India.[80] Many of his insights apply to Basel missionaries as well and he shows the influence of the BMTI on the British institutes. Chester Terpstra's study of David Bogue (1750–1825), a founding member of the LMS, delineates the specific focus of missionary training he developed as early as 1795.[81] Finally, two articles describe the training at the BMTI specifically; Tobias Eiselen's chapter in a book on the NMG and Haller's article in the *Missions-Magazin* from 1897.[82] Both focus on the period after 1850 when institutional regulation and supervision was considerably tightened. However, the basic emphases of the BMTI did not change; they were only more rigidly articulated and implemented under the new leadership. Haller's account represents an in-house perspective that endorses all practices uncritically which, in a way, is balanced by Eiselen's overly critical angle on anything related to order and control and his underlying tone of dismissal of Pietist spirituality and theology.

My analysis draws on insights from all these previous studies and asserts the importance of investigating the wide range of factors which influenced the preparation processes and in turn the attitudes and approaches of Basel missionaries sent to Africa. Similar to my thesis, Piggin observes an *erudite inflexibility* in many of the well-educated British missionaries in India.[83] Jon Miller's sociological investigation of internal contradictions and tensions in the Basel Mission uses cases of dismissal as starting point and highlights issues of class collaboration, social control, and organizational contradictions.[84] He cites both Piggin and sociological scholars to posit that *trained incapacity* contributed to the lack of "quick intelligence and flexibility," initiative, and creativity demanded by the ever changing challenges of the African context.[85] However, both these scholars ignore the perceptions, contributions, and responses of the non-western recipients to the missionary effort among them. My assessment of the Basel Mission training and intercultural engagement in Ghana builds on these briefly stated insights. It furthers them with a detailed analysis of the specific characteristics of the BMTI that contributed to the difficulties missionaries encountered in the cross-cultural

---

80. Piggin, *Making Evangelical Missionaries.*
81. Terpstra, "David Bogue."
82. Haller, "Leben im Missionshaus"; Eiselen, "Erziehung."
83. Piggin, *Making Evangelical Missionaries*, 248.
84. Miller, *Missionary Zeal.*
85. Ibid., 123–59.

context. More importantly, it advances previous evaluations of Protestant missionary preparation through a global historiographical approach that assigns prime importance to the impact of European missionary praxis on the African context and to African evaluations. I regard this perspective as indispensable for a viable appraisal of the training the missionaries received.

In the following, Part I analyses the BMTI as an intentional *Community of Practice*. Chapter 1 outlines the historical background of the Basel Mission, including developments that led to its founding, and explores the cultural, socio-economic, and religious factors that influenced the community learning approach of the BMTI. It examines the roots of Protestant missions in emphases of German Pietism and preceding educational models that inspired the Basel Mission founders to establish the BMTI as an intentional community. Chapter 2 traces influences of the general European image of Africa on the Basel Mission vision of Christian foreign mission that became the shared goal—the *domain of interest*—of this community. It further identifies specific Basel Mission ideas of mission work and the kind of people it required. Chapter 3 examines the varying backgrounds of participants in the Basel Mission and how each influenced the shared practice the organization embraced. It concludes with identifying the outcomes of Basel missionary preparation by discussing the relative impact of missionaries' background and BMTI training on their religious convictions and practical emphases.

Part II examines the engagement of missionaries thus trained in the African environment. Chapter 4 reviews the early nineteenth century context in Ghana, highlighting realities that impacted on Christian missions, and then examines indications for trained incapacity among the initial group of Basel missionaries (1828–1831). Specifically, conflicts among the team, lack of collaboration, and attitudes to chaplaincy are investigated. Chapter 5 focuses on Andreas Riis, the acclaimed founder of the Basel Mission in Ghana. It examines his specific background, ways he overcame trained incapacity by revising BMTI instilled perceptions, his ambiguous relationships with Africans, and the practical and political tensions he experienced which reveal indications for trained incapacity. Chapter 6 assesses the missionary attempts of the small team in the late 1830s suggesting trained incapacity as major factor in their failure to achieve organizational goals. Individual and organizational responses illustrate the wider historical development towards Christian mission as intentional replication of European culture which entailed trained incapacity. Finally, I offer conclusions from the historical case study, suggestions for its wider significance for preparing Christian missionaries, and some recommendations for counteracting the negative dynamic this study highlights.

PART I

The Community of Practice of the Basel Mission Training Institute

1

A Learning Community Shaped by German Pietism

THIS CHAPTER PROVIDES A historical background detailing the vision, movements, and influences that led to the establishment of the Basel Mission as a German initiative to engage in Protestant missions. It investigates the characteristics of German Pietism as significant inspiration towards Protestant mission and outlines the cultural, socio-economic, and religious factors that influenced the community learning approach that the BMTI adopted. I argue that the approach of the BMTI was shaped by the values and emphases of German Pietism and essentially constituted the kind of learning community that the construct of *communities of practice* describes.

From its inception in 1815 the Evangelical Missionary Society at Basel, commonly referred to as the *Basel Mission*, focused on training German and Swiss missionaries to bring the Christian message to regions outside Western Europe. Even after 1822, when they had started their own work, the BMTI continued to prepare considerable numbers of candidates for other societies. The motivations, emphases, and practices of the Basel Mission, both in its approaches to training missionaries and the subsequent cross-cultural engagement in Africa cannot be understood without the social, political, and religious developments that produced and molded this organization and its support networks. Specifically, since it had its roots in the European and global networks of German Pietism, the emphases and impulses of this movement are foundational. Not only did its missionary impulse birth the first Protestant missions in the

Danish-Halle mission in India and the Moravian missions in the West-Indies and Greenland, its educational emphasis also shaped approaches to training that essentially constituted *communities of practice*; groups of people "who engage in a process of collective learning in a shared domain of human endeavor."[1]

The definition "allows for, but does not assume, intentionality" but the Basel Mission leaders purposely designed the BMTI as a learning community which was focused on formation of shared ideas of character and specific practices as well as intellectual learning. This educational design built on previous approaches to missionary training at Halle University, in the Moravian community, and by "one-man-academies" like David Bogue's in Britain and Johannes Jänicke's in Berlin who trained many of the first missionaries for the newly established Protestant missionary societies.

THE MISSIONARY IMPULSE OF GERMAN PIETISM

German Pietism began as a reform movement that called for personal and societal transformation in response to the utter devastation and demoralization of the Thirty Years War (1618–1648). Philipp Jakob Spener (1635–1705) earned the designation "father of Pietism" with his *Pia Desideria* (published 1675) which offered candid critique of prevailing conditions and suggestions for reform addressed to civil authorities, clergy, and common people.[2] His core concern was the "inner religion" of individual believers who needed New Birth and a faith "whose expressions are the fruits of life." The proposal for realization of the priesthood of all believers was *collegia pietatis,* meetings in which believers read and discussed the Bible together "in order to discover its simple meaning and whatever might be useful for the edification of all" to teach, warn, convert, and edify each other. These conventicles and the "religion of the inner man" which finds expression in moral life became trademarks of Pietism across its different expressions. In Germany, with the exception of what has been termed "Radical Pietism," this movement was "a response from within the church to a felt spiritual need" which for the most part remained in state churches.[3]

---

1. Wenger, *Introduction*.
2. Spener, *Pia Desideria*.
3. Ward, *Evangelical Awakening*, 58. On "Radical Pietism" see the important study Schneider, *German Radical Pietism*.

Protestant missionary engagement began with Spener's protégé and successor August Herrmann Francke (1663–1727), who implemented his ideas at the new university in Halle, and his godson Count Ludwig von Zinzendorf (1700–1760) and the Moravian community in Herrnhut. In 1706 the first Halle trained missionaries arrived in the Danish colony Tranquebar in South India and their reports—published from 1710— raised missionary passion and support throughout Pietist circles.[4] From 1727 Moravian evangelistic bands and travelling evangelists started new groups wherever they went; and in 1732 the first Moravian missionaries went to the West-Indies and Greenland.[5]

These first Protestant missions were the result of the fact that Pietism promoted a personal, moral, and active understanding of Christianity that is inherently missionary and inspired local and foreign missions. This is typically lost in research on the disagreements within, varying religious expressions, and theological motifs of the movement. An exception is Vogt who suggested four tendencies in Pietism which facilitated its missionary impulse: the view of the Bible as instruction for present action, the ideal of the apostolic age that judged the established church as "fallen," Pietist eschatology that expected the conversion of Jews and "heathen" as condition for Christ's return, and the emphasis on personal faith experience which carried with it the responsibility of the "revived" to work towards the renewal of those who are not.[6] Vogt's analysis shows that it is more helpful for an understanding of Pietism's missional impulse to focus on common marks of this diverse movement as they have been articulated for example by Wallmann and Lehmann.[7] Then the essen-

---

4. Lehmann, *It Began at Tranquebar*; Clarke, *History of the S. P. C. K*, 59–76; Sattler and Francke, *God's Glory, Neighbor's Good*, 78. According to Sattler, Francke performed three major functions in this mission to India, "he trained and sent the missionaries who labored there, he was the mission's intellectual and spiritual leader, and he inspired Christians in Europe to make the mission an object of their prayers and contributions."

5. Zimmerling, *Pioniere*, 30–44; Stoeffler, *German Pietism*, 159–65. For accounts on the Moravian missions, see Beck, *Brüder in vielen Völkern*; Müller, *200 Jahre Brüdermission*; Schattschneider, *Five Hundred Years*.

6. Vogt, "Mission der Brüdergemeine," 211–13.

7. Wallmann identified as Pietist characteristics the centrality of the Bible and biblical devotion which led to the formation of groups in which the pious gathered, often chiliastic "hopes for better times," and sanctification as requirement for true Christianity beyond justification. See Wallmann, *Der Pietismus*; Wallmann. "Was ist Pietismus?" Lehmann posited religious private edification in small circles, awareness of a unique spiritual tradition, and the brotherhood of true believers as marks of historic

tially missionary nature of German Pietism and the impetus to Protestant missionary engagement it provided become obvious in each of its main emphases: individual conversion experience, sanctification, social action, Bible reading, education, and fellowship groups.

Individual Conversion Experience

Pietist spirituality was an experiential faith with strong emphasis on conversion and personal transformation of the believer. Faith as trust of the individual in the work of Christ lived out in a holy life and in continued repentance of sins was the understanding of "true Christianity."[8] Pietists insisted on a personal encounter with God—often described very emotionally—and transformation of the "inner man" as well as outward life. This theology of experience included a new emphasis on the Holy Spirit in guiding individuals and speaking to people.[9]

Conversion as personal emotional experience became a powerful motivation for mission. It ignited the desire to share this encounter and encourage others to also enter into it. It introduced a foundational move from the traditional external calling (*vocation externa*) of ministers by the territorial ruler to a subjective internal calling (*vocation interna*) by the voice of God in the heart of the individual which assigned the responsibility for Christian mission to all revived believers.[10] The rationale for mission no longer rested on the duty of Christian rulers to care for the spirituality of their subjects but mission became the responsibility of all Christians. Furthermore, it became directed not only to those of other faiths (including other Christian confessions) but also to people within the church who had not encountered God in this personal way. This individualistic understanding of the Christian faith is obvious in the

Pietism, and later also added the theological hope for better times. See Lehmann, *Pietismus und weltliche Ordnung*, 15–17; Lehmann, "Grenzüberschreitungen," 16–18.

8. Arndt, *True Christianity*. First published in 1606, this book by Johann Arndt (1555–1621) was the most influential devotional book among Pietists. One of the chapter headings reads: "He who does not follow Christ in faith, holiness, and continued repentance cannot be delivered from the blindness of his heart but must abide in eternal darkness, nor can he have a true knowledge of Christ or fellowship with him" (Part I, chapter heading 37, p.162).

9. For example, Spener states that listening to sermons or reading the Bible, the word was to "penetrate to our heart, so that we may hear the Holy Spirit speak there, that is, with vibrant emotion and comfort feel the sealing of the Spirit and the power of the Word." See Spener, *Pia Desideria*, 117.

10. cf. Zimmerling, *Pioniere*, 12.

autobiographies of BMTI applicants who typically described their conversion experience in emotional terms and clearly articulated a personal divine calling to serve in foreign missions.

Pietist ecclesiology was in danger of ignoring the corporate character of much of biblical teaching and reduce the church to "a union of pious individuals or an aggregate of saved souls."[11] On the other hand, the Pietist distinction between the visible and invisible church facilitated a closer affinity and sense of brotherhood with believers of any denominational, regional, or even national background than with non-pious believers in their own denominations. This enabled Pietist Christians to collaborate especially in the missionary enterprise with those from other national and denominational settings.[12] The Basel Mission leaders were involved in numerous relationships of this kind.

Regeneration and Sanctification

Pietists preferred the image of regeneration (or new birth) to describe Christian salvation, followed naturally by sanctification. For them it was "by no means enough to have knowledge of the Christian faith, for Christianity consists rather of practice" which meant above all "fervent love, . . . first toward one another and then toward all men," that had to be shown in practical actions of selfless service.[13] Personal transformation in moral behavior was seen as proof of conversion and included critique against vices like drunkenness, lawsuits, and oppressive business practices.[14]

Which behaviors specifically constituted a sanctified life varied in different groups, but the conviction that sanctification is crucial to true Christianity was shared. Over time the distinctive Pietist morality often comprised of rules of action and abstention that included a preoccupation with specifics and a denial of the "pleasures of the world." This has attracted vigorous critique centered on the dangers of legalism and judging people's faith by their actions. Some of the interpersonal tensions in the

---

11. Ibid., 37; Brown, *Understanding Pietism*, 142–48.

12. Lehmann, for example, emphasizes this "brotherhood of true believers" as distinct mark from the beginning and later the "truly international character . . . of all activities that were planned, organized and carried through by the Basel Christianity Society and their affiliated societies." See Lehmann, *Pietismus und weltliche Ordnung*, 16–17; Lehmann, "Mobilization," 197.

13. Spener, *Pia Desideria*, 95–97. See also Wallmann, "Was ist Pietismus," 20–22.

14. Spener, *Pia Desideria*, 58–67.

BMTI reveal that this emphasis could also lead to judgmental attitudes towards other pious Christians whose ethical practice differed.

Spener's advice on dealing with "unbelievers and heretics" illustrates how this emphasis inspired mission. He insisted on the need to pray earnestly that God may enlighten non-believers and take pains not to offend them, but when the opportunity arises to "indicate decently but forcefully how their errors conflict with the word of God."[15] Believers must also practice "heartfelt love toward all unbelievers and heretics," not stake everything on debate but realize that purity of doctrine is also maintained by "true repentance and holiness of life." Prominence is given to a life style that does not offend but rather invites nonbelievers and persuades others not only of truth but also of areas of unwholesome living. Pietists were convinced that the better life they lived very practically would attract the non-pious to their faith. This expectation is also present strongly in the Basel Mission. It is expressed for example in the repeated instructions to departing missionaries "to live in all things a life that does not offend" because their lives were "the most impressive and vivid sermon."[16]

Social Action Inspired by Eschatology

One significant trait of the changed Christian life was caring for those in need which resulted in Pietist involvement both on a personal and an institutional level in practical social action. Francke's social and educational institutions in Halle are well known. For him "one of the most important aspects of the life of faith was a new and profound concern for the neighbor."[17] Over Lutheran Orthodox preoccupation with right doctrine Pietists emphasized an active faith that stimulated the establishment of orphanages, schools for the poor, and other institutions for the marginalized as well as pastors and individual Christians personally helping those around them. The model Christian community in Korntal included schools and charitable institutions like homes for poor and delinquent children; and later in the nineteenth century, Johann Hinrich Wichern (1808–1881) and Konrad Wilhelm Löhe (1808–1872) instituted what became known as "Inner Mission" which included services to seamen,

---

15. Ibid., 97–102.

16. BMA D-10.3,3a1) Instructions 1828, 7 (I.4.) and 11 (III); MM 1830, 470–71, 478.

17. Stoeffler, *German Pietism*, 20–21.

unemployed, prisoners, and needy children as well as efforts "towards improved pastoral care for the masses in the growing cities."[18]

Pietist eschatology motivated this social action even though its emphasis changed considerably over time. Spener's "hope for better times" inspired an optimistic view of the future that envisioned reform of the church and the world through changed human lives and produced action towards transformation of society. But by the early nineteenth century economic and political revolutions and the rise of rationalism sidelined and disillusioned Pietists and led to reactions of opposition and withdrawal. Social activism and foreign mission became expressions of preparing for the imminent return of the Lord which the times suggested. Lehmann shows that fighting the perceived evil of the times by working for the Kingdom of God included action in Europe and mission in foreign regions which came to be seen as a precondition of the Second Coming.[19]

Pietists worked at alleviating social hardships, called for spiritual repentance and ethical separation, but (especially in Württemberg) became politically "the quiet people" characterized by defensiveness and insulation.[20] Inspired by various apocalyptic prophecies Pietists increasingly saw their activities as an alternative to developments around them. Some opted for separation and even emigration to the imagined safe havens of Russia, Israel, and America; but most worked for the establishment of the *Kingdom of God* at home. War, economic hardships and the revolting crowds destroying traditional order were interpreted as judgments of God. Pietists saw the underlying reason in the sinfulness and rampant immorality of the people and their lack of faith and fear of God. Therefore, the solution had to be less political or social, but primarily religious. They sought to further this objective by the spread of Bibles, educating people in their institutes, the prolific publication of literature, and missionary engagement.[21] Revolutions and war only served to increase the sense of mission to bring the gospel to a dark world that needed the word of God and messengers who called for repentance.

---

18. Latourette, *History of Christianity*, 1136. On Korntal see Lehmann, *Pietismus und weltliche Ordnung*, 176–87.

19. Lehmann, "Mobilization," 189–91.

20. Fulbrook, *Piety and Politics*, 151.

21. Lehmann, *Pietismus und weltliche Ordnung*, 135–267. Lehmann explores in detail Pietist activism motivated by this work for the "Kingdom of God in Württemberg" which he traces to the influence of the famous and respected preacher Ludwig Hofacker (1798–1728).

Philanthropy was also a major motivation for missionary involvement overseas. Helping the "poor heathen" in their pitiable state and bringing the gospel light into the "dark world of heathenism" were openly articulated as reasons to send missionaries. The June 1816 petition to the authorities in Basel for permission to start the BMTI declared:

> The final purpose of our little missionary institute is to train a number of upright pupils . . . who will work philanthropically for the heathen world in the mission fields of the Protestant governments in Asia and Africa among the barbaric peoples promoting Protestant Christianity and bourgeois civilization.[22]

This text also highlights a common critique of the movement, namely the assumption that "bourgeois civilization" was what non-European people needed together with the Christian faith.[23] Even in Europe, Scharfe argues, philanthropic activities only helped the poor charitably but did not address the root cause of antagonism between the social classes.[24] This is not the place to discuss whether or not that was the root cause but it can certainly be said that the philanthropic emphasis had a tendency to be paternalistic and often did little to effect structural changes in society. Pietist activism alleviated much socioeconomic hardship in unsettled times, but it also favored the old order and idealized rural life. Having lost most political influence in Europe Pietists became all the more active in building communities after their Christian ideal overseas.

The Bible and Devotional Literature

Pietists upheld the Bible as supreme authority over doctrine and church symbols and stressed the practical purposes of Bible study. Out of the profound conviction that the devotional aspects of religious life are of prime importance they launched a massive program of disseminating the Bible, various devotional books and tracts, and later missionary literature as well. Brown notes that Pietists

> believed the Bible had been communicated to man in order to edify, console, encourage, warn, reprimand, and help the church

---

22. BMA, Q-1-2.1 Plan der Missionsanstalt.

23. For example, Njoku critiques the "spirit and attitude of cultural superiority" of missionaries in Africa in Njoku, "The Missionary Factor," 228–29.

24. Scharfe, *Religion des Volkes*, 144–45.

and its members as well as to lead men and women to God by bringing about repentance and change. For Pietists the Bible became a devotional resource rather than a source of doctrine, a guide to life rather than just the source of belief and faith.[25]

The work of the Holy Spirit in illuminating Scripture, awakening true faith, and enabling right understanding was emphasized because through this "internal testimony of the Spirit" the believer was enlightened to understand what the unbeliever would not. Against the dangers of exclusivist and subjective revelations or narrow and simplistic interpretations by lay people Pietist theologians emphasized biblical theology and exegesis in the original languages. In this way, Pietism not only inspired the private reading and study of the Bible, it also gave significant impetus to biblical scholarship. The most prominent scholar of Pietist Bible interpretation was Johann Albrecht Bengel (1687–1752) whose commentary on the New Testament original texts was translated into many languages and influenced Wesleyan, Holiness, and Pentecostal exegesis. Exegetical work in biblical languages also had a central place at the BMTI.

This high regard for the Bible inspired a passion to get a copy into every house. Pietists printed and distributed the Scriptures and later joined the parallel movement in Britain founding Bible Societies on the continent following the establishment of the British and Foreign Bible Society in 1804. By 1826 "more than two million Bibles had been printed and distributed in practically all European languages and in practically all lands ruled by Europeans."[26] In Germany, as early as 1697 Francke started a publishing house in Halle which by 1738 already had 600 titles, including tracts, Latin books for theologians, and the mission reports from India in addition to the Bible.[27] The *Canstein Bible House*, inspired by Francke and instituted 1710 by Carl Hildebrand von Canstein (1667–1719), printed about two million Bibles and one million New Testaments in the first hundred years, "thus for the first time in Protestant history making the Bible really a book of the people."[28] Later a similar center

---

25. Brown, *Understanding Pietism*, 67–68.
26. Lehmann, "Mobilization," 192.
27. Beyreuther, *Kirche in Bewegung*, 96.
28. Stoeffler, *German Pietism*, 55. The German translation used was Martin Luther's, which had assumed rather normative status, even though especially Francke felt free to critique it and identified badly translated passages in his *Theological Observations*, which he published from 1695 onwards. See Brown, *Understanding Pietism*, 77. Lehmann, furthermore makes the political argument that in the nineteenth century

of biblical and mission literature emerged in Southern Germany with the *Calw Publishing House*, founded in 1833 by Christian Gottlob Barth (1799–1862) who was also a staunch supporter of the Basel Mission.

The desire to spread the gospel through distributing Bibles provided a powerful missionary impulse. Outside Europe it also inspired a passion for Bible translation into vernacular languages which was from the beginning central to Protestant missions. Emphasis on the Bible and literature also fostered the prominence of education in Pietism. People who were to be transformed by the Bible had to be able to read.

Education as Means of Transformation

A major activity of Pietists was to establish educational institutions and contribute to better school systems. Spener challenged the way church leaders were trained in his time and suggested substantial reforms. He condemned the unchristian academic lifestyle and called on professors to live exemplary lives and "pay attention to the life as well as the studies of the students entrusted to them."[29] He also posed training should include "exercises through which students become . . . experienced in those things which belong to practice and . . . edification," and "practice [of] those things with which the students will have to deal when they are in the ministry" like preaching purposeful sermons. Character and ministry formation was more important for clergy than academic achievement and integral to Spener's reform program which sought to counteract the doctrinal rigidity of scholastic Orthodoxy and the low state of morality in church and society.

Francke developed and systematized innovative educational thinking and many of his foundations were new schools. He believed the personal and institutional corruption in society was rooted in a faulty educational system and his twofold plan to counteract this was "to set up a model educational community on all levels" and to supply from Halle "both teachers and pastors . . . , [who] might be imbued with the same zeal for religious and moral renewal."[30] His comprehensive educational program included separate schools for political and military leaders, the

"in the German states, the German Bible in the translation of Martin Luther, and this was the version printed by all nineteenth-century German Bible societies, was believed to be the best protection against French Enlightenment, French Rationalism, French revolutionary spirit, and French despotism." See Lehmann, "Mobilization," 192.

29. Spener, *Pia Desideria*, 103–17.
30. Stoeffler, *German Pietism*, 25.

professional and merchant class, ordinary German citizens (both boys and girls), and free schools for the poor. Both, education in schools and theological training emphasized the formation of Christian character. Francke advocated that "for students of theology a rigorous intellectual discipline must be supplemented by a constant conscious striving to bring every aspect of life into harmony with God's law."[31] Pietist educational thought pioneered by Francke "was the forbearer of middle class pedagogical traditions which intended a comprehensive restructuring of the society through education" and shaped the German school system well into the twentieth century.[32]

Pietist initiatives were marked by pedagogical involvement that focused on biblical study, character development, and practical skills, often resulting in the founding of educational institutions. Nineteenth century examples with links to the Basel Mission were the boarding schools for boys and girls in Korntal and the *Institute for Teacher Training and Care of Poor Children* in Beugen.[33] Within the church, the educational emphasis was expressed in groups of mutual edification and through the renewal of catechist teaching for children and young people.[34]

Even though most scholars overlook the importance of education in Pietism the social, economic, and missiological implications of this element were considerable. Education itself became a missionary venture because it was seen as a means to instill Christian values and character in future leaders of a society that was seriously lacking in morals, both in Europe and overseas. This approach can be criticized as a questionable attempt to educate people to faith, especially as in practice such efforts tend to focus on moral rules and people learn to behave in certain ways

---

31. Ibid., 29.

32. Weimer and Jacobi, *Geschichte der Pädagogik*, 91. There is an English version of this book which was originally published in 1902, but despite its claim to be a translation, at least in the section on "Educational Ideas of the Pietists" it is not a translation, more a paraphrased summary of the original work by Weimer. See Weimer, *Concise History of Education*.

33. Christian Heinrich Zeller (1779–1860) collaborated with Christian Friedrich Spittler (1782–1867) who was also instrumental in the Christian Society and in the founding of the Basel Mission, in founding this school in 1820. See, for example, Hauss, "Die sozialpädagogische Arbeit."

34. The beginnings of religious instruction of the next generation go back to Martin Luther's time, but with the rise of Protestant scholasticism the need to educate the common people had been neglected. Pietists established Sunday school (in 1682) and confirmation (in 1723). See Haug, *Reich Gottes im Schwabenland*, 230.

while they may lack the inner conviction which should be the foundation of such actions. The emphasis also created a new hierarchy on the basis of educational attainment (notably Bible knowledge) among believers. It was this dynamic that made prominent leaders of Pietist conventicles very influential in the Basel Mission.

However, Pietism also insisted that everybody can be educated. At a time when orphans, girls, and children of the poor did not receive formal education Pietists built schools for them and expected them to be able to learn just as well as the children of nobility. In distant lands too, Pietist missionaries generally had a very high view of the ability of non-European people to learn and understand, a view which was not shared by all Europeans, especially with regard to Africans. Francke's pedagogical methods were revolutionary for the time, in that he eschewed the usual beatings and methods of punishment and put great importance on the exemplary life of teachers. On the other hand Zinzendorf's anti-intellectual tendencies are often emphasized which overlooks the fact that he also "fostered the rapid development of schools during the eighteenth-century Moravian movement."[35] More accurately, it would have to be said that Moravian approaches differed in being more inclusive of "all aspects of one's everyday life as education," but they had the same passion for transformation by education.[36]

The founders of one of the first British missions, the London Missionary Society, initially regarded spiritual qualifications, knowledge of the Bible, common sense, and practical skills as sufficient prerequisite for missionaries while formal education was considered unnecessary.[37] However, this is not true for German Pietists. Their high regard of education also influenced their approach to missionary preparation. Similar to pastoral ministry, they believed education was necessary for a missionary to acquire the needed knowledge, abilities, and qualities. The very first Protestant missionaries were Halle university graduates and it was a logical continuation of Pietist educational emphasis that their contribution to the nascent nineteenth century missionary movement was in the area of missionary training.

---

35. Vogt, "Headless and Un-Erudite."

36. Lempa, "Moravian Education," 282.

37. Walls, *Missionary Movement*, 162–63; Lovett, *London Missionary Society*, 26–29, 43–44.

Conventicles—Communities of Mutual Edification

When Spener first suggested that common people should be introduced to Scripture through daily readings and regular meetings beyond the Sunday services, his desire was for individual church members to grow in their understanding of doctrine and practice of piety.[38] This passion for reform in the church that included emphases on the priesthood of all believers, personal practice of Christianity, and fellowships of mutual edification resonated with many and sparked the instigation of such groups across Germany and beyond.[39] The conventicles—typically held on Sunday afternoons and including songs, prayer, and reading the Bible, letters from Pietist leaders, and later also mission reports—were a major innovation in church life and became powerful instruments for mobilizing the laity. Lehmann highlights the importance of community to Pietists and concludes that

> in theory, an individual Christian could become a member of God's Kingdom without joining a pietist conventicle. In the practical religious life of . . . Württemberg villages and towns, however, the kind of piety [that was] considered adequate for membership of God's Kingdom could only be found and expressed in close contact with the community of other true Christians as organized in the conventicles, . . . in which Pietist patriarchs decided theological, ethical, and many other matters.[40]

Several developments can be traced to these fellowships. As people began to meet and correspond with groups in other regions they transcended the rigid territorial parish borders and became conscious of the international and interdenominational breadth of Christianity. Lehmann outlines different forms of religious community building among Pietists and concludes that the primary dividing line they drew was "between the revived, pious, believing children of God . . . and the "children of the world."[41] He adds that this line went right through churches and even families. But the flipside was the "brotherhood of believers" among

---

38. These Pietist fellowships are variously known as *collegia pietatis*, conventicles, *ecclesiolae*, or *collegia philobiblica*.

39. Stoeffler, *German Pietism*, 71–87. Stoeffler traces the geographical expansion of the Spener-Halle movement to Berlin, Prussia, Pomerania, Saxony, Silesia, Hannover, the north, the west and the south of Germany as well as Scandinavia, America (the first Pietist group migrated in 1694 to Pennsylvania), Switzerland, and Russia.

40. Lehmann, "Community and Work," 88.

41. Lehmann, "Grenzüberschreitungen," 16.

the revived and pious from all churches and nations for whom foreign mission became a dominant common enterprise.[42]

The Southwestern German duchy of Württemberg emerged as a major center of Pietism where it became a "folk religion" both, intellectually respectable and a genuine grass-roots movement. The personal ministry and scholarship of Albrecht Bengel and political tolerance facilitated this. Bengel's exegetical studies were widely influential. Through him Tübingen University became a major center of Pietism (where incidentally most BMTI teachers were trained), and his eschatological speculations contributed to motivate Pietists' social and missionary action. Politically, the rapidly growing numbers of conventicles became acceptable with the *General Rescript* (1743) which "granted the right of private religious meetings to all who seemed qualified to hold them" but under the supervision of pastors.[43] Scharfe critiques Württemberg conventicles as instruments of lifelong social control that socialized members into their values and morality by means of supervision, control, and the communal pressures of patriarchal society.[44] Sociologically, Scharfe's criticism could be made of any close-knit community that encourages conformity to group values, but it highlights the danger of the fellowships to foster a homogeneous *community of practice* that is strongly shaped by its cultural context. The large percentage of participants that originated in Württemberg increased the probability of a similar dynamic in the BMTI.

The involvement of every believer that conventicles encouraged became a driving force of mission both, at home among the many that had no personal experience of the faith and overseas when Protestant Europeans became more aware of the wider world. As Pietism fostered lay participation, lay people could and did get involved in the life of the church and mission. They distributed the tracts and Bibles, paid for their printing, sold the mission magazine, led the monthly meetings, and collected financial offerings for the mission societies. Christian Friedrich Spittler (1782–1867), the driving force in founding the BMTI, was a lay person, trained as administrative assistant, not a theologian. The Members of the Basel Mission's governing board were mostly lay people, wealthy merchants and other influential burghers in the city of Basel, and the missionary volunteers were young lay men. All these activities were

---

42. As Lehmann points out in a more recent article; see Lehmann, "Mobilization," 191–94.

43. Stoeffler, *German Pietism*, 88–130.

44. Scharfe, *Religion des Volkes*, 63.

encouraged in the conventicles, prayed for, and often planned and carried out together.

The voluntary society subverted old church structures and first made lay people "of real significance above parish or congregational level."[45] This enabled the advance of mission beyond the denominational restraint. Foundations for this development were laid in the emphasis on fellowships of mutual edification which gave permission to believers of any social background to associate, and share ideas and purpose. By the nineteenth century a dominant mutual interest became the support of foreign mission. Support associations were a variation of conventicles for the specific purpose to disseminate news from mission fields, pray for the ministries and peoples, raise financial support, and challenge young people to join the missions.

In some contexts the fellowship was taken further. The Moravians "developed a particularly intensive form of religious community."[46] Their settlements practiced close accountability in daily meetings and prayer. Similar ideas of developing model Christian community guided the establishment of independent villages in Korntal (1819) and Wilhelmsdorf (1824) by Gottlieb Wilhelm Hoffmann (1771–1846), the father of the second Director of the Basel Mission.[47] Furthermore, model villages and local fellowships gained significance also as places of retreat as Pietists became more estranged from general socio-political developments. Such model Christian communities became a common pattern of mission. Moravians founded similar settlements wherever they migrated. Latourette referred to them as the Protestant version of monastic communities with the same dynamic that motivated and enabled missionary outreach at home and abroad.[48] Strong emphasis on model Christian community was also reflected in the Basel Mission, first in the goals for life and work in the BMTI and later in the mission stations in Africa.

45. Walls, *Missionary Movement*, 241–54.

46. Lehmann, "Grenzüberschreitungen," 13.

47. Lehmann, *Pietismus und weltliche Ordnung*, 177–87. Lehmann's detailed account of the political and socio-economic dynamics that led to the founding of Korntal shows that it was primarily motivated by an attempt to stem emigration from Württemberg.

48. Latourette, *Three Centuries of Advance*, 47. I find this perspective on Moravian missions more convincing than Vogt's suggestion that they represented "less a church but in certain respects already the prototype of a free mission society;" which is not to deny the influence Moravian missions undoubtedly had on subsequent Protestant efforts. See Vogt, "Mission der Brüdergemeine," 222; Schattschneider, "William Carey."

FOUNDING A GERMAN MISSION SOCIETY

The founding of the Basel Mission came out of the missionary impulses of Pietism and its impetus towards exchange with the like-minded in a "brotherhood of believers" across ecclesiastical borders. Ward points out that this "separation of religious life from ecclesiastical life" is at the root of a disregard for differences that sought relationships and cooperation with *true Christians* of any tradition or nationality.[49] Tracing the international networks of pious believers is difficult because of the parochial and national character of most history writing.[50] However, there are numerous examples of networking through the circulation of information by letters, personal contacts, and the press and through the translation of literature which ensured continuing mutual influences between the revived circles everywhere.[51] Halle-trained missionaries worked in Danish colonies and later under the British SPCK, Anglophone revivals were influenced by Moravians, Moravian missions spread through Zinzendorf's international journeys, and German training institutions provided missionaries with Lutheran ordination for Anglican British and Reformed Dutch societies. The "fortunate subversion of the church" that led to the founding of specific societies for missionary work in Britain happened in German Pietism long before.[52] These examples also show how the networks of communication between pious individuals and groups across ecclesiastical and national lines were motivated by, fostered, and enabled missionary activity.

Basel as International Pious Center

On the continent, Basel emerged as a significant Pietist center because of its strategic position, geographically and ecclesiastically, its proximity to Württemberg, relative political freedom, and the presence of diverse groups and ideas. Basel also had an influential wealthy middle class

---

49. Ward, *Evangelical Awakening*, 46–53.

50. Several authors comment on this reason for the difficulty to trace networks; for example, Jenkins, "An Early Experiment," 50; O'Brien, "A Transatlantic Community of Saints," 811–12.

51. Ward, *Evangelical Awakening*, 1–53; O'Brien, "A Transatlantic Community of Saints." See also the section on "Pietist forms of communication and networks" in Jakubowski-Tiessen, "Eigenkultur," 203–6.

52. Walls, *Missionary Movement*, 241–54. Vogt also highlights the importance of Pietist international networks for the development of a global Protestant missionary vision in Vogt, "Mission der Brüdergemeine," 209–11.

impacted by Pietism which became the driving force for an association of the various Pietist groups across Europe. This *(German) Christian Society* was founded in 1780 as network for mutual encouragement and promotion of Pietist values. Numerous particular societies and individual leaders joined and their correspondence shows the ecumenical and international relationships that ensued.[53] Basel was the administrative and visionary center from where the secretaries edited the letters and tracts suggested for dissemination, and sent monthly handwritten confidential reports to the members.[54] Excerpts were printed in a monthly journal. The *Gatherings for Lovers of Christian Truth* not only covered apologetic and edificatory subjects but increasingly promoted foreign missions.

The membership and relationships of the *Christian Society* foreshadowed the dynamics which later evolved in the Basel Mission. First, while local societies typically had a supporting pastor, the majority of those gathering to read the journal and corresponding with Basel were dedicated lay men. Sociologically, they originated in the middle class, most were merchants and artisans, and only a few came from the upper classes of government or academia. Finally, Lutherans, Reformed, and even Catholics were working together.[55] It is also significant that all the secretaries were from Württemberg and while a theologian was preferred, a lay person with considerable administrative and visionary gifts became the longest standing and most influential secretary, Christian Friedrich Spittler. This close cooperation between influential lay leaders in Basel, and dedicated participants from Germany became characteristic for the Basel Mission as well. Two secretaries of the Christian Society, Karl Friedrich Adolph Steinkopf (1773–1859)—secretary 1796–1801 and subsequently pastor of the German Lutheran church in London (1801–1859) with close links to the British revived circles—and Spittler, took the lead in

---

53. Even though it predominantly included the German speaking networks, the Society became known as *Christentumsgesellschaft* (Christian Society). See Staehelin, *Christentumsgesellschaft*, Vol. 1, 15–83. Staehelin, *Christentumsgesellschaft*, Vol. 2, 245–63 is a list of correspondents from 1813. Staehelin's two volumes contain the annual reports and transcripts of a wide selection of letters between members.

54. Staehelin, *Christentumsgesellschaft*, Vol.2, 4. About the Christian Society see also Weigelt, "Diasporaarbeit," 125–40; Brecht et al., eds., *Die Basler Christentumsgesellschaft*.

55. Weigelt, "Der Pietismus," 713. For the Catholic connections, see Staehelin, *Christentumsgesellschaft*, Vol. 2, 6, 66–67 (references to the Catholic pastor, Johannes Goßner, who even functioned as the secretary of the Christian Society for a period); Weigelt, "Diasporaarbeit," 129.

directing German pious circles towards enthusiastic involvement in foreign missions.[56]

Fresh Inspiration from the German Revival Movement

A significant contributing factor and source of missionary personnel was the renewed turn to personal religion known as the Revival Movement (*Erweckungsbewegung*) which spread across the continent from 1800 onwards.[57] Here the sometimes confusing details are not of concern, only that it was an ongoing phenomenon during the nineteenth century, invigorated Pietist values and practices in German Christianity, and reached various social strata.[58] Most importantly, the revived were inspired by the call to support foreign mission. They met monthly to read mission news and pray, supported foreign mission financially, and their young men volunteered for missionary service. Involvement in foreign missions became the central activity of pious believers. Lehmann ascribes this to three factors relating to eschatology, improved logistics, and the inclusion of lay people. First, for Pietists the preaching of the gospel to the heathen was an important precondition for the return of Christ; second the recent advances in transportation, geography, linguistics and medicine made the mission venture easier. Finally, foreign mission opened opportunities for simple provincial people to be involved in a fascinating global activity which became very attractive in the face of difficult economic circumstances and the decline of Christianity at home.[59]

The inclusion of lay people is a very significant factor in German missionary engagement because it provided the committed volunteers British societies were lacking. Through their global networks the scientific advances became accessible to Pietists at a time when Germany was still lagging behind in development. Those same networks provided the information which inspired fascination with foreign lands and ignited optimism about success for Christian missions. The Pietist revived were

---

56. For the crucial role of these two men, see Lehmann, "Mobilization."

57. The German revival was a religious response to the destruction, poverty, and suffering caused by revolutions and Napoleon's wars. It was a multi-facetted movement that emerged almost everywhere in German speaking Europe at different times. It had diverse expressions and various local leaders and related to events in Anglophone countries, Switzerland, France, and the Netherlands. See Benrath, "Die Erweckung"; Beyreuther, *Die Erweckungsbewegung*.

58. Holborn, *History of Modern Germany*, 494.

59. Lehmann, "Die neue Lage," 8–9.

the section of German Christianity who caught this vision; many in Germany became active in the Bible and Tract Societies, but foreign mission was what only the revival movement did.⁶⁰

Concrete Steps to Support Foreign Mission

The first concrete steps towards engaging in foreign mission came about through the existing relationships with evangelical revived circles in London. In 1798 the Christian Society entered into communication with the "Mission Society in London."⁶¹ Two leaders, Basel University professor Johann Wernhard Herzog (1726–1815) and Baron Friedrich von Schirnding (1754–1812) from Berlin became members of the LMS Board of Directors in the same year.⁶² Von Schirnding initiated a missionary training institute in Berlin which was established in 1800 with Johannes Jänicke (1748–1827), pastor of the Bohemian church in Berlin since 1792, as director.⁶³ This first missionary training institution in Germany supplied a considerable number of missionaries, mostly for the LMS and CMS.⁶⁴

In the meantime, in Basel the new secretary of the Christian Society, Spittler shared the vision of a similar institute in the South as early as around 1806.⁶⁵ However, in the face of the dire war situation and lack of support by other leaders, it was not until 1815 that the plan materialized.⁶⁶ Then the deliverance from Napoleon's troops was perceived as

---

60. Benrath, "Die Erweckung," 155.

61. Staehelin, *Christentumsgesellschaft*, Vol. 2, 5. A transcript of the actual letter is on pp.405–8.

62. Staehelin, *Christentumsgesellschaft*, Vol. 1, 40, 67. Herzog was Director of the Christian Society from 1780 to 1813.

63. Little is known of Baron von Schirnding, but from 1798 he functioned as director for the LMS in Germany and he is consistently mentioned as the visionary and principal sponsor of Jänicke's institute. See Ledderhose, *Johann Jänicke*, 95–96; Raupp, "August Karl Friedrich Freiherr von Schirnding."

64. Weigelt, "Der Pietismus," 709; Walls, *Cross-Cultural Proces*, 206–11.

65. Schlatter, *Heimatgeschichte*, 13. In 1801 Spittler, as a non-theologian, was given the administrative and bookkeeping side of the work assisting the first secretary. In 1808, however, he became the full secretary of the society and remained in this position for the remainder of its existence. He shared his vision of a mission training institute in Basel with Christian Gottlieb Blumhardt during the time of his secretaryship for the society (1803–1807). See Blumhardt's letter from September 6, 1815 cited in Staehelin, *Christentumsgesellschaft*, Vol.2, 296.

66. The *Historical Description of the Events leading up to the founding of a*

divine sign to focus on God's work in a fresh way. In July 1815 Spittler obtained permission to establish the suggested institute unexpectedly quickly from the city authorities and in September a governing Board constituted itself to found the Basel Mission. The former secretary of the Christian Society, Christian Gottlieb Blumhardt (1779–1838), accepted the position as Director. He provided the first curriculum, volunteers applied, support was promised by the friends in London, and on August 26, 1816 the Missionary Training Institute in Basel began its work with seven young men.[67]

The international character of the Basel Mission—with the director and the majority of the students typically originating from outside Switzerland—necessitated an ongoing negotiation process with city officials about residence permits and other political matters.[68] Spittler made it a point in the initial request to address potential concerns of the Basel authorities with dissenting religious groups. He emphasized that

---

Missionary Institute in Basel from September 1815 alludes to the distress the city of Basel had just experienced. In the course of Napoleon's retreat the allied armies had camped out in the city from December 1813 to June 1814. Not only had they depleted food supplies, they also brought Typhoid fever which killed numerous soldiers and civilians. The following year French troops threatened Switzerland, the battle line went along the Northern borders of Basel and when from March to August 1815 in several bombardments nobody was killed it was interpreted by the Pietist leaders as divine deliverance. See "Historische Darstellung dessen, was zur Gründung einer Missions-Anstalt in Basel geschah" in Staehelin, *Christentumsgesellschaft*, Vol. 2, 299–302. This is a transcript of the handwritten record which is the first entry in the book of minutes of Board meetings of the Basel Mission and precedes the minutes of the constituting meeting. This account was probably authored by Spittler and is signed by the founding members as a "true record of the events" (BMA, KP 1, 1–9. Minutes from September 25, 1815. See also the summary in BMA, Q-2-2-1).

67. Details of founding the Basel Mission are given by: Ostertag, *Entstehungsgeschichte*; Schick, *Vorboten und Bahnbrecher*; Schlatter, *Heimatgeschichte*. See also BMA, Q-2-1.1 "Anfänge des Basler Missions Instituts" (The Beginnings of the Basel Mission Institute). This folder contains the original application documents to the city council as well as the official approval letters and a copy of the Plan of the Missions Institute. On the support promised by the CMS see Eugene Stock, *The History of the Church Missionary Society: Its Environment, its Men and its Work* (London: Church Missionary Society, 1899), 120. In this 1816 report the CMS assigns an annual support of 100 Pounds to the Basel Mission.

68. The application also requested that teachers and students of the institute would be granted residence permits. On June 4, 1816 Blumhardt received official permission to reside in Basel and take on his position. "Heimatscheine" (official documents confirming a person's home village), proofs of completed military service in their home states and residence permits for Basel in the Personnel Files of missionaries testify to this ongoing political aspect engendered by the locale of the school.

the institute would offer teaching that was "according to the Protestant creed" to prepare young men for service in mission fields established "by the Protestant governments" as agents of the spread of "Protestant Christianity":

> The final purpose of our little missionary institute is to train a number of upright pupils through purposeful teaching in languages, sciences and the spiritual religion according to our Protestant profession . . . who will work charitably for the heathen world in the mission fields of the Protestant governments in Asia and Africa among the barbaric peoples promoting Protestant Christianity and bourgeois civilization.[69]

This application also shows very clearly that rather than establishing itself as another sending mission society, the Basel Mission initially focused solely on preparing missionaries. It is curious how little attention has been given to the significant educational traditions Pietists developed in their various institutions.[70] This project addresses this gap at least in part by examining the largest and arguably most influential school for training foreign missionaries that was initiated by German Pietists. The motivations for this educational focus and how preceding ideas and experiments of missionary training served as models are significant for understanding the kind of learning community which ensued in the BMTI.

Missionary Training—A Focus Inspired by Pietism

The founders of the Basel Mission do not explain the rationale for their decision to start a training institute other than reasons that could have also been brought forward for a mission agency.[71] The only argument for a school was the reference to the aging director in Berlin and the probability that this school would discontinue after his passing. Nevertheless,

---

69. BMA, Q-1-2.1 "Plan der Missionsanstalt"

70. Benrath, "Die Erweckung," 155. Benrath points out the need for more independent research into the educational traditions Pietists developed. Since his writing, however, some studies have been published. See especially the edited volume on Moravian Education: Lempa and Peucker, Self, Community, World.

71. The Historical Description lists among the considerations which led to founding the Mission Institute in Basel the great number of unreached heathen in the world, the command and example of our Lord, the fact that the director of the Berlin Institute was aging, the preparation of the way by the work of the Bible Societies, a number of reasons why Basel is an ideal place and finally the provision of the needed official permission, teacher, finances, curriculum and leadership (BMA, KP 1, 1–9).

several arguments can be put forward to support the view that shared Pietist emphases motivated the focus on training missionaries for other societies to send.

International Pietist networking facilitated complementary benefits for German leaders and the young mission societies. While the British missions had the means to send people but lacked men who would go, the Christian Society had the volunteers but lacked the resources to deploy missionaries because Germany lagged behind economically and in seafaring enterprise. Precedence had been set in Berlin, from where in fourteen years about thirty men had been sent by non-German societies. For the Basel Mission leaders this implied that volunteers were available, their training was possible, and their employment with other societies was bringing good results.[72]

Moreover, German and Swizz supporters of foreign missions did not feel the need to begin their own work because of the close relationships with their European brothers in the vision. They saw their role as preparing German youth to support the efforts of already existing societies "by which the German missionaries would be trained further and consequently sent out."[73] This is a highly interesting perspective because it presupposes a view of the world without empire in mind. German nationalism was just beginning to emerge and German unification was led by Prussia. Other regions, especially conservative Württemberg, were reluctant to join. Moreover, Pietists passionately opposed many of the related developments like the secularization of schools and loss of ecclesiastical authority over the life of the nation in general. Even when national thinking intensified in the late nineteenth century, studies of German missionaries reveal intense reservations against colonial governments and show many areas of contention and opposition to colonial policies and practice.[74]

Another reason for this self-evident focus on training lies in the Pietist emphasis on education from its inception. Since Spener and Francke Pietists developed curricula, influenced educational policies, and promoted general education.[75] Their tripartite emphasis on faith, intellect,

---

72. *Historical Description* BMA, KP 1, 2

73. Spittler's petition to the city council in July 1815 (BMA, Q-1–2.1).

74. See for example: Halldén, *Culture Policy*.

75. Schmalenberg, *Pietismus, Schule, Religionsunterricht*. Schmalenberg shows how Pietist Christian emphases were reflected in eighteenth century German school legislation. He traces their emphasis on faith and behavior in addition to intellect.

and behavior can also be observed in the BMTI. However, by the late eighteenth century schools in Germany became increasingly secularized and Pietists' influence restricted to their own institutions.[76] These they continued to pursue with undiminished vision for neglected youth and conviction that "schools should be . . . plantations of Christianity and evangelical truth and love."[77] The same men who envisioned these educational ventures founded the BMTI. For them training volunteers was a natural way to meet the need for more missionaries.

Finally, the founders' personal experience of education was a major reason why educating young people for mission was obvious for them. They belonged to the pious—and educated—middle class supporting the Christian Society: merchants, artisans, bankers, pastors, teachers, and theologians.[78] Lehmann identifies the "far-reaching intellectual and cultural influence of the pious middle classes" from before the seventeenth century who had their own view of the world and way of life before the religious revival movements of Puritanism, Jansenism, and Pietism absorbed them.[79] This specific worldview and lifestyle continued as they became Pietists. Their views of the courts as sinful and reprehensible and of the common people as immoral and undisciplined persisted alongside their confidence in education as a means of transforming people towards Christian ways. In the Basel Mission the pious middle classes in Basel and Württemberg worked together to establish and lead the organization. For both groups education was essential to develop the skills, knowledge, and character they perceived as necessary for ministry in foreign lands. They rejected the secularization of schools, but they regarded exercise of

76. Lehmann, "Die neue Lage," 17. In 1809–1810 Prussia introduced universal schooling and the educational structure that became the German school system which included a universal people's school (*Volksschule*), a high school (*Gymansium*) that prepared for academia, and universities. See Holborn, *History of Modern Germany*, 474–75. In Germany the pious never had the economic strength nor did they penetrate society in the same way as Evangelicals in America to sustain independent schools.

77. The speaker at the opening of the Beuggen institute for training teachers for the poor in 1820 expressed Pietist opposition to the secularized methods and curriculum in public education. He emphasized that "schools should be Christian schools, plantations of Christianity and evangelical truth and love" because this was the only way the "ailing school system can be healed." See Staehelin, *Christentumsgesellschaft*, Vol. 2, 388.

78. Wellenreuther points out that the new German missionary initiatives in the nineteenth century were generally led by the upper middle class in Wellenreuther, "Pietismus und Mission," 173.

79. Lehmann, "Pious Middle Classes."

the mind and good general education as important in addition to Bible study, personal piety, and Christian character. The way they implemented this in the BMTI was influenced by previous models.

PREVIOUS EDUCATIONAL APPROACHES AS MODELS FOR THE BMTI

The mission's founders themselves cite Francke's work in Halle, the Moravian institutes, and Johannes Jänicke in Berlin as previous enterprises that served as models.[80] Furthermore, it is probable that Jänicke was influenced by Bogue, whose academy was also known to the Basel Mission.[81] Wellenreuther states the obvious when he observes that "Halle only sent studied and ordained theologians" and the Moravians relied on artisans who as a rule were not ordained or educated in the protestant state churches.[82] The Basel Mission adopted elements of both approaches to missionary preparation and added their own emphases.

Francke—Academia with Character Formation

While the *Historical Summary* only mentions Francke as inspiration for trusting God in the venture, the BMTI educational approach reveals great indebtedness to his ideas. Francke is acknowledged for innovations in child education—including girls and the poor, rejecting harsh punishment, attending to individual needs and abilities, and teaching in the vernacular—but particularly his emphasis on developing practical skills, character, and spirituality in addition to academia is seen in the BMTI. For him the aim of education was the glory of God through "genuine piety and Christian wisdom" (*wahre Gottseligkeit und christliche Klugheit*).[83] *Piety* (a living faith that expresses itself in love and service to others) and *Christian wisdom* (avoiding temptations, using one's gifts, and knowing how to help others) required an education that combined development of

---

80. Staehelin, *Christentumsgesellschaft*, Vol. 2, 299, 301. Also: BMA, KP 1, 1–9 and Q-1–2.1

81. Indications are that several letters in the Christian Society reports mention him and Blumhardt cites Bogue's speech at the LMS annual meeting in 1820 in his 1821 annual report (MM 1821, 131).

82. Wellenreuther, "Pietismus und Mission," 170.

83. Francke, "Kurtzer und Einfältiger Unterricht."

the intellect with the formation of Christian character and practical skills that enable one to serve others.[84]

In Halle theological students were used as teachers in the schools, admonished to exemplify "godliness" and "Christian wisdom" in their own lives, and expected to join one of the *collegia biblica,* groups for devotional Bible study, guidance by tutors, and mutual encouragement. Francke's *Ideas about Theological Studies* emphasized that it is not enough to become learned, "the foundation must be an upright life in Christ [because] both piety and erudition is discredited by indecent moral behavior, [and finally] you also need wisdom and understanding in all your conduct."[85]

Key methods employed towards the non-academic goals involved students' engagement in practical ministry and living with tutors. This educational format inspired the establishment of the *Stift* in Tübingen where theological students also lived together under the supervision of tutors. While both Halle and Tübingen University served the clergy in Germany and were not framed as missionary training schools, the first Protestant missionaries were trained in Halle and most BMTI teachers studied in Tübingen which influenced their approach in Basel.

BMTI intellectual demands came close to the university course in Halle and like Francke, the leaders saw studies not as an end in themselves but emphasized ministry skills.[86] The focus on usefulness of acquired knowledge included exercises in teaching (*catechesis*), preaching, report writing, and drawing maps. But contrary to Halle, BMTI applicants originated mostly from rural communities and had very limited previous schooling.[87] This necessitated a lower academic level and eventually led to the establishment of a pre-school to ensure elementary education before students could enter the actual missionary training. However, while

---

84. Bunge, "Education and the Child," 260–61.

85. Francke, "Idea Studiosi Theologiae," 388.

86. For example, Blumhardt referred to "the practical-theological tendency of the Spener-Francke School" in support and as model for the "true understanding and use of scripture" practiced in the BMTI. See MM 1828, 383.

87. Both, Blumhardt and Hoffmann frequently emphasized the need for applicants with intellectual abilities to the supporting groups that recurrently recommended pious but not very schooled young men. See, for example, Blumhardt in MM 1821, 128 and Hoffmann in MM 1849, 384–87. Incidentally, this contradicts Wellenreuther's claim that in the first decades the Basel Mission "following the older model of the Moravians did not normally make educational demands of the applicants." See Wellenreuther, "Pietismus und Mission," 173.

56　Part I: The Community of Practice

intellectual requirements were high, this never was at the expense of the formation of Christian character and individual spirituality in a tight community—similar to the Moravians.

The Moravians—Spirituality in Community

The Moravian church sent dedicated missionaries from the 1730s onwards. They were shaped by the theology and practices of the Moravian communal approach to living pious Christianity. While formal training for mission was not deemed necessary, participating in this unique religious community was critical to the preparation process. For Moravians "all of life's tasks and challenges become occasions for worship and . . . in turn transformed into acts of religiously motivated service."[88] This service included a "universality of the calling to witness;" everyone who had met Christ was called to testify and the church as a whole was to carry out mission, not civil governments or only professional theologians.[89]

The Moravian community had monastic characteristics with shared resources and strong regulation of civil and religious life. While there was personal freedom and the use of individual gifts was encouraged, there was also "the expectation of radical conformation into the existing community and readiness to serve;" it was a "community school of dedicated and disciplined deployment."[90] They had numerous meetings for mutual edification including morning and evening devotions, several Sunday services, the famous 24/7 prayer watch, and intimate meetings of two or three in "bands or classes." The community was led by a "conference of elders" that oversaw daily events, administered advice or reproof, visited the sick, and assisted the poor. It was a general atmosphere of prayer and

---

88. Stoeffler, *German Pietism*, 139, 154. Lempa refers to this dynamic as "education toward a liturgical life." See Lempa, "Moravian Education," 281–85.

89. Zimmerling, *Pioniere*, 33. See also Vogt, "Mission der Brüdergemeine," 213–22. Vogt articulates this understanding of "mission as task of the whole church to which every member could be called by God" in contrast to the professionalized approach in Halle who sent only ordained theologians as missionaries. He also points out other differences between the two missiological approaches, like Halle's single focus on India in the East versus the Moravian "multitude of mission fields" primarily in the Western transatlantic region and Halle missionaries' emphasis on systematic teaching of converts versus Moravian emphasis on simplicity, warmth and heart-felt testimony to Christ. Wellenreuther, furthermore, highlights that these differences were rooted in their varying understanding of conversion and repentance. See Wellenreuther, "Pietismus und Mission," 169–72.

90. Beck, *Brüder in vielen Völkern*, 32.

religious conversation in the context of communal service through their crafts and the charitable institutions for children, the poor and the sick.[91]

Zinzendorf instructed the single men in composition, medicine, geography, and languages, and so trained "artisans to be lay missionaries fit for action."[92] Moravian missionaries were expected to support themselves with their agricultural skills and trades in the same way the community did. Practical skills, personal piety, Bible knowledge, and a divine calling recognized by the community were regarded as sufficient preparation and they tended to establish the same kind of communities wherever they went, thereby "transforming the fate of migration into the action of mission to the heathen."[93]

Like the Moravians the BMTI valued practical trades and communal spirituality with daily devotional meetings and oversight by elders. Similar expectations of a prayerful atmosphere and conformity to house rules resembled Moravian closeness and accountability.[94] However, in contrast to the Moravians, the BMTI community did not include women (apart from the director's wife and servants), its participants came from considerably more mixed backgrounds, and academic learning was valued much higher.

Bogue and Jänicke—Private Education in "Academies"

Terpstra outlines the characteristics of pastoral training for British independent churches in "academies" led by a local pastor who gathered a small number of interested students.[95] His study of David Bogue reveals close parallels between this school and Jänicke's Mission Institute in Ber-

91. Langton, *Moravian Church*, 73–78; Stoeffler, *German Pietism*, 139–40.

92. Beck, *Brüder in vielen Völkern*, 28.

93. Becker, *Zinzendorf*.

94. The directors referred to the BMTI as a "testing ground" for true spirituality, character formation, and discipline; for example Blumhardt in MM 1828, 385–89 and Hoffmann in MM 1845, 117.

95. Terpstra, "David Bogue," 21–26. Before describing the Gosport Academy in detail he explains: "The Act of Uniformity of 1662 and the Statutes of the Universities of Oxford and Cambridge left non-conformists outside the schools as well as the churches. Many of the ejected clergy had been professors at the Universities and, for financial reasons as well as for the education of dissenters' children and future ministers, continued teaching, not, however, in the Universities so closely associated with the established church, but in what have been termed 'academies.'" See also MacLachlan, *English Education*; Mercer, "Dissenting Academies"; Parker, *Dissenting Academies*; Smith, *Birth of Modern Education*.

lin. The most important are the small size, the private meeting place, and leadership by a single teacher-pastor.

Bogue's "academy" began as small private school in his parsonage in Gosport. It taught a three year program. He was the first to suggest that "the education of a missionary must be in many respects widely different from that of those who preach in Christian countries" and introduced a series of lectures for missionaries "suitable for their foreign career."[96] These lectures represented the first systematic curriculum for missionary training. Apart from biblical-theological subjects Bogue emphasized to missionary candidates the need of learning native languages and regarded Rhetoric, "Universal Grammar," and biblical languages as helpful preparation. He promoted Preaching, Reasoning, Conversation, Catechizing, and translation and writing of Christian literature as "means of conveying Christian knowledge." Missionaries had to expect temptations, difficulties, oppositions, and discouragements which demanded perseverance, diligence, wisdom, and above all spiritual qualities, a clear calling, and the right motives. The content of these lectures reveals the assumption of Europe as Christian territory and the prevailing negative view and paucity of knowledge of non-European cultures. But this was a first attempt to provide a preparation that takes into account specific challenges faced by ministry engagement in contexts vastly different from the candidates' background. Bogue made his *Missionary Appeal* already in 1794, but initially most LMS leaders regarded training for missionaries as dispensable.[97] Only after the majority of the first thirty LMS missionaries deserted the ministry within five years under the pressures of intercultural work was Bogue's insistence on the need for specialized education for foreign missionaries heeded.[98] In 1800 the LMS made his school its principal training place.

---

96. Terpstra, "David Bogue," 39. He made the *Missionary Appeal* in a letter from August 26, 1794, published in *Evangelical Magazine*, 1794, 378–80. Terpstra identifies Bogue as "pioneer in education" with specific reference to his *missionary lectures*. Piggin also summarizes these lectures. See ibid., 103–33; Piggin, *Making Evangelical Missionaries*, 175–81.

97. The "Rules for the Examination of Missionaries" from 1795 state that it "is not necessary that every missionary should be a learned man" and that "godly men who understand mechanic arts may be of signal use to this undertaking as missionaries, especially in the South Sea Islands, Africa, and other uncivilized parts of the world. See Lovett, *London Missionary Society*, 43–44.

98. Lovett describes the failures frankly. Bogue was instrumental in the founding of the LMS, one of the Board members, and the director of the Gosport Academy where

In the meantime, the sharing of information and personnel in the Christian Society meant that German Pietists were cognizant of the lessons learned in the LMS' early years and Bogue's academy.[99] This led to the first association of British missionary societies with German volunteers and training. Baron von Schirnding, a board member of the LMS, sponsored Johannes Jänicke to begin a similar school in Berlin in 1800.[100] Jänicke also was a member of the Christian Society and his younger brother Joseph Daniel Jänicke (1759–1800) had been a missionary with the SPCK in India since 1788. He became involved with printing a Bohemian Bible and later founded the Berlin Mission Society (1823).[101] Most graduates of his school in Berlin became missionaries with the LMS and later the CMS. By his death, he had trained more than eighty missionaries.[102]

Very little is known of the inner workings of this school. However, the educational parallels and personal relationships make it probable that Jänicke took his model from Bogue's academy. The curriculum covered *Realien* (reading, writing, arithmetic, basic sciences), English, Latin, Greek, Hebrew, Systematic Theology, writing sermons, music, and drawing. Schick acknowledges influences of revived spiritual life in Britain, the Danish-Halle Mission, and the Moravians, but claims Jänicke's own personality and example as preacher, apologist, and counselor impacted his students most.[103] Like Bogue he integrated teaching with community living. The modeling of a strong leader, focus on personal spirituality, and

---

he trained ministers for the Independent Ministry. His appeal was originally published in *Evangelical Magazine* 1794, 378–80 and is cited in Terpstra, "David Bogue," 153–56; Lovett, *London Missionary Society*, 6–10; Piggin, *Making Evangelical Missionaries*.

99. The sermons held at the LMS inauguration in 1795 were translated into German and published in 1797. The German Christian Society initiated an ongoing relationship with the LMS leadership from 1798, and the chairman of the German Christian Society Wernhard Herzog and the chairman of the Berlin society Baron Friedrich von Schirnding became members of the LMS Board of Directors. Staehelin, *Christentumsgesellschaft*, Vol. 1, 405–8, 467.

100. Staehelin claims that von Schirnding founded the school and commissioned Jänicke with its leadership. A letter from Jänicke which Schick and Ledderhose cite clearly shows they collaborated on the founding and Jänicke led the school from its inception. Staehelin, *Christentumsgesellschaft*, Vol. 2, 83, 128; Schick, *Vorboten und Bahnbrecher*, 258–60; Ledderhose, *Johann Jänicke*, 95–99. See also Vogt, "Mission der Brüdergemeine," 232–33. Vogt emphasizes the Moravian connections of both men.

101. Jackson, "Jänicke," 255–56.

102. Bundy, "Jänicke, Johannes."

103. Schick, *Vorboten und Bahnbrecher*, 259–60.

practicing the skills needed in ministry constituted a holistic formational experience for students.

In the BMTI the relationships between the Director and the students had much of the characteristics of an academy, especially in the early years. But the decision making Board provided a wider basis and greater stability to the organization. Originally, Spittler envisioned a similar set-up to Jänicke's in Berlin with his friend Blumhardt as the sole teacher.[104] However, Blumhardt emphasized organizational needs such as a building for the school, procedures for screening students, and economic security for the director. He suggested "a small group of proven, sober-minded, and experienced men who would be the human pillars and sponsors of the whole."[105] Steinkopf, the Pastor of the German church in London, also recommended "a small committee of truly upright and wise men that would discuss all important issues of such a big and important enterprise" and ensure the economic security of the director and the whole institute.[106]

Following this advice Spittler convinced Pastor Niklaus von Brunn (1766–1846) to become the institute's president—a position he held until 1838. They invited other "men of standing" who on September 25, 1815 founded the Basel Mission and constituted its first *Committee*.[107] This structure consequently led to recognition by these men that the missionary institute they established in actuality was, "no longer the business of individual private men, but a formal missionary society, in which they had accepted mutual responsibility and liability in all desirable or disagreeable eventualities."[108] The Basel Mission began solely as a training institute, a formal constitution was not drafted until 1820, and only in 1821 they sent the first missionaries; but organizationally it was a missionary society from the start.

In the Board meetings of October 1815 Steinkopf promised support from the British societies for training missionaries in Basel. He had already mediated between the CMS and Jänicke who supplied their first

---

104. A view he expressed clearly in a letter from November 25, 1815. Cited by Ostertag, *Entstehungsgeschichte*, 317.

105. Letter from September 6, 1815. Cited by ibid., 312–14.

106. Letter from September 20, 1815. Cited by ibid., 319.

107. *La Comité*—the French word was typically used for the Basel Mission governing Board.

108. BMA, Q-1-2.1 *Anfänge des Basler Missions Instituts*, Historische Darstellung, 5–6; identical with BMA, KP 1, 9 from September 25, 1818.

missionaries, and continued this function between Basel and the British missions.[109] These meetings also confirmed Blumhardt as director and sent out a communiqué to the corresponding members of the Christian Society requesting support from individuals and groups for this new venture.[110]

The small group of ten to fifteen students envisioned initially implied a similar set-up to Jänicke's. However, the Basel Mission was instituted more formally anticipating a larger organization. A governing Board directed the affairs of the BMTI that had final authority over all proceedings. The *Inspector* (Director) was the executive officer who reported to the Board. He exerted considerable influence through the strong bonds which life and work in close community created with the students, but he was not an independent leader and as the school grew additional teachers were employed. The interdenominational and international relationships of the founders from the start ensured a wider support structure and potential for advocacy, finances, prayer, and personnel across Europe.

While the founders cite the previous efforts as models and similarities are obvious, the BMTI represented a distinctive approach to missionary training. Schlatter summarizes it as a "middle way between the . . . two older German missions"—neither the [Moravian] vibrant personal Christianity nor scientific [Halle University] education was regarded as adequate missionary training.[111] The Basel Mission emphasized the need for specialized academic education, but also stressed the missionary's "inner relationship with his God and converted heart, which in the final analysis are independent of his level of education."

In light of educational theories, the approaches to missionary preparation that inspired the BMTI had one thing in common; they all advocated integral, experiential training. They not only assumed the social dynamics of learning but factored them in as deliberate educational means. Community relationships were regarded as important for desired goals such as personal piety, Christian values, behaviors, and ministerial

---

109. Stock, the historian of the CMS, recounts the initial difficulties of the society to find English volunteers and Steinkopf's mediation with the Berlin Seminary that trained 17 of the first 24 missionaries the CMS sent out. Stock, *Church Missionary Society*, 81–91.

110. BMA, KP 1, 15 from October 6, 1815. No.3. The text of the call for support, financially and in prayer, is printed in Staehelin, *Christentumsgesellschaft*, Vol. 2, 308–10.

111. Schlatter, *Heimatgeschichte*, 30–31.

skills, attitudes, and motivations. These were esteemed higher than academic sophistication. The Basel Mission leaders implemented a model that was also very intentional about establishing a learning community.

COMMUNITY AS MEANS OF LEARNING IN THE BMTI

A group of people becomes a *community of practice* when they use communal learning processes to develop practices regarded as conducive to common interests. In the BMTI such learning as a community was prioritized. Candidates and teachers lived together sharing daily life from morning devotions to evening prayers, over meals, and on preaching trips, as well as working together in classes and practically in the gardens and workshops. Figure 1 shows an image of the Leonhardsgraben building—used from 1820 to 1860—that reflects the ideal of tranquility, order, diligent work, quiet reflection, harmony, and agricultural landscaping that was upheld in the BMTI Community.[112] The house accommodated about forty students, the Director's family, classrooms, meeting rooms for the Board and the teachers, servant quarters, and guest rooms. Figure 2 shows a plan on the back of the image that indicates the location and usage of various rooms.

Figure 1
"Mission House in Basel" Leonhardsgraben

---

112. "Mission house in Basel." Max Beck, Schaffhausen, Switzerland. BMA, QS-30.018.0006: *BMArchives*. Online: http://www.bmarchives.org/items/show/81915. The Basel Mission Archive holds a rich and highly interesting collection of historical images. It is searchable at http://basel.bmpix.org/archive. For any use of the images, permission needs to be obtained from mission21, Missionsstrasse 21, CH-4003 Basel, Switzerland, info@bmpix.org. There are several depictions of the Leonhardsgraben house, all of which precede photography and reveal the idealized image of the BMTI community.

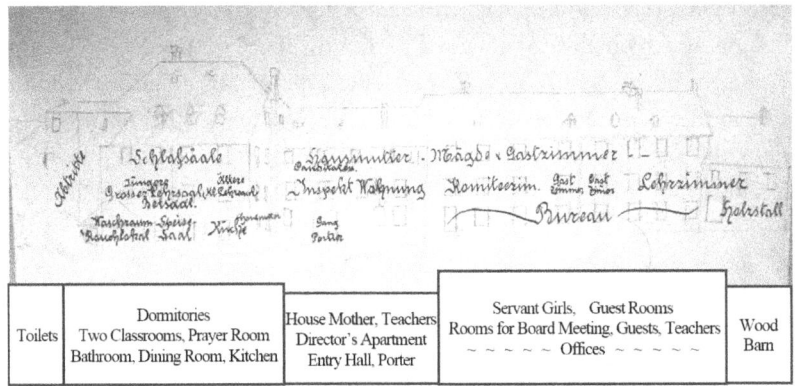

Figure 2
Room Plan of the Mission House Leonhardsgraben

The community of the boarding school was designed to encourage conformity to commonly held values and conduct—the *shared practice* of the organization that will be discussed in detail below. It purposefully fostered attitudes, character qualities, academic learning, and practical abilities which were regarded as vital for missionaries. Student evaluations indicate the priorities; they listed "Spiritual Life," "Missionary Fervor," "Ability" (a general category that comprised cognitive, social, and practical capacities), "Preaching and Teaching" as well as "Knowledge."[113]

The first two directors agreed on this community learning focus. Blumhardt spoke of the institute as a "nursery of the Holy Spirit" and a Christian family. Ludwig Friedrich Wilhelm Hoffmann (1806–1873), Inspector from 1839 to 1850, promoted residential seminary training as an ideal balance between academic university studies and apprenticeships.

The BMTI as "Nursery of the Holy Spirit"

Blumhardt's 1816 plan included a full daily schedule, provision for participation in Sunday services, and gave a central place to "Christian edification and means to foster living Christianity [and] promoting the practice of love for all people in the first place among each other."[114] His

---

113. "Knowledge" was divided into "Theology," "Languages" and "Realien" (covering various aspects that could be termed sciences and their practical application). Evaluations were recorded in the Board meeting minutes at the end of every term. See for example BMA, KP 15, 87–91 from January, 13 1841 which lists several students who were later sent to Africa.

114. BMA, KP 1, 24–45 from 7 März 1816. "Plan des Missions Instituts." This is

"House-Rule" (*Hausordnung*) from December 1818 was a foundational document which always remained part of the increasingly detailed regulations of life at the BMTI.[115] The specific rules of this document and its role in the practice of the BMTI community will be discussed below. For now, the significant observation is Blumhardt's characterization of the institute as a "nursery of the Holy Spirit" where not compulsion and coercion but "the law of God's freedom in everyone's heart" modeled God's order. He reasons:

> In nature, the Bible and human history, God is a God of order. If any individual or association devoted to a common purpose wants to please Him and take part in His blessing, this can only be on the path of order, which His wisdom has drawn in legible strokes in the nature of things and in the heart of man.

It is, however, not by the observance of rules but by the work of the Holy Spirit in human hearts that love for God's order grows and people live consistently after his ways. Candidates therefore, should already have this attitude and the purpose of training was to establish them firmly in it, so that—accustomed to accountability to God above all human rules—they would honor God on the mission field distant from familiar support.[116]

Miller cites this passage to engage in an impassioned discussion of the "hermeneutics of freedom and control" in which he explores the intellectual and emotional tensions involved in the simultaneous focus on outside imposed order and self-regulation.[117] His tone is disapproving of the authoritarian structure and in an effort to make a case for coerced uniformity at the seminary he misapplies Blumhardt's observation that seminarians would be "completely torn away from their previous ties."[118] In the actual context Blumhardt refers not to the seminary, but to the situation overseas, when missionaries would be far away from home and any communication would take weeks, possibly months. Therefore, he felt it was important that during the training students were established in

---

the official record of the document Blumhardt drafted. See also BMA, Q-1-2.1 "Plan der Missionsanstalt."

115. The rules were adopted in December 1818 and published in MM 1819, 641–43; a copy is recorded in KP 3, 13–16 from December 1819 when the 18 students in the BMTI at the time signed it.

116. For this argument see also MM 1828, 385–89.

117. Miller, *Missionary Zeal*, 115–21.

118. Ibid., 46–49. This misrepresentation occurs twice, on 48 and 118.

Pietist convictions and practice, so they would hold on to them in situations that separated them from most of the support they were used to.

More significantly, the seminarians shared the German Pietist convictions of their leaders and saw the BMTI training as opportunity to prepare for the challenges of missionary work. It is exactly this dynamic of mutually shared convictions that fostered the kind of communal learning the *communities of practice* framework highlights: establishing and perfecting a specific practice through communal interaction. All participants at the BMTI worked towards a common vision of Christian practice and mission outside Europe. The following chapters will show this in more detail.

Another related image to Blumhardt's ideas of community as means to instill attitudes and conduct was "planting a Christian family life *in which every individual sees themselves as happy part of the whole.*"[119] In this image too, the idea is that of a group of people living and working together, each member playing their part, to establish a community that represented their ideal of Christian life. In 1828 and 1838 Blumhardt used almost identical language to argue against expansion of the school and opting for quality over quantity.[120] Greater numbers of students in his view would be detrimental to "fulfill the real purpose of the mission-school, namely formation for the missionary profession and the melting of souls into one man in Christ."

Blumhardt stressed that the "Christian-disciplinary character" of the school was crucial to develop "fitness of life in the spirit," the ability to live out the biblical truth, which is more important than accumulating academic knowledge.[121] However, Blumhardt's presentation of rules as merely "necessary border posts and fences against misuse of spiritual freedom" proved unrealistic. Over the years regulations increased in response to various issues and organizational needs.[122] By the 1860s the House-Order listed thirty-nine paragraphs that regulated details of BMTI life.[123] Also, while both, Blumhardt and Hoffmann emphasized that there

119. MM 1838, 355. Emphasis mine.
120. MM 1838, 354–55 and MM 1828, 379–80.
121. MM 1828, 384–85.
122. MM 1819, 642. Major revisions and additions happened for example in 1837 when regulations regarding the teachers' conference, visitors in the house, and the marriage of missionaries were added (KP 14, 48–49 and 54 from November 8 and December 27, 1937).
123. BMA, Q-9, 31 #12 "Hausordnung der evangelischen Missions-Anstalt." This

were no punishments at the BMTI, in reality, the disciplinary action of dismissal constituted a considerable deterrent for students to refuse compliance.

Figure 3
The First Three Directors of the Basel Mission: Blumhardt, Hoffmann, Josenhans[124]

Hoffmann's Reflections on Seminary Education

The second director articulated the community learning approach of the BMTI in different terms, but his ideas indicate very similar priorities. In 1853 Hoffmann reflected on "the principle of seminary education" and defended this educational approach against both, those who would rather

---

version is prefaced with the "Old House Rule"; fifteen paragraphs already in force since Blumhardt's time and the added thirty-nine paragraphs are suggestions for the "New House Rule" from 1860 which were for the most part implemented. The new House-Order had over fifty pages.

124. BMA, QS-30.022.0056: "Hoffmann, Blumhardt, Josenhans." Creator unknown, *BMArchives*, http://www.bmarchives.org/items/show/82236, accessed May 21, 2015. The image depicts Blumhardt on top, Hoffmann on the bottom left, and Josenhans on the bottom right.

send pious artisans without further schooling and those who preferred academically trained theologians.[125] In his view the institute practiced just the right balance between encouraging strong personal spirituality—necessary in challenging missionary contexts—and the community spirit correcting "haphazard behavior of unbroken individuality" which proved detrimental overseas. Furthermore, this communal education was the best context to accurately judge candidates' "true piety and real inner life from God."

Hoffmann acknowledged that "seminary life with its regulated education and paternalism" was not conducive to the development of "practical personalities" for the independent missionary life with its incessantly arbitrary conditions. However, he felt that in Basel the "mixture of young men from farming and artisan background with young merchants, teachers, and university students" balanced practical and theoretical education. These statements show a remarkable self-awareness on the Director's part of the possibility of trained incapacity, acknowledging that BMTI graduates were facing difficulties in cross-cultural contexts because of a lack of flexibility induced by their training. But this did not lead him to revise the community learning approach that was characterized by considerable regulation and paternalism.

Finally, for Hoffmann the purpose of the institute was not to train missionary character but to assess the individual's divine calling. Those who were not found to be called by the test of the fitness of their "character, attitude, inclinations, and abilities" were "released into their former occupation." Like Blumhardt, he prioritized personal, spiritual, and ministry formation, expected candidates to already display pious faith and conduct upon entry, and saw the inevitable "effect of the community spirit upon the individual student" as a positive correction of extreme individual expressions and ideas by "the objectivity of the whole" community.

CONCLUSION

Both Directors demonstrate that they regarded the BMTI as a learning community along the lines of a *community of practice*. They designed an integral training approach that intentionally used communal learning as means to develop skills, attitudes, and practices the participants endorsed. These values were strongly influenced by their Pietist background,

---

125. Hoffmann, *Eilf Jahre*, 74–81.

especially the emphases on fellowship groups, sanctification, and education as a means of life transformation.

The BMTI reflected the earlier, less egalitarian understanding of *communities of practice*. As new participants, recently accepted candidates embarked on a process of increasing their competence in the generally accepted practice and thereby moved from peripheral to full participation. Notwithstanding the address as "brothers," senior students functioned as guides and supervisors over novices while teachers and Board members watched and evaluated all trainees. This hierarchical structure was integral to the BMTI community. The leaders were patriarchal figures, the students their "sons"—a perception of their relationship exhibited in written communication even long after they graduated.[126]

This shows that the reach of the Basel Mission community of practice did not end with graduation from the BMTI. In the minds of both, the leaders and the missionaries it involved a lifetime commitment. Early on this was just a mutual understanding but later it became formalized in a written agreement.[127] The mission promised free board, lodging, teaching, and anything else needed for their preparation, the missionaries in turn pledged availability to the society "forever and unconditionally" even though it accepted no "legally binding" obligation to employ, send out, pay, or generally support them. It was "a relationship of pure personal trust, in the final analysis built on faith alone." Their faith and common interest united them beyond organizational contracts or regulations. It is to this shared *domain of interest*, the passion for Christian mission in non-European lands we have to turn now.

---

126. Letters from missionaries in Africa are usually addressed to the "Dearest Inspector" or the "Dearest Fathers" in the Board.

127. BMA, QS-3-17 "Broschüren für Kandidaten" (*Brochures for Candidates*) A1a) "Bedingungen des Eintritts in die Evangelische Missions-Anstalt zu Basel" (*Conditions for Entry into the Evangelical Mission-Institute in Basel*) § 1 g). In this folder there are several variations of the Entry Conditions. The earlier versions are undated, but a virtually identical text was published in JB 1860, 23–24.

2

A Shared Vision of Christian Foreign Mission

FOR A COMMUNITY LEARNING approach to be a *community of practice*, the participants need a shared *domain of interest*. This represents the common vision, goal, or problems the community attempts to address. This chapter examines the shared vision for Christian foreign mission that motivated the Basel Mission with particular focus on Africa. It traces influences of the European image of Africa (and generally the non-Western world) and resulting ideas of Christian missionary work. However, the expressions of this domain of interest in the Basel Mission will be shown to reveal specific emphases which originated in their German Pietist background.

Apart from published articles and reports, primary sources for this investigation are the directions to missionaries about to leave Europe that were typically read in public at the annual conference. The first detailed instructions were given in June 1821 to the initial four sent to India and Russia. They reflect a foundational general statement of motivations and emphases.[1] The 1827 instructions for the missionaries to Liberia extensively articulated an approach to African mission that was subsequently published.[2] The first group sent to the Gold Coast in 1828 was referred back to this document and their directives explicitly complementary.[3]

1. MM 1821, 171–83.

2. MM 1830, 451–82 Appendix III. Interestingly, these instructions to the first group that was sent to Liberia in October 1827 were published in the *Missions-Magazin* as an appendix in 1830. The same issue reported the beginnings of the work in Ghana and the death of three of the four men sent there in 1828.

3. BMA, D-10.3,3a1) "Provisional instructions for our four brothers departing for

Finally, the comprehensive instructions for the new beginning in 1842 reflect the experience gained until then and subsequent instructions were regarded as supplementary.[4] These documents articulate specific expectations of relationships missionaries were to pursue and practical ministry they were to attempt which reveal ideas of "mission work" in Africa, attitudes toward African people and culture, and ideals concerning "missionary character." Instructions were the final word-on-the-way, both, a job description and exhortation to graduates ready to leave. It can be safely assumed that they expressed major emphases in the teaching and life of the institute. This makes them invaluable sources of the organizations' driving motivations and priorities.

THE MISSIONARY CAUSE AS SHARED DOMAIN OF INTEREST

> It is not without a deep yearning of love that we can think of the poor Negro people in its condition of total disarray and deep savagery, not without the longing . . . that it would please the Lord, who bought them too at the high price of his blood, to open a little gate . . . through which a small company of our German brothers can enter as messengers of salvation and peace to bring healing and blessing among these torn Negro tribes . . . and work towards the salvation and welfare of this deeply mistreated people.[5]

These words—spoken to the first missionaries sent to Africa—clearly expressed the reasons for all parties to be involved in the Basel Mission.[6] They agreed on the dire condition of peoples outside the sphere of European and Pietist Christianity and felt compelled to alleviate it. In this passion for Christian mission they assented to the "fairly homogeneous ideology" at the start of Protestant missions across Europe.[7]

---

the Danish Gold Coast in autumn of 1828, Salbach, Henke, Schmidt and Holzwarth" 1828, 1–2.

4. BMA, Q-3-3,26 "Instructionen von 1848–1876." The title of this book is misleading; it actually contains handwritten copies of all instructions to the Gold Coast missionaries beginning with April 1842.

5. MM 1830, 452.

6. In a similar vein, the initial call for support in 1815 cited "the love for our common Lord and Savior, his honor and the love for the poor heathen whose salvation we seek to further" as motivations to begin and support the institute. See Staehelin, *Christentumsgesellschaft, Vol. 2*, 310.

7. Kalu, "Church Presence in Africa," 17.

Addo-Fenning confirms the common convictions of Puritans in Great Britain and Pietists on the continent as they embarked on the missionary movement. He highlights their pious characteristics, namely, "that God spoke directly to each one of his children in the events of their lives, in the words of the Bible, and especially in (their) feelings as they prayed and read the Bible," and the emphasis on "a life of stricter puritanical behavior than that of their non-pietist neighbors."[8]

In Britain the birth of the Protestant missionary movement coincided with the public campaign against the Atlantic slave trade. "Supporters of the one movement were usually supporters of the other; and the parliamentary leaders against the slave trade were evangelical humanitarians who were mostly enthusiastic supporters of missions."[9] While in Germany there was no abolition movement, the overlap of strong humanitarian opposition to slavery that motivated an effort "to bring healing . . . to this deeply mistreated people" with traditional Pietist passion for Christian mission is clearly articulated in the above statement by the Basel Mission Director. That BMTI students shared this core motivation for involvement is obvious in their applications which frequently emphasize a burden to bring salvation to "so many people who still live in darkness."[10]

The "missionary cause" was the shared domain of interest, defined as bringing the Christian message to distant lands that were considered bastions of darkness in desperate need of this light. In 1816 Blumhardt posed "the condition of the world as proof for the necessity of mission" and cited "zeal for God's honor," "love for fellow humans," and "the honor of the Christian church" as reasons to support mission.[11] These themes recur throughout speeches and publications, not only in the Basel Mission but throughout the European Protestant missionary movement. For example, the CMS leader John Venn (1759–1813) described a "true missionary" as one "deeply affected by the sinful and ruined state of . . . the Heathen, [who] devotes his life . . . to promote their salvation. . . . He considers not his life dear, so that he may glorify God. . . . Daily studying the word of life . . . he holds it forth as a light to illuminate the darkness of the world around him."[12] Similarly, at the first public conference in 1821

8. Addo-Fenning, "Christian Missions," 194.

9. Walls, *Cross-Cultural Process*, 95.

10. See for example the application letters of Johann Christian Dieterle and Hans Nicolai Riis (BMA, PF 248 and PF 247).

11. MM 1816, 194–234.

12. His speech at the Valedictory Meeting on January 13, 1806, cited in Stock,

the Basel Mission President closed with a rallying call to the "brotherhood" of those who support "the cause of the Lord, the work of mission, [namely] the spread of the gospel among non-Christian peoples."[13] He stressed the organization's interdenominational orientation for the sake of the cause: denominational preferences were put aside for "the creed in their hearts that fits all church forms," Jesus Christ.[14]

This common cause brought together such diverse groups as Lutheran Württemberg theologians and pious villagers, Reformed Basel aristocrats and merchants, and Anglican British clergy. They joined forces and overcame their differences because they shared this vision of true Christianity reaching non-Christian peoples around the world as well as those who in their view had forgotten it in Europe, the Middle East, and North Africa. In the support fellowships the need of the "heathen world" was continuously upheld, the *Missions-Magazin* provided candidates with necessary details and visions of desperate darkness and dire need, as well as exemplars of dedicated missionaries who sacrificed their lives for the cause. "Missionary passion" was an indispensible quality of applicants to the BMTI and constituted one of the criteria of students' evaluations.[15] The Directors and teachers of the BMTI also came from pious fellowships, motivated by the same passion, and Board members, convinced to stand upon God's promises and advance his work, were "ruled by a spirit of pure interest in the cause."[16] Finally, CMS leaders represented the Evangelical wing of the Anglican Church and had the same principal interest in spreading the personal Christianity Pietist Germans advocated.

This does not imply that there were no tensions and differences—there were, especially about specific strategies to carry out the task—but the cause provided a shared motivation for engagement in Protestant foreign mission. A major contributing factor to this motivation was the image of the non-Western world, in particular of Africa, that had

---

Church Missionary Society, 85–86.

13. MM 1821, 154–60.

14. Ibid., 129. Schlatter reports that F. Cunningham came to the inaugural annual conference as representative of the British partner society (*Heimatgeschichte*, 70).

15. German "Missionssinn." See for example the student evaluations from December 18, 1839 in BMA, KP 14, 208–12 and from January 13, 1841 in BMA, KP 15, 87–91.

16. Hoffmann, *Eilf Jahre*, 27–28. The Director argues the pure motives of the Board members in this section, emphasizing that they put the cause of mission above personal interests and opinions.

developed throughout Europe. It shaped ideas of missionary work and determined the kind of candidates societies were seeking. The Basel Mission was part of the networks across Europe and clearly influenced by this general mood.

PERCEPTIONS OF AFRICA THAT MOTIVATED MISSION

> Perhaps the most striking aspect of the British image of Africa in the early nineteenth century was its variance from the African reality, as we now understand it. . . . The image of Africa, in short, was largely created in Europe to suit European needs. . . . When these needs allowed, it might touch on reality. . . . Otherwise the European *Afrikaanschauung* was part of a European *weltanschauung*.[17]

This conclusion of Philip Curtin's detailed study of the emergence of "the image of Africa" in Britain highlights the core issue, namely, that it was European ideas, interests, and developments that shaped European perceptions of Africa in the nineteenth century. Curtin's evaluation is relevant to the Basel Mission because of their close relationships with influential British circles. Furthermore, literature was often translated into German and information regularly exchanged, especially in the mission minded circles. This is illustrated by Blumhardt's article on "The Danish Possessions in West-Africa."[18] He cites extensively from the earlier Danish report by Monrad (1780–1825) who in turn refers to previous Danish, Dutch, and British authors.[19] This shows that fundamentally these perceptions were shared across Europe. Specifically, the factors that contributed to a collective Africa image and conclusions Europeans drew need attention.

---

17. Curtin, *Image of Africa*, 479.

18. Blumhardt. "Die Dänischen Besitzungen in Westafrika."

19. Monrad, *Description*. Monrad (1780–1825) was Danish chaplain in the Gold Coast from 1805 to 1809. The Danish original of his account was published in 1822. Blumhardt refers to both, the Danish and German publication of the book (MM 1827, 526). Winsnes confirms that the book was translated into German in 1824 by H.C. Wolf [and] published in Weimar as the 37th volume of *Neue Bibliothek d. wichtigsten Reisebeschreibungen* in her Translator's Introduction, see Monrad, *Description*, 12.

Impressed by Difference: Eurocentric Evaluations of Africa

Curtin ably demonstrates that the generally negative evaluation of Africa and its people "was very largely drawn from Europe's first impressions taken during the earlier and formative decades" and had hardened by the 1850s.[20] The Ghanaian scholar Kwame Bediako confirms that this image did not originate with nineteenth century missionaries and can only be understood by considering "the quality of European contact with Africa in the preceding centuries," namely, that is was predominantly through the transatlantic slave trade.[21] Early travel reports from Africa reveal "moderate xenophobia" and Eurocentric conclusions from (superficial) observations of African environment and life. What struck explorers and traders alike was the physical and cultural difference. The conclusions they drew were based on comparison with their own values and virtues. As a result, they invariably assessed African culture as "barbarism" in contrast to European "culture."[22] In addition, these evaluations were rooted in the fact that "before AD 1800 the chief contact of Negro Africa with European peoples was through the traffic in slaves."[23] This meant that Africans were judged by encounters with and reports of victims of the Atlantic slave trade, their cultural uprootedness, social struggles, and broken English.

As Hastings points out, missionaries too, were impressed by "the darkness of the continent" signified by "lack of religion and sound morals," ignorance, and a "general pitiful condition made worse by the barbarity of the slave trade."[24] Letters from Basel missionaries confirm this Eurocentric description of first impressions.[25] While Hastings stresses the foreigners' ignorance and advocates anthropological missionary training, it is disconcerting that he still evinces a similar sweeping evaluation of Africa in 1967 when he maintains that "there was plenty to horrify one in

---

20. Curtin, *Image of Africa*, vi–vii.
21. Bediako, *Theology and Identity*, 226–27.
22. Curtin, *Image of Africa*, 115.
23. Latourette, *Three Centuries of Advance*, 240.
24. Hastings, *Church and Mission in Modern Africa*, 60–61.
25. For example, Holzwarth offers the generalized description of Africans as "a poor, corrupted people" in 1829 (BMA, D-1,1 Christiansborg 1829 #2). In 1832 Andreas Riis emphasizes the laziness of Africans and attributes their harsh treatment by Europeans as partly due to their lying and stealing (BMA, D-1,1 Christiansborg 1832 #12b). Jaeger in the same letter describes the atmosphere in Africa as "spiritually unhealthy as if it was poisoned" (BMA, D-1,1 Christiansborg 1832 #12c).

the pre-Christian state of Africa" and emphasizes the cruelty of African kingdoms and "fear everywhere, above all, fear of sorcery."

In their descriptions Basel missionaries frequently made direct comparisons with European (German) conditions. From the features of landscapes and buildings to characteristics of moral and social life, they used their own context of origin as lens to evaluate African realities. To their credit, these judgments were not always negative, but predominantly they were, especially in regard to African social life and religious traditions. Like their British counterparts, Basel missionaries had fairly clear ideas about "the dire condition of the heathen world" and the "despicable conditions and utter darkness" of Africa.[26] But missionary letters also reveal typical Pietist German evaluations, like their preoccupation with the noise and commotion of African festivals that was so contrary to the quiet life they idealized.[27]

These Eurocentric conclusions from first encounters show a stronger correlation with the cultural self-centeredness of the people involved than the dominant political and anti-colonial critiques often allow. This is significant for understanding the Basel missionaries' encounter in Africa. Political collaboration with their own colonial government was not an issue for these German missionaries working in an area claimed by Danish and later under British control. Rather, the cultural self-centeredness they brought and the general European mood of the time affected their (mostly negative) image of Africa. Context of origin, preparation processes, and general historical moods are factors which influence cross-cultural missionaries' attitudes and practice everywhere and at all times. This observation points to a wider relevance of this study even for present day contexts.

Reporting and the Image of the Dark Continent

The increase of knowledge of Africa between 1790 and 1830 "was greater than that of any comparable period," but the quality of reporting contributed much to cementing the image of Africa as "dark continent," not only strange and incomprehensible, but savage, backward, and inferior

---

26. See the articles on Africa in MM 1827, 523–43 and MM 1839, 179–343.

27. Riis complains about this in a letter from 6 June 1832 (BMA, D-1,1 Christiansborg 1832 # 12b) and Widmann in a letter from November 6, 1843 (BMA, D-1,2 Goldküste 1843 #11).

to Europe.[28] Ignorance was often combined with cultural arrogance. Furthermore, frequent sickness and fast travel made most reporting, if not culture-bound, naïve and superficial. But "it was taken seriously [because] it was almost the only information available."[29] There were exceptions to the typical ridicule and negative stereotyping of African appearance and customs—Curtin mentions especially Winterbottom and Bowdich—but they were typically dismissed by European reviewers.[30] Such reports were also read in Germany and from the early 1800s journals emerged with the latest translations of other European as well as German travel reports.[31]

The timing Curtin identifies indicates that during the period of this study some aspects of the perception of Africa were still in flux. Missionary reporting contributed to establishing the image of the "dark continent" and gained disproportionate influence through pioneering new areas and the popularity of all literature on the non-Western world.[32] Basel Missionaries were among the pioneers of European engagement with African societies whose reports and evaluations contributed to shaping the generalized image in Europe. Missionaries were expected to regularly communicate home.[33] They summarized activities, shared opinions, and kept diaries that recorded "the daily joyful and sad experiences, important insights, . . . and general impressions . . . regarding their quiet mission business."[34] Numerous letters give evidence to the faithful

---

28. Curtin, *Image of Africa*, 198.

29. Ibid., 208.

30. Winterbottom, *Account of the Native Africans*; Curtin, *Image of Africa*, 211–13; Bowdich, *Mission from Cape Coast Castle to Ashantee*. Proof that such reports were also read in Germany is the fact that both authors' books were translated and published within less than two years: Winterbottom, *Thomas Winterbottom's Nachrichten*; Bowdich, *Mission der englisch-afrikanischen Compagnie*.

31. Two dominant journals were the *Journal für die neuesten Land- und Seereisen* (Journal of the latest Land and Sea Travels), published in Berlin from 1808, and the *Neue Bibliothek der wichtigsten Reisebeschreibungen*" (New Library of the most important Travel Descriptions) that commenced in 1818.

32. Curtin, *Image of Africa*, 413. Curtin asserts that from 1830 onwards missionary publications were read by far more people than scholarly works.

33. Curtin cites Wesleyan-Methodist instructions "to keep a Journal and to send home frequently [accounts] of labors, success, and prospects . . . and "give such details of a religious kind, as may be generally interesting to the friends of the Missions at home."

34. MM 1830, 472. See also BMA, D-10.3,3a1. Instructions 1828, 13 (IV.2.) and Q-3-3,26 Instructionen 1842 §41 and §43; 1844 Allgemeine Regeln §9.

observance of this directive which was also a means of accountability and information for the Board.

Basel Mission instructions to report show a clear development from inquisitiveness and acknowledgment of lacking information about Africa to more assertive directives based on established convictions. At the beginning, the missionaries were told to travel as circumstances allowed and gather information about the peoples and conditions in Africa to facilitate more informed decision making by the Board.[35] However, from 1842 onwards reconnaissance trips were no longer encouraged, in fact, the missionaries were cautioned about them as detrimental to their health.[36] This is one illustration for policy decisions the leaders made based on earlier evaluations. That does not mean they necessarily followed the recommendations of their field personnel. In fact, there are several important junctures where the Board in Basel went against the (better) judgment of the missionaries to follow their preconceptions. The ensuing struggles relating to missionary marriages and the question of house slaves present examples.[37]

Beyond the internal organizational use of missionary reports, they played an important role in raising the missionary passion (and monetary contributions) of supporters and inspiring new missionary candidates. Curtin's observation of "the link between publicity and fund raising" was also true for the Basel Mission.[38] For this purpose, as well as the validation of their labor and sacrifice, publications upheld the image of dire need, savagery, and spiritual darkness in contrast to the missionaries' perseverance, sacrifices, and faith. Selectiveness that stressed "those aspects of African culture most likely to be shocking to their readers" can also be observed in Basel Mission publications. Such readings were the staple diet of BMTI students. Their applications show that they already arrived with ideas of the difficult conditions outside Europe.

35. MM 1830, 477; BMA, D-10.3,3a1. Instructions 1828, 10–11 (III).

36. BMA, Q-3-3,26 Instructionen 1842 §31.

37. The primary book that engages the marriages of Basel missionaries is: Konrad, *Missionsbräute*. On the house slaves issue see Peter Haenger, *Slaves and Slave Holders*; Vogelsanger, *Pietismus und Afrikanische Kultur*.

38. Curtin, *Image of Africa*, 326. Lehmann confirms that the *Missions-Magazin* soon after its launch in 1816 "was widely read and served as a major vehicle for raising funds for the Basel mission. Most of the articles in this mission journal described the hard and dangerous work of missionaries in foreign, exotic countries. They satisfied the appetite for hero-worship as well as for adventure." Lehmann, "Mobilization," 193.

A Collective Image of "the African"

During the first half of the nineteenth century a general image emerged that invariably saw African life and culture as backward savage, and even evil. While some recognized individual Africans' achievements, this image was based on generalizations about "an abstract and collective 'Negro'"; individual Africans were "men not especially different from men elsewhere, while 'the African' in his collective image is an inhuman savage."[39] This generalization for the most part was ignorant of or ignored the diversity of African cultures because "specific customs of specific peoples counted for much less than their cultural difference from Europeans."[40] It also became a lens through which thereafter Europeans perceived what they saw in Africa, including most missionaries.

In the Basel Mission a similar collective image of Africans can be detected. One of the clearest indications is the fact that the instructions for the missionaries sent to Liberia were seen as valid and binding for those sent to Guinea as well. Furthermore, published articles reveal a stereotyped Africa image.[41] An example is Blumhardt's lament that the masses of Africa, an estimated population of 150 million, "still lie for the most part buried in the depths of darkest ignorance and superstition."[42]

By the early nineteenth century Europeans almost universally assumed, that "all parts of the world outside the bounds of Christendom were in a state of primitive savagery."[43] They only discussed the causes of the condition and its remedies.

IN SEARCH FOR EXPLANATIONS—EUROCENTRIC CONCLUSIONS

Most Europeans attributed African "barbarism" to some combination of race, climate, and the slave trade, while Christians offered additional religious explanations.

---

39. Curtin, *Image of Africa*, 36.

40. Ibid., 115. Curtin observes that projects for Africa either ignored ethnographic information or "buried [it] under largely imaginative concepts of men-in-general, 'the barbarian,' or 'the savage.'"

41. For example: MM 1827 Vol. 4, Appendix V, 523–43 and MM 1839 Vol. 2, 179–343.

42. MM 1839, 181.

43. Warren, *Social History*, 87.

Race and Contemporary Science

Occupied with physical differences, Europeans associated African's appearance with their way of life and status of slavery. Thus, "racial views became unconsciously linked with social views and with the common assessment of African culture."[44] One of the intellectual assumptions of the time claimed that all creation was arranged in a "Great Chain of Being" and could be classified into a linear hierarchy.[45] Suggestions of the exact classification of humans differed, but skin color (and other physical attributes) became a major criterion of distinction and invariably Europeans were identified as pinnacle and Africans as nadir.[46] The most common typology distinguished Caucasians, Mongolians, and Negros.[47] Numerous references in Basel Mission sources to Africans as "Negros" confirm that they adopted this typology.

STAGES OF CIVILIZATION

In social history, the idea of Progress flowed from the Great Chain. In light of the massive developments in science and unprecedented economic growth in Europe, it seemed reasonable "to see progress in the succession of living things through time, or a 'temporalizing' of the Great Chain."[48] Some went as far as posing separate origins for human races (polygenesis), a notion pious Christians rejected. The latter held on to a single origin of humans (monogenesis) based on the biblical creation account. But their descriptions of non-Europeans show that missionaries adopted universal European thought about progress which held "that non-Western civilizations represented earlier stages in human progress" and assumed European culture "as the only true civilization, the only one epitomizing mankind's path of progress."[49] The most common typol-

---

44. Curtin, *Image of Africa*, 30.

45. For the development of this idea see Lovejoy, *Great Chain of Being*; Marks, "Great Chain of Being." Marks emphasizes that while the idea originated with ancient Greek philosophers, it "represented an imposition of medieval European political relations upon the natural world" and became the normative way of thinking about nature in medieval Christian Europe.

46. For details on various theories see Curtin, *Image of Africa*, 227–43.

47. One of the clearest Euro-centric descriptions of this hierarchy is: Cuvier et al., *Cuvier's Animal Kingdom*, 49–53. The first of sixteen volumes covers humans and was originally published in 1827.

48. Marks, "Great Chain of Being," 69.

49. Curtin, *Image of Africa*, 63–64, 244–58.

ogy distinguished civilized, barbarians, and savages. Again, invariably, African societies were judged as savage, primitive early stages of human progress and often presumed to be fairly static. The Basel Mission endorsed these concepts as the frequent depiction of Africans as "savage" confirms. For example, the 1827 instruction portrays Africa as "in a state of total disarray and deep savagery" and Director Hoffmann describes African culture and traditional religion as a condition of "misery" and "moral savagery" in 1842.[50]

Furthermore, their perception of other societies was shaped by Pietist historiography that presumed pious religion as foundation of a people who partake in history. Schnurr's careful analysis of "Images of History" in German revival literature demonstrates that in their view "the Kingdom of God . . . describes the historical action of God with his people and includes church history as well as the biblical history."[51] Pietists consequently assumed that people without Christianity were outside world history and without culture. References to Africa as "wild and uncultured land" in Basel Mission sources illustrate this perspective.[52] This Eurocentric distinction between developed, cultured "historical" peoples and barbarian, uncivilized peoples outside history reflects contemporary thought. But Pietists were also critical of European engagement "overseas" and judged those who mistreated, oppressed, or destroyed others as "white (!) barbarians."[53] For them it was the pious version of righteousness "that exalts a people."

The distinction pious believers made between the "Christian world" and the "Heathen world" put Africa firmly in the latter, but they identified darkness also in the former. Holtwick's analysis of motivations and goals of the protestant missionary awakening suffers from gaps and inaccuracies concerning the British movement, but he is correct in pointing to the German Pietist diagnosis of a crisis in European Christianity.[54] Basel Mission leaders confirm their perception of darkness in both worlds

---

50. MM 1830,452; Hoffmann, *Missionsgesellschaft*, 56.

51. Schnurr, *Weltreiche und Wahrheitszeugen*, especially 231–36 and 295–300. Significantly, Schnurr's detailed case study is Barth's "World History" which was a textbook at the BMTI because of his close relationship with the Basel Mission: Barth, *Die allgemeine Weltgeschichte*.

52. For example: MM 1830, 458.

53. Schnurr, *Weltreiche und Wahrheitszeugen*, 299. Citing from a report of the Berlin Mission Society from 1840. Emphasis in original.

54. Holtwick, "Licht und Schatten."

by their efforts to spread the "light" both, through foreign mission and advancing true Christianity in Europe. However, West-Africa is invariably depicted as the abode of "millions of Negros in deep darkness" who demand urgent missionary engagement because of sheer numbers and depth of need.[55]

Literacy as Indicator of Intellect and Culture

One presumed sign of cultural backwardness was the lack of written language. As Bediako comments, whilst Indians and Chinese "could be accounted "civilized" pagans by virtue of being literate, Africans were believed to be without literature, arts, sciences, government, [and] laws."[56] A contemporary commentator denounced Asante history, "like that of all other savages who can neither read nor write, the history of a day, and little worthy of notice."[57] In Germany attitudes were similar. The Basel missionary Zimmermann calls attention to the practice to evaluate Africans and their language "by the deplorable Negro-English of West-India and Sierra Leone."[58] His observation confirms that liberated African slaves' limited English was used to draw conclusions about African languages. Basel Mission instructions describe African vernaculars as poor and lacking terminology to express spiritual ideas adequately, possessing only a "small store of ideas and terms."[59]

These evaluations led to underestimation of African languages (along with inadequate understanding of African religiosity). Early collections of vocabulary were flawed and before 1830 "most orthography was so careless and unstandardized . . . that the pioneer work had little or no permanent value."[60] In the Basel Mission too, early missionaries did

---

55. MM 1827, 343.

56. Bediako, *Theology and Identity*, 230.

57. *Quarterly Review*, 22.286 (1820) cited in Curtin, *Image of Africa*, 213. The article is a review of Bowdich that critiques him for attempting to write seriously about African languages or traditions, cf. Bowdich, *Mission from Cape Coast Castle to Ashantee*.

58. Zimmermann, "Die Lichtseiten des Negerlebens," 89. Zimmermann (1825–1876) arrived in Ghana in 1850, married the West Indian teacher Catherine Mulgrave in 1851, and became one of the eminent linguists in the Basel Mission in Africa. He is acclaimed for his linguistic work in the Ga language. In this article he criticizes the wide-spread dismissiveness of African languages and culture.

59. MM 1830, 469; BMA, D-10.3,3a1) Instructions 1828, 12 (III).

60. Curtin, *Image of Africa*, 221, 392–94.

not attain fluency in Ghanaian languages. This was in part due to their untimely deaths and other practical impediments, but they also found the languages more complicated than expected. Even after eight years, the acclaimed pioneer Andreas Riis (1804–1854) had not acquired the language well enough to speak without an interpreter.[61] His nephew, Hans Nicolai Riis (1822–1890) was the first missionary specifically assigned to analyze Twi, but he never realized that it—like many West-African languages—was a tonal language.[62] Only in 1852 a trained linguist was sent to Ghana. Johann Gottlieb Christaller (1827–1895) was exceptionally gifted and his linguistic work very influential upon Ghanaian Christianity. But the point here is how long it took the mission to take African languages seriously.

Related to the presumed primitive stage of African civilization and languages because of the lack of written literature was the evaluation of African intellectual abilities. Basel Mission instructions depicted them as simple, marked by childlike ignorance, and lacking most basic foundations. Educational work was deemed necessary because of the "complete lack of intellectual foundations and previous knowledge" for comprehending the message of salvation.[63] In presenting the gospel, the missionaries were advised to consider the "limited ability of Negros to grasp things" and to avoid abstract terms or preaching as they would in Europe, but to speak "simple, childlike and plainly" and use illustrations and parables.[64] African simplicity and ignorance was not necessarily seen as negative. In comparison with "nit-picking Hindu Brahmans and quarrelsome Muslim Mullahs, . . . Negro good-naturedness, thoughtlessness, and foolishness" was just childish immaturity that needed a "loving, fatherly, benevolent" approach.[65] Not surprisingly, this attitude justified missionary paternalism.

Despite these dark and limited perceptions, Basel missionaries never doubted the humanity of Africans or their ability to learn. Their

---

61. BMA, D-1,2 Akropong #15 Widmann May 26, 1845. Widmann wrote this in a rather accusatory tone because of the tensions with the senior missionary at the time, but stating a fact that is confirmed by Opoku who graciously comments that Riis's "largely futile endeavors" in learning Twi showed "that he really cared [for] and respected the Africans" in Opoku, *Riis, the Builder*, 87–89.

62. Curtin, *Image of Africa*, 393–94.

63. MM 1830, 465.

64. MM 1830, 469; BMA, D-10.3,3a1. Instructions 1828, 10 No. III.

65. MM 1830, 470–71.

extensive educational effort shows the conviction that African ignorance was a result of their environment and lack of exposure rather than an inherent inability. Missionaries were advised to submit to African political authorities as God instituted order as much as colonial governments, support their rule and keep their laws, and request of African coworkers the same.[66] In 1842 Georg Thompson (1819–1889), the African who had been brought up in Germany and trained in the BMTI, was referred to as brother and fellow missionary, and converted native Africans were to become evangelists and leaders.[67] Finally, instructions admonished missionaries not only to learn vernaculars but also to seek relationships with Africans and to study African customs and thinking closely.[68] The latter had the potential to transform missionary perceptions but frequently it cemented negative presumptions about African traditions.

One significant implication of the low view of African intellect was the general practice of mission societies to send the less qualified to Africa.[69] Early on this was also common in the Basel Mission. For example, a student with "poor ability" and "much obtuseness in heart and mind" and several who were excused from some academic classes were assigned to Africa.[70] Director Hoffmann articulated the practice in 1842, stating that students who failed academic studies could not be used in Asia but possibly in Africa or other less civilized regions.[71] However, later he strongly opposed this notion. In 1853 he posited that the existence of written literature actually makes work in Asia easier and where such literature did not exist better (rather than less) educated missionaries were required.[72] In passionate words he argued that the widely held perception was erroneous and "had led to much wasted energy and time,

66. MM 1830, 480–81.

67. BMA, Q-3-3,26 Instructionen 1842 §§ 2, 9, 19, and 23 on Thompson; 1844 Sebald et al. §13.

68. MM 1830, 457 and 469.

69. Njoku, "Missionary Factor," 198–99.

70. Georg Stanger was originally assigned to Africa, but eventually sent to India (Student evaluations from January 13, 1841 in BMA, KP 15, 87; KP 14, 15 from March 29, 1837 for his assignment to Africa; for his ministry in India see the list of basic facts on the three missionaries with the name Stanger in BMA, PF 254 Stanger, Joh.). Meischel, Johannes Stanger, and Dieterle, missionaries sent to Ghana, were excused from various academic lessons by the teacher conference on October 17, 1845 (BMA, QS-7-1b Lehrerkonferenz Protokolle 19 Okt 1845—7 Nov 1861).

71. Hoffmann, *Missionsgesellschaft*, 33.

72. Hoffmann, *Eilf Jahre*, 95–96.

and delayed success." This reevaluation significantly affected the Basel Mission engagement in Ghana. It brought the linguist Christaller and the educational expert Johann Gottlieb Auer (1832–1874) who inspired the school system that Ghana used into the twentieth century.

Deductions from the Tropical Climate

European perceptions of the tropical climate influenced the missionary enterprise in several ways. The myth of "tropical exuberance" dominated as explanation for the apparent laziness and immorality of Africans and contributed to misconceptions about African agriculture. Furthermore, the atrocious death rates of Europeans preoccupied medical speculations.

Myths of Tropical Exuberance and African Character

Tropical exuberance meant the conviction that the warm and supposedly vastly rich climate promised great wealth, but also bred indolence in its inhabitants.[73] One typical description claimed that "the Gold-coast, as well as all tropical Africa, is capable of affording incalculable advantages, if the inhabitants can be excited to industry."[74] Curtin shows that this myth of incalculable wealth waiting to be harvested persisted even long after agricultural experiments in Sierra Leone had failed miserably.[75]

While British schemes focused on more or less large scale projects in the Sierra Leone settlement and later regions of today's Nigeria, the Basel Mission's vision was directed towards local Africans. Their existing agriculture was judged as very imperfect and missionaries were instructed to teach Africans to cultivate their land more efficiently.[76] This employed European (German) agricultural wisdom (that disregarded African systems of shifting cultivation and land tenure) and assumed African laziness.

Conclusions from tropical exuberance alleged a stereotyped "African character," different in significant ways from Europeans. The lush environment was believed to cause both African indolence and extreme passions.[77] The latter included the perceived revengefulness and violence

---

73. Curtin, *Image of Africa*, 58–62.
74. Meredith, *Account of the Gold Coast*, vi.
75. Curtin, *Image of Africa*, 254, 123–32.
76. MM 1827, 503; MM 1830, 462.
77. Curtin, *Image of Africa*, 222–23. Curtin lists presumed African vices of "indolence, ferocity, cowardice and superstition" and African virtues were held to be "mild

of African customs as well as exuberant emotions and a presumed sexual prowess which pious Christians naturally condemned as immorality. Polygamy stood out as indicator for African savagery and the repression of women, a social evil to be eradicated.[78]

These assessments are also evident in the Basel Mission. For example, in 1827 Blumhardt saw African savagery specifically in laziness, selfishness, greed, glorification of drunkenness, violent traditions of torture and killing, moral degradedness, and sexual permissiveness.[79] The latter he also condemned of European traders and soldiers which shows that moral condemnations were informed by Pietist virtues that also disapproved of contemporary European vices. Culturally German and pious criteria were used to measure African realities; an evaluation that not only was unflattering, but also had the effect that Christian missionary action was built on a very flawed perception of Africa. Their assumptions fostered a condescending attitude and wholesale dismissal of African traditions and skills.

Tropical Climate and European Health

Among traders, missionaries, and soldiers alike European mortality in West Africa was about four times higher than in India or the West-Indies.[80] The Basel Mission like other Europeans was preoccupied with improving their workers' chances of survival and generally followed accepted contemporary wisdom. Personal hygiene, certain food and clothing, geographical locations, and building styles were considered to improve Europeans' health, staying in the sun and strenuous physical exercise was seen as detrimental.[81] Specific advice varied but only medical breakthroughs in the midcentury effected a significant change in survival rates.

---

manners, a peaceful disposition, politeness, charity, respect for the aged, and sometimes gratitude and nobility of character."

78. For a typical evaluation of polygamy see Winterbottom, *Account of Native Africans*, 144–48.

79. MM 1827, Appendix V, especially 531 and 539–41.

80. Curtin, *Image of Africa*, 71. Curtin discusses "rules for healthy tropical life," various treatments of fevers, and the apparent immunity of Africans on 71–87 and devotes whole chapters to "the problem of survival" (177–97) and developments in tropical medicine (343–62).

81. BMA, Q-3-3,26 Instructionen 1842 §7; 1844 Sebald et al. §4.

Basel missionaries were instructed to prioritize ensuring their survival in the "notoriously dangerous tropical climate." Directives assumed an acclimatization period and advised missionaries to learn from other Europeans on the coast.[82] In 1827 Blumhardt posits the coast as healthier because there were no forests and "the wind can blow more freely."[83] However, after 1840 missionaries were to move up to the healthier climate of Akuropon as quickly as possible—a change of mind that reflected European "medical topography" but also Riis's experience in preceding years.[84] Similarly, considerations regarding location and establishment of a mission station accepted universal European wisdom in which "clearing the brush was the most popular anti-fever measure of all."[85] But the "preparatory activities" of building houses, organizing daily living and household keeping, farming and gardening with the goal to provide necessities also reflected rural German ideals of economic self-sufficiency.[86] Finally, considerations related to missionaries' survival contributed to the reluctance to send women (presumed weaker than men) and Basel Mission policies not to allow marriages before the men had proved themselves for at least two years.[87]

THE RELIGIOUS MOTIVATION OF CHRISTIAN MISSIONARIES

Curtin poses the valid question why—in the face of mortality rates and known facts about the climate—Europeans were still willing to go to West-Africa.[88] Continuing "dreams of untold wealth" were an ongoing motivation and before 1830 most were soldiers recruited "to serve on the coast in commutation of punishment in Britain." Curtin mentions the "special religious zeal" of missionaries but focuses on the "personal optimism" of travelers and progress in science and technology. However, to assess Christian missionaries their profound religious motivation is crucial. As Warren observed, without this "inner-direction" it is impossible to understand the compulsion to follow a course of action "which to

---

82. MM 1830, 457.

83. Blumhardt, "Die Dänischen Besitzungen," 527.

84. BMA, Q-3-3,26 Instructionen 1842 §8; 1844 Sebald et al. §3; 1846 Meischel et al. §5.

85. Curtin, *Image of Africa*, 190.

86. MM 1830, 458–62.

87. BMA, Q-3-3,26 Allgemeine Regeln 1844 §8.

88. Curtin, *Image of Africa*, 181.

others may seem wildly inopportune, extremely dangerous, and possibly subversive to the 'natural order of things.'"[89] Latourette also asserted that "only devotion and faith sprung from profound religious conviction are sufficient to account for the continued offering of men and women for the task."[90]

Basel Mission sources are replete with references to the "holy profession" of the missionaries that was also a difficult vocation in which they would face many privations and obstacles.[91] It was a divine calling not to be taken lightly. When a candidate volunteered, the leaders would "exhort him to fervent prayer, strict self-examination, and thorough knowledge of the mission work and its difficulties."[92] Applicants express emotionally the seriousness of their decision and submission to God's will.[93] Upon departure to Africa missionaries were advised to pray fervently and continuously, especially during the voyage and the first months in Africa.[94] Along with such personal spirituality went the admonition to single-minded devotion and submission to God and his will. This inner state of contentment was believed to also foster physical stamina and increase the likelihood of their survival.[95] Thus, the religious convictions that drove participants in the Basel Mission need further examination to understand the missionary passion that united this community of practice. They were informed by biblical explanations for the state of the non-European world.

The Bible as Guide for Christian Explanations

Protestants missionaries believed in a common created origin of all people but they shared the contemporary negative evaluation of non-European

89. Warren, *Social History*, 44–47.
90. Latourette, *Great Century*, 461.
91. For example: MM 1821, 172–73; MM 1830, 541.
92. Blumhardt, "Charakter eines Missionars," 7.
93. Examples of Ghana missionaries are: Andreas Riis and Dieterle (BMA, PF 124 and 248). Johannes Stanger (BMA, PF 254) volunteered to follow in the footsteps of his brother who had died in Africa within eighteen months.
94. BMA, Q-3-3,26 Instructionen 1850, Steimle und Süß, §4 and 1851 Mader §4. The missionaries were instructed to spend their time on the ship (in addition to practicing languages and sharing the gospel with the other passengers) "in quiet communion with the Lord and in prayer and supplication for health, strength, wisdom and faithfulness and for the blessed advance of the mission."
95. MM 1830, 455–56.

cultures. However, different from many others, their conclusions were based primarily on readings of the Bible, in particular regarding the origin and eternal destiny of "savages."

Human in Sin: Progressive Degradation

Convinced of the utter depravity of non-western peoples, pious Christians concluded that this was humanity without God, the result of unrestrained original sin. The dispersion of peoples from Babel (Gen 11:1–9) was interpreted as migration away from God leading to a progressive degradation of religion. Different world religions, then, were thought "to represent different stages and directions of degeneration from the original biblical state of pure revealed religion."[96] Once people ceased to believe in one God, idolatry was believed to produce cumulative moral degradation as Rom 1:18–32 seemed to suggest.

Birgit Meyer has shown that this thesis that posed African peoples as originally monotheist but fallen from it was common in German Pietist circles.[97] Statements of the "utter brokenness and deep barbarization" of the "poor negro people" which motivated the Basel Mission express these ideas.[98] Furthermore, missionaries in Africa identified "remnants of a lost more correct understanding of the divine and the afterworld which had been mixed with the imaginations of a mind now alienated from God."[99]

This concept prompted the condemnation of other people's religious traditions. In fact, Stanley asserts that all religions apart from Protestant Christianity were classified as idolatrous.[100] More accurately, any religion other than pious Christianity—which incidentally, included not only Catholics but also non-Pietist Protestants—was a target of missionary zeal.

---

96. Gunson, *Messengers of Grace*, 199; Stanley, *Bible and Flag*, 64. See also Curtin, *Image of Africa*, 53, 420.

97. Meyer, *Translating the Devil*, 57–60.

98. The 1826 instructions described Africans this way (MM 1830, 452).

99. For example, H. N. Riis claimed in his annual report of 1846 that Akan religion reflected such remnants (BMA, JB 1847, 244).

100. Stanley, *Bible and Flag*, 64.

African Religious Traditions as Cause for Immorality

The intensely negative judgment of African religion in particular originated not only in the certitude that heathen religious systems were the products of fallen humanity, but was aggravated by the conviction that idolatry caused savagery. With the foregone conclusion that African cultures represented the lowest stage of progress, "gradual degradation" provided a rationale for the evil of cultural practices. For example, Beecham—convinced that domestic slavery and polygamy were "two of the greatest temporal evils by which Africa is afflicted"—identified the cause in their sanctioning by Akan beliefs and concluded that a "careful examination of the national religion unfolds the true source of the barbarous practices which so extensively prevail."[101] Cruickshank in similar manner describes idolatry as deification of "the worst passions of our nature" that aggravates natural depravity.[102] Thus, for most missionaries African religion was "a positive evil depressing society below the moral level attainable by unaided natural reason."[103]

In Germany too, "the moral condition of Africans [was] seen as at least as appalling if not even more dismal than their religion."[104] Zimmermann observed that missionaries bring this appraisal to Africa and usually keep it. Basel Mission sources typically depict African religion as "blind superstition" and "fetish service" evincing the same condemnation and misconstruing widespread in Europe. Indicative for the presumed connection between African religion and immorality is Blumhardt's concurrent treatment of them.[105] He iterates "the abominations of the degenerated and debased human nature" which are to be expected of a people with the religious ideas and practices just described.

---

101. Beecham, *Ashantee and the Gold Coast*, 250–55.

102. Cruickshank, *Eighteen Years*, Vol. 2, 257.

103. Curtin, *Image of Africa*, 406–7.

104. Zimmermann, "Die Lichtseiten des Negerlebens," 87. German Text: "Für ebenso tief stehend, ja noch tiefer, als den religiösen, hält man ihren sittlichen Zustand. Der Missionar bringt diesen Maßstab mit und mag ihn lange behalten und vertheidigen."

105. Blumhardt, "Die Dänischen Besitzungen," 534–41. Another example is his articulation of the contrast between the "moral degradation and great need of the heathen peoples" and "the glory of the divine global salvation effort" their mission participated in (Annual Report in MM 1838, 363).

However, Basel instructions did not encourage the common derision, violation, and confrontation.[106] Missionaries were advised to be careful in their dealings with "fetish priests," not to oppose them as enemies or ridicule them and thereby arouse anger and enforce the "blind superstition of the people."[107] Instead, they were to act confident of "the higher dignity and . . . superiority of the living testimony of Jesus Christ." Their lives were to be a witness to the truth through "unselfish love, straightforward simplicity, unity among them, and zealous service for the true benefit of Africans."

Nevertheless, the wholesale condemnation of African religious tradition and life encouraged a "crusade against idolatry" and a "war between cultures" which has been amply critiqued for its insensitivity toward and destruction of indigenous cultures and the detrimental consequences for African Christian identity.[108] Basel missionaries' depiction of African priests as money-greedy deceivers and African environment as realm of darkness indicate a similar judgmental attitude to their British counterparts.

HAM'S SONS—AFRICANS AS HUMANITY CURSED

The confrontation was justified, because—in the case of Africa—the heathen not only represented fallen and degraded humanity, but were positively cursed. This verdict was based on the biblical version of European race typologies which drew a direct line from the account of Noah's sons (Gen 9:18—10:32) to contemporary racial differences and divided humanity into the descendants of Japheth, Shem, and Ham. It assigned Africans to Ham and believed them to be under the curse recounted in Gen 9:18–27.[109] The curse on Africans was identified in their immoral

---

106. Njolu points out that flouting African religious observances and taboos, and violating sacred places and objects, "were the rule rather than the exception among the Christian missionaries both Catholic and Protestant." See Njoku, "Missionary Factor," 196.

107. BMA, D-10.3,3a1. Instructions 1828,11.

108. See, for example, Kalu, "Church Presence in Africa," 18–19; Stanley, *Bible and Flag*, 63–65; Bediako, *Theology and Identity*, 225–66; Bediako, *Christianity in Africa*, 1–88. Cruickshank also presented fetish worship as "the struggle . . . between the two great principles of barbarism and civilization." See Cruickshank, *Eighteen Years, Vol. 2*, 298–99.

109. Curtin, *Image of Africa*, 37–39, 403–4; Gunson, *Messengers of Grace*, 199, 206.

life style (by European judgment) and the fact that they were subdued as slaves of other peoples.

This theological classification of the world's peoples was taught at the BMTI as Schnurr's analysis of one of the text books shows.[110] Barth's *General World History* ascribed the knowledge of God to the Semites and a sad fate of "hopeless servitude" to the descendants of cursed Ham, the progenitor of Africa. Presumed consequences of this curse were "an immoral life style and the fact that Africans rarely achieved the status of cultured peoples." Expressions of these concepts in Basel Mission rhetoric are manifold. In 1827 Blumhardt pondered the "mysterious curse of Ham" evinced even by the dangerous African climate and wild life.[111] By 1839, Hoffmann reached the conclusion "that the judgments of God, which lay upon these sons of Ham because of an ancient curse were not easily . . . wiped away."[112] But he also expressed the hope that "God had begun to extend the tents of Shem and Japheth into the banished regions of Ham until these 'servants of all servants' are saved." As this statement shows, for Pietists the Christian faith overcame the curse and alleviated all distinctions due to the "salvation historical universality of the gospel." Once people become Christians, they are adopted into God's family irrespective of who they are.[113]

It is one indication for the trained incapacity this study posits in the Basel Mission that application letters typically did not mention the Hamite curse, but after the BMTI training many missionaries used this framework to explain their impressions in Africa. For example, in 1843 Widmann expressed his conviction that "God's holy will included the salvation and sanctification of the sons of Ham."[114] The 1848 report articulates bluntly the view of Africa as cursed land in demonic darkness which obviously shaped the missionaries' perceptions:

> We fight peculiar difficulties in this dark and cursed land; often we seem to tangibly feel the curse and the power of darkness

---

110. Schnurr, *Weltreiche und Wahrheitszeugen*, 197–262; Barth, *Die allgemeine Weltgeschichte*.

111. MM 1827, 528 (after a lengthy account of tropical diseases).

112. MM1839 Vol 2, 180–81. This is the preface to Blumhardt. "West-Afrika."

113. Schnurr, *Weltreiche und Wahrheitszeugen*, 303–4.

114. BMA, D-1,2 Goldküste-1843 #11 Widmann letter November 6, 1843 cited in JB 1844, 192.

heavily lying upon us, as if one could grasp the spiritual dark power, so that sometimes courage wants to fail us.[115]

Nevertheless, for German Pietists those who are not true Christians of *all* races were outside salvation history and, as mentioned above, they identified spiritual darkness also at home, where secularization and political upheavals were seen as signs of God's judgment and a need for "inner mission."[116]

The "Perishing Heathen"

From these biblical explanations of Africa's condition it is clear that for pious Christians Africans' fate could only be eternal perdition. Njoku observes that "Missionaries were essentially believers" who attached great importance personally to their Christian faith and came to the mission to share it.[117] Their methods and attitudes can be critiqued, but the "zealous piety" that drove them was based on sincere belief in "the reality of the afterlife as described in the Christian narratives." The resulting conviction that the "heathen" were perishing "imparted a sense of absolute urgency and priority to the missionary imperative."[118] Warren calls this motivation "divine pity" identifying a "profound otherworldly concern for the souls of men" in early Catholic and Puritan missionaries and claiming it as "an authentic element in the missionary movement" still in his time.[119]

Evidence for this concern is abundant in the Basel Mission. They set out to proclaim God "among peoples who do not know God yet [and] sit in . . . the shadow of death" and they could not find peace while "millions of immortal souls rush to eternal destruction without Christ."[120] Missionaries were sent to Africa to "attempt to win immortal souls through faith in Christ for his kingdom and eternal glory."[121] In 1850 the undiminished

---

115. BMA, D-1,2 Akropong 1848 #27 Annual Report from December 1848 by Widmann, Dieterle and Mohr, cited in MM 1849, 127.

116. Lehmann, *Pietismus und weltliche Ordnung*, 135–67; Schnurr, *Weltreiche und Wahrheitszeugen*, 305–7.

117. Njoku, "Missionary Factor," 198–99.

118. Stanley, *Bible and Flag*, 67.

119. Warren, *Social History*, 77–78.

120. MM 1821, 174, 179.

121. BMA, D-10.3,3a1. Instructions 1828,1.

passion was "that God would grant the missionaries success in "saving many souls for the eternal home."[122]

The urgent effort to save multitudes in non-European lands presumed eternally lost was also rooted in traditional Pietist eschatology that inspired social action and mission.[123] In Germany, Bengel's prediction of the Parousia and the Millennium in 1836 created an obsession with that date which motivated emigration and various local and foreign missionary activities.[124] While the Basel Mission did not join this fixation, they too were motivated by an expectation of the imminent return of Christ. For them pious faith characterized those who are saved eternally. Therefore missionary activity was necessary everywhere outside Pietist Christianity—in Europe and beyond.

European Mistreatment

Finally, the African condition was attributed by many to the experience of slavery. According to Curtin the slave trade was "the most hotly debated of the possible causes of African barbarism" and only after its official abolition in Britain a new line of argument admitted "that *coastal* Africa was savage, made so by the evil influence of the slave trade."[125] The long process of ending slavery in the British colonies is a clear indication for the prevalent reluctance, not least for economic reasons.[126] Humanitarians and evangelical Christians were the most vocal advocates of abolition in Britain.[127] They appealed on moral grounds to Christian responsibility to alleviate the suffering slavery caused and on economic grounds that

---

122. BMA, Q-3-3,26 Instructionen Steimle and Süß (Nov 1850), 125 (§ 7).

123. Stanley adds that the missionary movement "was born out of a conviction that the church stood on the brink of the last days of history. Christians expected that the work of foreign missions would initiate a turning of the 'heathen' to Christ on such a scale that the kingdoms of this world would become in actuality the kingdom of Christ." Stanley, *Bible and Flag*, 74.

124. Lehmann, *Pietismus und weltliche Ordnung*, 68–75, 188–267.

125. Curtin, *Image of Africa*, 254–56. Emphasis in original. The immorality of slavery was by no means a settled issue in Britain with its official abolition, and the trade still had its defenders in the early nineteenth century.

126. See, for example, Drescher, *Mighty Experiment*; Walvin, *Black Ivory*.

127. Curtin, *Image of Africa*, 52. See also Drescher, *Econocide*. Contrary to a widely accepted thesis, Drescher makes the interesting argument that the humanitarian mobilization of Britain's public which led to abolition was actually detrimental to Britain's economic interests at the time because British slavery was at the height of its potential.

trading with Africa would be more profitable than trading in Africans. Incidentally, the same men initiated Protestant mission societies.[128]

Divine Pity and Restitution as Motivation

The fervent sentiment against slavery in pious circles across Europe added strong impetus to their passion for Christian mission in Africa as a way of restitution for the wrongs committed by Europeans. For example, in the 1804 instructions to its first two missionaries the CMS clearly stated this motivation to engage in West-Africa:

> The Western coast of Africa ... has not only, in common with other heathen countries, received from us our diseases and our vices, but it has ever been the chief theatre of the inhuman Slave Trade.... The wickedness and wretchedness consequent upon this trade of blood have deeply and extensively infected these shores.... We desire, therefore, while we pray and labor for the removal of this evil, to make Western Africa the best remuneration in our power for its manifold wrongs.[129]

Basel Mission leaders concurred. Debating the possibility to begin an African mission, the Board cited "the outrageous need of West-Africa ... where Christianity has to ameliorate a terrible debt."[130] The first missionaries they sent were strongly exhorted

> to never forget on every step in the Negro world how shamefully the poor Negros have been treated for centuries by men who called themselves Christians and how much glaring injustice has to be ameliorated by your unselfishly loving, forbearing, and forgiving behavior.... You owe these mistreated creatures inexhaustible patience and excessive charitable love, if at least to some degree the thousand bloody wounds should be healed which have been inflicted on their people for centuries by the dirty greed and cruel malice of Europeans.[131]

---

128. Groves, *Planting of Christianity*, Vol. 1, 178–232. The significance of this connection in Britain between evangelical revival, the anti-slavery movement, and protestant missions is pointed out by many scholars. For example: Ajayi, *Christian Missions in Nigeria*, 9–10; Bediako, *Theology and Identity*, 227; Hanciles, "Back to Africa," 194; Walls, *Cross-Cultural Process*, 94–96.

129. Stock, *Church Missionary Society*, 95.

130. BMA, KP 27 April 1825, cited in Schlatter, *Basler Mission in Afrika*, 8.

131. MM 1830, 454 and 471–72.

A Shared Vision of Christian Foreign Mission

Thus, in the Basel Mission as in Britain, the enterprise "was activated as much by a profound sense of grief at the harm done to Africa and Africans . . . as by a rediscovery of the Great Commission."[132]

The "outrageous misery of the poor Negros" and the guilt Christian peoples have to pay off persisted as major motivations, and pious Christianity was seen as the remedy. For example, in 1842 Hoffmann listed among the considerations for not giving up on the mission the vivid descriptions of West-Africa's destitution by the sole surviving missionary and counteracting the horrors of the slave trade through preaching the Gospel and introducing Christian morals.[133] Love and pity were repeatedly entreated as appropriate missionary attitudes. Warren termed the initial inspiration of European Christian missions "divine pity," a "conviction about the lost state of natural man," but also shows that from early on another thrust of "material concern" can be observed, a "this worldly" concern that inevitably made missionaries "agents of social change."[134] In pious Christians' response to the vices of slavery the idea of the "perishing heathen" combined with disgust about European mistreatment of Africans to amplify a motivation of pity and amelioration. However, the envisioned change was informed by European values. This fact is greatly significant for the trained incapacity this study seeks to identify because typically it was European—and in the Basel Mission German Pietist—perceptions of progress that directed the missionaries' social change efforts.

The condemnation of slavery as inherently evil extended to any form of bonded relationships which incidentally included traditional domestic indenture in Ghana. For Europeans it was among the "greatest temporal evils by which Africa is afflicted" and the Basel Mission pursued a strict policy of abolishment which eventually caused serious tensions between African believers, the more experienced missionaries, and the home Board.[135] However, as far as political agitation for abolition in Europe is concerned, this was a British preoccupation. It had the sympathies of

---

132. Bediako, *Theology and Identity*, 227.

133. Hoffmann, *Missionsgesellschaft*, 57.

134. Warren, *Social History*, 77–80. One example he cites are Jesuit missionaries in the seventeenth and eighteenth century working towards "the conversion of the Indians and their protection against the vices and exploitation of the colonies." Cf. Latourette, *Three Centuries of Advance*, 154–55.

135. Beecham, *Ashantee and the Gold Coast*, 255; Haenger, *Slaves and Slave Holders* Vogelsanger, *Pietismus und Afrikanische Kultur*.

the Basel Mission leaders, but in their context the government was not involved in trading slaves and their Pietist mentality eschewed political involvement.

THE COAST AS CORRUPT AND FASCINATION WITH ASHANTI

Finally, condemnation of the slave trade also prompted an evaluation of coastal settlements as corrupted by slavery and European misconduct. This supported the common "sharp distinction between the 'superior' peoples of the interior and the 'degraded' nations of the coast" which resulted in Ghana in a preoccupation with the Asante.[136] Bowdich's glowing description after the 1817 expedition to Kumasi and later Beecham's account—based on the journals by mixed race Methodist missionary Thomas Birch Freeman (1809–1890)—contributed to European imaginations about this powerful inland state.[137]

In the Basel Mission, Ashanti fascination was held in check by their missionary Andreas Riis's sobering account. He travelled to Kumasi in 1839 on the heels of Freeman, but, contrary to him, was not granted an audience with the Ashantehene (the title of the King) and concluded that "the time was not yet ripe for a mission to the Ashanti."[138] Based primarily on his recommendation, the less known Akuropon, where he had made connections, became the main Basel Mission station. This focus on small beginnings where success was more likely also reflected the shrewd wisdom of the Board members and characteristic German Pietist virtues.

Curtin underlines "the existing dislike of partly-Westernized Africans" and British partiality towards and against certain African tribes.[139] The Basel Mission displayed some similar tendencies, but their primary issue with coastal settlements rested on a religiously motivated ethical evaluation. Coastal Africans were seen as morally corrupted as a result of a combination of African sexual permissiveness and misbehavior of

---

136. Curtin, *Image of Africa*, 226, 255. Curtin points out that this was a curious choice in the face of the constant threat the Ashanti represented to the British. Today this dominant Ghanaian kingdom and people is typically referred to as "Asante" but the majority of historical sources use "Ashanti."

137. Beecham, *Ashantee and the Gold Coast*; Freeman, *Journals of Various Visits*; Bowdich, *Mission from Cape Coast Castle to Ashantee*.

138. BMA, KP July 7, 1840. Freeman had been in Kumasi in April 1839. Riis's description of the Kumasi trip from 10 November 1839 to 13 January 1840 was published in MM 1840 III, 174–238.

139. Curtin, *Image of Africa*, 226.

"even poorer European men."[140] The moral conduct of Europeans and mixed race "mulattos" on the coast was the main point of grievance in Basel missionaries' reports. The seamen, soldiers, and traders who braced arduous voyages, the hostile climate, and harsh conditions in Africa were drawn by economic fortunes in the trade of intoxicating drinks and guns for gold and slaves.[141] Their behavior was seen as deterrent to Christianity and often invited the scathing critique of Basel missionaries.[142] They wanted to plant churches among the native African population because they felt that a fruitful approach to Africans with the gospel could only be made in areas outside the negative influence of raucous and profit-hungry Europeans.[143]

IDEAS OF "MISSION WORK" IN AFRICA

So far the analysis has shown that the Domain of Interest that inspired the Basel Mission was driven by Eurocentric evaluations and pious biblical convictions. The passion for the "missionary cause" originated above all in the religious conviction of the "perishing heathen" that was informed by assumptions of African degradation and savagery common throughout Europe. But it was also shaped by the German Pietist background of Basel leaders and missionaries. This becomes even clearer in their specific ideas of "mission work" in Africa.

In defense of the extended BMTI course Blumhardt outlined in 1829 the "unfathomable needs" in Africa and the "manifold tasks" required to meet them.[144] A "planting of the Kingdom of God in the darknesses of heathendom" began with building a hut and learning the local language. Schools had to be built to "proclaim the word of salvation to an ignorant people in darkness," teachers trained, school books acquired, and the Bible translated, printed, and distributed. The "naked and helpless children" needed "food and clothes produced from the native soil." Even-

140. Blumhardt, "Die Dänischen Besitzungen," 541.

141. Ibid., 532, 540.

142. The diaries and letters of the first Basel Missionaries in the Gold Coast attest to this evaluation of what they saw by their Pietist standards. See, for example, Henke's description of the "mulattos" in strong terms as a bad lot and the Europeans as rotten, living in polygamist relationships and having no true faith (BMA, D-1,1 Christiansborg 1830 # 2 Henke May 20, 1830).

143. Wurm, "Anfänge," 138–50. See also the Board meetings that discuss the beginning of an African mission in April and May 1826 (BMA, KP 1826).

144. MM 1829, 353–56.

tually Africans were expected to be "ashamed of the wild life and desire instruction." As they settle near the missionary in a village, "thousand needs arise which the wild bush people did not know before." The missionary is teacher and guide as natives learn to "plough, plant gardens, build huts, dig wells, breed livestock, and one civil craft after another." Thus, Blumhardt concludes, "the first planting of the gospel of Christ has drawn us inevitably into the full activities of the civilized world." However, while these activities were essential, the most important work was the "fruitful spread of the knowledge of God and Christ Jesus in the wildness of the heathen world." This required missionary preparation to focus on the Christian life of candidates regarded as vital to face the challenges overseas including "deprivation and difficulties, opposition and enmity, coping with strange customs, new ways of thinking, prejudices and foolishness, and disappointed hopes."[145]

This detailed account of the Basel Mission's ideas of missionary work corresponds with the various instructions to missionaries and reveals general European presumptions including the total lack in Africa of intellectual foundations and physical amenities considered part of a "civilized" life. It also illustrates the strong roots of the Basel Mission in rural artisanship, their focus on vernacular languages, and unrealistic expectations regarding African responses.

The Gospel of Civilization

Many scholars express astonishment at the unbridled cultural arrogance of nineteenth and twentieth century Europe. For example, Kalu notes that "missionaries came with an amazing degree of confidence in the supremacy of Christianity and European social and economic order."[146] Curtin highlights that to the tendency of most civilizations to overvalue their own way of life and undervalue that of others, "another, less common belief" was added: "Most Europeans thought their own way of life represented values of universal application."[147] He suggests the roots of this belief "in the theoretical universality of the Christian religion and the injunction to preach the gospel among the heathen." Njoku critically remarks that in spite of the moral appeal of the abolitionists, the obligation to pass on the Christian faith in Africa "was construed . . . as a kind

---

145. MM 1818, 8.

146. Kalu, "Church Presence in Africa," 18.

147. Curtin, *Image of Africa*, 259.

of remedy for the slave trade and as a civilizing mission" and "not exactly *mea culpa*."[148] He notes that it "was often cast in zealous and self-righteous forms" and refers to various authors who show that Christianization and "civilization" were inseparable.[149]

European Culture as Christian Society

For Europeans of the time the logical deduction of their assessment of the non-European world was a felt responsibility to spread "civilization." Since other peoples, especially in Africa, were "in general poor, barbarous, naked pagans, as destitute of civilization as . . . of true religion," the mission of Christian nations was "to carry the banner of civilization into . . . heathen lands."[150] As Stanley pointed out, "the close association in missionary thinking between Christianity and civilization" assumed confidence in human progress, non-Western cultures as positively evil, and European culture as Christian.[151] Blumhardt's exposition illustrates this "tabula rasa" approach, which presumed a non-existing local culture and German rural life as Christian, and envisioned the imposition of a completely new way of life. Behind the perceived "moral duty" to spread civilization was the assumed superiority of European culture and its identification with Christianity.

The Gospel as Means of Civilization or Preparing the Ground for its Reception

For pious missionaries an additional factor was their religious conviction. They took for granted that civilization was necessary, but in addition they had "an extraordinary faith in the power of the Evangelical gospel to affect men's minds so that they would promptly assume the social system of northern Europe."[152] The clearest illustration of this in Britain is the result of a Committee of the House of Commons that considered measures regarding the "aborigines" of British settlements.[153] The Secretaries

---

148. Njoku, "Missionary Factor," 194, 215. His emphasis.

149. Curtin, *Image of Africa*, 259–61, 415, 420, 422; Jacobs, *Black Americans*, 5–6.

150. Bediako, *Theology and Identity*, 230; Busia, "Introduction," 6–7; Carey, *An Enquiry*, 63.

151. Stanley, *Bible and Flag*, 160–62. Stanley adds that rapid growth of the church in Sierra Leone was seen as evidence that "it worked."

152. Gunson, *Messengers of Grace*, 268–69.

153. Coates et al., *Christianity the Means of Civilization*.

of the CMS, the Wesleyan Missionary Society, and the LMS were asked to comment on whether civilization should lead the way to the introduction of Christianity or Christianity would introduce civilization. The consensus was that undoubtedly Christianity was the instrument by which to bring about "civilization in the sense of moral and social improvement of a people." For the CMS Secretary Dandeson Coates (d. 1846) the gospel was "a divine influence on the human mind" that would make people "peaceable, honest, sober, industrious, and orderly, humble, self-denying, philanthropic, beneficent."[154] The LMS Secretary William Ellis (1794–1872) furthermore emphatically proclaimed that "in proportion as individuals receiving Christianity yield themselves to its influence . . . they must be civilized. No man can become a Christian, in the true sense of the term, however savage he may have been before, without becoming a civilized man."[155] Beyond the notable agreement on what constituted civilization, there was consensus on the power of Christianity to effect it.

The Basel Mission record is more ambiguous. The agricultural imagery of Africa as "wild and uncultured land" prevailed. From this followed the conviction that it had to be cleared and prepared for the reception of Christianity. Cultivation included European style buildings, agriculture, and household keeping to ready the "wild thorn field of the Negro world that has been lying fallow for centuries" for the understanding and acceptance of the gospel.[156] In keeping with European views, African life was perceived as unhealthy, rough, lazy, and unproductive. Therefore "planting the cause of Christ" had to include teaching "the poor Negros not only to read and write, but also to work their land *to make them receptive and worthy for admission into the kingdom of God* through proclamation of the gospel."[157]

"Oekonomie," as the Basel Mission termed this "ground breaking" mission work, was to ensure the survival of missionaries and to model a presumed better Christian life which would attract Africans. Repeated references to the missionaries' life as the most impressive sermon testify to this intention in the Basel Mission.[158] Ideals of German rural economy and Pietism about healthy and moral existence shaped this endeavor.

---

154. Ibid., 99–100. On Coates see also Shenk, "Coates, Dandeson."
155. Coates, Beecham, and Ellis, *Christianity the Means of Civilization*, 174–75.
156. MM 1830, 458.
157. MM 1830, 462. Emphasis mine.
158. BMA D-10.3,3a1. Instructions 1828, 7 (I.4.), 11 (III); MM 1830, 470–71, 478.

This model Christian life was also the expected pattern for new believers, based on similar convictions as their British colleagues of the transforming power of the gospel. The approach fostered the establishment of mission stations (in Ghana known as "Salems") to shield converts from the "pagan" influences of "uncivilized" African village and family life. Already the 1826 instructions on a fitting location to settle assumed the need to set up an independent "station" for their work.[159] The consequent effect of separating African believers from their community has been amply critiqued since.[160]

Over time, increasingly "culture work" was also aimed at the economic support of converts. However, this does not neutralize the importance the Basel Mission attached to evangelism and establishing churches. In 1853 Director Hoffmann expressed the tension between economic activities to ensure a livelihood for local believers and the "true mission work" of "converting the heathen to the living God." The solution he contemplated for India (and challenged his readers to consider) was European merchants who invest in Indian agriculture, sugar production, or coffee plantations.[161] This would free the missionaries for their primary task.

Lack of Response Leading to Indirect Methods

Initial optimism about African responses waned eventually. Curtin points to the resilience of West-African cultures to prolonged contact with "civilization" and discusses increased European focus on "more direct attempts at culture change."[162] For the missionaries and African Christian scholars later these were "indirect methods of evangelization" and reflected the shift to "material concern" which made Christian missions a social service.[163] Njoku refers to "extra-doctrinal techniques for

---

159. MM 1830, 458–60.

160. For example, Mobley, *Ghanaian's Image*, 73–80.

161. Hoffmann, *Eilf Jahre*, 55–56.

162. Curtin, *Image of Africa*, 418–19.

163. Ajayi, *Christian Missions in Nigeria*, 126–65; Warren, *Social History*, 77–95; Kimble, *Political History*, 151–61. Ajayi describes the "Civilization around the Mission House" which in Nigeria included linguistic studies, education (primary, industrial and missionary agents), apprenticeship schemes, building, printing, and medical work. Warren identifies this shift as "material concern" and Kimble emphasizes the missionaries' social change agency by treating the impact of Christian missions in Ghana under the heading of "Social Change."

conversion" that included the introduction of Western style education and medical care, and "the recruitment of local hands in the missionary project [including] interpreters, catechists, teachers, and domestic hands."[164]

Basel leaders always had a strong preference for agriculture and practical trades that reflected the German village economy most missionaries originated from. But while they saw the need to "prepare the fallow ground" from the beginning, a similar development towards a greater emphasis—certainly in terms of time and energy spent—on civilization activities can be observed.[165] Most significantly, the "new approach" from 1843 onwards responded to the failure to achieve organizational goals with a more intentional civilization effort.[166]

In the Basel Mission—like other contemporary European Protestant missions—indirect methods were primarily educational. By 1850 Basel Mission strategy was to socialize a new generation into European culture in the face of unresponsive adults. Schlatter summarizes that they realized "educating the youth was the right way to build a church."[167] The consequence of this shift was increased imposition of European practices and values. Besides schools, Basel Mission indirect strategies included technical training in agriculture and artisanship, and intentional separate "Christian" settlements. However, medical work was a minor activity until the 1880s.[168] For the Basel Mission "church work" remained the priority—at least in terms of importance attached—and a large part of "school work" aimed at raising African agents as teachers and evangelists.

British Grand Schemes versus Basel Mission Humble Values

In Britain many enthusiastic supporters of missions were also parliamentary leaders opposing the slave trade and "practical politicians who combined their moral stance against slavery with economic arguments

---

164. Njoku, "Missionary Factor," 204–7.

165. Several of the missionaries complain that they do not get around to "proper mission work," i.e., preaching and evangelizing because of the amount of time they spent teaching in the school and working practically in the stations. For example, BMA, D-1,3 Ussu 1850 #10 Zimmermann letter July 29, 1850.

166. This is very apparent in the instructions for this group: BMA, Q-3-3,26 Instruktionen 1842.

167. Schlatter, *Basler Mission in Afrika*, 44–45.

168. Ibid., 187–89. Schlatter recounts the beginning of medical work in the early 1880s.

against slave trade as an economic institution."[169] Dominant among them was Thomas Fowell Buxton (1786–1845) who incidentally also chaired the above mentioned parliamentary commission on "Aborigines' rights, Christianity, and Civilization." In 1840, Buxton published the widely read *The African Slave Trade and Its Remedy* which presented his vision to ameliorate Europe's debt while building profitable African economy through "calling forth its own resources"—both, economic and human— and promoting "legitimate trade."[170] He recommended intensifying the campaign against the slave trade, establishing and encouraging legitimate commerce, promoting and teaching agriculture, and imparting moral and religious instruction.[171] While he attached importance to the latter, his main argument was economic and political. The publicity of Buxton's program, its adoption by British government, and the subsequent first Niger expedition in 1841 had far reaching consequences for British involvement in Africa, despite the latter's failure and loss of life.[172] Eventually the result was British annexation of African regions.

DISSIMILAR POLITICAL CONTEXT

While attitudes and arguments often sounded similar, in Britain the Protestant missionary movement was intricately linked to government policies and colonial interests in ways the Basel Mission was not. Similar dynamics did not emerge in Germany before its fractured multitude of states united in the late nineteenth century. Before, continental Pietists were less optimistic and nationalism was less developed than in Britain.[173] German maritime and colonial involvement was still in the future. Moreover, for the German missionaries in Ghana nationalist dynamics

---

169. Walls, *Cross-Cultural Process*, 95.

170. Buxton, *African Slave Trade*, 301–43.

171. Ibid., 518. See also Curtin, *Image of Africa*, 298–302.

172. Curtin, *Image of Africa*, 302–4; Schön and Crowther, *Journals*. Curtin sums up, "the unusual enthusiasm of 1840 and 1841 provided the impetus for a new round of African activity [which] remained even after the general enthusiasm died away. In time, it was to alter the whole of British relations with West Africa."

173. Schnurr, *Weltreiche und Wahrheitszeugen*, 307–15. Schnurr emphasizes that regional allegiances and identities were stronger than German nationalism, especially in Württemberg. See also Barth's depiction of Württemberg as "promised land" in deliberate parallelism to Israel in his history of the duchy: Barth, *Geschichte von Württemberg*.

never applied because they worked under Danish and from 1850 British government.

Furthermore, Southern German Pietists had lost most political influence and generally adopted a retreat mentality.[174] They regarded the revolutionary movements of the 1830s and 1840s as unruly and immoral disturbance of the God-ordained order and tended to look at all political activity with suspicion. Pietist groups and activities were seen as a counter force to the immoral and secularist developments of the wider society. Above mentioned Basel Mission references to the corruption and need of true Christianity in Europe testify to this attitude.

Nonetheless, the traditional intersection of German Pietist missionary vision with Danish political and ecclesiastical interests can be detected in the Basel Mission. One indication is Blumhardt's extensive citing of the Danish Chaplain Monrad's account of the Gold Coast.[175] More importantly, the Basel Mission collaborated with Danish authorities to establish their work in Guinea. They had to rely on Danish protection and in the early years their missionaries filled the vacant Chaplaincy in the Danish settlement. Furthermore, it can be argued that the support of the Danish merchant Georg August Lutterodt (1790–1854) contributed to Andreas Riis's survival, the first Basel missionary to last longer than three years. Riis was of Danish origin, established a friendship with Lutterodt early on, received supplies through him, and frequently recuperated on his plantation.[176] As we will see, because of his Danish nationality Riis struggled to maintain political neutrality and in 1844 the Danish governor purported the Basel Mission as Denmark's contribution to African civilization.[177] All this indicates that if any political connection can

174. Fulbrook, *Piety and Politics*, 130–52.

175. Blumhardt, "Die Dänischen Besitzungen." Hans Christian Monrad (1780–1825) was chaplain in the Danish Gold Coast for four years (1805–1809) and published his account in 1822. The German translation was published in 1824. See the introduction by his translator, Selena Axelrod Winsnes, in Monrad, *Description*, 6–13.

176. Opoku, *Riis, the Builder*, 7–9, 15–19; Wurm, "Anfänge," 244. Riis's letters from June 6 and 20, August 10, and December 2, 1832 (BMA, D-1,2 Christiansborg 1832 # 12–15). Lutterodt's stint as acting governor in Christiansborg was from July 5, 1844 to October 9, 1844. See http://www.worldstatesmen.org/Ghana.html. This website uses a misspelling of his name as "Lutterdot." See also Riis's letter from February 27, 1835, (BMA, D-1,2 Christiansborg 1835 # 7, excerpts printed in HB 1835, 61–65) and his diary from March 19 to October 7, 1835 in which he described the journey to Akuropon, welcoming reception by the Okuapemhene and his first months of settling there (D-1,2 "Christiansborg 1835 #11, excerpts printed in MM 1836, 510–64).

177. "Remarks concerning the Danish-Guinean possessions" June 30, 1844 and

be established, it was with the Danish government, neither the German nor the Swiss.

HUMILITY AS PERSONAL AND ORGANIZATIONAL VALUE

German Pietism fostered a value of smallness and "faithfulness in little things" which is reflected in the founding document of the BMTI and various later statements.[178] Spittler's 1816 petition outlines the "purpose of our small mission institute" and Blumhardt hopes in 1826 that God would "open a little gate" for a "small group" of German missionaries in Africa.[179] A further indication of this value is the repeated argument for quality over quantity against an enlargement of the institute.[180] Consequently, in their relationship with the CMS on several occasions a discomfort can be detected with higher education and grand schemes that smelled of pride and were contrary to the Basel Mission's emphatic value of humility, not only in its candidates—as several authors emphasize—but also as an organization.[181]

AN AMBIGUOUS ATTITUDE TO TRADE

The Basel Mission was furthermore reluctant about grand schemes of commerce because so much in the realities of African trade offended their moral values. Initially they investigated the necessity and options of economic support of the mission through exchanging goods, but it was accompanied by stern warnings not to let this barter tarnish missionary work and character.[182] The "importance of their holy profession" called for guarding "against getting mixed up with political concerns, trade issues or other merely temporary things" and remembering that they were "not businessmen, servants of the state, preachers of an existing (state) church, or government employed teachers" but "messengers

---

letter July 25, 1844 in Carstensen, *Closing the Books*, 58–60, 78, 84.

178. Lehmann, *Pietismus und weltliche Ordnung*, 73.

179. BMA, Q-1-2.1 "Anfänge des Basler Missions Instituts"; MM 1830, 452. Emphasis mine.

180. MM 1838, 354–55 and MM 1828, 379–80.

181. Blumhardt's statement on "Missionary Character" in 1818 is a prime example of the humility value (MM 1818, 2–11). Examples for very critical analyses of this value as organizational control of the missionaries are Eiselen, *Erziehung*; Miller, *Missionary Zeal*.

182. BMA, D-10.3,3a1. Instructions 1828, 14–15 (IV, 4).

of Jesus Christ in the heathen world."[183] Trade remained an ambiguous undertaking that was always feared to interfere with the ethical testimony of the missionaries. Goods most commonly used by contemporary merchants, like fire arms and brandy, were explicitly excluded.[184]

In 1842 Hoffmann refers to "a description, recently published in England, of the atrocities of the slave trade and its result, that only the *preaching of the gospel and of Christian morals* in Africa can uproot this poisoned tree."[185] This is clearly a reference to Buxton's proposal with the significant omission of British government action and commerce as the remedy.[186] The Director's elective citation clearly indicates where the Basel Mission's priorities lay. Not in grand schemes to promote legitimate trade (and European economic interests) and eradicate the slave trade through British military and political action in West-Africa, but in "preaching the gospel and Christian morals." When the Basel Mission eventually established some trade, the purpose was primarily the support of the mission.[187] The secondary wish "to eliminate, if possible, the firms which were introducing liquor and gunpowder" was not fulfilled.[188]

Thus, it is clear that trade was an afterthought in the Basel Mission and motivated by economic viability of the missionary settlement and developing African artisanship, not by European commerce. Only after German Pietist village economy did not achieve the envisioned self-supported Christian communities they began to seriously pursue larger scale cultivation of crops like coffee and cocoa. Walls is correct in saying that the Basel Mission "laid the foundations of Ghana's cocoa industry" because they introduced the seeds in the country, but citing them as example of economic mission policies that were designed to discourage

---

183. BMA, D-10.3,3a1. Instructions 1828, 7 (I, 4). See also MM 1821, 178.

184. BMA, Q-3-3,26 Instruktionen 1842 §36.

185. Hoffmann, *Missionsgesellschaft*, 58–59. Emphasis in original.

186. It is not likely referring to the 1837 Commission's report, because he continues to add that "the total failure of the great enterprise on the Niger river" was another argument to follow up any already existing points of connection—which for the Basel Mission at this point were the favorable Danish king and Riis's positive evaluation of Akropong as the most likely location to promise success for the mission.

187. Schlatter, *Basler Mission in Afrika*, 91. Schlatter recounts the considerations for sending the first merchant, Hermann Rottmann (b. 1832) in 1854 as (1) to assist the material support of the mission and (2) to work against the trade in alcohol and weapons on the coast.

188. Eppler, *Geschichte der Basler Mission*, 204; Latourette, *Great Century*, 446.

slave trade can be disputed.[189] The Basel Mission only very reluctantly embraced trade in cash crops and mostly out of felt need to support the growing mission and church.

The Importance of "Language Work" in Vernacular

For all Protestant missionaries linguistic work was a priority. While they disagreed on strategies of training African agents and technical education, there was great unanimity about the importance of literacy.[190] The roots for this are obviously in the Protestant reformation with its strong emphasis on the authority of Scripture accompanied by the desire to make the Bible accessible to ordinary believers in their language. Furthermore, the pious revivals in Britain and on the continent fervently renewed this passion. As we saw above, this gave the impetus to founding Bible Societies and efforts to print and distribute Bibles. Consequently, in Africa where most languages were unwritten, learning, analyzing, developing orthography and grammars, and producing Bible translations in vernacular languages became a priority. Two assumptions were behind this effort. First that people should hear the gospel and read the Bible in their mother tongue and second, that literacy is essential to understanding and living Christianity. Both are articulated in the Basel Mission.

The first missionaries were instructed to pursue systematic study of a major African language because "it is always better when the great deeds of God are proclaimed to people in their own language." But a group should be at least 100,000 people to merit the effort to "elevate its language to a written and religious language and thereby ensure its continued existence."[191] Blumhardt's outline of mission work clearly evinces the priority of language learning and linguistic work.[192] Hoffmann regarded fluency in the local African language as condition for any effective further ministry and assigned one missionary specifically to develop dictionaries and grammars, both for the purpose of aiding future missionaries in learning the language and to be used in translating the Bible and other literature.[193]

189. Walls, *Cross-Cultural Process*, 96.
190. Ajayi, *Christian Missions in Nigeria*, 126.
191. BMA, D-10.3,3a1. Instructions 1828, 12 (III).
192. MM 1829, 354.
193. BMA, Q-3-3,26 Instructionen 1842 §§23–28; 1844 Sebald et al. §7, 10, 12 and 13; 1846 Meischel et al. §§3 and 6; 1849 Locher and Zimmermann § 13; 1850 Steimle

It can be argued that the Basel Mission had an even higher value for linguistic work than other societies. German Pietism emphasized people hearing and reading the Christian message in their mother tongue as the most effective way to impact individuals. Furthermore, in this area too, the lack of colonial interests in Ghana influenced Basel Mission priorities. They focused on vernaculars and resisted pressures from European governments and Africans alike to offer education in colonial languages. This also implied that in Ghana Basel missionaries never expected Africans to learn German. In the colonial context of Danish and British rule those languages were employed in chaplaincy and until the missionaries had sufficient fluency in an African language. However, examples of African agents' ability to join the training in Basel also indicates that young Africans who worked as house helpers in the missionaries' families did acquire some German in the process.[194]

The success of Basel missionaries in attaining fluency in African languages did not always match their priority for language learning, as we will see. However, the roots of these convictions in European presumptions about literacy and their influence on the BMTI curriculum are significant.

Literacy as Condition for Christianity

The articulated rationale reveals the assumption that literacy elevates a culture and is a necessary precondition for Christianity. Ajayi describes the major effort at teaching literacy as aspect of the "civilization around the mission house."[195] It was part of civilization efforts that implied the general European dismissal of oral African traditions as inferior and entailed the introduction of European school education.

But missionary literary work also inspired scholarship on non-European languages. BMTI graduates were among the most significant contributors to the scientific study of African languages, both in Ghana and in the CMS work.[196] From the 1840s a school of scientific linguists developed in Germany. Its most prominent scholar, Karl Richard Lepsius

---

and Süß §5; 1851 Mader §§4, 7, 9–10; 1852 Christaller §§1, 9–10; 1852 Steinhauser §3.

194. For example, the half-brothers David Asante (1834–1892) and Wilhelm Ofori (c. 1843–1862) who were brought to Basel in 1857 and 1860 respectively. Ofori died there in 1862, but Asante was the first successful Ghanaian graduate from the BMTI. See HB 1862, 31–34; Abun-Nasr, *David Asante*.

195. Ajayi, *Christian Missions in Nigeria*, 126–32.

196. Curtin, *Image of Africa*, 392–400.

(1810–1884) produced a universal phonetic orthography that was adopted by all major mission societies in 1854.[197] Lepsius's hope for his effort to develop an "alphabet combining simplicity and precision" was not only to assist missionaries, but also that "the natives will themselves teach one another to read and write without the perpetual aid of European teachers" because "in this way only can we hope for the Evangelization of that vast continent."[198] While he expected African agency to be central to Christianization—an unusual insight for his time—he also presumed that people need to become literate to become Christians. The statements above show that the Basel Mission shared this assumption.

Language Learning in the BMTI

Literacy as priority of Christian mission stimulated a strong focus on languages in the BMTI curriculum. Students from fairly low educational background were taught to better read and write their own vernacular (German). Biblical languages provided the foundation for hermeneutics and the syllabus included English because of the partnership with the CMS. Other languages were added on account of their presumed helpfulness for learning vernaculars in Africa and India. The erroneous assumption of Arabic as foundational for West-Africa and Sanskrit for Indian languages reveals the prevalent ignorance of non-European contexts.[199]

All these languages were learnt by the use of written aids, dictionaries, and grammars, which established this as the normative approach to learning a foreign language. Consequently, in Africa the missionaries also depended on written materials for language learning. Grammatical analysis and word lists developed by missionaries were seen as the best means to learn vernaculars for those who followed the first pioneers.[200] However, the failure to take African languages seriously led to little qualified personnel producing grammars that tended to assume European patterns of language—certainly initially—which made them quite useless.[201]

197. Kemp, "Universal Phonetic Alphabet," 1579; Lepsius, *Standard Alphabet*.

198. Ibid., iv–v.

199. Annual Report (*Jahresbericht*) JB 1840, 52. The argument for Arabic in Africa was the spread of "the rule of Muslim priests and wizards."

200. MM 1830, 463–64. This instruction to the first missionaries sent to Africa claims that the grammatical analysis of the first missionaries "will make it tremendously easier" for those who follow to learn the language.

201. Curtin confirms that, generally, before 1830 those producing materials were so lacking in broad linguistic background, that their work had "little or no permanent

This approach also ignored the relational character of language and its primary role as means of oral communication. They could not imagine and were not prepared to learn languages by oral means and solely through relationships with speakers of the language. Consequently, the missionaries struggled to extract word lists and identify grammatical patterns from African helpers and took a long time to acquire fluency in vernaculars. More seriously, this also entailed a delay of the primary means for African appropriation of the Christian message, its expression in their mother tongue.

Regarding German missionaries' level of English a brief comment on remarks in British sources is necessary. For example, Mesthrie observes that a surprising number of first generation missionaries in South Africa "were continental Europeans with little knowledge of English" and cites a letter from 1827 in very poor English by a Saxony-born missionary.[202] It is also often emphasized that the first two German CMS missionaries did not know English and had to learn it in London.[203] However, both comments refer not to BMTI graduates but to Germans trained by Jänicke in Berlin. Nevertheless, it is accurate that the CMS complained about Basel missionaries' level of general education. But this needs to be balanced with the fact that these comments are from the 1820s when the British impatiently demanded missionaries before they had completed the three year course. Furthermore, BMTI trained personnel of the CMS like Jakob Friedrich Schön (1803–1889), Sigismund Wilhelm Kölle (1820–1902), and David Hinderer (1819–1890) made major linguistic contributions in West-Africa.[204] This indicates that ultimately the emphasis on language learning in the BMTI may have been the least disabling aspect of their training as the missionaries deployed in Africa.

"MISSIONARY CHARACTER"—THE KIND OF PEOPLE NEEDED FOR AFRICA

The shared ideas of mission work in the Basel Mission led to clear notions of the kind of people they felt would accomplish the task. In Blumhardt's

---

value." Curtin, *Image of Africa*, 221.

202. Mesthrie, "Contact Linguistics and World Englishes," 282–83.

203. Cox, *British Missionary Enterprise*, 88.

204. Ajayi, *Christian Missions in Nigeria*, 127–30; Curtin, *Image of Africa*, 293–300. See also Schöen, *Grammatical Elements of the Ibo Language*; Schoen, *Grammar of the Mende Language*; Schoen, *Dictionary of the Hausa language*; Olabimtan, "Hinderer, David"; Lohmann, "Koelle."

words, missionaries needed both, "true heaven-mindedness" and "excellent cognitive capacities."[205]

"True Heaven-Mindedness"

Because the "perishing heathen" were the prime motivation for Protestant mission outside Europe and to sustain them through the physical challenges, missionaries needed to be people with deep religious conviction. For the Basel Mission this included aspects of spirituality and character.

Spirituality: Converted, Pious, and Contemplative

As we saw above, pious believers' response to the privations and hardships of foreign missionary life was a profoundly religious one. In their view, it demanded not only a strong sense of divine calling and zeal for the task, but also self-denial, readiness for sacrifice, and rootedness in spiritual life. Basel missionaries were strongly impressed with the need for "thorough conversion," personal piety, devotion to God, and extended times of prayer and contemplating Scripture.[206] This individualist emotional spirituality was encouraged throughout the BMTI training through exhortations, a generally quiet atmosphere, and times and rooms set aside for personal prayer.[207] In Africa, as we will see, the lack of "quiet atmosphere" became frequently one of their personal struggles.

The admonition to exercise "daily dedication to the Lord and his work" and "fervent prayer" was also given to missionaries as a "fellowship of brothers."[208] Together they were to commit themselves to God and their unity was to strengthen them and become a testimony to the people around. Instructions presume a weekly "conference" of the missionaries and explicitly ask them to share from their diaries. It goes without saying that those were also times of praying, singing, and reading the

---

205. Blumhardt, *Charakter eines Missionars*. German: "wahrhaft himmlischer Sinn" and "ausgezeichnete Verstandeskräfte." Unless indicated otherwise, the following citations are from this article.

206. MM 1821, 172–73; BMA, D-10.3,3a1. Instructions 1828, 9 (II); MM 1830, 478–79.

207. One of the rubrics of student evaluations was "Spiritual Life" (*Geistliches Leben*) which included comments on practiced spirituality, personality, and the quality of relationships with other students. For example, BMA, KP 15, 97–92 from January, 13, 1841.

208. BMA, D-10.3,3a1. Instructions 1828, 9 (II). See also MM 1830, 478–79.

Bible together.[209] This communal aspect to BMTI spirituality reflected the Pietist conventicles, but its implementation in Africa had unexpected challenges.

Character: Humility, Pious Morality, and No Ulterior Motives

A major emphasis of Blumhardt's article on *Missionary Character* is the need for humility. He emphasizes personal spirituality, humility, and self-examination of moral life and motivations to volunteer for this "holy and exalted profession. On the field "a right mind, clear insight, self-control, untiring patience, gracious friendliness, and knowledge of the human heart" were seen as indispensible. "Knowledge of the human heart" referred particularly to the sinfulness, weakness, and lack of humility of the missionary himself. This reflected the Pietist emphasis on sanctification as proof of true conversion. The stress on morality also relates to the convictions that missionaries' lives were the most convincing sermon and mistrust resulting from previous mistreatment could best be overcome by friendliness, charity, and forbearing towards Africans.[210] Despite the definite paternalistic tone, these were attitudes not shared by many and more typical of German Pietism than other expressions of Christianity.

Finally, ulterior motives of economic or social advancement and adventure were regarded as detrimental to their work, and missionary applicants were warned that they would not carry them through the expected challenges. Consequently, even though in effect the BMTI training brought advantages to many candidates, indications to them as motivation to apply are extremely rare.

"Excellent Capacities"

Abilities the Basel Mission saw as indispensable for missionaries concerned physical constitution, practical skills, and intellect.

Physical Health and Perseverance

Born out of the ideas of tropical climate, the mission emphasized that missionaries needed to be healthy and have a strong physical constitution. Accordingly, health issues were a major reason students left the

---

209. MM 1830, 473 and 477.
210. MM 1830, 470–71.

BMTI within the probation period of six months.[211] Incidentally, this also challenges the strong case some scholars build on dismissals for insubordination.[212] However, a closer look at these resignations and student complaints about the work load also reveals that their physical endurance was primarily measured by the ability to persevere through extended hours of study they were not used to.[213] This is a highly questionable measurement, given that in Africa, tropical sicknesses and physical work offered the greatest challenges to missionaries' health. A level of recognition of this contradiction is revealed by changes in the BMTI schedule that introduced short times for physical exercise.[214]

Practical Skills as Artisans and Farmers

Furthermore, the practical skills to plant stations that could sustain the missionaries and ensure their survival were regarded essential. In the Basel Mission this was defined in German village terms and thus focused on agricultural and technical skills. As Blumhardt outlined in 1829, these proficiencies were also necessary to eventually teach African converts the "civilized" life. Hence, the background of most candidates in rural communities and artisanship was a welcome fact to Basel Mission leaders, not the challenge the CMS felt who desired clerically trained workers—at least initially.[215]

Intellectual Abilities

Besides practical skills, intellectual capacities qualified the ideal missionary. They enabled him to cope with the extensive curriculum that included several languages. In Africa missionaries would need wisdom to make decisions regarding their ministry and to become "teachers

---

211. The statistics in Annual Reports of the 1820s and 1830s in the *Missions-Magazin* show that physical struggles were the primary reason students were "sent back to their former occupation." For example, MM 1829, 349.

212. Foremost among these is Miller, *Missionary Zeal*.

213. After listing the dismissals for health reasons of that year, the Director offers in 1830 a defense of the strenuousness of the program at the BMTI because of its character and virtue building effect (MM 1830, 366–68).

214. BMA, QS-3-4 "Stundenpläne 1816–1955." This folder contains weekly schedules of the year 1816/17 and from 1839 to 1955. See also the various documents of the House-Order in BMA, QS-9.31.

215. Stock, *Church Missionary Society*, 86–91; Walls, "Protestant Missionary Awakening," 37.

and preachers to the ignorant." A sufficient level of intelligence was also perceived to help missionaries distinguish between the two pitfalls of "faithless anxiety" and "thoughtless carelessness" regarding their health in Africa.[216]

These ideas about the qualifications of a missionary also illustrate the ongoing tension in the Basel Mission between the indispensable Pietist spirituality and religious practice, and the mental abilities which were also deemed necessary and often lacking among applicants. The following chapter investigates this dynamic more closely and its roots in the preferences of various participants in the BMTI community of practice.

CONCLUSION—SHARED DOMAIN OF INTEREST AND TRAINED INCAPACITY

This chapter investigated the "domain of interest" of the Basel Mission community of practice. It became obvious that their motivations and approaches towards Christian mission in Africa were strongly influenced by the general historical context. Their ideas were shaped by the contemporary image of Africa and suggested remedies for its perceived savagery in wider European humanitarian and missionary circles. With them the Basel Mission opposed slavery as inhuman and felt a Christian obligation to counteract its destructive effects in Africa and compensate European guilt through introducing Christianity and European civilization. Furthermore, with other pious Christians they shared the driving passion to safe the "perishing heathen" from the spiritual and moral darkness they judged them to inhabit. These commonalities enabled the collaboration with British Evangelical leaders.

However, the expressions of this domain of interest in Basel Mission publications and their instructions to missionaries in Africa reveal specific emphases which were shaped by their German Pietist background. Contrary to British Evangelical politicians' campaigning for "legitimate trade" to replace the slave trade, the Basel Mission was reluctant to adopt trade as a major policy and generally preferred political non-involvement. While their evaluations of conditions in Africa and ideas of ministry reflected general European assumptions of cultural superiority, the Basel Mission was influenced more strongly by German Pietist priorities. Its leaders articulated the missionary work in agricultural terms and privileged self-supportive village economy through agriculture and technical

---

216. MM 1830, 457; BMA, Q-3-3,26 Instruktionen 1842 §7.

skills over commerce. The workers they sought had to bring these practical skills and Pietist religious convictions and practice.

Before a closer examination of the practice of this community an important concern needs to be addressed, namely whether the similarity of attitudes to Africa and ideas of Christian mission to general European perceptions and Protestant missionary praxis invalidates the thesis of *trained incapacity* in the Basel Mission. Any response to this concern depends to a large degree on the meaning one attaches to "trained" in the concept.

The sociologists who defined the framework are very clear that what they refer to goes beyond the common perception of training as deliberate educational interventions. Veblen posed that the proclivity of businessmen to evaluate their actions solely from the perspective of pecuniary gain originated in the *experience and education* of the business world. Burke asserted that attitudes, behaviors and thinking established by previous *experience and education* which formerly served people well needed to change in the face of new contemporary challenges. Merton, finally claimed that "actions based upon *training and skills that have been successfully applied in the past* may result in inappropriate responses under changed conditions."[217] Thus, the incapacity identified here is based on mental frameworks which are shaped by various means, including socialization, experience, and intentional instruction.

Applying this to the question at hand then, far from being an argument against the trained incapacity posited in the Basel Mission, the widespread similarity of assessments and approaches among European Christians indicates that this trained incapacity was rampant throughout nineteenth century Protestant missions. The whole movement was imbued with it. Across denominational and national borders the pious in the churches adopted similar ideas. They followed closely each other's experience, successes, and failures—albeit continental Christians were probably more aware of British developments than vice versa—and mutually influenced each other. They collaborated in the implementation of their vision and this shared domain of interest shaped their work in Africa and what specific intentional training efforts groups employed for their workers.

The "training" of missionaries in Africa comprised of a wide range of preparatory processes. As Njoku rightly pointed out, they were not

---

217. Merton, *Social Theory*, 198. Emphases mine.

simply "products of the seminary" but socialization into their context of origin—including the prevalent spirit of cultural superiority—was "a critically important dimension of the education of the missionary."[218] As the following chapters show, Pietism of the Württemberg variety and rural culture provided this informal education for most of the Basel missionaries and was a dominant factor in shaping the intentional efforts at the BMTI.

The findings from the Basel Mission so far suggest that communities of practice are influenced by the wider historical context as well as the specific objectives and background of their participants. Their domain of interest is shaped be the general historical environment and with that ideas of the "practice" needed to address it. However, this does not preclude specific emphases of particular groups. The following chapter examines the participants in the Basel Mission enterprise and how their various backgrounds impacted on the practices of the BMTI.

218. Njoku, "Missionary Factor," 200–1.

3

Diverse Participants with a Shared Practice

IN A COMMUNITY OF *practice* participants develop a "shared practice" by interacting over time.[1] Sustained interaction was guaranteed in the BMTI. As they lived and worked in the community for up to six years, missionaries increased competence in knowledge, conduct, and practical skills inspired by the shared domain of interest. The curriculum demanded extensive studies and the general organization of life fostered specific spiritual and ethical practices. Beyond the institute, continuous dealings between leaders, British contacts, and supporters throughout Germany guaranteed the exchange of ideas as the previous chapter indicated. This chapter examines the distinct context of origin of the participants in the Basel Mission enterprise and how each impacted the organization's practices. I will demonstrate that in spite of significant socio-economic, cultural, and religious differences between the various contributing groups, the BMTI constituted a basically homogeneous community of practice that embraced shared theological emphases and socio-ethical convictions. A brief overview of developments in the BMTI from its inception to the mid-century sets the stage for this analysis.

---

1. Wenger, "Introduction." Wenger defines: "Members of a community of practice are practitioners. They develop a shared repertoire of resources: experiences, stories, tools, ways of addressing recurring problems—in short a shared practice. This takes time and sustained interaction."

GROWTH AND ADJUSTMENTS

Blumhardt's *Plan of a Missionary Training Institute* from 1815 outlined a three year curriculum which included memorization and study of the Bible teaching, and preaching, Christian ethics, mission history, and various basic sciences (non-European Geography, Arithmetic, Biology, Medicine).[2] The references to mission history and non-European geography were the only indication that this went beyond contemporary German school curricula. English and Dutch were taught because of the prospective employment of graduates with other societies, but biblical languages took a minor place. The founders imagined ten to fifteen students living with the *Inspector* (Director) who would be their teacher and mentor.[3] In May 1816 a building was purchased for this small boarding school.[4]

Falling well short of the intended three year training, the first two missionaries went with the Dutch society in April 1818 and another two with the CMS that fall. However, soon the demand for higher educated missionaries came from the British leaders who felt missionaries needed the academic education required for clerical ordination. Steinkopf, the mediator in all negotiations with the CMS, communicated in June 1818 that the *Episcopal Mission Society* (the term typically used for the CMS) "can only accept further candidates from our Institute who possess a scientific education (knowledge of Latin, Greek, and Hebrew) besides Christian heart abilities, and also a certain level of general education." For six such students they would provide the finances.[5] This was the beginning of an ongoing negotiation process between the values of academic studies and heart religion in the BMTI.

Most students from the second intake in 1818 graduated in 1821, thereby completing the three year curriculum. Two of this group went as

2. BMA, Q-2-1.1 "Anfänge des Basler Missions Instituts" (*The Beginnings of the Basel Mission Institute*). This folder contains the documents relating to the founding of the BMTI including a copy of the *Plan of the Missions Institute*. The official record of the "Plan" is in the Board minutes book in BMA, KP 1, 24–45 from March 7, 1816. The "Plan" was drawn up in 1815, adopted by the Board in March 1816 and approved by the educational authorities of the city in June 1816.

3. BMA, KP 1, 26.

4. BMA, KP 1, 51 from May 27, 1816. The comment that the *Panthier* had "a comfortable, healthy location and offered room for an apartment for the missions teacher and 15–20 students" already indicated a vision for expansion.

5. BMA, KP 2, 65 from July 27, 1818. These minutes include a summary of the letter.

the first Basel missionaries to Russia. The drafting of a constitution and the first public conference in 1821 reflected the growing importance of mission support associations as a source of funding, prayer, advocacy, and personnel for the further development of the organization and aspirations to establish independent fields overseas. Rising numbers of applications and the unbroken demand for more workers motivated the purchase of a larger house in 1819.[6] This Mission-House on Leonhardsgraben was dedicated in June 1820 and accommodated the BMTI until 1860. In 1821 they were settled in the new house, more missionaries were still needed and applications plentiful. Consequently, a much larger intake doubled their numbers with an average of around forty students from that year onwards until the number doubled again in 1860. The first instructor to assist Blumhardt was also employed in 1821.

In addition to the Russian Caucasus the Basel Mission began work in Liberia (1827–1832), the Gold Coast (1828), India (1834), and China (1847). This growth eventually led to delegating tasks to sub-committees. The *Oversight and Examination Commission* oversaw educational aspects including student applications and evaluations, the curriculum, and general supervision of "the spiritual and scientific state of the institution." The *Accounting Commission* was responsible for book keeping, and other committees for correspondence, administration, and practical maintenance of the Institute.[7]

The first leadership transition took place after Blumhardt's death in December 1838. Like his predecessor, Wilhelm Hoffmann hailed from one of the leading Pietist families in South-West Germany. He introduced the Preparatory School in 1844 to provide basic schooling for the many applicants whose previous education lacked the foundations needed for the BMTI curriculum. Hoffmann also expanded Basel Mission affiliations beyond Pietist groups into the circles of the nineteenth-century German revival movement. In 1850 Joseph Josenhans became the Director (until 1879). He led the mission into much stronger organizational conformity and presided over the beginnings of commercial activities.

---

6. Schlatter, *Heimatgeschichte*, 69–70. Schlatter also reports, that because of necessary renovations the school moved to a hotel, the "Badischer Hof" during 1819–1820.

7. Ibid., 132. Schlatter cites BMA, KP 5, 4ff and 113ff from 1821. Later committees were introduced for "Industry" (responsible for material needs overseas), for the education of missionaries' children, and for collecting donations. The various committees and their members were listed from 1853 onwards in an overview at the beginning of the annual reports. See BMA, Y2 (*Jahresberichte*).

As the Basel Mission expanded and developed relationships with international partners and support groups, gathered experience in training young volunteers, and extended into independent ministries, adjustments were made but basic emphases remained unchanged. They were shaped by the shared passion for foreign mission and common convictions regarding pious spirituality and character, practical ministry skills, and knowledge required for Christian missionaries. However, each of the participating groups shaped the practice at the BMTI in specific ways.

DIVERSE PARTICIPANTS INFLUENCING PRACTICE

Studies of the impact of European missions in the nineteenth century typically limit the discussion to either organizational policies or missionaries' background. Warren, for example, outlines incisively the socio-economic milieu of missionaries as part of the wider development of "the social emancipation of the underprivileged classes" in Britain.[8] Altena describes in detail the context German missionaries originated from, but brushes over the impact of training institutions in a few pages.[9] Jenkins explores the influence of Basel missionaries' village background on their engagement in Africa.[10] Other studies—typically the earlier, Euro-centric histories—limit their perspective to recounting mission leadership's thought processes and decisions. For instance, for Eppler, Ostertag, and Schick the history of the Basel Mission consists of the Board's actions embellished with detailed biographies of influential members.[11] Miller offers an insightful analysis of organizational dynamics in the Basel Mission, but limits it to relationships between the Board and the "rank and file."[12] The few studies that investigate the BMTI show similar tendencies. Schlatter and Haller acknowledge some tensions, in particular between students from different regions and with support societies, but overall endorse Board decisions as beneficial for the organization.[13] Then again,

---

8. Warren, *Social History*, 36–57.

9. Altena, *Ein Häuflein Christen*.

10. Jenkins, "Villagers as Missionaries."

11. Eppler, *Geschichte der Basler Mission*; Ostertag, *Entstehungsgeschichte*; Schick, *Vorboten und Bahnbrecher*.

12. Miller, *Missionary Zeal*, 35–80.

13. Haller, "Leben im Missionshaus"; Schlatter, *Heimatgeschichte*.

Eiselen, Vogelsanger, and Morgenthaler critique the authoritarian leadership of the Board tacitly assuming the superiority of democratic rule.[14]

By contrast, this chapter explores the background and relationships of all participants in the BMTI community, in order to identify how each contributed to its practice. Every group influenced BMTI proceedings, curriculum, goals, and decision making, while they also shared a religious and socio-ethical consensus. The *Committee* or leadership Board represented the group of men who founded the mission and continued to determine its course. It included the *Inspector*, the Director of the school, who with other teachers interacted daily with the students. The demands and expectations of the CMS shaped some BMTI practices. Finally, Mission Support-Societies contributed not only finances but also concerns that needed to be addressed and the missionary candidates' context of origin.

THE COMMITTEE: LEADING WITH BENIGN AUTHORITY

> The Committee was and is the beating heart, the proper guiding life-center of the [Basel Missionary] Society.[15]

The second Director spoke very highly of the *Committee*, the standing of these men in society, their true Christianity, unity in diversity, and the orderliness and quality of decision processes. Hoffmann did not believe that any German city could have provided an equally qualified group of men with true faith, independent wealth and influence, business experience, and political wisdom.[16] The founding members included clergy, a university professor, a merchant, and an administrator. They were already well acquainted through shared passion for pious Christianity and involvement in the Christian Society. In 1842 most Board members had served more than ten years, several since the beginning. At that point there were three pastors, five with business and finance expertise (two also City Council members), Secretary Spittler, and the Director.[17] By 1900 forty different men had served on the Board, all of whom closely

---

14. Eiselen, "Erziehung"; Morgenthaler, "Die Verfassung der Basler Mission"; Vogelsanger, *Pietismus und Afrikanische Kultur*.

15. Hoffmann, *Eilf Jahre*, 20.

16. Ibid., 17–20.

17. Hoffmann, *Missionsgesellschaft*, 79.

related by family ties and most Basel citizens of position and financial strength.[18]

In Basel pious Christianity was strong and the mission had influential supporters, but there were other practical reasons for preferring Basel citizens. The frequency of meetings—typically weekly—and the desire for regular personal observation of students necessitated physical proximity. Indeed, Board members interacted almost daily with the affairs and people of the Mission-House through visits and some as instructors. Students visited their houses and ministered in their churches and fellowships. This provided ample opportunities to assess students whose evaluations were based on Board members' judgments in addition to the director's reports.

New members were appointed by the existing Board. Hoffman commended the continuity of personnel and unity of decision making this self-constituting procedure facilitated—features which naturally are critiqued today.[19] However, for the Basel Mission leaders this was a deliberate policy which assumed that "those who carry within the true spirit of mission, nurture it in others, and establish ministries originating in this spirit, (humanly speaking) are obviously most qualified to judge whether others have this spirit" because this way "the true attitude and spirit is preserved, the unity of intention and action, principles and experience is maintained."[20] The organizational arrangements and constitution of the Board ensured continuity and aimed at establishing a homogeneous community in spite of the international and interdenominational rhetoric and origin of participants. Creative change, flexibility, and adaptability were not encouraged by these structures which—as we will see—had detrimental implications for intercultural engagement. In particular, the Board members' sociopolitical and economic standing in the city and their religious convictions influenced processes of the BMTI.

"Basler Daig" and "Frommes Basel"

Still today, the politically and economically dominant families of the city are referred to as *der Daig*, the "dough" that sticks together and keeps

---

18. Miller, *Missionary Zeal*, 41–42.

19. Eiselen, "Erziehung," 48–49; Vogelsanger, *Pietismus und Afrikanische Kultur*, 40–42; Hoffmann, *Eilf Jahre*, 22.

20. Hoffmann, *Missionsgesellschaft*, 80. See also Hoffmann, *Eilf Jahre*, 21.

among themselves, their social circle, their influence, and their money.²¹ They immigrated in the sixteenth and seventeenth centuries—many as Protestant refugees from Catholic persecution, made money in trade, new textile industries, and later the banking sector, and became very influential politically.²² Because of their status and role in the city they are often described as *aristocrats* or *patricians* in spite of the republican Swiss form of governance.²³ This small group of rich merchants, fabric owners, and bankers were closely related through purposeful marriage policies and dominated Basel economically, socially, and culturally until WWI.²⁴ They founded, supported, and led most political and social institutions of the nineteenth century. Their wealth and influence also benefited the Basel Mission, ensuring necessary permissions from the city government and financial support for the mission. The pastors on the Board belonged to the same families, and even though they tended to be less well-off, these "most orthodox ministers of the established state church . . . exerted considerable influence on the life of the city."²⁵

---

21. The word is the German *Teig* (dough) but could also be interpreted as *Deich* (dike). In 2008 I saw proof for the use of the term in the advertisement for a restaurant guide which simply said, "Worin blättert der Daig?" (What is the *Daig* reading?), assuming that this would be an incentive to buy the guide. Stoll clarifies the original meaning of the word as *Deich* depicting the wall and moat which used to fortify the city and the social group it referred to originally as the families of noble knights which used to live alongside the wall ready to defend the city. But the modern *Daig* depicts the bourgeois families of new industrial wealth who replaced the old aristocracy who left or died out. See Stoll, "Die Bedeutung des Basler Daigs." *Daig* even made it into the German Wikipedia where it is defined as "the common expression . . . for those families of Basel's upper class who possess citizen rights for generations, . . . a social group which is notable by its distinct self-distancing both upward (towards the Middle and Lower class) and sideways (towards the newly rich)." This is ironic as they themselves were the "newly rich" in years past. See "Daig."

22. See "Historical Lexicon of Switzerland," www.hls-dhs-dss.ch. This online dictionary includes family registers that combine genealogical information from various chronicles and lists the common names like Sarasin, Merian, Burckhardt, La Roche, Christ, Iselin, Preiswerk, most of which are dominant among the Basel Mission Board members and supporters. An investigation of these families shows their migratory origin in Basel. See also Gossman, *Basel in the Age of Burckhardt*, 13–107.

23. Schlatter, *Heimatgeschichte*, 133. In 1916 the official historian of the Basel Mission stated that the Board members "naturally" came from the "aristocratic circles" of the city.

24. Degen and Sarasin, "Basel (-Stadt)."

25. Gossman, *Basel in the Age of Burckhardt*, 49.

The Basel elite brought to the Basel Mission a conservative business mind that favored financial and practical scrutiny and frugality. One of the implications for Basel Mission engagement in Africa was the parsimonious support initially given to the missionaries and the expectations imposed on them to quickly establish themselves as independent of major assistance from Basel.[26] This expectation also reflected European ideas of tropical abundance and, as we will see, proved impossible to implement and a great strain on the missionaries.[27]

The *Daig* was also strongly impacted by Pietism and the nineteenth century revivals, and commonly referred to as *Frommes Basel* (Pious Basel).[28] They saw no contradiction between the pursuit of profit through trade and manufacturing, and religiosity embodying both, conservative and revivalist values.[29] In *Pious Basel*, a "peculiar geographical location, combined with a proudly defended heritage of Reformation humanism, eighteenth century pietism, and a long-standing . . . tradition of cultural conservatism," which together gave Basel "a unique and almost wholly skeptical attitude toward the phenomena of dechristianization and secularization emanating from other universities and urban centers" in contemporary Europe.[30] They valued learning highly, "not in the . . . sense of *Wissenschaft* (Science), but rather as the modest handmaiden of Christian truth and ethical character formation." Howard's analysis shows the tension that rose between Pietist elite families and the University of Basel over the appointment of W. M. L. de Wette (1780–1849) as Professor of Theology in 1822. Significantly, those who opposed the secular, critical

---

26. The first group sent to Africa (Liberia) in 1827 was instructed to establish gardens and farms in order to "win the necessities of life for the missionary family from their own soil" (MM 1830, 462).

27. For complaints and the eventual revision of this policy, see Schlatter, *Basler Mission in Afrika*, 16, 27; Wurm, "*Anfänge*," 245–46.

28. The depiction could be an honorific term or a polemic insult, but it acknowledged the fact that from the late eighteenth century Basel was "a city characterized by Pietist and awakened piety." See Hebeisen, *Leidenschaftlich fromm*; Kuhn and Sallmann, eds., *Das "Fromme Basel."*

29. Raith and Baumann, "Christentum in der Nordwestschweiz." Gossmann cites a satiric contemporary observer writing, "Basel is the city of miracles, where the rich can enter the Kingdom of Heaven more easily than a camel can pass through the eye of a needle. There is a high price on piety. It can almost substitute for wealth." *Schweizerische National-Zeitung*, 4 January, 1844, cited in Gossman, *Basel in the Age of Burckhardt*, 59.

30. Howard, *Religion and the Rise of Historicism*, 110–36. He uses Gossmann's analysis in Gossman, "Basel."

scientific approach to biblical theological studies de Wette represented were also supporters of the Basel Mission. Howard cites Spittler as the "most vocal critic" and Simon La Roche (1786–1861) was one of four faculty members who protested against the appointment. Both were signatories of the Basel Mission founding document, remained on the Board for decades, and La Roche became its president in 1838.[31]

The few German members on the Board shared religious convictions with Basel leaders. For both rational theology and critical methods of biblical interpretation opposed true Christianity. In Germany, at Tübingen University Pietist students—like the second director of the Basel Mission and the BMTI teacher Johann Christoph Blumhardt—sided with "supernaturalist" defense of traditional church doctrine against "rationalist" theologians.[32] In very much the same way, Basel Pietists perceived secular criticisms of the church as a threat, felt that "practical, pious wisdom was under attack in the modern world" and "called for a restored understanding of the divine limitations placed on human thought."[33] Consequently, at the BMTI the leaders were united in their opposition to the emerging trends at theological institutions and developed a strongly anti-rationalist biblical curriculum that emphasized Bible knowledge and ethical formation.

Patriarchal Regiment

In 1853 Hoffmann argued at length for the practicality and advantages of the "strict aristocratic, almost monarchical constitution of the Basel Mission" that kept leadership in the hands of a few wealthy influential Basel citizens and only granted an advisory role to the most prominent leaders of support societies.[34] He commended the "well regulated, orderly proceedings and smooth collaboration" of men from very different professions and the consistency facilitated by long-standing familiarity. Hoffmann strongly resisted suggestions of majority vote and decision making powers for support societies as undesirable and alarming. Democratic rule for this mission director would lead to lack of decisiveness

---

31. Howard, *Religion and the Rise of Historicism*, 121. La Roche was President of the Basel Mission for sixteen years (1838–1854).

32. Ising, *Johann Christoph Blumhardt*, 37–39.

33. Howard, *Religion and the Rise of Historicism*, 116–17.

34. Hoffmann, *Eilf Jahre*, 16–30.

and emotional decisions, based on lack of information and long-term perspective.

Even within the Board decisions were not made by majority vote, but for all important issues they desired unanimous agreement which could lead to repeated similar debates, especially on personnel and strategies. Schlatter in 1916 still felt that the patriarchal rule of the Board, independent from "the easily aroused and not always thoroughly informed" mission friends, was a commendable situation. He saw the practice of unanimous decision making as safe guard for "appropriate and trustworthy decisions" which had "undeniable advantages," in spite of the time repeated consideration could take.[35] This delay in decision making affected the missionaries in Africa who often did not receive responses to their requests for many months.

The Board's patriarchal regiment is typically condemned by recent scholars. Morgenthaler sharply denounces the lack of participation granted to support societies.[36] Vogelsanger, citing Eiselen, concurs with his assessment, that the mission leadership could not imagine anybody from a lower social standing with less education making appropriate decisions and so "there was no room for any participation by other groups involved in the project."[37] These strong positions need to be challenged because, firstly, they are inaccurate. While support societies were not officially on the Board and at times contested their lack of participation, they provided many highly influential advisors.[38] More importantly, such

---

35. Schlatter, *Heimatgeschichte*, 133. Only after 1945 the patriarchal Board was replaced by a democratically organized association and since 2001 the *mission* 21 which is a collaboration of the former Basel Mission, the Evangelical Mission in Kwango, and the Moravian Mission. They present themselves as "a community of churches and organisations which connects people from different cultures and countries" and strongly emphasize equal partnership with partner churches in Africa, Asia and Latin America, "theological and cultural exchange, as well as projects in development cooperation within fields such as the reduction of poverty, health care, women and gender, education and the advancement of peace." See "Our Mission." http://www.mission-21.org/en/mission-21/our-mission/; Jenkins, "Basler Mission."

36. Morgenthaler, "Die Verfassung der Basler Mission."

37. Eiselen, "Erziehung," 49; Vogelsanger, *Pietismus und Afrikanische Kultur*, 41–43.

38. These included the chair of the large society in Stuttgart, the merchant Johann Jakob Häring (1775–1838), the founder of Calw Publishing House, Christian Gottlob Barth, the co-founder and inspector of the Institute for Teacher Training and Care of Poor Children in Beugen, Christian Heinrich Zeller (1779–1860) and the professor of Physics and later presiding pastor in Schaffhausen, David Spleiß (1786–1854). See

criticism fails to consider the historical context because it idealizes democracy. However, at the time, and especially among Pietists, democratic rule was not generally accepted as superior political system. As we saw above, they opposed such aspirations of contemporary revolutionaries as disruption of God constituted order.

Furthermore, in Basel political leadership was perceived as duty and privilege, and because there was only a token remuneration active participation in government was "effectively restricted . . . to citizens of means."[39] Members of the city council were treated with great deference and the constitution "ensured . . . that those already in power determined their successors" and the wealthy elite families maintained political power. Parallels to the attitudes and proceedings in the Basel Mission Board are unmistakable. As Miller put it, their "firm hegemony in the organization . . . matched the economic and political influence and social prestige to which they were accustomed in the larger society."[40] They saw their work, as an extension of societal responsibilities. Their Pietist stance added to this the religious conviction that they had been entrusted with a holy task and providentially put in the position to fulfill it.

Most participants of the BMTI community shared the conviction that this group of men had been divinely mandated and providentially prepared for leadership by education and social standing, and treated them with much deference.[41] Miller incisively analyzes this charismatic and traditional reasoning that legitimized unequal social roles.[42] He adds a bureaucratic dynamic; the implementation of structures and rules which reflected the "shared objectives and reciprocal confidence" and were not

---

Ising, *Johann Christoph Blumhardt*, 8, 80–83; Schlatter, *Heimatgeschichte*, 134–35.

39. The analysis of Basel city *Honoratiorenregiment* (honorable rule) summarized here is offered by Gossman, *Basel in the Age of Burckhardt*, 31–32.

40. Miller, "Class Collaboration," 36.

41. Hoffmann illustrates the general agreement that by divine guidance the mission was established in Basel, that the leading men had good intentions and were driven by passion for the divine cause not their personal interests, and most importantly they were "the true, by God himself constituted leadership of the mission" who acted upon God's promises and furthered God's work." See Hoffmann, *Eilf Jahre*, 27.

42. Miller, *Missionary Zeal*, 86–109. In this section he uses Max Weber's three types of authority (*charismatic* based on new revelation, *traditional* based on what has always been, and *bureaucratic* based on legal or imposed rules) to show how "Württemberg Pietism provided . . . a system of bridging beliefs" which enabled a reconciliation of "charismatic, traditional and bureaucratic modes of decision making" and legitimized the claim to authority by the Board and Director with the rank-and-file missionaries.

128 Part I: The Community of Practice

perceived as tools of oppression and exploitation. Interestingly, searching for evidence of the latter, Miller fails to find it and concludes that "the Committee never violated the moral pledges it made to the seminarians" regarding social honor and economic security. This validates the participants' "reciprocal confidence" against such criticism.

Committee Influences on BMTI Practice

Patriarchal regiment is strongly evident in BMTI practice. The House-Order presents Board members and teachers as patriarchal leaders to whom obedience and submission was due, but who were also entrusted with the care and best possible training of the candidates.[43] The Board's "fatherly care and love" included giving advice and ensuring missionaries' physical and spiritual wellbeing. Accommodation, clothing, food, and teaching were provided. In return, missionaries were expected to trust the leaders' wisdom and willingly obey. The word "Zöglinge" is most frequently used for the students (besides *brothers*). It depicts novices—most often children or apprentices—who need training, education, instruction to become mature and skilled.[44] The title implied a subordinate and dependent position but also the care of superiors. It was widely used for various types of trainees including theology students. More importantly, the roles of fathers, teachers, and pastors as authority figures were integral to the communities Basel missionaries originated from. In the BMTI, Board members and teachers took on those social roles. Consequently, students' obedience and submission to Board rules and decisions was demanded by the House-Order and typically imposed when disagreements arose. There was provision for voluntary resignations, but the leadership reserved the right to discharge anyone who proved "unfit for missionary work."

Patriarchal authority needs to be balanced with the honest care which permeates Board considerations. This internal tension between uncompromising convictions and concern for personal and spiritual development of candidates is revealed in prolonged reluctance to dismiss students who failed expectations.[45] Miller's sociological analysis high-

43. The longest paragraph in the House-Order dealt with the "behavior of the brothers towards the Mission-Committee" and outlined their duties and rights (BMA, QS-9.31 #11 §14).

44. The closest English translation is "pupils."

45. For example, Bargas was a student who entered in March 1837 and quickly showed weak academically and physically, but he was not dismissed until December

lights the benefits gained by Board members, like religious satisfaction, business connections, and enhanced social prestige.⁴⁶ While those likely contributed to Basel elite involvement, there is a sense of deep concern which reveals an emotional commitment of the Board members to the "rank and file" beyond any personal benefits.

This also comes through in the various provisions for patriarchal supervision. Teachers reported weekly to the Director "important incidents" in the house.⁴⁷ They visited students' rooms to assist their studies, give advice, and watch over their private lives, faithful use of time, and generally appropriate silence. The weekly teachers' conferences discussed students' behavior, academic and spiritual progress, and general proceedings.⁴⁸ Later, the "Durchgang" required regular individual student teacher meetings to sort out any differences, for "mutual confidential sharing," admonition if necessary, and spiritual counseling.⁴⁹ Thus, it is clear that leaders and teachers were concerned about students' personal and spiritual as well as their academic development. Most candidates had grown up in a context where authority figures would relate in a similar way, occasionally taking a young person aside to offer advice and admonition, and ask questions about their inner life.⁵⁰ Hence, BMTI students

---

1839. See BMA, KP March 29, 1837 (report of Bargas's acceptance into the BMTI), June 13, 1838 (one of the reports of Bargas's academic, theological and physical weakness), December 11, 1839 (final dismissal of Bargas). Similar prolonged considerations and repeated conversations with the students were also conducted between March and July 1839 when Forchhammer and Schifterling had disagreements with the other candidates. Both were at one point dismissed, but Forchhammer was restored and even employed as a teacher for a short time. See BMA, KP February 18, March 13, 20, April 4, 10, 17, July 31. However, eventually Forchhammer did leave the Basel Mission. See KP September 11, October 18, 1839.

46. Miller, "Class Collaboration"; Miller, *Missionary Zeal*, 72–80.

47. BMA, QS-9.31 #11 §1. With the addition of several other teachers to the director in the 1820s the position of the "Wöchner" (responsible teacher for the week) was instituted. In the 1860s the new House-Order assigned this title to a student, and the role became more one of a servant to the teachers and administrator of the various permissions students needed (BMA, QS-9.31 #12, B, III, 31).

48. BMA, QS-7-1a "Lehrerkonferenz Protokolle" contains the minutes of these meetings.

49. Haller, "Leben im Missionshaus," 234.

50. One example is Johann Christian Dieterle's account in his application letter of his older brother making him recite Bible verses and admonishing him about his life and faith. (BMA, PF 248).

did not perceive the tension modern readers feel in the fact that superiors would also act as counselors and confidants.

Two important aspects of the Board's "patriarchal rule" are pertinent to interpreting the practice that emerged in Basel. The Committee members had the social standing, economic resources, and political power that enabled them to act, which caused others to expect their leadership. They were convinced of their benevolent motives and true seeking of the will of God in their decisions and actions. Consequently, it was a small step to presume that their perspectives were guided by God and they should lead this venture. Secondly, all other participants also took their leadership for granted. The British leaders would naturally deal with those they already had relationships with and who were in a similar social place, the support societies looked to Basel already as a center of Pietist leadership, the students had grown up in a cultural context where elders governed all areas of life, and the Director, originating from the same context, unquestioningly assumed the role of leader and counselor over those younger in age and in the faith. In other words, there was a shared cultural understanding of each participant's social role that supported the hierarchical structures which resulted in the "patriarchal rule" contemporaries corroborated with but which scholars from the very different context of late twentieth century Europe (that idealizes egalitarianism and democracy) condemn. It is important to recognize the cultural shaping of both these responses and to evaluate the BMTI community of practice within its own context. For everybody involved, these dynamics made perfect sense and fit with their religious and social expectations.

While this contributed to the strength and homogeneity of the Basel Mission community, it also held great potential for trained incapacity. The general consensus on social dynamics meant that these perceptions were not challenged but reinforced at the BMTI. Consequently, the missionaries arrived in Africa with strong convictions about proper relationships between people of varying social position and educational attainment that influenced their approach to African realities. In that context they perceived themselves of higher social status expecting Africans to assume roles of followers, pupils, and apprentices. The tensions and misconceptions this caused were predictable.

THE INSPECTOR AND TEACHERS: APPLYING THE SEMINARY MODEL

At the outset the Board saw Blumhardt as advisor and asked him to take on "the supervision and leadership of the new mission institute."[51] He created the first curriculum, outlined the inner workings, and continued to develop the school.[52] As applications increased other teachers were employed, but the *Inspector* remained dominant. In fact, the first Director had so much clout that his successor called his time an "absolute monarchy" and felt compelled to "bring the Committee into its true position as actually ruling institution."[53] This did not stop Hoffmann from pushing through the changes he felt necessary which included the introduction of the preparatory school and general expansion of the BMTI.

The *Rule of an Inspector*—articulated at Hoffmann's appointment in 1839—required "complete commitment of his time and strength to the holy mission work" which included general oversight and leadership of the institute, all its students and employees, under the supervision of the Committee, of which he was a member.[54] Except practical maintenance and financial administration, the total responsibility for the seminary was on the shoulders of the Director. He was the central person who related to all other participants, the supporting groups, missionaries, other societies, and the Board. In fact, rather than the Committee, it could be argued that the Inspector was "the beating heart" of the Basel Mission. He was part of the patriarchal leadership and his background and understanding of Christian mission decisively shaped BMTI practice.

---

51. Ostertag, *Entstehungsgeschichte*, 326. The appointment letter from October 6, 1815.

52. BMA, KP 1, 31–43. *Plan of the Mission-Institute*. Especially the sections on *Disciplinary Organization* (Disziplinar-Einrichtung) and *Mission-Teacher* (Missions-Lehrer).

53. In a letter from December 6, 1849 to Christian Gottlob Barth (1799–1862), a long time supporter and advisor to the Basel Mission whose classes at the university students took (1836–1839), cited by Schlatter, *Heimatgeschichte*, 149. See also Hoffmann, *Eilf Jahre*, 28–29.

54. BMA, KP 14, 117 from February 1, 1839. Hoffmann's own account of his duties lists the execution of Board decisions, correspondence with overseas stations, support societies, other mission societies and official authorities, the general leadership of the institute, coordinating applications and attending to publications. See Hoffmann, *Missionsgesellschaft*, 83.

Prominent German Pietist Families

The Directors and most teachers hailed from prominent German families in the Christian Society.[55] Beyond personal friendships, they shared the Pietist faith, apologetic efforts against Catholicism, Enlightenment philosophy and liberation movements, and passion for foreign mission. Furthermore, many were also related through kinship and marriage. For example, the teachers Johann Blumhardt and Jakob Heinrich Staudt (1808–1884) were married to sisters, the daughters of Karl Köllner (1790–1853), a staunch supporter of the Basel Mission.[56] The Blumhardt family was dominant in Stuttgart—the largest and most influential support society—and the Hoffmanns had co-founded the Christian colony Korntal and were closely befriended with the Josenhans family. Inspector Hoffmann was a class-mate and friend of Johann Blumhardt and had grown up with his successor Joseph Josenhans.

Throughout the nineteenth century the Inspectors were theologians from Württemberg. Most assistant instructors were *candidates,* recent theological graduates who taught briefly before entering ministry. The few long-term teachers, like Johann Blumhardt, Heinrich Staudt, and Paul Albert Ostertag became influential lifelong advisors.[57] They mo-

---

55. See Staehelin's "Introduction of the more important Persons in the World of the Christian Society" which lists most of the BMTI instructors, its Directors, Committee members, and the leaders of support societies throughout Europe. Staehelin, *Christentumsgesellschaft, Vol. 2,* 31–160. Exceptions were the few theologians from the Basel circles of the Christian Society and other Europeans like Peter Fjellstedt (1802–1881), the Swedish BMTI graduate who taught for a couple of years (1828–1831) before he went to India. Fjellstedt later started a Swedish Missionary Society in Lund and "became the pioneer architect of Swedish missions." See Ising, *Johann Christoph Blumhardt,* 464; Schlatter, *Heimatgeschichte,* 119; Walls, "Protestant Missionary Awakening," 43.

56. Three of Karl and Maria Köllner's daughters married Basel men, the third one was the India missionary Johannes Häberlin (1808–1849). The Köllner family provides an interesting illustration for the networks and relationships in Pietist circles. Originally from Idstein near Frankfurt, Wilhelm Köllner (1760–1835) came to Basel in 1818 and was a regular in meetings of the society. His son, Karl Köllner was involved with Basel Mission associated groups from his early twenties. In 1845 he became Director of the charitable institutions in Korntal. Both father and son Köllner were prolific correspondents in the Christian Society and close friends of Spittler, the Hoffmann family, and many others. See Scheffbruch, "Carl Köllner."

57. Johann Christoph Blumhardt taught from 1830 to 1837, Heinrich Staudt from 1832 to 1843 and Paul Albert Ostertag (1810–1871) from 1837 to 1871. Ostertag also was a Board member from 1848, edited the new *Evangelisches Missions-Magazin* from 1857 and authored a historical account of the beginnings of the Basel Mission at its

Diverse Participants with a Shared Practice 133

tivated their congregations to support missions, sent young men to be trained, spoke at Annual Conferences, and were consulted on important decisions.

Vogelsanger refers to the director and teachers as intermediaries.[58] While their education and the leading role of their families raised their social status, they shared the socio-economic background of most students. Growing up in Pietist fellowships in rural Germany meant that pious emphases of decent behavior, regular family devotions, and weekly meetings shaped the young men as much as prevalent poverty.[59] Famine years (1816–17, 1848–49, 1851–52), sickness, economic changes, and the aftermath of war put early demands on youths to deal with spiritual and material needs. For example, Director Blumhardt had to give up schooling for some time to support his family working as a cobbler.[60] Only the provision of free education—covering tuition, room, and board—for those who passed the *Landexamen*, an examination for future pastors, enabled youth with intellectual abilities to enter theological studies.[61]

Pietist families fostered social involvement, condemned rationalist philosophy and secularization, had a growing sense of chiliastic urgency, and disseminated information on foreign missions. All this contributed to passionate activism in evangelism, Bible distribution, and missionary support. These passions are reflected in the frequent travels and publication activities of Basel Mission Directors. Blumhardt spearheaded the *Missions-Magazin* as means to disseminate global missionary information.[62] Hoffmann advertised foreign mission through his writings, speak-

---

fiftieth anniversary. See Ostertag, *Entstehungsgeschichte*.

58. Vogelsanger, *Pietismus und Afrikanische Kultur*, 46; Miller, *Missionary Zeal*, 40–41.

59. Ising, *Johann Christoph Blumhardt*. Ising's account of Director Blumhardt's relative and later teacher at the BMTI, Johann Blumhardt, gives a picture of the life and experience of these men prior to their involvement with the Basel Mission. Johann Blumhardt is often referred to as the director's nephew, but Ising clarifies that Christian Gottlieb Blumhardt was a cousin of his father, Johann Georg Friedrich Blumhardt (1777–1822). The Blumhardts are another family which illustrates the wide network of interrelationships among the men and women involved in the Basel Mission.

60. Ostertag, *Entstehungsgeschichte*, 59–91. This section is an account of Blumhardt's youth by the author who knew the director personally.

61. Ising, *Johann Christoph Blumhardt*, 13–14. Ising points out that both, Johan Blumhardt and Wilhelm Hoffmann were only able to attend seminary because they passed this examination at the conclusion of *Gymnasium* (High School).

62. Bundy, *Blumhardt, Christian Gottlieb*.

ing engagements, and teaching at the university which expanded the influence of the Basel Mission beyond Pietists to other revived groups.[63] Directors also typically went on extended summer trips. This pattern influenced ideas of itinerant ministry for the missionaries in Africa which proved unhelpful in that very different context.

School Experience in German Seminaries

Upon his arrival in Basel Hoffmann observed that the general design of the BMTI "was taken from the Württemberg seminaries where the theologians of the country were trained"—a fact that made him feel at home from the beginning.[64] All Directors and most instructors had attended these seminaries.

Württemberg schools had a "somewhat rough" tone that handled things "in a manner more police like than positive and encouraging."[65] A rigorously regimented time table and frequent tests made for a "situation marked by continuous demand and self effort." The day was filled with study, strict dress codes applied—jacket, vest, trousers, boots and cap in "decent, dark color"—and activities during limited "recreation" times were also regulated, with visiting taverns, theatre, card playing, and smoking strictly forbidden. Punishments ranged from assignment of additional work and restriction of privileges to confinement and expulsion. However, at the time, cautions for teachers to "apply discipline sparingly" represented "a corrective to overly strict disciplinarian practice." Recent graduates functioned as teaching assistants and oversaw students outside classes.

The curriculum emphasized classical languages, mathematics, and history. In Tübingen three years theology followed two years of general studies, and university lectures were supplemented by the *Stift* curriculum. Johann Blumhardt and Wilhelm Hoffmann attended this boarding

63. Bundy, "*Hoffmann*"; Hanst, "Hoffmann." Examples for Hoffmann's mission related publications are: Hoffmann, *Die Erziehung des weiblichen Geschlechts*; Hoffmann, *Missionsgesellschaft*; Hoffmann, *Missions-Fragen*; Hoffmann, *Eilf Jahre*.

64. Hoffmann, *Eilf Jahre*, 16.

65. Ising provides a detailed description of what seminary education was like in his biography of Johann Christoph Blumhardt who went to both lower seminary (1820–1824) and the Tübingen *Stift* (1824–1929) with Wilhelm Hoffmann and was himself an instructor at the BMTI for seven years (1830–1837). The *Stift* was a boarding school for theological students attached to the university. See Ising, *Johann Christoph Blumhardt*, 10–22, 31–58. The following descriptions and citations are taken from these sections.

school for theological students together (1824–1829). They were part of the *Pia*, the Pietist "Union of Christian Students" and added to private studies edifying literature like Arndt's *True Christianity*. Theologically, they were exposed to the debate between rationalist theologies and *supernaturalists*. Pious students sided with supernaturalist rejection of critical rationalist views.[66] The *Pia* members were also uncomfortable with Student Unions calling for a Republic and dissociated from political activities, concerned about the disruption of public order student revolts at German universities represented.

The seminary included practice of public speaking, beginning with memorized sermons, exercises in teaching, and preaching. Instruction in Bible history, doctrine, and morals, daily devotional times, and regular Sunday services focused on applying the teaching to practical Christian living. This education put strong demands on intellect and memory but also emphasized the practical equipment of future pastors. In addition, Pietist students studied devotional literature and practiced spiritual disciplines, especially prayer, solitude, and Bible reading.

BMTI Characteristics Reflecting German Seminaries

In all this the parallels in the BMTI are obvious. As Hoffmann put it, from the Württemberg seminaries the institute had "adopted the good without retaining the faults" avoiding the latter by "the highest principle that everything built on the true conversion of the students which could be and had to be presumed."[67] Affinities with German seminaries included the prominence of ancient languages and heavy study load, the practical ministry emphasis, strictly regulated daily schedule, and the boarding school set-up with its supervisory characteristics. However, the BMTI selection criteria ensured that students invariably originated with the pious groups.

Similar to German seminaries, BMTI schedules reveal fully planned days.[68] Beyond up to thirty class hours weekly, there were obligatory

---

66. Schnurr, *Weltreiche und Wahrheitszeugen*, 151–52. Hoffmann wrote a 400 page rebuttal of the critical treatment of the *Life of Jesus* by David Friedrich Strauß (1808–1874): Hoffmann, *Das Leben Jesu*. For an English translation of Strauß, see Strauss, *Life of Jesus*. Around the same time Director Blumhardt stressed that such rationalist approaches contradicted revealed biblical faith and were not part of the BMTI curriculum in his annual report. See MM 1836, 372–75.

67. Hoffmann, *Eilf Jahre*, 16.

68. BMA, QS-9.31 #11 §3. See also BMA, QS-3-4 "Stundenpläne 1816–1955." This

daily devotions, evening meetings, assigned physical work in the gardens and workshops, and students were expected to spend several hours in personal studies and devotion.[69] Private reading was essentially restricted to devotional literature, mission reports, and the Bible. Communal living with teachers guaranteed constant oversight. Furthermore, specific roles were assigned to students to watch each other's private life, efficient use of time, and general keeping of silence and order.[70] These characteristics deeply convinced students of the values of order, diligence, and constant industriousness. Consequently, they developed quite judgmental attitudes towards anybody not displaying these qualities. In this way the BMTI practice reinforced European prejudice and affected Basel missionaries' assessments of Europeans and Africans in Ghana as undisciplined and indolent.

The extensive BMTI curriculum reflected German seminaries. As we saw above, languages were a priority. In addition to Hebrew, Greek, and Latin as in the seminaries, the BMTI taught English and later added Sanskrit and Arabic.[71] Such language study was expected to help missionaries preach and translate the Bible and other Christian texts into vernaculars, but its strong reliance on written aids did not consider learning oral vernaculars in Africa.[72] Furthermore, the BMTI covered Old and New Testament exegesis, "Bible Analysis," Systematic Theology, and Biblical History which led seamlessly into World History and Church History. The historical subjects reveal the assumption of Pietist historiography which placed non-Christian peoples outside of history and civilization, thus validating general European evaluations discussed above.[73] Any doubts students may have had about the position of African

---

folder contains weekly schedules of the year 1816–17 and from 1839 to 1955.

69. The House-Order demanded "faithful and diligent" attendance and absence needed valid reasons and prior permission (BMA, QS-9.31 #11 §5).

70. BMA, QS-9.31 #11 §2, a, 1–5 and §4, 7. Weekly reports by the "Senior" are in BMA, QS-4 "Wochenberichte."

71. MM 1839, 391–99. In this inaugural report Hoffmann offers a particularly detailed description of the BMTI curriculum and the reasoning behind it. Latin was regarded as necessary because biblical-theological commentaries were typically written in Latin. Hoffmann explicitly mentioned Bengel's *Gnomon* in his defense of keeping Latin in the syllabus. See also Hoffmann, *Eilf Jahre*, 94.

72. MM 1838, 358.

73. Schnurr, *Weltreiche und Wahrheitszeugen*, 157–63, 275–85. Hoffmann's outline of the BMTI curriculum confirms and illustrates Schnurr's incisive analysis of pious historiography.

peoples were eliminated at the BMTI. Consequently, the training served to reinforce and establish unhelpful attitudes which shaped missionary engagement in Africa.

Pressing this extensive curriculum into three years quickly proved impossible.[74] In 1821 a fourth year was introduced. Later Hoffmann advocated for a two year preparatory school to cover the basic education most applicants were lacking. When this was implemented in 1844 it extended the BMTI for most students to six years.[75] Nevertheless, the prevailing emphasis the Director, instructors, and Board agreed upon was Pietist spiritual and character formation. For this purpose the boarding set-up was well suited and all stressed this distinction from universities.

Practical ministry preparation also paralleled German seminaries and covered instruction on and practicing teaching, preaching, and leading devotions. It privileged memorized material from Bible verses to devotions and sermons by pious German pastors. In the final year students composed short teachings and had weekly evaluated preaching practice before teachers and fellow students.[76] This preparation that heavily used homilies by acknowledged Pietist leaders was seen as "the most suitable for the proclamation of the blessed gospel in the heathen world."[77] However, it is doubtful that sermons written for a European audience were going to resonate with Africans. Another idealized pattern was itinerant preaching. This was practiced on vacation trips. It also served the purpose that support societies met the missionaries and students rehearsed writing the kind of reports expected from the mission fields. All these practices were typical in Germany, but their usefulness in the dissimilar cultural environment of foreign mission—where European illustrations and applications were not likely to make much sense and traveling affect-

---

74. Elementary and secondary education followed by two levels of seminary meant that Hoffmann for example had about sixteen years of schooling (nine of these in seminary).

75. Hoffmann, *Eilf Jahre*, 81–86. See also his Annual Report from 1844 in MM 1844, 197–99. Hoffmann complained that BMTI students were expected to cover in four years basic German elementary education as well as general and theological training up to university level.

76. MM 1830, 375; MM 1840, 56. These annual reports commend principals of local schools for opening up their schools for catechetical exercises. The House-Order paragraph on preaching practices details that all resident teachers and students were obliged to attend. It also regulates the handling of occasional invitations to preach in local churches (BMA, QS-9.31 #13).

77. MM 1830, 377–78; MM 1839, 393–94.

ed European's health—is questionable. Thus, the ministry preparation given to BMTI students had the propensity to create trained incapacity in their intended context.

THE BRITISH PARTNER: CMS DEMANDS FOR ERUDITION

The CMS was the main employer of BMTI graduates outside the Basel Mission. Even though the British partners were not directly participating in the BMTI community, they nevertheless influenced its practice considerably. Therefore the relationship needs to be briefly considered without presuming to provide a comprehensive analysis.

It is surprising how little scholarly attention is given to this important alliance.[78] The CMS did not have any missionaries to send for almost five years after its founding and relief from this "absurd situation" finally came from Germans trained by Jänicke and later the BMTI became a major supplier of personnel.[79] Jenkins identifies 102 Basel-trained missionaries sent out by the CMS between 1819 and 1858.[80] Whereas the CMS historian Stock minimizes mention of Basel missionaries mostly to acknowledging their dedication, Basel Mission authors present a cordial cooperation that generally conceals the tensions, negotiations, and often struggle involved.[81] But they did cooperate regardless of their disagreements, because of their shared passion for Christian mission.[82]

---

78. Three recent articles explore the CMS collaboration with the Basel Mission: Becker, "Basel Missionaries Cooperating"; Jenkins, "An Early Experiment"; Kirchberger, "Fellow-Labourers."

79. Walls, "Protestant Missionary Awakening," 37; Stock, *Church Missionary Society*, 68–91. The CMS was founded in 1799 and sent its first missionaries—two German graduates from Berlin—in January 1804. See also Pinnington. "Church Principles." Pinnington bemoaned the lack of an analysis of "the actual relations between Salisbury Square and the continental missionary societies which supplied for so long so many of the greatest C.M.S. missionaries."

80. Jenkins, "Early Experiment."

81. See also Becker, "Basel Missionaries Cooperating." Becker's paper is an incisive analysis of the differences in the way the relationship was presented in CMS and Basel Mission publications.

82. Walls, "Protestant Missionary Awakening," 40–43.

Developments and Tensions in the Relationship

From the beginning Steinkopf mediated the promise of financial support by the CMS in exchange for personnel.[83] In his caution that they should be "men with talent, knowledge, and ability to learn languages" is a hint of British reservations towards German missionaries based on their experience with Berlin graduates. They wanted people better trained academically than was typical of German candidates.[84] In October 1818 CMS representatives visited Basel and the two societies entered into a formal agreement.[85] The BMTI would provide a certain number of men in exchange for a contribution towards their training (annually £25 per student). The Basel Mission also agreed to add Latin and biblical languages to the curriculum to meet the request for "scientifically educated missionaries . . . who . . . could engage the world [in East India] and would not offend church authorities." This deal was "frequently updated, confirmed as late as 1861, and apparently never formally revoked," and basically remained the same.[86] The clear prospect of fields of service strengthened the confidence of supporting circles and brought more applicants. Both the expanded curriculum and larger class necessitated the employment of the first additional instructor.[87] The growth also

---

83. Steinkopf was the Pastor of the German Lutheran Savoy Church in London, a member of the Bible and Tract Society and its representative on the continent. He communicated to Blumhardt on August 3, 1816 (three weeks before the opening of the BMTI) the decision by the CMS to financially support the new venture and their promise to take on graduates under the condition that they were "young men of talent who combined with unfeigned piety and compulsion by the love of Christ also natural abilities (especially in learning languages) and knowledge." Cited in Schlatter, *Heimatgeschichte*, 61–62. For the first grant of £100 see also Stock, *Church Missionary Society*, 120. For the important role German Protestant clergy in London played for Anglo-German relationships, see Kirchberger, "Fellow-Labourers."

84. The CMS continually struggled with the gap between the German volunteers from simple rural background and the theologically educated clergy the British leaders really would have wanted to employ. Andrew Walls discusses this struggle from the perspective of the CMS leaders and how the precedence of Halle trained and Lutheran ordained missionaries with the SPCK in India led to the acceptance of the first German missionaries from Berlin. Walls, "Missionary Vocation," 164–70. For details see also Stock, *Church Missionary Society*, 73–91.

85. BMA, KP October 6, 1818.

86. Jenkins, "Early Experiment," 57; Schlatter, *Heimatgeschichte*, 63–64. Adjustments concerned numbers of missionaries and the amount of money exchanged.

87. Kaspar Schlatter (1796–1862) was the first of many pastoral candidates who accepted this task. He taught at the BMTI from 1819 to 1823 before he served as a pastor in various churches in Germany. See Staehelin, *Christentumsgesellschaft*, Vol. 2, 129.

required the purchase of larger quarters. However, increased academic work caused the first complaints about the study load and eventually the introduction of a preparatory class.

A detailed contract resulted from Director Blumhardt's visit in England in 1822. CMS requests for higher general and theological education led for a brief period (1822–1824) to a two-tier course, one following the more academic curriculum, the other for "catechists and school teachers after the way of the Moravians" which was, however, soon dropped in favor of the academic course for all students.[88] This episode reflected ideas of more or less civilized non-European nations requiring differently qualified missionaries, a notion the Basel Mission never embraced to the extent it was held in Britain.

Stock's reduction of this important visit by Blumhardt to a footnote that leaves the contract unmentioned is an indication for the unequal relationship.[89] He also ignores subsequent frictions over the level of English and Lutheran ordination that almost ended the relationship in 1824 (were it not for the fact that the British were in dire need of workers), serious tensions over the soundness of BMTI theology (1827), Blumhardt's second visit to London when he was again confronted with critique on the deficiencies of his graduates (1833), the extended stay of teacher Ostertag in England during which the feasibility of the relationship was discussed yet again (1838), and even the humiliating doctrinal examination of Director Hoffmann in 1846.[90] There were also visits by CMS officials in Basel, but overall the impression remains that the Basel Mission made the concessions while CMS leaders continued to raise concerns.

Becker suggests prejudices about the other country and projection of problems at home onto the other side as reasons for misunderstandings.[91] Pinnington discusses at length the tensions over Episcopal ordination, Anglican liturgy, and church discipline.[92] He concludes that even though "personal relations between the Societies always remained cordial, the way in which the C.M.S. interpreted their role caused much

---

88. Schlatter, *Heimatgeschichte*, 72–75. This episode never was to the liking of the Basel Mission leaders, mainly because of the separation it caused in the student body.

89. Stock, *Church Missionary Society*, 120, 263.

90. While the official CMS historian all but ignores the relationship, the official Basel Mission historian, Schlatter recounts the perennial negotiations in detail. See Schlatter, *Heimatgeschichte*, 72–86.

91. Becker, "Basel Missionaries Cooperating," 3–8.

92. Pinnington, *Church Principles in the Early Years*.

pain and anxiety to the Germans." Eventually, the CMS established their own training institute (1825) and Basel missionaries received Anglican ordination (from 1826) after a period there to improve their English and ensure doctrinal compatibility.[93] The Basel leadership accepted the practicality of this in view of the difficulties their missionaries had experienced overseas from Anglican authorities, but they were not prepared to force it upon their graduates, rather "recommend it to their free and joyful decision."[94] Most, but not all of those designated to work with the CMS, decided to accept these conditions for the sake of the missionary cause.[95]

Ecclesiastical and cultural issues are revealed in the process.[96] The more clerically minded in England struggled with the Basel Mission's independent and non-confessional stance, in spite of the satisfaction which personal encounters typically brought.[97] Becker points to the "explicitly supra-denominational" character of the Basel Mission in contrast to the focus on the Church of England of the CMS which demanded that their "missionaries had to be or to become Anglican." Furthermore, Kirchberger highlights the important fact, that one of the main discrepancies between the Germans and British was that "British missionary activities were part of a broad variety of components of British expansionism."[98] Consequently, British missions were placed within the multi-dimensional expansion of the British Empire. Germans were not part of such

---

93. The *Church Missionary Institution* in Islington opened January 31, 1825 and eventually ""more missionaries were trained there than in any other institution in Britain." Piggin, *Making Evangelical Missionaries*, 189–97. See also Stock, *Church Missionary Society*, 264–66. On Germans receiving Anglican ordination after receiving "further training in England," see ibid., 245, 263.

94. Pinnington, *Church Principles in the Early Years*: 528. Pinnington cites a letter by Blumhardt to Coates from November, 29, 1828.

95. BMA, QS-3-18, Mappe 9 *Erklärungen* (Declarations) is a folder of signed documents indicating students' agreements to work with CMS ecclesiological particularities.

96. Jenkins, "Early Experiment," 59–61. I essentially follow his argument in this section. Becker makes a similar case in her analysis of the different representations in the two societies' publications.

97. Becker observes that "whenever difficulties between the societies arose, personal meetings of the leaders . . . managed to dissolve the problems. Whenever the officials of the societies went for a longer period without meeting, misunderstandings tended to arise, and, in the end, this resulted in indifference to the cooperation. See Becker, "Basel Missionaries Cooperating," 1, 7–8.

98. Kirchberger, "Fellow-Labourers," 88–89.

a dynamic (before the 1880s) and German missionaries who joined the British effort were not comfortable with this enmeshment in political and economic interests.

The cultural issues were recognized to a degree by both organizations. British prejudices regarding the "well-known general apostasy of the German Protestant church" were—for a time—dissolved in 1827. However, the Basel Mission decided that it was prudent to establish separate mission fields "in order to avoid the disrupting collisions which are generated so easily, even in pious souls, by their different ways of life and upbringing."[99] Misunderstandings and frictions were at least in part also due to the German's inadequate English language skills as they struggled to respond to complicated theological questions about their doctrinal orthodoxy. Finally, the culturally expected practice in the Basel Mission "of men in the field to keep an eye on each other and report on their brothers' deviant behavior" often caused tensions and would have seemed "strange and dysfunctional" to the CMS leadership.[100] Jenkins concludes that conflicts

> were due to the inherent tension in mission between the claim to be representing a higher, better, more accurate truth, and the difficulty, in the hurly-burly of everyday intercultural and interconfessional relations, to recognize that one's own—or even one's church's—grasp of the truth is conditional and imperfect.[101]

This issue relates to a central argument in this study; namely, that the training religious organizations devise is typically designed to foster their particular "grasp on the truth" with little recognition that it is culturally shaped, "conditional and imperfect." Consequently, the people who receive this preparation lack the flexibility necessary in diverse cultural contexts. They tend to criticize what is different and replicate what they were taught which indicates trained incapacity.

Unfortunately, this lesson was not adequately learnt by either society in this "experiment in inter-European missionary cooperation" and

---

99. Schlatter, *Heimatgeschichte*, 76–78. Schlatter cites from Blumhardt's report published in MM 1828, 376–378. For the same sentiments expressed by CMS officials, see Jenkins, "Early Experiment," 60. Jenkins cites a document by William Jowett (1787–1855), the CMS Clerical Secretary in BMA, QK/GB/CMS.

100. Jenkins makes both these points convincingly, building on Miller's analysis in Miller, *Missionary Zeal*, 163–65.

101. Jenkins, "Early Experiment," 63.

ultimately the relationship died a "quiet death."[102] Demands for more equal cooperation after 1850 were not heard and eventually the two organizations went separate ways. By that time there were sufficient British applicants for the CMS and the Basel Mission had established independent ministries that needed workers. Furthermore, the rise of confessional assertiveness and growing nationalistic sentiments on both sides prevented a continuation of this pan-Protestant collaboration of Pietist and Evangelical circles.[103]

Impact of the Partnership with the CMS

The most obvious impact of the partnership with the CMS on BMTI practice were changes to the curriculum because of their demands for better educated missionaries. The language requirements and generally the amount and length of the curriculum were raised to a level much beyond the original *Plan* and from the intended three years to eventually up to six years. Basel Mission leaders repeatedly had to defend the level and amount of studies towards the support constituencies who felt that this erudition was detrimental to the religious passion which should characterize missionaries. The Board and Directors valued higher education and endorsed the need for well trained men, but they also stressed the priority of "practical preparation for . . . Christian life if the teaching was not going to miss its purpose."[104] Eventually, the frequent tensions with the British partners most likely contributed to the decision to establish independent ministries.

---

102. Ibid., 63–65. Jenkins cites more self-confidence of the British missionary movement and "heightened confessional consciousness" and growing nationalism on the continent as reasons.

103. See also Becker, "Basel Missionaries Cooperating," 4. She lists as reasons primarily that they did not need each other anymore, aided by the end of "good personal understanding and intense interaction between the mission leaders on a personal level," and increased "distrust of the theology, piety and lifestyles of the Germans [which] became particularly virulent in this time of rising nationalism."

104. MM 1829, 353–54, 356. In this report Blumhardt also cited the feedback of missionaries who expressed "regret not to have spent more time in preparation and acquired even more thorough and versatile knowledge" in defense of the BMTI curriculum. A decade later Director Hoffmann stated that in addition to "true and thorough conversion" and a good life testimony, BMTI applicants needed to evince "the intellectual capacities necessary for the various difficult tasks a missionary has to deal with" and explicitly refuted the claim that "many sciences are unnecessary for a missionary to the Heathen" (MM 1839, 383–85).

Additionally, BMTI graduates with the CMS maintained relationships with Basel and their reports were regularly printed in Basel Mission publications. Their experience and descriptions, and the information they gathered shaped the understanding of the non-European world that developed in Basel, as well as ideas of how to approach the work and best prepare for it. This is confirmed by Kirchberger's conclusion that transfer of ideas took place through missionaries who related back to Germany selectively that "which they regarded as positive and admirable and in which they felt their home country to be deficient."[105] By contrast, the CMS incorporated German missionaries into the British system. Becker identifies as "predominant themes" of CMS publications "the glory of God and the blessing God had bestowed on England, which England now had to impart to the world." This nationalist British presentation of Christian mission stood in stark contrast to the "predominant theme of the Basel Mission [which] was the entity of the whole world."[106] Becker goes as far as to identify in this a "fundamentally different approach to the missionary task." This difference was a major cause of their tensions.

In addition to British suspicious of the interdenominational stance and possible influences from German rationalistic theology, the fact that BMTI graduates often did not attain the desired erudition and lacked grasp of English were factors that strained relationships. Ironically, over time many of the Basel-trained missionaries became known for their scholarship in language analysis and translation work.[107] Notwithstanding the acknowledgment of their achievements, the general attitude of CMS leaders was rather condescending, over the years—as they needed them less—decreasing in sensitivity and increasingly imposing. On the other hand, submission to Anglican Bishops and ecclesiastical forms was difficult for the Basel missionaries.

Ironically, when the *Church Missionary Institution* was established, many common characteristics indicate that it was modeled after the BMTI. CMS leaders resisted calls for higher education and decided that the institution "was to be less of a College and more of a Home, and

---

105. Kirchberger, "Fellow-Labourers," 92.

106. Becker, "Basel Missionaries Cooperating," 8–9.

107. One consequence of the practice to send the better educated personnel to India was that "Germans soon took leadership in African linguistics" with famous names like Jakob Friedrich Schön (1803–1889) in Nigeria, Sigmund Kölle (1823–1902) in the Middle East and Sierra Leone, and Johann Gottlieb Christaller (1827–1895) in Ghana—all BMTI graduates. See Walls, "Protestant Missionary Awakening," 38.

the academical element was to be distinctly subordinate to the spiritual element."[108] These priorities were identical with those at the BMTI and confirm the "indirect influence on the minds of [the CMS] committee [of] the example of the Missionary Seminary in Basel."[109]

Eventually, both societies sent out what the CMS called "artisans" and the Basel Mission "supporting missionaries" (*Hilfsmissionare*), craftsmen with little academic education. They were sent to support the "missionaries" and train local believers in their craft. On the field—predictably—the distinction was not easily maintained and some of the "supporting missionaries" became successful church planters.[110]

These facts illustrate that their collaboration was rooted in the sense of common purpose which linked the diverse groups that championed "true" Christianity. In spite of national, cultural, and ecclesiastical differences, they agreed on much and were passionate about the same vision. Pietists on the continent and Evangelicals in Britain equally opposed secularizing tendencies and rationalistic theology. Both regarded personal conversion and spirituality, a moral life style, and missionary zeal as essential qualifications for missionaries, more important in the final analysis than academic achievements.[111] It was the Evangelical faction in the Anglican Church which supported the CMS. They shared core emphases of personal religion with the Basel leaders who conversely also recognized the importance of education.

---

108. Stock, *Church Missionary Society*, 266.

109. Piggin, *Making Evangelical Missionaries*, 192.

110. One example in the Basel Mission is Joseph Mohr (1814–1884), who founded a station in Ghana and became a senior missionary serving twenty-six years (BMA, Personnel File (PF) *Mohr, Franz Joseph* and BV 236). Mohr started the BMTI but was dismissed for lack of academic ability. Eventually he was re-admitted and sent to Ghana as support-missionary. A report about his readmission to join his former fellow students in Ghana was published in MM 1846, 152.

111. Walls, "Protestant Missionary Awakening," 40–43. Andrew Walls makes a strong case for the common ground of the diverse groups of Pietism and Evangelicalism on both sides of the English Channel who in spite of their differences all "acknowledged the primacy of personal religion [and] sought to express 'real' Christianity" and therefore worked together in the Protestant missionary movement. See also Jenkins, "Early Experiment," 56. Jenkins muses about the differences Basel-trained missionaries may have exhibited in the fields, but he cautions about exaggerating such differences in light of "the evangelical, pietist, activist heritage that they had in common."

146   Part I: The Community of Practice

THE SUPPORT SOCIETIES: HOTBED OF MISSIONARIES

In the eighteenth century, groups began to form to support the foreign missions of Halle and the Moravians.[112] Reading the latest reports, praying for non-European regions, and collecting funds became a regular feature of most fellowships.[113] Consequently, the Basel Mission appeal for support in 1815 addressed a prepared audience and the first and strongest response came from Württemberg, the German center of Pietism.[114] By 1819 fifteen Support-Societies (*Hilfsvereine*) had guaranteed the expenses for twenty-eight students.[115] Basel Mission Support-Societies committed to "the mission cause generally and to contribute to the ... missionary school in particular."[116] They distributed mission publications and sponsored at least one student who corresponded regularly with his local society, both, from Basel and later the field.

Support-societies did not make decisions in the Basel Mission which has raised scholarly criticism. For example, Eiselen cites Hoffmann's

112. The "Halle Reports" of the mission in India were a major factor in spreading missionary passion across Europe. The year 1710 is typically the date given for the first Halle Reports because that year the Canstein Institute was established. Lehmann explicates that the first report from India was already published in 1707 but he also uses the 1710 date in his summary section. See Lehmann, *It Began at Tranquebar*, 90, 103. Other important impetuses were Ziegenbalg's Deputation (1714–1715) and Samuel Urlsperger's fundraising effort in Württemberg (1715–1718).

113. Actual societies to support missions in prayer and financially in exchange for regular information began in Switzerland in the 1730s and Germany in the 1790s. For Switzerland, see Wernle, *Der schweizerische Protestantismus*, 463–66; for Germany, Raupp, *Mission in Quellentexten*, 238, 255. The "Mustard Seed Mission-Society" in Ostfriesland (1798) and the group in Elberfeld (1799) were founded in response to the appeal to the "Brothers in Germany who love the Lord Jesus sincerely" by the founder of the Mustard Seed society, Georg Siegmund Stracke (1751–1814) and the then pastor of the German Savoy Church in London, Johann Gottlieb Burckhardt (1756–1800), in 1798. Raupp's important collection of transcripts of German texts related to mission is the first to publish this appeal which was believed to be lost. It is a significant illustration of the close networks between British and German missionary interest.

114. Already in 1742 the first Württemberger, Johann Martin Mack (1715–1784), had become a Moravian Missionary. See: Raupp. "Ein vergnügter Herrnhuter."

115. The first Basel Mission support group was founded in 1816 by the mayor of Leonberg, Gottlieb Wilhelm Hoffmann (1771–1846) and his friend Johann Friedrich Josenhans (1760–1850). Both families later provided a Director of the mission. See Ising, *Johann Christoph Blumhardt*, 68, 72; Schlatter, *Heimatgeschichte*, 38, citing their letter from April 16, 1816. Blumhardt states this progress in his end-of-the-year-report to the committee: "Die Missionsgesellschaft in ihren äußeren Verhältnissen am Schlusse des Jahres 1819"; final Version in BMA, KP 4, 1–12 from January 10, 1820.

116. MM 1818, 629–31. These are the first rules concerning Support-Societies.

statement that the "right" of a support society was to "daily pray ... for the mission, disseminate the tidings of mission, ... and collect as many donations as possible," in order to emphasize that they were not to participate in decisions on acceptance of students, choice of mission stations, or placement of missionaries.[117] Morgenthaler investigated the participation of Support-Society leaders at annual General Conferences.[118] He also concludes that they had no decision making powers and these meetings were merely an avenue for information and addressing concerns. However, even when supporters were given a voice, no major critique was raised.[119] Generally, they regarded Basel as the natural center and the organization in capable hands and did not desire democratic rule. Support-Society leaders highlighted perceived dangers in the academic focus of the BMTT—which they saw as "erudite bustle and harmful intellectualism"—and otherwise relatively minor issues.[120] Their relationship between these associations and the Basel Mission invites more detailed study. However, for this project the main interest is their impact on the BMTI practice through personnel and influence.

The "Directory of Brothers" lists basic information about Basel missionaries. All "brothers" were single men and their birthplaces confirm the centers of pious Christianity as their context of origin.[121] Table 1 lists the home states of the 1112 applicants who were accepted into the BMTI between 1816 and 1881. It shows clearly the dominance of Southwest Germany (Württemberg and Baden) which provided almost

117. Eiselen, "Erziehung," 51. He cites Hoffmann, *Eilf Jahre*, 24.

118. BMA, Q-2-1-3 Morgenthaler, "Die Verfassung der Basler Mission."

119. The only time there actually was an animated discussion was in 1847 when the Special Conference was convened for the first time since 1843. Wilhelm Stern (1792–1873), Director of the Teacher Seminary in Karlsruhe had given voice to desires for a more organized relationship between the German societies and Basel. His suggestion of an advisory council consisting of elected representatives from the support societies was discussed by the twenty-six "trusted friends" whom the Board had invited. The outcome was that no such council was needed but the Special Conference became a standing part of the annual festivities as an avenue of open exchange and clarification of any questions or misunderstandings. Stern's letter from May 9, 1847 and the minutes of the Special Conference on June 29, 1847 are cited in Schlatter, *Heimatgeschichte*, 167–70.

120. Hoffmann, *Eilf Jahre*, 106.

121. BMA, *Brüderverzeichnis* (BV). Only in the 1850s single women were also sent out, who were then recorded in the "Directory of Sisters" (*Schwesternverzeichnis*) but did not receive the BMTI training. Names and background of women who went as "missionary brides" were recorded with their husbands.

148   Part I: The Community of Practice

55 percent of all students. This basic distribution is similar for those sent to Ghana (and their wives) in the first twenty-five years (Table 2). Among this group the proportion from Germany is even higher, especially when considering that the area of Denmark several originated from was culturally German.[122] Thus, most students, as well as the directors and teachers at the BMTI originated from the German Support-Societies.

Table 1
Geographical Origin of BMTI Students until 1881[123]

Region of Origin	No.	Percent
Württemberg	505	45.4%
Baden	105	9.5%
Alsace	36	3.2%
Other areas in Germany	173	15.6%
All from Germany	**819**	**73.7%**
Switzerland	203	18.2%
Other parts of Europe (Russia, Denmark, Sweden, France, Hungary, Greece, Holland, England, Austria, Norway)	50	4.5%
From other parts of the world (Armenia, Africa, India, China America)	40	3.6%
All accepted applicants until end 1881	**1112**	**100%**

---

122. Andreas and Anna Riis, Peter Jäger (1808–1832) and Hans Nicolai Riis came from Schleswig, a German region under Danish governance at the time (BV 106, 124, 247). Another student from the same region was Christian Gottlieb Forchhammer (b. 1814), BV 178. In his record the remark that this was in Denmark (which is obviously added later in A. Riis's entry) is missing. Furthermore, in the biographies of these missionaries their German Pietist worldview and upbringing is quite apparent.

123. Based on data in MM 1882, 155; cited in Schlatter, *Heimatgeschichte*, 260.

Table 2
Geographical Origin of Basel Missionaries in Ghana 1828–1854[124]

Region of Origin	"Missionaries"		All (with women)	
Württemberg	11	40.8%	16	45.8%
Baden	2	7.4%	2	5.7%
Bavaria	2	7.4%	3	8.6%
Prussia	2	7.4%	2	5.7%
Other areas in Germany	4	14.8%	4	11.4%
All Germany	21	77.8%	27	77.2%
Switzerland	2	7.4%	2	5.7%
Other parts of Europe (Denmark)	3	11.1%	4	11.4%
From other parts of the world (African)	1	3.7%	2	5.7%
All	27	100%	35	100%

Further influence came through Support-Societies' financial and practical support, and respected leaders of large groups like Stuttgart and the Christian colony Korntal carried much weight as outspoken advocates.[125] Arguably the most prominent individual was Christian Gottlob Barth, co-founder of the Tübingen Support-Society (1819), assiduous writer, publisher, and mission speaker.[126] Stuttgart, Korntal, and Barth were in Württemberg, undeniably the most influential region in the Basel Mission. It financed one third of its budget and provided more than half of

124. Based on data in BMA, BV.

125. By 1876 over fifty male and female missionaries had come from the Korntal community and its boarding schools. Raupp, "Vorwärts für das Reich Gottes," 30.

126. Schlatter, *Heimatgeschichte*, 122; Frohnmeyer, "Barth, Christian Gottlob"; Ising, *Möttlinger Amtsvorgänger*; Lehmann, *Pietismus und weltliche Ordnung*, 189–92; Raupp, *Christian Gottlob Barth*. Raupp characterizes him as the "Mission pope" and "secret Inspector of the Basel Mission" and key figure of the "antimodern" international revivalist movement of the nineteenth century. Barth's *Bible Stories for Schools and Families* became the "standard work for the conversion of the heathen" and his *General World History* a text book of Pietist Historiography. The *Bible Stories* were published from 1832 and had been translated into eighty-seven languages by 1945, including Ga and Twi in Ghana. See Barth, *General History*; Schnurr, *Weltreiche und Wahrheitszeugen*. From his pastorate in Möttlingen (1824–1838) Barth also sent a number of young men to be trained. Basel missionaries in Ghana who came on Barth's recommendation were Johann Georg Widmann and the brothers Andreas and Johannes Stanger (BMA, PF 178, 202, 254).

its missionaries.[127] Therefore, the blending of rural German culture and socio-economic conditions with Pietist religious emphases in this region needs closer investigation.

Dualist Worldview and Rural Ideals

Although Pietists always were a minority, even in Württemberg, their influence as guarantors of traditional life and stability while adjusting to changing contexts was greater than their numbers.[128] In the process of the rise of "a lower class Pietism" as true grassroots movement, strong cultural traditions, chiliastic expectations, theological apprehensions of developments in universities and state churches, religious condemnation of political uprisings and secular (lack of) ethics, and economic hardship in the context of urban industrial developments contributed to a retreat mentality which idealized traditional rural values and structures.[129] Socioeconomically Württemberg Pietists came to perceive the self-sufficient subsistence agriculture village community as Christian ideal and ethically they endorsed behaviors that reflected the values of this context. Theologically these attitudes and perceptions built on an interpretation of the Bible that posited a clear separation between the Kingdom of God and the Kingdom of the World.

Birgit Meyer's astute analysis of the famous picture *The Broad and the Narrow Path* shows the "crude dualism" of Württemberg Pietist worldview.[130] The drawing purports to present a view of life and history from God's perspective based on Matt 7:13–14, that gains authority through biblical citations which explicate numerous minute details. It shows a strict separation of two ways to live with respective eternal outcomes. On the left is the populated *wide path*, its entrance framed by the gods of wine and love. It leads past "worldly pleasures" (drinking, gambling, theater, dancing) and vices (greed, selfishness, desecrating the Sabbath, stealing, murder) and ends in an inferno of war and a crumbling city in flames crowned by a pair of scales from which souls tumble into the fires.

---

127. Raupp, "Vorwärts für das Reich Gottes." 31–32. See also EMM 1907, 217. This report states that 52 percent of the male Basel missionaries originated from Württemberg.

128. Trautwein estimates their share in the old duchy's heartland as "c.7–8 percent of the adult protestant population." Trautwein, *Religiosität und Sozialstruktur*, 51.

129. Fulbrook, *Piety and Politics*, 151; Lehmann, *Pietismus und weltliche Ordnung*, 121, 135–39.

130. Meyer, *Translating the Devil*, 31–38.

By contrast, the *narrow path* is entered by few through a tiny door, leads past a cross on a rock gushing out water, massive church and Sunday School buildings uphill. There are no entertainments here but a *Child Rescue Institute* and a *Deaconesses House,* and the devil in form of a lion attacking a warrior on the path that culminates in a steep climb and loses itself in a city in bright clouds. Even though the lithograph originated in Württemberg, its popularity across Europe and America demonstrates the resonance this dualistic allegorical imagery had in all Evangelical and Pietist circles.[131]

Pietists were deeply convicted of the dualism represented by this metaphorical painting and determined to avoid worldly defilement and to build the Kingdom of God. This expressed itself in moralizing ethics, a spiritual dichotomy between God and the devil, and the evaluation of political developments by whether they advanced the Kingdom of God or not. Despite many contributions to socioeconomic betterment in the changing times, Pietists favored the old order and idealized rural communities and virtues.

God's Village Ideal versus Evil Cities

The contrast between godly soberness, frugality, and industry in the rural environment and the wild pleasures and vices of the city is illustrated in the two ways image. Large buildings of the kind that were springing up in the new urban centers frame the broad path and the final judgment destroys a metropolis with approaching train while the narrow path mostly leads through a natural landscape. The city is perceived as immoral, lewd, violent, decadent, and full of temptations. From the Württemberg perspective the microcosm of the village was a relatively intact community in contrast to the fragmentation and secularization of urban society. Increased critique of traditional religion among the educated, emancipatory workers' movements, the urban "dechurching" and ethical decline

---

131. There are several variations of this image. I came across it both in Germany and in Ghana. It is based on an original lithograph designed in the 1860s by Charlotte Reihlen (1805–1868), cofounder of the *Deaconesses Institute* and a girl's school in Stuttgart. Gawin Kirkham (1832–1892), the Secretary of the *Open-Air Mission of London* saw the Dutch version of the picture in 1868 in Amsterdam, brought it back to England, used it extensively in open air preaching, and translated it into English. An "Explanation" of the origin by Kirkland himself cites a son and a daughter of Charlotte Reihlen and traces an earlier version of the image back to G. W. Hoffmann, the founder of Korntal. See Millward, "Broad and Narrow Way."

with extremes like alcoholism and prostitution were seen as dark threat, not only to proven ways of life, but also to true Christianity.[132]

Pietist response was a "self-limitation to the rural" that idealized village culture and retreated into Christian fellowships and associations. The traditional patriarchal society and agricultural economy that demanded a tight knit community characterized by mutual responsibility, clear hierarchy, hard work, orderliness, tidiness, diligence, and a simple frugal lifestyle became regarded as expression of biblical norms and virtues. Increased poverty—among other factors, through overpopulation and the inheritance practice of *Realteilung*—forced greater mobility and complementary trades (wine growing, traditional crafts, day labor, even inn keeping) upon people.[133] However, Pietists "did not try to flee the economic situation of the traditional village, but rather idealized its practicality along with the economic and social independence of its structures."[134] The Christian settlement in Korntal, patterned after a traditional village, was an attempt to implement this vision. The settlers were selected from "quiet, conscientious, diligent, and largely without means" Pietist believers and included representatives of "all important professions" including two teachers, many artisans and mostly farmers.[135]

Many studies emphasize the cultural embeddedness of this expression of Christianity that is not unexpected.[136] More surprising is the fact that the "commercial aristocrats" of the Basel elite also embraced this village ideal—at least for the "simple folk" both at home and in the "heathen world."[137] This reflected the general view of non-European peoples, especially in Africa. Furthermore, the BMTI leaders shared its moral values and the Support-Societies always advocated for practical preparation and spiritual formation against increased studies. Thus, into the twentieth

---

132. Altena, *Ein Häuflein Christen*, 233–36.

133. *Realteilung* (equal partition) was common inheritance practice in Southern Germany. It divided the land in equal parts among all children. While enhancing people's attachment to the land, it also deprived them of full subsistence farming. See Köhle-Hezinger, "Die enge und die weite Welt," 45–47. Meyer, *Translating the Devil*, 223; Trautwein, *Religiosität und Sozialstruktur*, 18–19.

134. Jenkins, "Towards a Definition," 4–6; Jenkins, "Villagers as Missionaries," 427.

135. Lehmann, *Pietismus und weltliche Ordnung*, 177–78, 185.

136. For example, Lehmann, *Pietismus und weltliche Ordnung*; Meyer, *Translating the Devil*, 28–54; Scharfe, *Religion des Volkes*; Trautwein, *Religiosität und Sozialstruktur*.

137. Miller, *Missionary Zeal*, 100.

century "idealization of the traditional farming community remained basic to Basel Mission policy."[138]

Consequently, the "important professions" were farming and artisan skills, followed by teaching, which is reflected in the requirement of applicants to have a vocation or higher education—most brought the former.[139] At the BMTI, students were admonished to maintain physical fitness through "Exercise and Handiwork," not only because of expected hardships of unfamiliar travel and climate but also to practice skills required to establish pioneer mission stations.[140] Students used their crafts to maintain the buildings and grow food for the school.[141] During vacations they were encouraged to practice their trade and visit "friends in the countryside to gain insights of farming and other economic matters."[142] In this way, the BMTI aimed at establishing a model patterned after the Württemberg ideal of economically and socially independent tight communities that provided for their own needs and also showed charity to others.[143]

As we saw above, the Basel Mission adopted this rural ideal as goal of missionary work in Africa. However, the viability of building rural independent communities after German models in this different context

---

138. Jenkins, "Villagers as Missionaries," 428. Jenkins cites the African Secretary of the Basel Mission, Walter Oettli stating in the annual report of 1913 that "we know that a stable farming population is the kind of soil in which the Christian faith can root itself most easily" (*Jahresbericht der evangelischen Missions-Gesellschaft zu Basel 1913*, 111).

139. BMA, QS-3-17 (Brochures for Candidates); see also Annual Report 1860, 23–24 (an official document streamlining what had been practice more or less from the beginning) and Hoffmann, *Missionsgesellschaft*, 24–30.

140. BMA, QS-9.31 #11 §6, 1. The House-Order admonished that "much depends in the ministry of the Lord in the heathen world on maintaining health and enduring physical strength."

141. Haller, "Leben im Missionshaus," 211. Haller points out that everyone was expected to be useful in these areas and non-artisans were expected to learn a practical skill during their training in Basel.

142. BMA, KP 1, 30–31. In this first outline of the BMTI training Blumhardt expressed that generally, "a certain practical deftness and correct judgment" would be more useful than erudition.

143. As the institute grew, it became a practice to help the poor on a daily basis. See BMA, QS-9.31 #12 "Haus-Ordnung der evangelischen Missions-Anstalt in Basel" Buchdruckerei von C. Schultze 1860 [date added in hand writing], III, 11. This paragraph regulated the tasks of the "Almoner" (*Armenpfleger*) who oversaw every day after lunch the orderly distribution of leftover food, used clothes, and occasionally even money to those who came with their needs to the house.

was questionable, especially as they ignored any existing African patterns of community life, agriculture, and artisanship. The rural ideal BMTI training established in missionaries convinced them of the universal validity of their cultural traditions in ways that made intercultural incapacity very probable.

Even though situated in Basel, the BMTI leaders intentionally limited student exposure to the city. The House-Order regulated relationships with people outside the mission house, reasoning that "very much depends in our missionary school on avoiding even the appearance of evil."[144] This included refraining from unnecessary visits and wandering about in Basel. Students were instructed to return straight away after Sunday services, not to extend visits to acquaintances (which they should keep to a few truly godly relationships), and report who they visited. These regulations reveal the perception of the city as a place of evil and temptations, best avoided by pious believers. They show that even the mission leaders—some of whom were involved in the city council—held reservations about urban influence on missionary candidates.

In Africa, the negative perception of cities added to the common unfavorable evaluation of coastal settlements. It instilled in the missionaries a discomfort and inability to engage these emerging urban communities which—as we will see—impeded their intercultural engagement.

"Quietistic Disapproval" of Political Authorities

The dualist worldview also affected evaluations of political developments. Increasing urbanization and industrialization fell under the negative assessment of cities, but political revolutions disturbed the divine order as Pietists perceived it. They worked at alleviating social hardships but became politically characterized by defensiveness and insulation. In mostly rural Württemberg conventicles enjoyed toleration by the authorities.[145] Consequently, Pietists supported their king's authority. They preferred political non-involvement and principally perceived rulers as God-instituted authorities, but favored those who supported their cause. Fulbrook convincingly argues the relationship of Württemberg Pietists with the "worldly order" as "quietistic disapproval" that was not provoked into

---

144. BMA, QS-9.31 #11 §11, 1 and 2.
145. Stoeffler, *German Pietism*, 88–130.

Diverse Participants with a Shared Practice 155

political action because they were incorporated into the state church and "tolerated in their religious orientations and organizations."[146]

Her comparison with England and Prussia also demonstrates the noteworthy difference this attitude represented from European contemporaries. Significant for this study is in particular the contrast to British evangelicals' close engagement with African politics of their nation. In the Basel Mission there was no such identification with any one government. Their international character and Pietist values fostered a high value of political neutrality that is evinced clearly in missionary directives. However, as we will see, Pietist evaluation of political authorities by whether they would advance their cause extended in Ghana to African rulers and colonial governors. Officials' support of missionary work (or lack thereof) became a primary criterion for attitudes towards them. This was likely to create various difficulties for the missionaries' ministry. Both, evaluations of political authorities and urban settlements were exacerbated by Württemberg moralism.

Moralism: Ethics Shaped by Rural Pietist Virtues

The two paths image illustrated the dichotomy Pietists perceived between true Christian life and "the world." It identified many of "the middle things which by that time were fixed and canonized" by placing physical pleasures and amusements on the broad path.[147] "Middle things" or *adiaphora* are matters which are neither commanded nor forbidden in the Bible. However, throughout history Christians defined permissible behavior—typically as appropriation of the faith in specific contexts. As Scharfe astutely analyzed, the Württemberg "fixing of middle things" had extremes that provoked ridicule from those outside the movement; notably, the view of basic needs (food, drink, sexuality) as sinful and "pronounced techniques of asceticism and self-mortification" this led to. Generally, Pietists were recognized by their simple dark clothes, neat appearance, serious faces, humble demeanor, frugality, and industriousness.[148]

Lehman demonstrated that in many ways Pietist ethical emphases fit with realities and challenges people faced, and "by idealizing a life of

---

146. Fulbrook, *Piety and Politics*, 130–52. In the Württemberg section she builds heavily on Lehmann's thorough analysis in Lehmann, *Pietismus und weltliche Ordnung*.

147. Scharfe, *Religion des Volkes*, 77–90.

148. Ibid., 48–57. In this section Scharfe demonstrates this "modeling of the person." Pictures of Basel Mission personnel confirm this impression.

modesty and simplicity, the leaders of Pietism made it easier for their followers to cope with the harshness of life."[149] Beyond coping, they provided a spiritual theological rationale for the attitudes and patterns of behavior necessary for survival. In a context with few other options this created strong confidence in these values and freed up energies for passionate activism. Württemberg Pietism represented an appropriation of the faith within its rural culture and idealized culturally shaped values and virtues. Scharfe emphasizes that in conventicles cultural patterns of patriarchal authority and ideas of virtue were intensified and their survival ensured—even as the conditions in the world around were drastically changing, implying that Pietists refused to face contemporary realities.[150] By contrast, Meyer highlights that individual self-control and ascetic ethics also had contextual relevance in the new industrial economy that required from workers many of the same virtues.[151] Yet "on a conscious level" Pietists opposed "the modernity and rationality professed by rational and liberal theologians, liberal philosophers, democrats and socialists." Meyer concludes that they subscribed to a "somewhat paradoxical modern conservatism."

Württemberg Pietist ethics were reflected in the BMTI in numerous ways. Students were strongly admonished to order, cleanliness, diligence, and frugality because "without strict order and cleanliness of . . . the individual it is impossible for the brotherhood to live together beneficially."[152] House-Rules commanded economy and care with all possessions and efficient use of time and energy.[153] However, any signs of pride or ambition were shunned. Such lack of humility could contribute to dismissals. For example, one student was dismissed for displaying self-righteousness and "a spirit of studiousness that diminished heart and soul."[154] Control of sensuality is reflected in unchaste behaviors eschewed in the BMTI.

149. Lehmann, "Community and Work," 96.

150. Scharfe, *Religion des Volkes*, 62–64.

151. Meyer, *Translating the Devil*, 33, 51. In a different section Scharfe makes similar observations: Scharfe, *Religion des Volkes*, 87–89.

152. BMA, QS-9.31 #11 §4. This paragraph specifically refers to keeping "strict order around their desk, wardrobe and bed" and "diligently washing to keep their bodies clean and healthy."

153. Ibid. §11, 5. This paragraph advised care with clothes, linen, books, lights, paper and pens with a reminder that these provisions were love gifts from needy fellow Christians. A similar reference to "widows' mites" prohibited unnecessary correspondence as it wasted time and money.

154. BMA, KP 14, 134–42, Board minutes from March 13 to April 17, 1839.

They included lack of seriousness, waste of time or things, and unsanctioned relationships with people outside the institute; but most importantly, fraternization with "persons of the opposite gender" was "strictly prohibited."[155] The latter—if discovered—was immediate cause for dismissal, as was any kind of sexual misconduct. In their view, whoever acted this way had "by this action severed the link to his [missionary] profession and his circle of brothers."[156]

These ethical emphases were in the Basel Mission further motivated by the conviction that missionaries' lives were the best sermon. Therefore, the BMTI became a training ground for the attitudes and virtues which would not bring shame upon the mission nor discredit the gospel when they went overseas.[157] On many occasions the purpose of the BMTI as "continuous examination" and means to determine the suitability of candidates was articulated.[158] Consequently, BMTI students internalized strong ethical convictions that were shaped by German rural conditions.

The missionaries then used these virtues to evaluate everyone, including European Christians perceived to have relapsed. In Africa they became the lens by which African customs and behaviors were judged. This way BMTI training intensified general European judgments and preoccupations with African indolence, indulgence, and immorality. Thus, the imposition of European cultural virtues gained justification.

Validation of Students' Socioeconomic Background

In reflecting influence of Basel Mission supporters, the rural ideal of mission work also validated the students' background. Table 3 and 4 list the vocations of the 1112 applicants to the BMTI until 1881 and the twenty-seven sent to Ghana until 1854. These data confirm the general origin from rural artisan contexts. Considering that merchants and medical doctors did not receive the BMTI training because they were expected to support ordained missionaries, the percentage of students with artisan-farming background is even higher.[159] Even though professional crafts

155. BMA, QS-9.31 #11 §13, 6.

156. Examples for dismissals are Durban's immediate expulsion for "secret meetings with a servant girl" on September 7, 1839 (KP 14, 180) and Wildy's for masturbation on October 23, 1844 (KP 17, 175).

157. MM 1828, 388 is one section where Blumhardt developed this line of argument.

158. BMA, QS-9.31 #11 §14, 5.

159. Merchants and doctors were also not recruited in any significant numbers

dominate, artisan skills typically would have been supplemental to agricultural family economy, meaning that most had farming skills as well.

Table 3
Vocations of BMTI Applicants until 1881[160]

Practical Crafts		Other Professions	
Farmer, wine grower	143	Teacher	73
Weaver	98	Student	73
Shoemaker	69	Scribe	29
Woodworker	65	Candidate of Theology	16
Iron worker	50	Medical doctor	12
Taylor	46	**"Educated" Professions**	203 (19%)
Factory worker	19		
Baker	16		
Printer	16		
Book binder	15	**Merchants**	123 (11%)
Mechanic	15	*(did not attend BMTI)*	
Watchmaker	13		
Saddler	13		
Gardener	13		
Various other crafts	178		
Without profession	17		
Artisans and Farmers	**786 (70%)**		

BMTI candidates were single men in their late teens and early twenties.[161] They had some life and work experience, but most had only rudimentary schooling. While Württemberg officially introduced general education in 1649, economic pressures forced many children to help on the family farm and pick up a trade early in life.[162] Consequently, the level of

---

until after the middle of the century when trading companies and medical work were established on various fields.

160. Based on data in MM 1882, 155; cited in Schlatter, *Heimatgeschichte*, 260.

161. Entry requirements varied slightly over the years. The original "Plan" stipulated "10–15 pious men age 20 or above." In later documents the entry age ranges between 17 and 25. See various documents in BMA, QS-3-17 Brochures for Candidates.

162. Trautwein, *Religiosität und Sozialstruktur*, 20.

education obtained and/or remembered by the time students applied for the BMTI was typically short of what the leaders desired.[163]

Table 4
Vocations of Basel Missionaries in Ghana 1828–1854[164]

Profession/Craft		Profession	
Cabinetmaker, Carpenter	4	Merchant	1
Weaver	4	Scribe	2
Shoemaker	3	Student	2
Potter, pot maker	2	Teacher	2
Turner	1	"Educated"	7 (26%)
Ribbon weaver	1		
Rope maker	1		
Glass Blower, Glazier	1		
Baker	1		
Farmer	1		
Servant	1		
Artisans and Farmers	20 (74%)		

The humble background of most nineteenth-century missionaries has been highlighted by many scholars.[165] Urban industrial conditions and agricultural insecurity "were every inducement to the more enterprising to escape" and Warren posits—probably correctly—that Germany was "even more a country from which escape was desirable" and devastation of wars, disorganization of life, and widespread poverty were "at least a measure of explanation of the fact that the great majority of the first missionaries sent out by the CMS were Germans."[166] In Britain missionaries "belonged in very large measure to a distinctive and emerging class in society, that of the skilled mechanic" and Warren asserts that the missionary movement was part of "a far wider development—the social

---

163. Repeated appeals for a minimum school education of applicants testify to this. See, for example, Hoffmann's extensive defense of the need for sciences and therefore a minimum of intellectual abilities in applicants in the 1839 annual report: MM 1839, 384–87.

164. Based on data in BMA, BV.

165. For example Piggin, *Making Evangelical Missionaries*; Potter, "Social Origins"; Warren, *Social History*; Williams, "'Not Quite Gentlemen.'"

166. Warren, *Social History*, 50–52.

emancipation of the under-privileged classes."¹⁶⁷ Prospects of ordination and social advancement made becoming a missionary attractive.

Sharp class distinctions were a distinctive feature of British society, but most German volunteers were also "skilled mechanics" for whom becoming a missionary was an alternative to economic struggle and hardship. German villagers had limited options to break out of over-populated space and constant threat of indigence.¹⁶⁸ Journeymanship, military service, or "factory going" provided temporary escapes. The latter was unpopular among Pietists because of their negative view of industrial developments and morals in the cities, but journeymanship after completed apprenticeship was common.¹⁶⁹ The most drastic step was emigration, an option increasing numbers chose, especially the poorest or persecuted religious minorities. In the face of these alternatives, volunteering as missionary became increasingly attractive; especially as the BMTI offered considerable economic security and an education which rural youth could not afford otherwise.¹⁷⁰

Basel leaders recognized the possibility of socioeconomic incentives. For example, Hoffmann listed in 1839 as "ungodly motivations" the feeling "to be born for something better than ... the workbench," childhood imaginations of being a pastor one day, "enthusiasm about the great feats of missionaries," and the "desire to see the world."¹⁷¹ But, well aware that in this religious environment ambition and lack of humility would automatically disqualify them, applicants never openly expressed such motives. Instead, they emphasized their desire "to win poor souls

---

167. Ibid., 37–39. See also Piggin, *Making Evangelical Missionaries*, 28–54.

168. Köhle-Hezinger, "Die enge und die weite Welt." She expands on the options I summarize here.

169. Literally "going on travels" (*auf die Wanderschaft gehen*), journeymanship after completed apprenticeship were "wanderings" to gain experience in their trade through working with different masters. Some travelled considerable distances in several years, consequently saw the changes of the time firsthand, and gained a wider understanding than folks at home. Ghana missionary Dieterle, for example, spent five years between his apprenticeship and acceptance in Basel "in foreign parts," including Bavaria, Basel, and St. Louis, and did not go to France only because his *Heimatschein* (a document testifying the bearer's home village which was equivalent to an identity card) was invalid there (BMA, BV 248 *Lebenslauf*).

170. As we saw above, support societies committed to finance at least one student. Often there were relationships between specific local societies and students. The mission covered accommodation and basic needs of students, typically from the support of their home society.

171. MM 1839, 388.

for God's Kingdom," feelings of inadequacy and reluctance to volunteer "for such a great and holy task," and faith in God to carry through difficulties they may face.

However, too much is often made of socio-economic motivations. Miller for instance emphasizes "social ascendancy well beyond their modest material origins" and that BMTI training "offered an alternative path to the desirable profession of the pastorate."[172] He further shows that marital alliances of missionaries (and even more so their descendants) "were also socially advantageous." But such proof of material advantages was not yet visible to the early missionaries this study focuses on. By contrast, Trautwein's analysis demonstrates that Württemberg villagers survived by diversifying occupations and few were really destitute, especially among Pietists.[173] This means that beyond material advantages, other factors must have contributed to young men volunteering. Furthermore, the "considerable publicity" the missionary profession gained in Britain was not shared in Germany.[174] Here the missionary movement remained a marginal enterprise. However, in the Pietist and awakened circles who eagerly read missionary publications, becoming a missionary was increasingly an esteemed vocation and also offered an outlet for religious zeal.[175]

This religious motivation cannot be underestimated, as I argued above. The sacrifices and privations of missionaries in foreign lands were real and well publicized. It is hard to imagine that any singular advantage could have motivated the risk for life and limb becoming a missionary—especially in Africa—entailed.[176] In spite of some economic and educational benefits, the passion for this risky profession cannot be explained apart from the religious motivation explicitly articulated by applicants.

---

172. Miller, "Class Collaboration," 35, 44–48.

173. Trautwein, *Religiosität und Sozialstruktur*, 53–54. He asserts that Pietists' frugality and diligence made their circumstances often better than other contemporaries' situations. Often they had some family owned land which enabled families to maintain village citizenship. Citizenship in turn afforded rights of protection, using common property, and participation in village government.

174. Warren, *Social History*, 58–76. Warren shows the impact of political involvement by prominent evangelicals and evangelical revivals on the public image of missionaries in Britain.

175. These motivations are explored by Altena, *Ein Häuflein Christen*, 279–300; Miller, *Missionary Zeal*, 53–57. For motives in Britain see also Piggin, *Making Evangelical Missionaries*, 124–55.

176. Warren argues along identical lines in Warren, *Social History*, 51–53.

Besides, the discussion of motives carries limited significance for this research. More relevant is Miller's observation in passing that the recruits brought "valuable skills" to the mission.[177] They fit with the Basel Mission idea of mission work as "cultivating the wild thorny land" that envisioned the introduction of rural German building (and other artisan) skills and agriculture as preparatory necessity for schools and churches. Thus, the students' background was in the idealized rural context. Their artisan and farming skills were welcome and their socioeconomic background validated in the BMTI as divine order and "civilization."[178]

In this emphasis they differed, at least initially, from British ideas. Contrary to Miller's claim that the CMS "embraced the principle of internal class separation but . . . was unable to find enough recruits from appropriately modest background," it is clear from Stock's account that they desired clerically trained missionaries.[179] Only when educated volunteers were not forthcoming, the CMS resorted to German artisans. As we saw above, these differences in expectation of candidates caused continual tensions between the two organizations. Later in Britain the same sorts of people volunteered and were trained in similar institutions to the BMTI.[180] Incidentally, this coincided with the greater focus on "extra-doctrinal" methods across the movement in response to its early failures. While in the Basel Mission too, more effort was put into these methods, they privileged an agrarian rural ideal from the start.

Missionaries' Socialization Processes

BMTI applicants were required to submit handwritten autobiographical accounts which delineated their "outward and inner development" and specified the reasons for their application.[181] Most followed a stereotypical outline that was characteristic for "Pietist biography."[182] It emphasized

177. Miller, "Class Collaboration," 44.

178. It is significant in this context that the German term "Kulturarbeit" (*culture work*) can also be translated as "civilization activities."

179. Stock, *Church Missionary Society*, 58–91; Miller, "Class Collaboration," 42. See also Walls, "Missionary Vocation," 164–66. Walls summarizes the discussions within the CMS leadership about the feasibility of introducing a "lower order of unordained missionary," i.e., "catechists," but this scheme was abandoned.

180. Piggin, *Making Evangelical Missionaries*, 28–47; Warren, *Social History*, 36–57.

181. Hoffmann, *Missionsgesellschaft*, 25.

182. Schnurr, *Weltreiche und Wahrheitszeugen*, 127–29. See also Scharfe, *Religion*

their pious upbringing, a phase of rebellion, eventual emotional conversion, and subsequent struggles with temptations. For obvious reasons, missionary candidates added a description of the missionary passion that compelled them to volunteer, typically referring to their exposure to mission reports and literature.

PATRIARCHAL BENIGN AUTHORITIES

The accounts depict widening circles of social networks with similar patterns of benign patriarchal authority that controlled and watched children's physical and spiritual development. Fathers, teachers, pastors, conventicle leaders, and sometimes Christian friends or siblings admonished the youth about "the depravity of his heart and his need of the Savior."[183] Male authorities are described as strict, watchful, punishing transgressions. Mothers, by contrast, care and pray, but with the same passion to see their children become "true Christians."[184] Parental influence included "clear division of roles for all family members" and "a closely regulated, work-filled ... week that culminated in the general high point of Sunday with church service and fellowship meeting."[185] Teachers and pastors were important stimuli, their patriarchal authority and benign influence equally unquestioned. School education covered arithmetic, reading, writing, memorization, singing, and "faith teaching" (*Glaubenslehre*). In all subjects the Bible served as textbook and "religion occupied a ... dominant space."

Applicants often described confirmation and preceding Christian teaching as dominant in their Christian formation.[186] Thus, pastors "have to be seen as the most influential person after the parents" as long as they were not suspected of rationalist theology. Incidentally, this revealed

---

des Volkes, 56.

183. For example, conversations with "spiritual friends" visiting his parents' house influenced Andreas Riis, for him and Christian Dieterle an older brother was important, and his pastor (who happened to be Christian Gottlob Barth) left a strong impression on Johannes Stanger. See the respective autobiographical accounts (*Lebenslauf*) in BMA, PF 124 (Andreas Riis), PF 248 (Dieterle), PF 254 (Johannes Stanger).

184. There is no autobiography in Georg Widmann's file (PF 202) but the Director's summary of it emphasizes the lasting "pious impression upon his tender heart" which his Christian mother left early in his life (BMA, QS-1.44 *Petentenliste für Ostern 1836*, No. 31).

185. For this whole section see Altena, *Ein Häuflein Christen*, 238–40.

186. Christian Dieterle and Johannes Stanger are examples among the missionaries sent to Ghana (BMA, PF 248, PF 254).

Pietist evaluations of state church clergy which resulted in the oxymoron of "believing pastors" (*gläubige Pfarrer*) in contrast to clergy who did not embrace Pietist Christianity. Pietists supported and wanted their children to be taught by believing pastors. If a pastor was not pious enough, it could happen that a father would send his son to be confirmed in another village as in the case of the Ghana missionary H. N. Riis.[187] In Africa such judgments led to negative evaluations of "rationalist" chaplains which had consequences for their relationships.

Emphasis on Human Sinfulness

Pietist social authorities impressed rural moral virtues and strongly emphasized human sinfulness. However, as their upbringing typically prevented serious diversions from pious lifestyle, applicants make generalized statements about the "depraved condition" of their heart, "sundry disobediences," and "youthful carelessness" which necessitated a decisive humiliated turning to the Savior.[188] Specific transgressions were relatively minor offenses like talking during school lessons, wasting time playing, or thoughtless prayers.

Both, conviction of guilt and the experience of forgiveness were expected to be very emotional encounters. Scharfe claims that "internal brokenness" by means of "external humiliation" that impressed an undue sense of guilt upon children were "important preconditions for the complete integration into the Pietist community."[189] He reproves a tendency to "pathological self-condemnation and psychological self-punishment" which individualized guilt and "as ongoing preparedness to sacrifice prevented critique of reality." While these observations are incisive in pointing out the Pietist preoccupation with critical introspection, Scharfe fails to appreciate the religious motivation of Pietist parents' belief that anybody—including their children—was eternally lost, unless they experienced true conversion. BMTI candidates had internalized these convictions. Their accounts contrast the good intentions of parents, teachers, and pastors with their own evil desires.

Meyer demonstrates that "the Pietist notion of sin as bad behavior resulting from a bad inner state" was at dissonance with African

---

187. BMA, PF 247 *Lebenslauf*.

188. See for example the autobiographical accounts of Andreas Riis, Christian Dieterle, and Johannes Stanger in BMA, PF 124, PF 248, PF 254.

189. Scharfe, *Religion des Volkes*, 57–62.

perceptions of evil "above all in terms of agony—people's suffering from and struggle against hostile, anti-life forces."[190] Her analysis of Pietist engagement with Ewe religion highlights the contradiction between "the Pietist feeling of internal sinfulness" and Africans who saw evil "expressed through sickness and other forms of life destruction, and considered it the result of inappropriate behavior in a relationship, not as an individual state."[191] Furthermore, Pietist emphasis on human sinfulness was heightened by European images of Africa, resulting in a message that condemned African traditions and was thus not particular attractive. This contributed significantly to the initial failure of the mission in Africa.

Emotional Individual Conversion

For pious missionary candidates conversion logically followed as release from guilt, and reconciliation with the values and priorities of their upbringing. Jenkins suggests that conversion was a coming to terms with overriding authority figures and Eiselen adds that options for young men from this context were submission, liberation through rejection of the parents' religious expectations, or superseding them, for example, by becoming a missionary.[192] Rejection was unattractive as it meant loss of the entire social support system, but becoming a missionary became honorable with increasing popularity of mission. Jenkins adds as alternative motivations for conversion personal failure, sickness, and the attractiveness of solidarity in pious fellowships.

Invariably, the eventual turning to the Savior is portrayed as emotional, personal event, during which the person is strongly grieved over their appalling sinfulness and deeply moved by the grace of God. Sociologically it can be interpreted as "completion of the (Pietist) socialization process" or the "Pietist initiation ritual" which makes one not only a member of the Kingdom of God but also of the community of true

---

190. Meyer, *Translating the Devil*, 85–93. Meyer's astute analysis of the involvement of missionaries of the North German Mission Society in the Ewe area of Ghana is relevant for the Basel Missionaries in Guinea because of the fact that NGM missionaries were trained in Basel and also because of the similarities between Ewe and Akan religious ideas and traditions.

191. Ibid., 102.

192. Eiselen, "Erziehung," 66; Jenkins, "Towards a Definition," 15–16.

Christians.¹⁹³ It is portrayed as emotional revival that emphasized heartfelt faith over understanding.

BMTI applicants were expected to testify to a "true and thorough conversion" indicating a personal emotional encounter with God, their own sin, and overcoming temptations because the "one who wants to convert others, has to be truly and thoroughly converted himself, not just fleetingly touched ... but truly born again by the Holy Spirit."¹⁹⁴ Such entry requirements demonstrate that the BMTI presumed and reinforced students' religious socialization. They also confirm that individual emotional conversions were the goal of missionary work. In Africa missionary requests for individual repentance clashed with African ideas of "evil mainly as something undergone and to be countered by purifying rituals."¹⁹⁵ Consequently, the religious solutions Pietists offered addressed a European internal dilemma, but made little sense in Africa.

While Pietist conversion was an intensely personal and individual experience, it was not private, because it was expected to be followed by public testimony and proof of the inner change of heart in behavioral conformity to Pietist virtues. This transformation is depicted as a process of ongoing struggle with temptation, often including the taunting of colleagues and former associates. Many autobiographies describe the temptations—typically ascribed to Satan and caused by association with bad company—in more detail than the personal sin prior to conversion.¹⁹⁶ The accounts confirm the pious view of the Christian life as ongoing struggle with evil desires within and temptations without.

Demonization: Outside "True Christianity" Satan Rules

It is puzzling how little attention is given to the dualist conception of God and the devil among Pietists. They believed in "the real presence of the devil in his global struggle with God over every soul."¹⁹⁷ For them, "the

---

193. Altena, *Ein Häuflein Christen*, 229–30; Scharfe, *Religion des Volkes*, 57.

194. BMA, JB 1860, 23. Hoffmann states: "That a man who is not himself a new creature in Christ cannot lead others to salvation and to a new birth in Christ is such a simple thing that nobody can doubt it" (MM 1839, 383).

195. Meyer, *Translating the Devil*, 88. Meyer shows the contrasting anti-ritualist stance of Pietists.

196. Especially when the youth worked with non-pietist colleagues the struggle is depicted more serious after conversion, Examples are Christian Dieterle and Johannes Stanger (BMA, PF 248, PF 254).

197. Russell observes that "of all the movements of the eighteenth century only

devil was active both at home among lukewarm Christians [and] abroad among the heathens who had never heard God's word."[198] Many scholars discuss the exorcism performed by Johann Blumhardt on his church member Gottliebin Dittus (1815–1872) in 1842–43, but few expand on the central importance of the "image of the Devil and traditional diabology" in popular Pietist religion.[199] Rich demonic imagery prevailed in popular religion, in spite of theologians cautioning against overemphasizing evil. Meyer demonstrates that Blumhardt's own reflections reveal the dualistic conception of God and the devil central to his theology. She concludes that by "considering Satan to be the force behind popular beliefs and practices dealing with spirits, Blumhardt subordinated popular religion to Pietism without dismissing the former as irrational 'superstition.'" Pietism thus integrated the spirits "at the cost of diabolisation of popular religion and the exclusion of popular [magical] practices."[200]

In the two path image this dualist spirituality is symbolized by a lion attacking the Christian warrior. Satan was perceived to tempt believers in evil thoughts and actions.[201] Temptation was internal from the depravity of the human heart and external from opposition and corrupting "bad company." In order to stand against temptations, Pietists practiced pious

---

Pietism strongly upheld belief in Satan as attested in the Bible." See Russell, *Mephistopheles*, 131–32; Russell, *Prince of Darkness*, 207–8. Lehman accounts the Pietist opposition to a new liturgy in Württemberg in 1809–10 because of its failure to specifically mention the devil. He shows that they saw the change as "inspiration of hellish power" and a sign of the rule of unbelief in the land. See Lehmann, *Pietismus und weltliche Ordnung*, 162.

198. Lehmann, "Mobilization," 198. In this context Lehmann highlights the use of military language and the role eschatological convictions played in the urgency leaders like Spittler felt in all their actions for the advance of the Kingdom of God.

199. A noticeable exception is Meyer, *Translating the Devil*, 40–51. She affirms that psychologists, physicians and theologians studied Blumhardt's demonology without paying much attention to his relationship to popular religion without which an adequate understanding of Awakened Pietism is impossible. For one example of an author struggling with explaining the events from a modern mindset, rather than within contemporary diabology, see Ising, *Johann Christoph Blumhardt*, 162–88.

200. Meyer, *Translating the Devil*, 50.

201. For example, the Ghana missionary Johann Christian Dieterle (1816–1898) describes coldness towards his redeemer, singing bad songs with his colleagues, and unchaste images in his mind as temptations by Satan. Describing temptations at his work place, he states that "under such circumstances Satan tried to work more in my soul." (BMA, PF 248 Dieterle). This is a common feature in the life stories of missionary applicants.

168   Part I: The Community of Practice

spirituality and Bible reading, associated in fellowships, and engaged in mutual and patriarchal supervision.

Pious Contemplative Spirituality

The Pietist concept of internal temptation led to careful introspection and preoccupation with individual self-control and inner development.[202] It emphasized a quietist contemplative spirituality, extended times of prayer, and communal devotions.

Life at the BMTI fostered such spirituality. Students were required to engage in personal prayers, and "prayer chambers" provided a space for individual retreat throughout the day.[203] Generally, "every activity . . . should begin and end with a short song, prayer, and reading of scriptures," and this "spirit of true heartwarming devotion" was the real life source of the institute.[204] "Singing" class practiced hymns that emotionally expressed the faith, but with the appropriate seriousness and decency.[205] The "sober reverence" attached to worship eschewed drumming, clapping, or dancing which inevitably tainted missionaries' evaluation of African musical expressions. A quiet contemplative atmosphere was considered appropriate piety and necessary for successful studies.[206] During classes and study time "repeated gathering of mind and heart before God, protecting the soul from all diversions" was regarded the "anointing oil which sanctifies every scientific activity, protects from error, strengthens and cheers the inner man."[207]

---

202. See for example: Scharfe, *Religion des Volkes*, 64–72.

203. Personal prayers and chores were scheduled before the morning meeting. The new House-Order put the morning devotion at 7 am, but in the yearly timetables up to the mid-1850s it was at 6 am (BMA, QS-3-4 *Stundenpläne* 1816–1955).

204. BMA, QS-9.31 #11 §3, 2.

205. For example, the curriculum outlined in the annual report from 1838 (MM 1838, 356–57). Pietism is known to have inspired a flood of new spiritual songs. Ch. G. Barth was a contemporary known for composing many songs. Before him well-known Pietist composers were Gerhard Tersteegen (1697–1769), Joachim Neander (1650–1680), and Zinzendorf who is credited with 2000 spiritual songs. Pietist music would invite a separate study because of the numerous new songs that came out of this movement.

206. BMA, QS-9.31 #11 §1.

207. Ibid. §5, 4. The German word *Geist* can be translated "mind" or "spirit." Director Hoffmann felt that such personal spirituality and "pious enthusiasm for the holy purpose" were expected to "awaken, strengthen and enhance the abilities of the mind, enlighten judgment on every subject and clarify the memory" (MM 1839, 385). See

These conceptions were diametrically opposite to the impressions of African exuberance in Europe and the missionaries' observations of African expressions of spirituality and worship in Ghana. Predictably, their evaluations were less than favorable, eschewing the "noise and commotion" of African religious festivals.

Devotions and Bible Study

Beyond introspection, what Christians were exposed to was regarded as essential to overcome temptation. Pietists strictly regulated acceptable literature and above all used the Bible in all affairs of daily life as guideline. "Pious talk" made constant allegorical connections between biblical (often agricultural) imagery, daily life, and divine truths.[208] Scharfe shows how such "transgression into the heavenlies" created a link between ordinary experience and the divine that could be applied by any believer and used metaphors "not to concretize experiences which were difficult to grasp, but to connect daily experiences (often not at all difficult to grasp) with the divine." The mind thus occupied with the divine was believed to be less likely to be tempted.

Pious believers identified "signs from God" (*Winke Gottes*) and revelations of biblical truth in world events as well as personal experiences.[209] Finally, there was the practice to use biblical verses in a kind of "divination rituals." *Däumeln* (arbitrarily opening the Bible and pointing to a verse) und *Losen* (drawing Bible verses from a box) were widely used to determine specific divine guidance or promises.[210] In these ways the Bible became almost a magical text for reading daily life and historical events.

---

also Blumhardt in MM 1827, 357.

208. Meyer, *Translating the Devil*, 38–40; Scharfe, *Religion des Volkes*, 97–102. Scharfe calls this "transgression into the heavenlies" (*Transgression auf das Himmlische*) and cites many illustrations for "pious talk" (*frömmelndes Reden*). For example, a farmer is weeding and reminded of the need to remove the weeds of sin from his heart, the winegrower ties the shoots on sticks and prays that his soul might be tied safely to Jesus, another farmer harvests and thinks of being ready for the final harvest of the judgment day, someone holds a glass and is reminded of the fragility of life, or a woman washing dishes remembers the need of being cleansed from sin.

209. This contributed to the eschatological expectations widely spread among Pietists. See for example Stoeffler's comments on Bengel's predictions in Stoeffler, *German Pietism*, 102–3.

210. Scharfe, *Religion des Volkes*, 92–97. The similarity to the *Losung* (word for the day) of the Moravian community—which often was used as oracle for personal life situations—is striking. This booklet of daily biblical texts is still published every year,

Pietist biblical emphases at the BMTI are obvious. The day began and ended with community devotions which included reading and memorization of Scripture passages and biblical exhortations that aimed at personal responses, repentance from sins, and ongoing spiritual renewal. However, the curriculum championed extensive intellectual as well as devotional study of the Bible. Both, Blumhardt and Hoffmann emphasized the need for systematic biblical knowledge in addition to understanding the Bible as the "indispensable means of edification for our inner needs."[211] The extensive biblical curriculum testifies to intellectual engagement that also counteracted some of the more "magical" uses of the Bible in Württemberg. However, all agreed on the universal validity of pious interpretations, as Hoffmann's statement indicates that the Bible offered "the fundamental truths regarding earthly, divine, and human matters." Reflective of the BMTI balance was students' preaching practice. While it built on rigorous exegetical study, it was also expected to "offer true edification" for those present.[212]

Communities of Mutual and Patriarchal Supervision

Edification, protection, and encouragement to stand against temptations were provided by pious fellowship. Beyond family socialization, conventicles functioned as educational institutions guaranteeing Pietist subculture.[213] Mutual and patriarchal admonition encouraged behavioral conformity. Württemberg Pietists employed the traditional social hierarchy as control networks. Furthermore, everybody felt compelled to draw attention to others' shortcomings. This not only led to mutual supervision, but also to judgmental attitudes towards anybody who did not conform to Pietist virtues.

The BMTI adopted the emphasis on pious fellowship. Weekly attendance of meetings in Basel was to aid personal edification and spiritual

---

translated into many languages, and widely used. This extensive distribution of the *Losungen* also points to the influence of these ideas far beyond Germany.

211. Blumhardt saw Scripture as "the only and most fruitful source of Christian understanding of religion" which necessitated systematic biblical knowledge; but as the Word of God it was also the "indispensable means of edification" (MM 1830, 375–77). Hoffmann argued that the Bible offered "the fundamental truths regarding earthly, divine, and human matters" and as such was the source and foundation of all teaching and guideline to judge the usefulness of everything (MM 1839, 390).

212. BMA, QS-9.31 #11 §13.

213. Scharfe, *Religion des Volkes*, 62–64.

Diverse Participants with a Shared Practice 171

development.²¹⁴ More importantly, within the institute patterns of mutual surveillance and patriarchal supervision were employed. BMTI teachers and Board members were "fathers" watching the conduct of their pupils and the roles of *Senior* and *Famulus* functioned to ensure compliance with BMTI practice.²¹⁵ The weekly "Brothers-Conference" served mutual edification and conflict resolution. This involved open confession and acknowledgment of guilt which, if not provided, was invariably interpreted as lack of humility.

A telling illustration for the internal tensions this mutual supervision could cause and its potential to erode supportive relationships are the disturbances in early 1839.²¹⁶ At the center were the students Forchhammer and Schifterling whose concerns reveal the discomfort some felt about Württemberg's "narrow sanctimonious spirit." Refusing to respond to "brotherly punishment" and persisting in his complaint about harsh treatment by patronizing older students, Schifterling was dismissed. Forchhammer humbled himself and even was briefly employed as teacher.²¹⁷ Forgiveness came at the price of public confession of guilt. This is significant to understand the Basel missionaries' approach later to discipline African Christians. During the early mission in Africa, however, this dynamic became primarily a source of frustrations between missionaries.

Pietists' ideas of perennial struggles with sin called for humility as illustrated by the BMTI emphasis on character development through communal formation.²¹⁸ Contrary to interpretations that stress the Basel Mission's hierarchical structure as means of social control of students, this attitude was grounded in Pietist spiritual dualism and the context

---

214. BMA, QS-9.31 #11 §10; MM 1830, 375. Students were expected to regularly attended Sunday services and conventicles in Basel.

215. BMA, QS-9.31 #11 §2.

216. BMA, KP 14, 123–42. The Board meetings from February to April 1839 describe in detail the procedures the Board employed, its considerations and decisions in response to the tensions.

217. BMA, KP 14, 174 from July 31, 1839. Contrary to the BV 178 entry, Forchhammer was not dismissed in April 1839, but reconciled with the new inspector Hoffmann. The weekly student reports confirm him as a teacher in *Denkübungen* (Thinking Exercises) from July to October 1839 in BMA, QS-3-18 Mappe 1 *Wochenberichte*. But he also eventually left the Basel Mission. BMA, KP 14, 185 from October, 25, 1839 reports his departure from the Mission-House.

218. Humility as key to exemplary Christian living and missionary testimony permeates especially Blumhardt's writings. See MM 1828, 384–85; MM 1830, 369; Blumhardt, *Charakter eines Missionars*.

most students and teachers originated.[219] Consequently, BMTI dynamics served to reinforce patterns already espoused by its participants. The institute was a community of mutual edification and supervision very similar to Pietist fellowships, but the physical closeness, concentrated work, and extended time spent together intensified these social dynamics.

CONSENSUS AND HOMOGENEITY DESPITE DIVERSITY

The Basel Mission always took pride in its international and interdenominational character. The diverse background of Board members, Directors and teachers, the CMS, Support-Societies, and missionary candidates contributed to its practice in different ways. Nevertheless, they shared basic assumptions and were united around a common vision. Consequently, the BMTI became characterized by a basic homogeneity as well as compromise between varying interests for the sake of the mission cause. Typical for a community of practice, the practice that developed was uniquely shaped by the collaboration and therefore not identical with any one of the participants' backgrounds.

While more groups of participants can be identified, there were only three basic influences. Directors, teachers, students, and some Board members originated in the Support-Societies, mostly in Southern Germany. Therefore, Württemberg rural culture and distinct folk-religious Pietism was the dominant influence in the BMTI. However, students from other German regions, collaboration with British evangelical leaders, and the leadership of Basel aristocrats effected modifications.

The Basel elite, who constituted the majority on the Board, brought institutional structure and business mind to the organization. The CMS desire for academic qualification fit for ordination led to a more intellectual curriculum than most German supporters would have chosen, but Basel Mission leaders on principle concurred. They adopted wider European perceptions of the non-European world and the missionary task and used their educational experience to shape the syllabus and learning practices. Nevertheless, the influence of Support-Societies ensured the prevalence of German rural culture and Pietist emphases, in particular the socio-economic village ideal, patriarchal leadership, individualized dualistic spirituality, and ethical moralism.

---

219. Similar sociological critique is offered by Eiselen, "Erziehung," 49, 68–82; Miller, *Missionary Zeal*, 174–75, 109–15; Vogelsanger, *Pietismus und Afrikanische Kultur*, 41–48. Miller and Eiselen use the 1839 incidents to argue for organizational coercion of students.

From a sociological perspective "elective affinities in their beliefs, interests, and circumstances" brought these different participants together.[220] Miller emphasizes how everyone's interests were served by their membership. He lists as such for Board members the advance of economic and political interests and "reinforcement of their concern for community standing and their commitment to social and political conservatism," aside from gratifying religious zeal. Satisfied interests of the rank-and-file were the ability to avoid undesired options of emigration and urban industrial work in the face of increasing economic pressures and gain of "greater social honor" and "visible upward mobility," in addition to religious gratification. While Miller focuses on the non-religious interests, he admits the prominence of "the powerful personal zeal characteristic for Pietism [as] the ultimate source of the Basel Mission's moral energy." Throughout his insightful analysis of social dynamics he is reluctant to appreciate religious factors. However, while interests were served for everyone, the religious motivations were both the unifying factor of the BMTI community and the key to its foundational homogeneity. In the final analysis, all participants shared pious religious and ethical emphases, and the institute represented an intentional community of practice geared towards those emphases.

Consequently, the BMTI practice emphasized pious, practical, and scientific learning. It fostered Pietist spirituality and character, practical training of Christian ministry skills and "culture" building abilities, and academic studies with a focus on languages, the Bible, and scientific knowledge deemed helpful in non-European contexts. Student evaluations were divided into these areas. They listed "Spiritual Life," "Missionary Fervor," "Ability" (cognitive, social, and practical capacities), "Preaching and Teaching," and "Knowledge" divided into Theology, Languages, and "Realien" (basic physics, chemistry, mathematics, and geography).[221] Dismissals also fall into these three categories: Those "sent back to their previous occupation" failed morally, lacked mental abilities, or proved physically weak.[222] By 1840, sixty of 260 students were

---

220. Miller, *Missionary Zeal*, 72–80.

221. Evaluations were recorded in the Board minutes at the end of every term. See for example BMA, KP 15, 87–91 from January 13, 1841 which lists several students who were later sent to Africa; or the Minutes of Teacher Conferences from 1825 in BMA, QS-7-1a Lehrerkonferenz Protokolle, 5–32.

222. Haller, "Leben im Missionshaus," 241–42. This author, who was a teacher at the BMTI, further lists "the general impression of unsuitability for missionary service"

discharged, which means about twenty-three percent did not complete the BMTI.[223] While dismissals for moral failure have attracted attention, judged by the annual reports the majority left because of sickness or lack of ability. The outcomes of this preparation, the ways it shaped the missionary candidates and subsequently their engagement in Africa need brief consideration.

OUTCOMES OF BMTI PRACTICE—THE SHAPING OF BASEL MISSIONARIES

Missionary candidates spent up to six years in Basel which raises the important question how this community shaped their ideas and conduct. Jenkins suggests a close relationship between the village background of Württemberg missionaries and their social ideals in Africa, but asks whether "Basel Mission Seminary training and . . . the exposure to social life there would . . . wipe out any preexisting peasant formation resulting from their upbringing?"[224] The preceding analysis demonstrated that BMTI practice reflected German cultural traits and Pietist religious emphases already present in the applicants' socialization processes but added emphases and modifications.

A Selection Process Ensuring Homogeneity

Entry requirements for BMTI candidates demanded good health, elementary education, a vocation, thorough knowledge of the Bible, and faculties of mind and memory.[225] Students had to be single and unat-

---

as a reason.

223. MM 1840 III Insert "Verzeichnis der Zöglinge der evangelischen Missions-Anstalt zu Basel vom Jahr 1816 bis zum Jahr 1840" (*Register of the Pupils of the Evangelical Mission-Institute in Basel from the Year 1816 to the Year 1840*). This list omits students who were dismissed as a comparison with the Brothers-Register (which recorded students upon acceptance) shows. Haller also confirms that by his time (1897) only about two thirds of those accepted in the institute actually made it to the mission fields. He attributes the comparatively large number of dismissals from Basel to the fact that the students were older and the educational requirements higher than at other schools.

224. Jenkins, "Villagers as Missionaries," 429.

225. The conditions for acceptance at the BMTI were published repeatedly in the MM and other writings. There are various versions in BMA, QS-3-17 (Brochures for Candidates). See also Annual Report 1860, 23–24 (an official document streamlining what had been practice more or less from the beginning) and Hoffmann, *Missionsgesellschaft*, 24–30. Based on the applicant's autobiographical account and references by

tached, have parental permission and no obligations.[226] However, most important was evidence of personal conversion, moral life, missionary zeal, and divine calling. This shows the shared priorities of BMTI participants regarding necessary qualifications of missionaries. It ensured students' origin from the Pietist networks, thereby maintaining a homogeneous community that favored young men with Pietist values who testified to pious religious experiences.

Miller claims that Basel Mission leaders had "a positive preference for a uniform and relatively modest missionary recruitment base."[227] He concurs with Williams' argument that recruits from a lowly socioeconomic background would be "amendable to hierarchical discipline" and show gratitude for the social improvement the process of training presented by their acceptance of authority.[228] However, it was arguably less a deliberate decision by the leadership than an inevitable outcome of common convictions and relational networks between all participants, that BMTI students shared theological beliefs, religious practices, and missionary passion with their leaders.

Haller describes the Württemberg students as "characterized by seriousness in life, diligence and faithfulness in work, and obedience and respect for their teachers. However, sometimes they show a one-sided legalism that easily judges others unlovingly."[229] Coming from an insider, this statement confirms that the BMTI community was not solely shaped by this region. Württemberg moralizing tendencies were curbed by leaders' international, interdenominational outlook and students from other regions. Haller observes that despite the differences in "family, social status, educational level, aptitude, church background, and spiritual development, . . . the brotherhood is united in the common love for mission." While he idealizes the harmony, his statement reflects the shared passion that created a basic homogeneity in the BMTI.

---

his pastor or Support-Society leader the Board decided on acceptance.

226. Military service was the main issue regarding government obligations. It is an interesting observation that a man in his twenties was still under the authority of his parents. An example of this is the Ghana Missionary Joseph Mohr who in his diary states as a matter of fact his father's permission in 1838 (at age twenty-four) to live in Wilhelmsdorf (BMA, D-10.36, 9 *Tagebuch Joseph Mohr*).

227. Miller, *Missionary Zeal*, 46–49.

228. Williams, "Recruitment and Training." Williams adds, it was "naturally expected that they would repay their debt with loyalty to the organization that had accepted and so elevated them." See also Williams, "Not Quite Gentlemen."

229. Haller, "Leben im Missionshaus," 163.

Studies that draw direct conclusions from the South-German environment to German missionaries' overseas involvement presume an unchecked influence of Württemberg religiosity and culture.[230] However, Switzerland and other parts of Germany played significant roles, the prosperous commercial center of Basel had a global orientation, and even Württemberg Pietism was not monolithic.[231] Furthermore, Altena's analysis which builds on a wide range of missionary autobiographies from across Germany, confirms that commonalities far outweighed differences in the socialization process of Pietist youth.[232] BMTI applicants' testimonies corroborate their common pious origin, and their life stories leading up to the application show many parallels. This is true at least for those who were accepted, which is also an indication that certain accounts were preferred by the leadership. Autobiographical accounts that were accepted are not available and do not pertain to this study because those young men did not participate in the BMTI community of practice.

Villagers Gained Knowledge

The first obvious effect of BMTI training was the new information years of study and memorization gave the students. BMTI students learned what limited and faulty knowledge Basel Mission leaders had of the non-European world. As the analysis of the BMTI's domain of interest showed, this was strongly colored by British ideas and European cultural self-centeredness which evaluated especially Africa extremely negative. Scientific education covered basic contemporary geography, physics, chemistry, and medical knowledge. The contents of published articles and instructions to missionaries demonstrate that general speculations on tropical conditions and medical wisdom of the time were part of the BMTI curriculum. Most extensively the students engaged in learning languages. Both, content and methodology of language study assumed literate society as superior and thereby enforced the presumption that the ability to read and write was foundational to understanding the Christian

---

230. Examples for such conclusions are Jenkins and Vogelsanger, even though Jenkins wonders about the influence of the BMTI training: Jenkins, "Villagers as Missionaries"; Vogelsanger, *Pietismus und Afrikanische Kultur.*

231. Ising, *Johann Christoph Blumhardt*, 73. Ising concludes, that the Basel Mission was "in its element in this wide confessional spectrum and differs in this regard from more confessionally exclusive groups like the Lutheran Leipzig Mission or the Anglican CMS."

232. Altena, *Ein Häuflein Christen*, 191–300.

message. Judged by ongoing complaints about the low level of schooling in applicants, this presumption was amplified through the BMTI training. Furthermore, the institute established the importance of education in developing strong Christians and leaders. The intellectual challenge of the syllabus was assumed as necessary missionary preparation, proving perseverance, and indispensable qualification for a "teacher of the ignorant." Graduates adopted this conviction and consequently saw themselves as teachers in non-European contexts, even though they originated from relatively unschooled contexts.

The biblical-theological curriculum was extensive and generally confirmed the beliefs of students' upbringing. Rationalist developments in universities and state churches, political uprisings, and secularism were as much condemned in Basel as in the conventicles. But BMTI teaching also streamlined variations and established greater assurance of correct interpretations and doctrines which reduced missionaries' ability to embrace different positions. Regarding Württemberg students, it also curbed some common extremes.[233]

The substantive academic program the educated leadership from Germany and the Basel elite introduced became necessary also to meet CMS requirements for ordination. Typically, graduates ready to depart received German Lutheran ordination. Missionaries with the CMS agreed to further training in England where they were introduced to the Anglican context of their ministry. That the majority of those sent integrated well confirms the interdenominational spirit of the BMTI for the sake of the common cause.

Because of the extensive knowledge gained in missionary training Piggin argues that "erudite inflexibility" became a major issue of British missionaries in India.[234] However, this term is less accurate than "trained incapacity" because—certainly in the BMTI—knowledge was not the only, or even most significant factor that influenced graduates' inability to adjust to different contexts. Conversely, many of the internal tensions related to complaints about too much erudition. The BMTI practice al-

233. Hoffmann, *Eilf Jahre*, 104–13. Director Hoffmann refers to the curbing of extremes in several places. In this section he defended the considerations that had led to his appeal to the wider church and recounted changes of relationships with the traditional support base that ensued. He cites as a major reason for the complaint about too much erudition in the BMTI dissatisfaction with the changed tone of students regarding "popular eschatological sentiments and apocalyptic expectations," especially in the years leading up to 1836 (the year of Bengel's prediction of the *Parousia*).

234. Piggin, *Making Evangelical Missionaries*, 248.

ways also emphasized pious spirituality and affirmed the practical skills of students' rural artisan background. It was the BMTI unique mix of these three aspects which became the norm to be replicated with little room for deviation in other contexts. However, the inevitable effect of higher education and ordination was a rise in social status which affected cross-cultural engagement.

Education Leading to Upward Mobility and Role Reversal

While upward mobility effected by the BMTI education—certainly in the early period—was not a major motivating factor to apply, it constituted a fact.[235] Basel Mission leaders discouraged ulterior motives of socio-economic advancement, but recognized the effect that students "have been lifted out of their previous circumstances by the higher education of the mind" they had received and were no longer suited to return to their old existence.[236] For this reason and because of "the time, effort, and expenses" spent on them, those who physically disqualified for service in the tropics were typically employed in temperate climates, serving German migrant churches in the Caucasus and America or among Muslims and Jews in the Mediterranean. The marriage policies Miller observed were a tacit acknowledgment of the fact of upward mobility, even though it was decried as motivation. The education, advancement in age, and exposure to a wider perspective than the limited village community qualified BMTI graduates for the roles of patriarchal leaders. Trautwein observed a similar effect with lay leaders of the conventicles who became a "new elite" by virtue of their pious life style, Bible knowledge, humility, and ability to serve the community.[237] Further evidence is the title "missionary" given to all BMTI graduates, which incidentally included the

---

235. Miller, "Class Collaboration," 45–46. Miller concedes that "the exact extent to which the missionaries were attracted by the prospect of social 'betterment' cannot be established" but proceeds to outline the facts of education, ordination and marital alliances which effected social upward mobility of Basel missionaries. He cites various studies of British missionaries later in the century for "evidence that the hope of advancement came consciously into play in the thinking of the rank-and-file volunteers."

236. Hoffmann, *Eilf Jahre*, 71. See MM 1839, 388 for a list of "ungodly motivations" which included ambitions for socio-economic betterment and visions of success and exploration.

237. Trautwein, *Religiosität und Sozialstruktur*, 46–49.

few Africans trained there.[238] They continued to be "brothers" but they were no longer "Zöglinge" which indicated this social shift.

Intended or not, social upward mobility was a significant outcome of BMTI preparation and influenced the missionaries' intercultural engagement. Already at the institute students experienced social lift as they advanced through the years to positions of seniority and supervision of younger students. On visits back "home" they became admired missionary speakers and sometimes assumed pastoral roles. Consequently, BMTI graduates were convinced that they had the knowledge and skills to become guides of others, especially those deemed less educated and ignorant of technical skills and (true) religion. Their instructions also assumed that they would be "teachers of the ignorant" and pastors to the emerging church. Despite the strong humility value, this led to arrogant assumptions of teaching and leadership roles towards local Africans which—as we will see—became detrimental to the accomplishment of the mission, especially in relationships with African rulers.

Finally, Miller makes the interesting observation that this reproduction of Pietist patriarchal hierarchy in Africa was a compensation for organizational subordination; it "balanced the missionaries' subordination in one sphere (with respect to the Committee) by raising them to superordinate positions in another (with respect to the native converts)."[239] In their relationships with the Board missionaries remained "sons," submitted to clear systems of reporting and accountability, but towards non-European converts they assumed "patriarchal and charismatic dominance." More significantly, this did not constitute a change in basic values. The BMTI reinforced German Pietist social authority of benign patriarchs, but the position of graduates in this hierarchy shifted.

Biblical Validation for Pietist Socialization

Württemberg religious ideals and ethical emphases were the strongest influence in Basel missionary training. For the most part, values and virtues, biblical interpretations, relationships, and behaviors of this

---

238. For example George Thompson, the Liberian who was brought to Basel by Sessing, educated in Beugen and the BMTI, and sent to Ghana, was referred to as "missionary" in BMA, KP April 6, 1842. The Inspector is reported to have read out "the Instruction for the missionaries Riis, Widmann, and Thompson and the assistant missionary Halleur." See also BMA, Q-3-3,26 Instructionen 1842.

239. Miller, "Class Collaboration," 45n48. It indicates Miller's lack of concern for the African element in Ghana that he relegates this whole argument to a footnote.

socialization were affirmed. However, the fact that about half of the student body originated from other regions of Germany and beyond meant that BMTI practice was not identical with Württemberg Pietism. BMTI practice curbed peculiar behaviors and balanced allegorical biblical interpretations with rigorous exegetical studies.

Moreover, the BMTI curriculum streamlined ethical and biblical teaching and impressed a perception that what was taught was universally valid. Consequently, by and large Pietist perceptions were being validated. For example, in 1827 Blumhardt argued for a simple, direct reading of the Bible as more helpful than scientific study to meet "the moral needs of the human heart, which are in general the same in any climate and among every people"—the Bible alone represented "the holy law book for all peoples."[240] These statements assume that BMTI approaches to and readings of scripture represented universal human needs and laws. Very similarly, Hoffmann posited that the subject "Christian Ethics" presented the beliefs and ethics of the Bible which "are eternally valid truth and God's healing will for the world."[241] Thus, Basel Mission leaders were convinced that their particular interpretation of biblical faith and ethics was universally valid for all people everywhere. As the specific regulations show, it had distinctly cultural characteristics that championed order, obedience, diligence, cleanliness, frugality, and efficient use of time, energy, and resources. The BMTI practice represented the German Pietist "fixing of middle things" and students were impressed with assurance of its universal applicability.

The implications of this conviction are at the heart of the argument I put forward in this study. Such assurance of universal validity of a particular cultural expression of Christianity carries within a high propensity for incapacity to engage meaningfully with people of another cultural context. Basel Mission graduates evinced very judgmental attitudes towards non-Pietists, European administrators, traders, and soldiers in Africa, and Africans. Because their culturally shaped religious convictions and socio-ethical ideals were considered biblical teachings, there was no room for other appropriations of the Christian faith. Furthermore, their strongly individualistic piety elevated each missionary's convictions and led to judgmentalism even of each other and numerous tensions in missionary teams. This dynamic became established and amplified through

240. MM 1827, 358.
241. MM 1839, 397–98.

the BMTI practices of mutual supervision and reporting to superiors. Judgmental attitudes stemming from individualized religion, moralizing ethics, and dualist worldview created tensions among students, and strengthened the condemnation of other worldviews, especially those in Africa regarded as representing the lower stages of human development. The biblical validation of German rural values also enforced ideas of "culture" that justified the effort to replicate German rural models in foreign mission fields.

Standardization through Intentional Community of Practice

Definitions of trained incapacity identify experience and education as factors that can cause incapacity to engage new situations or changed conditions. In the Basel Mission the combination of socialization by previous experience and intentional educational intervention at the BMTI shaped missionary engagement with foreign contexts and unfamiliar circumstances. The essential homogeneity of the BMTI community guaranteed a streamlining of its practice as universal norm. Practical, theological, and ethical emphases were influenced largely by Pietist rural German culture, but a high educational value and wider European ideas of Africa and "mission work" in Africa were added. Most importantly, confidence in the biblical validation of the BMTI practice was instilled in its graduates which elevated it to the standard for all and everywhere. They graduated with a certainty and sense of superiority that made trained incapacity very likely in the cross-cultural encounter.

The potent resonance between the background of candidates and the ideals of Basel Mission leaders led to what Altena describes as the "standardization of missionary personnel."[242] Seminary training strengthened existing worldviews and priorities, and also "ensured that candidates adopted orientations and attitudes which were seen as essential by the mission leadership." He further comments that attitudes and practices so impressed on the candidates were "now and then more obstructive than conducive for the ministry overseas." This is a clear reference to the dynamic of *trained incapacity* which this study seeks to expand upon and confirm.

Overall the outcomes of BMTI preparation were missionaries with stronger convictions and rigidity than before. After successful conclusion of their training they had clearly defined understandings of both,

242. Altena, *Ein Häuflein Christen*, 192–93.

their own doctrines and the shortcomings of non-European religions and cultures, even though they typically had never encountered them. There was no self-awareness of the cultural shaping of these convictions and their rootedness in the particular appropriation of Christianity in rural German Pietism. The assumption of this cultural appropriation as universal truth was at the heart of the BMTI community of practice. Its streamlining of procedures, teachings, behaviors, and social dynamics in the final analysis reveals an essentially homogeneous community focused on ensuring continuity of and compliance with its shared practice. Common theological perspectives, religious practices, ethical emphases, and practical virtues were deepened and became the norm; the "biblical" way to see and do things that was regarded as universally applicable and accordingly prescribed for overseas engagement.

Profound religious compulsion and compassion, instilled and intensified by preparation processes, drove the missionaries. It was kindled by their dualist theology which allowed only for pious, moral, and Bible reading individual believers to be safe from eternal damnation. They were prepared to face any difficulties to replicate their model which after all was "true" Christianity, but they made little allowance for different expressions. Consequently, these missionaries' engagement with the disparate African context was likely to exhibit various levels of incapacity to adjust to life, build relationships, communicate the gospel meaningfully, and foster the development of culturally relevant communities of indigenous believers. The following chapters will assess indications for the presence and extent of this trained incapacity.

PART II

Indications for Trained Incapacity in the Beginnings of the Basel Mission in Ghana

4

The African Context and the Early Basel Mission (1828–1831)

EUROPEAN IDEAS AND EVALUATIONS shaped nineteenth-century Protestant missionary engagement in Africa and there were many common influences on European missionaries. Therefore, the Basel Mission in Ghana represents a familiar story in many ways. In this second part I examine the particular experience of this mission in its early stages in Africa, in order to identify indications for trained incapacity that can be traced to the preparation processes of Basel missionaries. More specifically, I will demonstrate that the religious convictions and practical emphases established in the BMTI community of practice impeded the missionaries' adjustment to the cross-cultural situation, the realization of organizational goals, and the emergence of an African appropriation of Christianity. This will be shown in the missionaries' attitudes, practices, and experience in the political, economic, social, and cultural context of early nineteenth century Ghana and African responses to the encounter. A comprehensive history of the Basel Mission in Ghana is beyond the scope of this study, as is a detailed analysis of the various missiological issues it raises. Rather, I examine the Basel missionaries' engagement to assess the presence and scope of trained incapacity. This chapter describes the African context and evaluates the first phase of the work in Ghana.

THE GOLD COAST IN THE NINETEENTH CENTURY

The entire nineteenth century can be regarded as a period of transition in Gold Coast history.[1] For centuries, economic relationships with Europeans were defined by the transatlantic slave trade. Between its abolition by European parliaments (Denmark 1803, Britain 1807, Netherlands 1814) and Britain's final submission of the Asante (1896) and colonial rule over most of today's Ghana (1902) a century of strive and transition passed. Limited and contested European control, shifting economic developments, and local African interests determined the context of Protestant missions during this period. Within this wider context the Basel missionaries worked in the Danish claimed area (until 1850) and the location of their primary base Akuropon was embroiled in disputes between various African factions.[2]

Shifting Economy: Replacing the Slave Trade

Fage emphasizes the importance of the slave trade and the difficulty in replacing it, economically and in people's minds "as a staple of the country's commercial ties with the outside world."[3] He posits that, at least in part, the Asante military drive southward was motivated by the desire to connect with those who still traded slaves. Boahen adds that the transition "generated a host of social problems" and caused economic hardships for those Africans as well as Europeans who had profited greatly.[4] The Basel missionary Henke observed in 1829 that "the shameful slave trade still operates secretly in our vicinity" which testifies to its persistent presence after official abolition.[5] Into the 1880s the trade continued in

---

1. Fage, *Ghana*, 57.

2. Akuropon (often spelled *Akropong*) is the capital of the region and the people called *Akuapem*. Alternative spellings are *Akwapim* or *Aquapim*. In citations I retain the authors' spellings.

3. Fage, *Ghana*, 58–71.

4. Boahen, "Politics in Ghana," 167, 179–180. Boahen recounts Asante pleas to British officials to revive the slave trade, because they did not know how to feed their prisoners of war who had been convenient pay for British goods. See also Dupuis, *Journal of a Residence in Ashantee*, 163–64, 171. Dupuis relates this request by the Asantehene in 1820.

5. MM 1829, 522. From excerpts of BMA, D-1,1 Christiansborg 1829, #1; Henke January 21, 1829. This letter includes his diary entries from October 11, 1828 to January 1829.

the Anlo-Ewe area east of the Volta River.[6] Alternatives were limited and only took root with abolition in the Americas, British commitment to the colony, and the emergence of lucrative replacements.

FAILED ATTEMPTS WITH PLANTATIONS WORKED BY "SERFS"

Already in 1788 the Danish physician and scientist Paul Erdman Isert (1755-1789)—appalled by what he saw on voyage via the West Indies and a keen observer of African life—attempted a plantation "similar to those in the Caribbean" in Akuropon.[7] He pioneered a European-African land agreement in this region and the concept of plantations in Africa, worked by "serfs" and managed by Europeans, to render the transatlantic slave trade superfluous. Isert's "serfs" were granted rights and protection West Indian slaves had not, including limited work hours and land to work for their own benefit. While his untimely death prevented the realization of this plan, by the 1830s there were Danish, British, and Dutch plantations experimenting with export crops such as cotton, coffee, and sugar.[8] Incidentally, this also indicates that the British remedy of "legitimate trade" from African production was inspired by these earlier Danish ideas.[9]

One Danish plantation owner was very significant for the survival of the Basel Mission in the country. George August Lutterodt (1790-1854) came to Africa as a youth, became a merchant, and married an African

---

6. Ward, *History of Ghana*, 227, 313–15. According to Ward the "ringleader in this traffic" in the Ada-Keta district was one Geraldo de Lema, the slave of a Brazilian slave dealer who "took possession of his master's name, property and wife, and carried on the business" after his death in 1862, enlisting "almost the whole Anlo people in his activities." Only in 1885 the Anlo were defeated and de Lema received a prolonged prison sentence.

7. Isert, *Letters*. See also Kwamena-Poh, *Akuapem State*, 96–102.

8. In the British region James Swanzy had a short-lived coffee plantation (1837–40) which (like Lutterodt's) was "quite happily based on 'pawned' labour" but stopped by the British Commissioner. See Kimble, *Political History*, 7–8. Bredwa-Mensa reports in the nineteenth century, "there were around ten Danish owned plantations, the majority of which were situated south of the Akwapim Ridge with a total area of approx. 1,100 acres. The number of enslaved workers varied considerably but the average was about forty . . . per plantation." Bredwa-Mensah et al., *Frederiksgave Plantation*, 24. Several failed Dutch attempts are reported by Nagtglas, *Een Woord aangaande de Vraag*, 6–11.

9. Buxton, *African Slave Trade*. Thomas Fowell Buxton (1786–1845) was the most influential promoter of the replacement of the slave trade by "legitimate trade" with the British parliament. In this much cited book he acknowledged his indebtedness to previous ideas.

woman.[10] As a long-term survivor he was frequently called upon service in the Danish administration. He met Andreas Riis soon after his arrival in Africa, introduced him to the king of Akuropon, and the Basel missionaries regularly recuperated on his plantation.[11] It can be assumed that this relationship influenced Riis's choice of Akuropon as mission station. He also followed similar patterns to Isert's in the employment of serfs. Eventually, all these European managed plantations ended in failure, not least because they failed to produce significant crops.[12] Hernæs cites a Danish official for the significant observation that successful "cultivation of colonial products . . . must probably be carried out by the natives themselves and to their direct advantage."[13] The increasing importance of palm oil exports produced by local farmers supports this evaluation.

African Ventures Shifting the Economy

Palm oil became next to gold dust the primary export product from the 1830s.[14] Consequently, British and Danish commercial interests conflicted in its main producing areas Akuapem and Krobo, which affected the Basel missionaries. Kimble shows that palm oil was "subject to remarkable fluctuations" of demand during the nineteenth century, but it remained an important commodity.[15] Cotton and coffee were ex-

---

10. Information about George Lutterodt is scanty. The life dates were given to me by a descendant of the trader, Philip Lutterrodt, in a personal email from October 14, 2009. He is in possession of a copy of his ancestor's birth certificate and family tree. They correspond with Riis's statement that Lutterrodt was already in Ghana for twenty-seven years in 1832 and Governor Carstensen's claim in 1846 that he came to Ghana at the age of fifteen. Storsveen, however, estimates his death in 1857. See BMA, D-1,1 Christiansborg 1832 #13 Jäger und Riis June 22, 1832; Translator's footnotes in Carstensen, *Closing the Books*, 2, 259. Lutterrodt managed the Danish warehouse for many years and even acted as Danish governor in the 1840s.

11. In Basel Mission sources Lutterodt's plantation is sometimes called *Frederiksgave*, which was the Danish royal plantation. Storsveen explains, that Lutterodt's private plantation was "close to Frederiksgave, [called "De forenede brødre" (The United Brothers)]." See ibid., 2, fn. 26. The ruins of Frederiksgave were restored 2005–2007 and an informative guide is available on http://www.frederiksgave.org. See also Bredwa-Mensah, Justesen, and Jørgensen, *Frederiksgave Plantation*.

12. Frederiksgave, for example, was given up as economic venture in 1836 and "increasingly became a health resort for ill Danish public servants from Christiansborg." See Bredwa-Mensah, Justesen, and Jørgensen, *Frederiksgave Plantation*, 6.

13. Hernæs, "Introduction," xii.

14. Ibid., xiii–xv.

15. Kimble, *Political History*, 4–7.

perimented with, but remained relatively small-scale, and trade north added to the traditional fish and salt European manufactured goods (predominantly textiles, spirits, and fire arms).[16] Independent merchants and a growing group of mixed-race and African small-scale traders were considerably helped by the advent of regular steam transport to Liverpool in 1852.[17] This greatly improved communication with Europe. Incidentally, it coincided with the change of leadership in Basel and the new director Josenhans's aspirations to streamline the organization. Faster and more reliable communication enabled him to strongly increase the Board's control over missionary activities in Africa.

In spite of these changes, Kimble maintains that, essentially, the economic system remained unaltered until the final quarter of the century. He cites as reasons limited extent of money economy and lack of easy communication. Traditional economy included subsistence agriculture, slave labor for manual work (legal until 1874), primitive means of transport (carriers, imported European animals for this purpose died), a limited range of goods produced and demands to be satisfied, corporate systems of land ownership, and "the whole network of social obligations with set limits upon individual acquisition of property."[18] His preference for individual initiative and European principles of economic advancement is apparent, but it is accurate that major economic changes were affected by British commitment to the colony (1874), subsequent larger scale gold mining and improved infrastructure, and, most importantly, by the introduction of cocoa. The latter was first imported and produced by Basel missionaries in the 1850s, but Tetteh Quashie (1842–1892) is rightly credited with providing the "economic leadership" that was widely emulated by African farmers and made the Gold Coast by 1911 the world's leading producer of cocoa.[19] Economic activities of the Basel Mission in Ghana must be evaluated by their role within these general developments.

---

16. Agbodeka, *African Politics*, 4–6.
17. Kimble, *Political History*, 5.
18. Ibid., 3, 9–10
19. Ibid., 33–34. See also BMA, D-10.1 *Ghana Manuskripte*, #13 (This file contains various articles and manuscripts on the history of cocoa in Ghana); Owusu-Ansah, *Historical Dictionary of Ghana*, 76–77, 214.

African States and European Administration: Theoretical Equality and Struggles for Dominance

Attempts to provide alternatives to the slave trade inevitably led to greater European involvement in Africa because "legitimate trade" needed peace and security inland. The eventual outcome was the establishment of European administration.[20] But commercial interests motivated political aspirations of African States too. Boahen, for example, explicates that the disputes between Asante and Fante "centered on the question of trade and trading routes."[21] Interrelationships between economic and political concerns also compelled Europeans to be drawn into African politics "far more deeply than men whose interest was essentially a commercial one ever desired to be involved."[22] Fage emphasizes the contribution to this development of "the emergence in the immediate hinterland of the Gold Coast of great states with an active policy of imperial aggrandizement" and highlights Akwamu and most dominantly Asante.[23]

AFRICAN ASPIRATIONS CAUSING BRITISH VACILLATING INTEREST

African scholars stress that African political activities affected European actions and that British growing influence was not the outcome of any

---

20. Agbodeka, *African Politics*, 10. Hernæs summarizes that after abolition European forts became gradually "the bridge heads of colonial ambitions, and the Europeans developed a growing interest in territorial control, more than partnership. 'Legitimate trade' required greater stability and peace, thus the need for control." Hernæs, "Introduction," xiii. See also Fage, *Ghana*, 62. Fage lists Christian mission, agricultural and industrial development, alternative trades, and the establishment of European administration as means Europeans employed to affect the social change regarded necessary "to achieve the extinction of the very idea of slavery as an institution in Africa."

21. Boahen, "Politics in Ghana," 168. A European illustration is the last Danish governor Carstensen's frank confession that the slave trade first brought his nation to the coast and determined the (in 1844 disadvantageous) location of Danish forts. The absence of a lucrative alternative was a major reason they eventually left. See Carstensen, *Closing the Books*, 76–79, "Remarks concerning the Danish-Guinean possessions" from June 30, 1844. Edward Carstensen (1815–1898) was Danish governor 1842–1850 and oversaw the handover of the Danish "possessions" to the British in 1850.

22. Fage, *Ghana*, 52–53.

23. Akwamu was a significant state c. 1640–1730 when Akuapem rose as a power in much the same region. See Kwamena-Poh, *Akuapem State*, 21–44; Wilks. "Rise of the Akwamu Empire"; Wilks, *Akwamu*. On Asante see Boahen, "Politics in Ghana"; Reindorf, *History*; Ward, *History of Ghana*, 147–312; Wilks, *Asante*.

clearly defined policy. Instead, their approach was "mere pragmatism and the growth was rather an accidental product of the uncoordinated and at times illegal activities of officials, traders, missionaries on the coast" which led to "periods of advance followed by periods of stagnation or even retrogression.[24] British action in the Gold Coast, especially in the first half of the nineteenth century, evinces this vacillating interest in response to Asante ambitions to regain allegiance from rebellious states and to trade directly with Europeans (not through the coastal Fante who clung to being middlemen). In 1824 the British, allied with Fante, suffered a painful defeat and—even though they had reversed military fortunes—in 1826 considered relinquishing the Gold Coast. Administration was given to a Company of Merchants in 1828 (the year the first Basel Missionaries arrived) but British government resumed control in 1843 and through the famous 1844 "Bond" that in reality was only a formal acknowledgement of already exercised jurisdiction.[25] Between 1858 and 1865 revolts over the introduction of a poll tax, Asante military campaigns pushing southwards again, and a Fante confederation attempting to set up self-governance led to renewed debates in Britain over withdrawal. Only in 1874 British military managed a decisive victory and declared the coastal stretch a British colony. Finally, in 1896 they took the Asante capital Kumasi and in 1902 added the "Northern Territories."[26]

Most significant for Christian mission was the de-facto governorship of George Maclean (1801–1847) as president of the Committee of Merchants from 1830 to 1847.[27] His shrewd leadership brought a period of peace to British-Fante-Asante relations, the introduction of European judicial system, and strong support for missionary activity. This benefited the Wesleyans (from 1835) and also the Basel Mission. Even though Basel missionaries settled to the East in Danish claimed regions, some of their

---

24. Boahen, "Politics in Ghana," 205. See also Agbodeka, *African Politics*. Agbodeka critiques earlier European authors and shows convincingly that African political activity in protest against British government and local African disputes "affected both the formulation and execution of British policy" in the late nineteenth century.

25. Boahen critically evaluates the importance of this agreement between the British and coastal African rulers and concludes that its importance "lies more in the myth that later grew around it than in its terms and impact." Boahen, "Politics in Ghana," 213–14.

26. Good summaries and analyses of this history that include the perspectives of the various African rulers and interest groups involved are: Agbodeka, *African Politics*; Boahen, "Politics in Ghana."

27. On Maclean see Boahen, "Politics in Ghana"; Metcalfe, *Maclean*.

provisions used British channels and their cause was strongly supported by Maclean. Basel missionaries testified to this, observing that "the English Governor Maclain [sic] will support the good work . . . in any way he can and every missionary may expect his friendly assistance."[28] However, for Andreas Riis this contributed to difficulties with Danish authorities.

Boahen's account is critical of evaluations by earlier (European) authors and clearly shows that British rule was incomplete.[29] Political interests and considerations of African rulers, individual characters involved, and regional issues were decisive to political and military outcomes. While he—as most Ghanaian historians—focuses on the British, Fante, and Asante, the political dynamics between the Danish and African rulers in Ga, Akuapem, Krobo, and Akwamu had very similar characteristics.[30] Hernæs welcomes Storsveen's recent English translation of the last Danish governor's reports as a resource for scholars "to avoid a rather problematic 'British bias' in interpreting European rivalries and local events on the Gold Coast in the mid-nineteenth century."[31] His introduction summarizes insightfully "the complex relations between the Danes, the British, and African societies in the eastern parts of present day Ghana." As this is the location of the first Basel Mission station, these events constitute important context.

African Disputes and Danish Intervention in Akuapem

The Akuapem kingdom was founded in 1733 by Akan from Akyem Abuakwa who assisted the native Guan in expelling their Akwamu overlords.[32] They introduced the Akan political system, but all but four of the seventeen traditional towns remained majority Guan. Kwamena-Poh offers the most comprehensive account of the region's complicated history in the eighteenth and nineteenth century.[33] He observes that "bases for political unity in Akuapem were difficult to find" because the people were

28. MM 1837, 541, citing Riis's letter in BMA, D-1,1 Akropong 1836 #6 Riis July 27, 1836.

29. Boahen, "Politics in Ghana."

30. This focus on the Asante and their encounter with British political and military presence is rooted in the subsequent British colonial takeover and the fact that the Asante were the most formidable African state in the region.

31. Hernæs, "Introduction," xxii.

32. Gilbert, *Christian Executiner*: 349; Middleton, "One Hundred and Fifty Years," 2–3.

33 Kwamena-Poh, *Akuapem State*.

divided by diverse languages, different festivals, and differing systems of inheritance.[34] The "wise and tolerant" Akyem rulers built their system on preexisting communities and created offices typically filled by "a relative who could be relied upon" to strengthen their authority. At various occasions "an external factor . . . affected the internal fissionary tendencies."[35] During the period of this study Akuapem "fissionary tendencies" and European rivalries interacted to create the most serious and prolonged conflict between the factions of the kingdom.

Interest in palm-oil fuelled British attempts in the 1830s to forge stronger ties with the mountain kingdoms that the Danes perceived within their sphere of influence. Consequently, Governor Frederik Segfried Mørch (1800–1839) pursued a more aggressive policy to expand Danish influence, but with little understanding for the internal factions and disputes.[36] As Kwamena-Poh demonstrates, African factors were quarrels between Akuapem and Krobo, division rulers revolting against the *Okuapemhene* (king of Akuapem) because of a breach of traditional custom, and the clever manipulation of the Danish governor by one of the division leaders, the Adontehene Kwafum.[37] Kwafum convinced Mørck to pursue a military campaign against Krobo (December 1835), depose the Okuampemhene Addo Dankwa (July 1836), and install Adum Tokori (January 1837).[38]

Contrary to Hernæs' claim, this did not bring stability to Akuapem, but divisions between Adum, Addo Dankwa, and another legitimate heir,

---

34. Ibid., 45–60.

35. Ibid., 60–61. One example for such "external factors" was when around 1780 "rivalry between the Danes and the Dutch to secure Akuapem as an ally in their quarrels at Accra" illustrated the "familiar pattern in the many local wars between the different European nations" to recruit African supporters.

36. Ibid., 62–71, 95–110. Mørch was governor from December 26, 1834 to March 18, 1839 (acting to August 19, 1837). See also Metcalfe, *Maclean*, 196–202.

37. See also Reindorf, *History*, 307–14. Like Middleton I use the word "king" advisedly. He states: "During the colonial period local rulers were referred to as 'chiefs' of various kinds. But the head of a state such as Akuapem is a 'king' by any proper anthropological and historical usage." See Middleton, "One Hundred and Fifty Years," 2, 16.

38. Addo Dankwa I (d.1839) is sometimes spelled *Adu Danquah*. In Danish and Basel Mission sources typically *Ado Dankwa* or sometimes *Adow Dangqua*. I follow the spelling of most recent scholarship which is also in line with his successors of the same name, including the recent Okuampemhene Addo Dankwa III. In citations I retain the author's spelling.

Owusu Akyem, leading to years of strife.[39] In December 1844 Governor Carstensen intervened by summoning Adum and Owusu Akyem to Christiansborg.[40] The meeting ended tragically with several murders, including Owusu Akyem's, followed by Adum's arrest and deportation to Copenhagen. Eventually, a man from outside the warring factions, Kwadade I, was installed in March 1846 marking the end of a decade of political unrest.[41] The Basel missionaries who settled in Akuapem observed and participated in these disputes in various ways. Closer analysis below will examine the character of their involvement and its impact on the mission. At the roots of European interventions—driven more by economic interests than concern for African situations—were faulty conceptions of African states and unjustified confidence in European influence in Africa.

EUROPEAN MISCONCEPTIONS OF AFRICAN RULERS

Ward highlights the European misconception that African rulers were despots and able "to decide and to act without an opportunity of consulting their constitutional advisers."[42] Missionaries shared these misconceptions. For example, Blumhardt saw "numerous despotic rulers" as moral obstacles to Christian mission in Africa, along with the slave trade and "constant bloody tribal wars."[43] In reality, African traditional society was an intricate system of kinship and responsibility. Ward emphasizes the importance of family, clan and village elders, a ruler's capacity to gauge the general sense of community opinion, and the deep rootedness of political organization within religion, in particular the worship of common ancestors. Even in politically centralized states, like those of the Akan groups, there were clearly defined rights and obligations.[44] The social status of an individual and royal rights of succession and inheritance were

---

39. Hernæs, "Introduction," xvii; Kwamena-Poh, *Akuapem State*, 64–66.

40. Christiansborg was the main Danish settlement and fort on the coast.

41. Kwamena-Poh, *Akuapem State*, 66–71. See also Carstensen's letters concerning the events from January 13, 1845, November 1, 1845 and March 2, 1846 in Carstensen, *Closing the Books*, 88–90, 154–55, 198–200. Carstensen refers to Owusu Akyem as *Ussu-Akim* and Kwadade as *Ohine Kuma*.

42. Ward, *History of Ghana*, 99–103.

43. MM 1827, 532; MM 1839 II, 182.

44. "Akan" has become the summary term for the various related societies in Southern Ghana and parts of the Côte d'Ivoire that belong to the Kwa language group. The Asante, Fante, Akyem, and Akuapem belong to this grouping.

"determined largely by lineage, kinship and age," and along a matrilineal system.[45] Rattray's detailed analysis of Asante constitutional law demonstrates that rulers were sovereign only within clearly defined boundaries and accountabilities. While a king was "ostensibly an autocratic ruler; in reality he was expected to do little or nothing without having previously consulted his counselors, who in turn conferred with the people in order to sound popular opinion."[46] These dynamics were important factors in the Akuapem disputes between 1835 and 1845. Without consideration for the communal nature of African leadership and the various groups of divergent origin missionaries and Danish governors saw only "tribal wars" and "despotic rulers," while African kings and aspirants to leadership negotiated the mood of their communities and potential advantages of aligning themselves with different foreign powers.

Lack of European Control Affecting Missionary Engagement

Scholars are unanimous about the lack of European control in Guinea during the period.[47] Before 1800 relations between Europeans and African political authorities were "generally those of equal partners in a commercial transaction" in which "various actors played a strategic game to gain advantages, and where neither party was able to dictate the rules."[48] Trading forts on the coast did not imply influence in the hinterland. Quite contrary, Europeans "were in no position to dominate" but paid rent for the land they occupied and gave gifts in exchange for good will.[49] The contracts or "notes" that regulated relationships were interpreted by Africans as "a kind of lease agreement as well as firm evidence that the Europeans officially acknowledged the sovereignty of the local states" re-

---

45. Kimble, *Political History*, 125–28.

46. Rattray, *Ashanti Law*, 84–87.

47. The Southern part of the West African coast is often referred to as *Guinea*. More specifically, the Danish documents refer to the Danish claims in today's Ghana as *(Danish) Guinea*. The English word comes from the Portuguese term *Guiné* which came into use from the mid fifteenth century to describe the lands south of the Senegal River inhabited by the *Guineus*, a generic term for black African peoples as opposed to North Africans, who were called *Azenegues* or *Moors*.

48. Curtin, *Image of Africa*, 7–8; Hernæs, "Introduction," xiii.

49. Ibid., xii; Ward, *History of Ghana*, 97–98; Curtin, *Image of Africa*, 7–9. For example, a report from 1820 lists rents and stipends to African officials paid by the British forts of over three thousand pounds sterling. Cited in Crooks, *Records Relating to the Gold Coast*, 126–34.

garding their land. Bredwa-Mensah recounts the appointment of an Akwamu civil servant "responsible for relationships with Christiansborg" and seen as "protector of the Danish governor and as the representative of the Danes in the capital, responsible for their behavior and punctual payments," and adds that this "signified . . . a perception of the Danes as subjects to the king."[50]

By 1830 "formal relations between European and African states were still conducted on the basis of theoretical equality" and the rights of African states in international law accepted.[51] However, Curtin adds that "legal sovereignty . . . was no guarantee for equal treatment" as the British began to claim a moral right to intervene in the slave trade that led to a "moral right to intervene in Africa for the sake of carrying civilization to the barbarians." Nevertheless, in reality "authority over the people of the coastal areas was never clearly defined and any jurisdiction enjoyed depended ultimately on the cooperation of the people."[52] Contemporary observers confirm this. Brodie Cruikshank (1814–1854), British official in Ghana 1834–1854, acknowledged that "nominally masters, we yet exercised no authority, or only such as the natives did not care to dispute."[53] Even the perception as "nominal masters" was not shared by African rulers. When the Danish sold their "possessions" in 1850, it is clear that they "were able to transfer not much more than buildings. . . . By all intents and purposes, the British inherited no more than a Danish sphere of influence, or certain *claims* of authority."[54]

In fact, even in the period of high imperialism after 1880 European control in Africa was never as complete as both, proponents and opponents of Western change agency in Africa often presume. Certainly in Ghana—last to succumb to British military might and first to gain independence just about sixty years later—such control was always dependent on the cooperation of the people, who continuously challenged British authority.[55]

---

50. Bredwa-Mensah, Justesen, and Jørgensen, *Frederiksgave Plantation*, 14–16.
51. Curtin, *Image of Africa*, 279–81.
52. Boahen, "Politics in Ghana," 205.
53. Cruickshank, *Eighteen Years*, Vol. 1, 32.
54. Hernæs, "Introduction," xi. Emphasis in original.
55. Kimble's study, for example, shows that there were many challenges to British authority even as they also influenced the emergence of a Ghanaian nationalism: Kimble, *Political History*.

The consequences for missionaries were significant. Lack of European control meant that during the early nineteenth century missionaries were "guests of indigenous rulers and peoples, not ... colonial agents;" they usually "relied heavily upon local populations for their security and basic material needs," and survival depended on "carefully cultivating alliances with local leaders."[56] Barker explores this dynamic "where the missionary frontier ran ahead of empire" in the Pacific islands with "some comparative notes on Africa." Walls confirms that until the 1880s, the norm in most of Africa was that "missionaries could operate only on terms laid down by African powers [who] were always in charge, and missionaries, however reluctantly, accepted this."[57] He adds "that missionaries often had to acknowledge that they were welcomed or tolerated for reasons other than the one that brought them, that of preaching the gospel." Such living "on terms set by someone else" required patience and compromise. Both are evident in Basel missionaries' experience; especially during the years of engagement without "success" in the form of African converts and in dealings with local religious leaders whose rituals the missionaries tolerated, at least initially.[58]

Coastal Settlements: Mixed Communities with Social Problems

Europeans—especially mission leaders—regarded African coastal settlements as corrupted by slave trade and European misconduct. There was good reason for this evaluation, and contemporary observers confirm it almost unanimously, despite their own prejudices. For example, Cruickshank describes African society as a "race of slaves" and argues "the instinctive slave-trading propensities of the African," but is appalled nevertheless by "European treachery and cruelty" and highlights the degrading effects of slavery on European and African alike.[59] Hans Chris-

---

56. Barker, "Missionary Frontier," 86–87.

57. Walls, Cross-Cultural Process, 96–97.

58. For example, the first four Basel missionaries did not refuse the traditional brandy for pouring libation to the priests who visited them because they felt they had to bow to "this evil custom of the land." Henke's diary entry from December 20, 1829, printed in MM 1829, 518 (BMA, D-1,1 Christiansborg 1829, #1; Henke letter January 21, 1829, including his diary from October 1828 to January 1829).

59. Cruickshank, Eighteen Years, Vol. 1, 290–345. Cruickshank was in the Gold Coast 1834–1854, a member of the first Legislative Council from when it was set up in 1850 until his death, the first Collector General from 1852–1854, and the Acting Governor for a year from August 1853. See also Busia's introduction to the reprint of Cruickshank's book: Busia, "Introduction."

tian Monrad (1780–1825), Danish chaplain 1805–1809, was a very keen observer and, as Debrunner rightly states, more sympathetic to Africans than his predecessors.⁶⁰ This makes him an important source for understanding conditions in Christiansborg. He bemoaned the corruption and "multiple misfortunes" European relationships had brought to Africans.⁶¹ Kimble incisively comments that contemporary observations "often tell us more about the observer than the contemporary scene" because accounts "tend to evoke either a golden age of social stability or a lurid nightmare of primitive stagnation and savagery."⁶² His analysis of the social problems of these "societies in transition" perceptively illuminates dynamics in the coastal settlements of nineteenth century Africa.

Europeans of Questionable Character

European forts were military and trading outposts manned by traders, administrators, and soldiers. The population in Danish posts "fluctuated considerably due to high mortality rates" with an average of thirty to forty in the eighteenth century, most of whom were soldiers. By the nineteenth century "there were only on average around ten expatriate Danes" who mostly lived in the forts, where they "engaged in administration and commerce, while a few were in charge of the army, now mainly consisting of Euro-Africans and a limited number of enslaved persons, their total figure rarely exceeding fifty."⁶³ Many contemporary observers judge the Europeans as men given to violence, drunkenness, and womanizing. For example, Isert saw them as "lascivious, gluttonous inebriates [who] ruined their health by consorting excessively with 'Venus, Ceres, and Bacchus.'"⁶⁴ In the 1820s Monrad describes frequent "brilliant banquets" excusing excessive drinking with "the enervating heat [and] heavy perspiration [that] make some cheering and strengthening drink necessary."⁶⁵

60. Debrunner, "Notable Danish Chaplains," 18.

61. Monrad, *Gemälde*, 60–61.

62. Kimble, *Political History*, 125. He cites Cruickshank for the latter and Hayford's description of Ghanaian society before European contact as "a system of self-government as perfect and efficient as the most forward nations of the earth to-day can possibly conceive" for the former. See Hayford, *Gold Coast Native Institutions*, 128–29.

63. Bredwa-Mensah et al., *Frederiksgave Plantation*, 18–19.

64. Winsnes' "Editor's Introduction" in Isert, *Letters*, 19–20. Isert's letter from April 20, 1786 is devoted to describe "how we ourselves act in the land in which both our blood and our habits change." See Ibid., 195–211, especially 207–10.

65. Monrad, *Description*, 263–64. This is the English translation of Monrad's 1822

The African Context and the Early Basel Mission (1828–1831)   199

The governors determined the atmosphere. While some were "well beloved and sincere Christians," others "ruled more despotically than the most absolute monarch in Europe."[66] The majority were the "merry-go-lucky types" who—expecting to die in Africa—focused on drink and women. Isert laments that due to frequent deaths, "people from the lowest ranks, such as soldiers, artisans, or cabin boys have risen to the rank of governor" and their government was "often a mixture of petty arrogance and cruelty." An illustration that untrained men still substituted in the 1840s is Lutterodt's frequent government service and stint as acting governor despite Carstensen's disapproval.[67]

Most Europeans took African wives. Unique on the coast, the Danes had regulated these unions. Rømer cites a ruling by Bishop Christian Worm (1672–1737) of Copenhagen in the 1730s that "all the Danes at Christiansborg 'are allowed to take to themselves a black woman, yet not more than one' on two conditions: that she be converted to Christianity; and that she be taken with her husband back to Denmark, if she wished to go."[68] Debrunner comments that this "amounted practically to a marriage according to native custom."[69] These marriages were seen as beneficial, because the European men would not be "so easily plagued by homesickness" and the women would take care of their needs and look after them in sickness.[70] They were advantageous for the African women too, because every European had to contribute "in proportion to his salary" to a "Mulatto Treasury" that monthly supported them and a school for their

---

book. Debrunner cites extensively from the German translation of 1824 in Debrunner, "Notable Danish Chaplains," 18–25.

66. Debrunner, "Notable Danish Chaplains," 20; Isert, *Letters*, 209; Monrad, *Gemälde*, 75. Monrad claims that when some governors left the natives "sacrificed to the sea at their departure, praying that they might perish in the waves."

67. Letter from January 22, 1846 in Carstensen, *Closing the Books*, 193–95.

68. As cited by Winsnes, "An Eye-Witness, Hearsay, Hands-On Report," 49. Ludewig Ferdinand Rømer (1714–1776) was a trader in Danish Guinea c. 1739–1750 and in 1760 published his book *Tilforladclig Efterretning otn Kysten Guinea* (A Reliable Account about the Guinea Coast). He adds that "on these conditions each one of our nation has his mistress." See also Monrad, *Description*, 269; Debrunner, *Christianity in Ghana*, 69–70; Rømer, *Reliable Account*, 185.

69. Debrunner, "Notable Danish Chaplains," 22. He cites Rømer's German translation, 213.

70. Isert, *Letters*, 208; Winsnes, "An Eye-Witness," 49.

children.⁷¹ The fund functioned until the handover to the British in 1850 and assisted the Basel Mission school and church in Osu.⁷²

While the mixed-race children were "christened and instructed in Christianity," their mothers typically were not, and the second condition of monogamy was also "frequently discarded;" so frequently, that Monrad asked, "Where is the European here who does not keep one or more concubines, among them even baptized Mulatto women?"⁷³ He is so exasperated with the promiscuity and indifference to Christian marriage that he exclaims, "nothing seems more ludicrous than chastity" in Guinea.

His statement appears to be confirmed by the mocking that men like him and Isert endured for their critique and refusal to participate.⁷⁴ As "no friend and defender of the slave trade," Monrad felt "redundant" and his "whole life in Guinea a terrible inner struggle [and] a string of bitter insults."⁷⁵ Tufuoh concludes, at Christiansborg, "the climate was far from favorable to missionary enterprise."⁷⁶ When the Basel missionaries arrived, they stepped into "a heritage of indifference and neglect" and drew similar conclusions as Monrad before them.

Multi-Cultural Communities Evincing Problems of Urbanization

European trade brought "a new concentration of population and of wealth" and the evolution of "extra-tribal communities around centers of European power."⁷⁷ Not only were the emerging towns near European forts extra-tribal, they were also mixed-race and multi-cultural. By the nineteenth century the Danish coastal towns had "a population between

---

71. Monrad, *Description*, 273. See also Isert, *Letters*, 208–9.

72. Carstensen, *Closing the Books*, 120, 247, 274, 296. Osu was the town that grew outside the Danish castle Christiansborg. From 1843 onwards the second major Basel Mission work developed here. In contemporary sources the name is typically spelled *Ussu*.

73. Debrunner, *Christianity in Ghana*, 23; Monrad, *Description*, 269–70.

74. Isert, *Letters*, 318–19. Jens Adolf Kiøge (1746–1789) was acting governor December 2, 1780 to April 21, 1788 and refers to this treatment of Isert in his obituary.

75. Monrad, *Gemälde*, 375–76.

76. Tufuoh, "Relations," 36–37. Tufuoh summarizes Debrunner's account of Monrad's writings and generally embraces the chaplain's evaluations.

77. Fage, *Ghana*, 52.

The African Context and the Early Basel Mission (1828–1831) 201

500 and 2,500, with an increasing number of Danish-African families."[78] Some merchants of Danish and Danish-African origin "had established their own merchant houses with up to approx. 200 enslaved persons attached." According to Monrad, Europeans associated with "the wealthy Mulattos and Negroes—who live in the European manner—as equals . . . since wealth is the measure of human worth here."[79] He acknowledges that egalitarian relationships had limitations, but his observation confirms the rise of African merchants. Conversely, the majority of economically less fortunate Africans made their living by performing various services, some in regular employment as artisans, servants, or soldiers. From this group Basel missionaries employed, for example, carpenters for their building work in Akuropon.[80]

Coastal towns were also multi-cultural communities. While they adopted European ways of appearance and trade, the girls tended to marry Europeans, and most boys became soldiers, "mulattos" retained African beliefs and customs.[81] Monrad mentions the belief in witches, describes persistent funeral customs, and concludes that Danish-Africans took part "in the customs of both Africans and Europeans being equally despised by both; by the first because they proudly lifted themselves above them, by the latter, because they wanted to lift themselves up to their level."

Evidence for European disdain for those Africans most influenced by European ways is plentiful, including Basel missionaries. For example, Henke posits that Africans' character was generally evil, including stealing, lying, and cheating, but "Negros are as a rule less corrupt where there are no Europeans."[82] However, so shortly after his arrival this was probably based less on his observations than a parroting of what he had learned. Furthermore, Kimble shows that from the 1860s political demands of government participation by educated Ghanaians contributed to British

---

78. Bredwa-Mensah et al., *Frederiksgave Plantation*, 19.

79. Monrad, *Description*, 271.

80. BMA, D-1,1 Christiansborg 1835 #11, Riis's diary from March 19 to October 7, 1835; MM 1836, 510–64; Akropong 1838 #8 Mürdter September 25, 1838.

81. Debrunner, "Notable Danish Chaplains," 23–24; Isert, *Letters*, 208; Monrad, *Gemälde*, 254.

82. BMA, D-1,1 Christiansborg 1829, #1; Henke January 21, 1829. Diary entry from December 18, 1828, printed in MM 1829, 518.

disparagement of "mulattos and semi-educated blacks" as "discontented and unprincipled natives."[83]

Beyond social and racial differences, coastal towns were multi-ethnic communities, both among Europeans and Africans. British James Town, Dutch Accra, and Danish Christiansborg were within two and a half miles, and despite political rivalry, all Europeans interacted regularly.[84] The African settlements around the forts, too, "took no account of the boundaries of the traditional native authorities," and their inhabitants included "permanent and transient emigrants from a number of states, some of them probably in the remote interior."[85] This mixed origin meant that "European language, customs, even religion, tended to become the only language, customs, and religion the community as a whole had in common." Fage insightfully comments that while there were African indigenous ways to "solve the divisions and conflicts of authority arising in such cosmopolitan communities," as a last resort, particularly in defending the community towards outsiders, "authority naturally tended to reside with the commander of the fort and its soldiers and guns, and the inhabitants would also naturally tend to side with their own particular group of Europeans in conflicts between the various European nationalities." However, the Akuapem conflict illustrates that Africans also used European rivalries to advance their interests.

The growing urban centers evinced practical and social problems of urbanization. Methods of government and sanitary arrangements "appropriate to villages soon proved inadequate for the expanding towns."[86] Contemporary descriptions paint a picture of few large houses, but the majority of dwellings "huddled together in the most crowded manner, and without the slightest regard to light, or air, or the convenience of approach."[87] Horton describes Accra as "native huts ... so completely jumbled up together that they present a confused mass."[88] Towns lacked properly laid out streets and sanitation. Prominent nationalist leader Casely Hayford (1866–1930) critiqued in 1903, the "effect of intercourse

---

83. Kimble, *Political History*, 89. See also Cutin's observation of the general dislike in Britain of partially-Westernized Africans in Curtin, *The Image of Africa*, 226, 265.

84. Monrad, for example, informs us of frequent feasting together: Monrad, *Description*, 263.

85. Fage, *Ghana*, 50–51.

86. Kimble, *Political History*, 141.

87. Cruickshank, *Eighteen Years, Vol. 1*, 23.

88. Horton, *West African Countries and People*, 125.

with Europeans on the . . . coast towns has been to disorganize their own former municipal arrangements, and to throw them back upon such haphazard provisions as the Government has felt inclined to make."[89] His critique of colonial government maintains that attempts to assert traditional authority in the "quarters" of early municipal organization were suppressed because they "tended to appear as a challenge to British rule."[90] Even local African rulers struggled to control or improve the lot of the population, because most owed them no allegiance as they immigrated from other African states. However, as Kimble insightfully shows, one of the major difficulties was "that of adjustment to an extended field of social relationships, where the 'stranger' or foreigner predominated" which led to a "breakdown of social restraints and moral values."[91]

Notwithstanding these urban challenges, this population became the group to mediate European influence. They displayed not only the negative effects of cultural diffusion and trade in brandy, weapons, and slaves, but were the first to be exposed to European school education, to take up posts in colonial military and governance, and to become Christians. However, as we will see, Basel missionaries' rural ideals prevented them from recognizing the significance of this mixed group of uprooted people.

Chaplains were not Missionaries

From the beginning Europeans brought with them chaplains. Dangerous voyages and tropical deaths meant that often it was difficult to find willing clergy and many were "woefully incompetent for their job."[92] In Danish Guinea appointment to the chaplaincy "was sometimes a punishment" and often "a sort of probation charge for supernumerary young candidates for the ministry."[93] Chaplaincy was primarily a service to Europeans on the coast eventually extending to their mixed-race offspring.

Early missionary efforts to Africans outside the immediate European sphere of influence were carried out by African or mixed-race chaplains, often educated in Europe. Kpobi reviews the impact of five

89. Hayford, *Gold Coast Native Institutions*, 111.

90. Kimble, *Political History*, 142.

91. Ibid., 144–46. Kimble's section on *Some Social Problems of Urbanization* incisively analyses the issues evident in the new African towns.

92. Kpobi, "African Chaplains," 153.

93. Debrunner, "Notable Danish Chaplains," 20.

"notable African chaplains" in the eighteenth century.[94] While the details fall outside the scope of this study, these chaplains show that the first missionaries to Africans in this area were other Africans. It is striking, however, that they all encountered numerous difficulties and were frustrated by their European superiors' apathy and resistance. Consequently, the most significant contributions they made were translations of Christian documents into Ga and Fante, but their efforts did not result in an African church.[95]

All three Protestant nations in this area did not see their chaplains' role beyond the ministry to Europeans and their mulatto families. Tufuoh confirms that Dutch, British, and Danish establishments showed "indifference and even hostility to all a missionary stood for," and "their rejection went with a manner of life marked by brutality and debauchery" that undermined any efforts to "convert the people to a religion with which the European was identified."[96] Monrad emphatically stated that "it is not correct to consider the chaplain in Guinea a missionary, since he is chaplain only for the Europeans there, for the Mulattos, and for Negros who have been baptized in Europe or America." He adds that as far as he was able to ascertain, "it has never been his contract to engage himself in the conversion of the natives to Christianity."[97]

When the position was filled, the chaplain's pastoral care involved primarily the consolation of dying Europeans, care for the mixed-race families, and teaching their children.[98] But indifference led to long stretches of vacancy. As late as 1843 Carstensen reports that he himself

---

94. Kpobi, "African Chaplains." The five men were Jacobus Elias Johannes Capitein (1717–1747) who was highly educated in Holland and worked in Elmina (1742–1747); Philip Quaicoo or Quaque (1741–1816) who was trained in England, ordained Anglican, and returned to Cape Coast where he worked for some fifty years; Christian Jacob Protten (1715–1769) who was educated in Denmark, sent back to Guinea by the Moravians, and worked intermittently in Elmina and Christiansborg for over thirty years; Frederick Pedersen Svane who was educated with Protten in Denmark and worked for ten years in Christiansborg (1736–1746) before he retired in Denmark, and lastly, Anton Wilhelm Amo (c.1700–1756) who studied at Halle University, became "one of the most celebrated African intellectuals of the eighteenth century," returned to his native Axim after about forty-five years. See also Debrunner, *Christianity in Ghana*, 60–83.

95. Most significant for the Basel Mission, Protten produced a dictionary and translations into Ga which were used by the first Basel missionaries. See MM 1827, 529; Wurm, "Anfänge," 140–41.

96. Tufuoh, "Relations," 36.

97. Monrad, *Description*, 271–72.

98. Debrunner, "Notable Danish Chaplains," 22, 24.

(as one of few governors who cared) had to prepare, baptize, and confirm some young people "as in previous periods when the absence of clerical personnel occurred."⁹⁹ After Monrad there was no replacement, and the Basel missionaries were invited in large part because of this need. They stepped into the spiritual heritage of Danish chaplains (whose accounts of conditions in Africa were text books in Basel), experienced similar challenges, and struggled to find ways to evangelize native Africans.¹⁰⁰

ESTABLISHING A MISSION IN "TRUE HEATHEN LANDS"

In April 1823 the Basel Mission Board first contemplated starting independent work in Africa.¹⁰¹ In contrast to Russia, Africa was perceived as "true heathen land" and more likely to ignite the passions of mission supporters. Faster church growth was reported from West-Africa and during those years ample funds were available to consider such an undertaking. They considered various options. An initial attempt made in Liberia (1827–1831) was impaired by quarrels between missionaries and weakened by frequent deaths. It also suffered from lack of support by the colonial administration and African American colonists. Constantly struggling to survive, the missionaries attempted work in Monrovia and among the Bassa, but eventually the Board gave up on Liberia. The one man who had lasted for almost four years, Georg Adam Kißling (1805–1865), transferred to the CMS in Sierra Leone where he worked for another thirty-three years.¹⁰²

This short-lived mission in Liberia became significant for Ghana because for this initial work the Basel leaders articulated instructions that expressed their motivations and ideas of mission work in Africa.¹⁰³ The

99. Report from June 26, 1843 in Carstensen, *Closing the Books*, 45.

100. An illustration of a Danish chaplain's account being used in Basel is Blumhardt's article on *The Danish Possessions in West Africa* that draws heavily on Monrad's account; Blumhardt, "Die Dänischen Besitzungen."

101. BMA, KP April 18, 1823. See also Schlatter, *Basler Mission in Afrika*, 4–5. From 1822 onwards the Basel Mission had followed closely the efforts of their graduates with the CMS in Sierra Leone. This was the first time the Board considered starting their own mission in Africa after the initial work in Russia was mostly among German immigrants.

102. Stock, *Church Missionary Society*, 263. For details on the Liberia mission see Schlatter, *Basler Mission in Afrika*, 9–16.

103. Published as appendix III in MM 1830, 451–82. "Excerpts from the Instruction for our Missionaries Working in the North-American Colony Liberia from October 1827"

first group sent to Guinea was referred back to this previous document and their directives explicitly described as complementary.[104]

The impetus for the Gold Coast came through "preacher Rönne from Lyngby near Copenhagen, the former teacher of the crown prince" and a supporter of the Basel Mission.[105] In March 1826 he related an invitation by the Danish governor of Guinea, Johan Christopher von Richelieu (1789–1858; governor 1823–1825). Distressed about conditions in Christiansborg, Richelieu had resumed worship services in the fort, conducting them himself, and established a school. Upon his return to Copenhagen, he requested Christian teachers for Africa and Rönne suggested missionaries from Basel. Over the following year the conditions for an involvement in Danish Guinea were settled.

From the beginning there was greater affinity in Basel for this venture than the concurrent one in Liberia. Here old bonds between German Pietists and revived circles in Denmark were renewed and again provided the avenue of cooperation between willing German activists and Danish ecclesiastical needs and logistical means.[106] While in Liberia support from Basel was minimal and letters were delayed by hostile government officials, in Ghana organizational precautions were taken to ensure safety and ongoing support for the missionaries.

However, the arrangement was a tradeoff between the mission's interests and those of the Danish government and church. The Danish Lutheran church wanted to provide chaplains for their settlements, while the Basel Mission envisioned planting churches among native Africans. Consequently, they did not want to become chaplains for the coastal

---

104. BMA, D-10.3,3a1. Instructions 1828, 1–2. These "Provisional Instructions" explicitly state that they should regard as valid for them as well "the general points concerning missionary character and … the work in heathen lands" of the previous instructions and re-read them from time to time.

105. Schlatter, *Basler Mission in Afrika*, 7, 20. Bone Falck Rönne (1764–1833) founded in 1821 a "Danish Missionary Society" to support missionary efforts of Danes in any missionary society. See Bahl, "Die dänische Missionsthätigkeit," 202; Stocks, "Die Mission in Dänemark," 86.

106. The historic Danish-Halle mission in India inspired the leaders involved. The Danish Missionary College was regarded as the heir of this history. The connection is indicated by the fact that the Basel initiative was initially mistaken by the Danish king as a venture of that institution. On June 3, 1827 the royal approval was given, but it was issued on the name of the Danish Missionary College. The leaders of the newly established Danish Missionary Society in Copenhagen had to plead and explain until the permission was given in their name and extended to several missionaries from only one originally. See Schlatter, *Basler Mission in Afrika*, 21; Wurm, "Anfänge," 141–42.

communities, nor did they cherish the thought of working under the authority of a Danish Lutheran bishop. On the other hand, missionaries needed protection and favor from the political, military, and ecclesiastical powers on site. Eventually the Board agreed to release one of their missionaries as chaplain in Christiansborg, the main Danish settlement, in exchange for assurances that their missionaries would be free to explore and begin work among Africans.[107]

In March 1827, four students were designated for Ghana, Johannes Philipp Henke (1798–1831), Carl Ferdinand Salbach (1799–1829), Johannes Gottlieb Schmid (1804–1829) and Gottlieb Holzwarth (1802–1829). Figure 4 depicts these four in 1828.[108] At the Annual Conference in June the missionaries to both Liberia and Guinea were commissioned. By fall the first group was on voyage to Liberia, while those assigned to Danish Guinea spent a year in Denmark to study the Danish language and school system. They received Danish Lutheran ordination in June 1828 and arrived in Christiansborg in December. Meanwhile, in Liberia all but one of their colleagues had died or left the country by January 1829.

Figure 4
"The First Gold Coast Missionaries" of the Basel Mission

107. For details of the negotiations see BMA, KP April 12 and May 10, 1826; Schlatter, *Basler Mission in Afrika*, 21–22; Wurm, "Anfänge," 138–50. The results were published in MM 1827 III: 406–12. This same article continues with the report of the invitation to and arrangement in Liberia—another indication of the close relationship of the two African ventures in the minds of Basel Mission leaders.

108. BMA, QS-30.022.0143: "The first Gold Coast missionaries, and Inspector Praetorius" (clipping). Unknown studio, December 1828, *BMArchives*, http://www.bmarchives.org/items/show/82323. Shown is only the top part of this image. The bottom part depicts the later Ghana missionaries Christian Dieterle, Gottlieb Christaller, and Andreas Riis, and Basel Mission inspector and secretary, Hermann Praetorius (1852–1883). This choice reveals later Basel Mission perspectives on the relative importance of certain persons.

Death also prevented the high hopes of their instructions from coming to fruition in Ghana. After eight months, three fell victim to the perennial fever and Henke alone was left. Receiving the tragic reports (only in June 1830), the Basel leadership questioned whether to continue the mission in Africa.[109] While they decided to abandon Liberia, three new missionaries were sent to Guinea.[110] Andreas Riis (1804–1854), Peter Petersen Jäger (1808–1832), and the physician Christian Friedrich Heinze (1804–1832) arrived in Christiansborg in March 1832. On route they received the news of Henke's death in November 1831.

In these initial three years nothing substantial had been achieved towards accomplishing the expressed objectives given to the missionaries at their departure.[111] No station had been acquired, no house built, no garden planted, and no African language learned. Teaching had been limited for the most part to mixed-race children and preaching to Europeans and their Danish-African families. Even the "life of the missionary as the best sermon" had not impressed upon the coastal community in a way that Africans were drawn to the church. In the following I will investigate some of the causes of this failure with a focus on ways in which the missionaries' preparation might have contributed to their inability to adjust to the circumstances, realize organizational goals, or facilitate a positive response to their message by Africans.

Conflicts Challenged the Ideal of Brotherhood

Long before the tropical climate claimed the first sacrifices, conflicts among the initial group jeopardized the mission. During their stay in Denmark the four young men had bitter disagreements and in detailed reports to Basel expressed intense sentiments of inability to work with each other.[112] In particular, tensions arose between Henke and the other

---

109. MM 1830, 409. This report by the Basel Mission leaders was already written and the sad news is an addendum followed by the request to their supporters to pray with them about this weighty decision.

110. BMA, KP April 6 and June 22, 1831. See also Schlatter, *Basler Mission in Afrika*, 15, 26.

111. Instructions 1827 in MM 1830, 458–72; BMA, D-10.3,3a1. Instructions 1828 (III) "Euer Missionsgeschäft auf jener Küste."

112. BMA, D-10.3,2 "Briefe der Brüder Cappeler, Henke, Holzwarth, Salbach, J.G. Schmidt." Most letters in this folder of about forty letters are by Henke, Holzwarth, Salbach, and Schmid from the period after they had left Basel and before they embarked for West Africa. Frequently, in the sources Schmid's name is spelled *Schmidt* and Henke's name is spelled *Hencke*.

three. They accused him of lack of brotherly spirit and he felt that they merely expressed feelings but could not point to specific facts that proved their accusations. In February 1828 they convened a conference during which they articulated but were not able to resolve their differences. The outcome was an extensive report, supported by personal letters from Salbach, Holzwarth, und Schmid that in effect requested Henke's removal from the team.[113] Director Blumhardt responded with strong exhortations. He demanded either Henke's voluntary resignation or their reconciliation, otherwise threatened to recall them all. They reconciled—at least for the moment.[114]

In Africa the animosities flared up again. Schmid wrote openly about his bitter feelings and broken Christian fellowship.[115] After Schmid's death Henke read his diary and commented on the margins. His comments and accompanying letter to the Director reveal the depth of ill feelings between these men who had been exhorted throughout their training to maintain a humble, brotherly spirit. Significantly, the contemporaneous effort in Liberia suffered from similar disunity. Nor was the problem limited to the first groups. Tensions in the missionary teams were a recurring concern. Later examples are the bitter differences and accusations leading to Andreas Riis's departure (1844–1845) and Friedrich Schiedt's dismissal (1847–1848). But "perennial palavers" also occurred over trivialities like how much paper someone used.[116] Considering the strong language of brotherhood and love employed in the BMTI and the Mission's publications and instructions, the frequent quarrels between the missionaries are a startling observation. Why would they have such difficulties getting along? After all, they shared a common vision and sense of calling and had spent years of preparation together. Attempts to answer these pressing questions are rare. Interestingly, while

---

113. BMA, D-10.3,2 Salbach, Schmid, and Holzwarth from February 23, 1828.

114. BMA, Copy Book No.2, 291 Letter by Blumhardt to Salbach, Henke, Schmid, Holzwarth from March 1, 1828 cited in Schlatter, *Basler Mission in Afrika*, 23–24. Schlatter's surprising frankness in reporting the conflict and Blumhardt's heartache about it illustrates his stance that supports leadership actions and typically faults the missionaries for any problems.

115. His diary of this period is in Schmid's personnel file in BMF, PF 64 "Schmid, Gottlob."

116. Rosine Widmann reports a squabble over wasting paper between her husband and Dieterle as illustration of wearying "perennial palavers." See BMA, D-10.4,9 "Tagebuch Rosine Widmann, geb. Binder, 1845–1849" (Diary of Rosine Widmann, née Binder 1845–1849), 114–115, entry March 3, 1849.

conflicts in missionary teams happened frequently and are today well recognized as cause of attrition, almost no attention has been given to explore reasons for such tensions in the nineteenth century.

Inter-Missions Rivalry: Not the Basel Mission Issue

African historians typically highlight the rivalry between different missionary groups that arose increasingly in the later nineteenth century. They identify the "fragmentation of Christianity in Africa" as consequence of "denominational rivalries" between European missionaries, and several scholars discuss specific examples in detail, especially in Nigeria and Sierra Leone.[117] As Njoku put it, "the theological and doctrinal voices were decidedly plural, and the various missionary groups came to Africa with a strong feeling of intolerant rivalry and mutual suspicion."[118] Ajayi highlights the change in attitudes in the last quarter of the nineteenth century as a result of the "scramble" of European nations "to stake out claims and secure possessions in Africa."[119] This confirms the observation in Ghana that denominational rivalry is not a factor in the earlier period this study covers. Here Methodists were associated with the British and Basel missionaries with the Danish regions, and to the end of the century the Basel Mission dominated in numbers and experience.[120]

There was one occasion, nevertheless, when denominational and national interests possibly played a role. In August 1843 a British Wesleyan missionary requested to establish a mission in Osu. The Danish governor Carstensen offered the opportunity to the Basel Mission instead, indicating full support. His reasoning was to "acknowledge that the Basel missionaries are the first to have access in this area" and "not until the Basel missionaries declare that they are not able to establish a

---

117. Avery, "Christianity in Sierra Leone," 108–9, 116; Ekechi, *Missionary Enterprise*; Tasie, *Christian Missionary Enterprise*, 202–34. Avery cites as a "factor in keeping low the percentage of Christians in Sierra Leone" in the late 1970s "the fragmentation of Christianity" as a result of the fact that "the Christians of the various denominations who have come tend to try to reproduce their home situations, and to urge allegiance to their particular brand of Christianity, rather than to Jesus Christ."

118. Njoku, "Missionary Factor," 195.

119. Ajayi, *Christian Missions in Nigeria*, 8, 233–73.

120. Bartels, *Roots of Ghana Methodism*, 118–26. The historian of the Methodist Church in Ghana reports on the strength in numbers and experience of the Basel missionaries over Methodists and Catholics in the 1890s. He omits the Bremen Mission in Eastern Ghana which was even less significant.

school in Ussu town, will the Establishment . . . not oppose an application from the Wesleyans."[121]

One could speculate that both Danish Lutherans and Pietist Basel missionaries were uncomfortable with the "different practice" of the Wesleyans, who they faulted as "enthusiasts" and "eccentrics."[122] Danish-British rivalry may also have contributed. However, Carstensen merely stated the prior presence of Basel missionaries and seemed quite prepared to allow a Methodist mission, if they declined. The Basel missionaries did send someone to Osu and it became their second major station in Ghana. But throughout the early years evidence for collaboration outweigh denominational rivalry. For instance, in the 1830s the Basel missionaries regularly communicated with the Wesleyan missionary in Cape Coast and he sent a translator to assist them.[123]

Reasons Suggested for Team Tensions

Disagreements among missionaries arose over practical decisions of ministry like the location of stations, most useful ministry approaches, and differing assessments of African customs and colonial situations. In Liberia Kißling felt the need to train Africans in Monrovia, while Sessing wanted to establish stations inland. In Ghana, similarly, Holzwarth and Henke hoped to train mixed-race Christians in Christiansborg to reach out to their African relatives, while Salbach and Schmid planned to begin a new work in Ningo, an African coastal settlement.[124] Because in Europe there was only limited and often flawed information about Africa, missionaries were typically unprepared for what they met and, as Barker rightly comments, in the beginning "had to invent procedures and standards as they went along, a process that occasioned no end of

---

121. Letter from August 26, 1843 in Carstensen, *Closing the Books*, 55–56.

122. Schlatter, *Basler Mission in Afrika*, 12. Schlatter comments on the inability of the Basel missionaries in Liberia "to endure the eccentricity of the Methodists" that affected their emotional and spiritual health. Later, Rosine Widmann expressed her discomfort with "the clapping of hands and generally strange" behaviors at a Wesleyan meeting she attended in London (BMA, D-10.4,9 "Tagebuch Rosine Widmann," 26, entry October 26, 1846).

123. BMA, D-1,1 Akropong und Ussu 1836 #6 Riis July 27, 1836; MM 1837, 536–50; Akropong 1838 #8 Mürdter September 25, 1838.

124. BMA, D-1,1 Christiansborg 1829, #5 and #7 Salbach from March 20 and June 30, 1829; excerpts printed in HB 1829, 63; HB 1830, 25–27; See also MM 1830, 407–8.

squabbling."¹²⁵ He focuses on the Pacific islands, but the observation holds true in Ghana.

However, this does not explain the emotional quarrels among Basel missionaries before they even reached Africa. Debrunner suggests personal issues when he emphasizes that the first missionaries "were no heroes" and describes Henke as harsh authoritarian and Schmid as "sensitive, sickly, emotionally unbalanced, though well-meaning."¹²⁶ Nevertheless, attributing the issues to the missionaries' character is more informative of the author's tendency to embrace Basel Mission official positions, than helpful to understand this perennial issue.

Mutual Surveillance Eroding Relationships

So far, Jon Miller's sociological study offers the most convincing explanation. Incidentally, his analysis also provides a strong indication for trained incapacity, because he traces the detrimental dynamics between missionaries to the practice of mutual surveillance at the BMTI.¹²⁷ In his words, "the 'mutual watchfulness' woven into the social relations among the missionaries both presumed and created interpersonal estrangement, [and] the bitterness this caused sometimes made it impossible for the missionaries to work together productively and caused recurrent injury to the organization." This means, a destructive "erosion of solidarity" was built into the BMTI practice. As described above, mutual watching and reporting to superiors was part of patriarchal supervision and integral to the shaping experiences of Basel missionaries from their childhood. However, the tightness and small size of the BMTI community intensified this dynamic.

Henke had already been "marked for attention by the 'mutual watchfulness' of his fellow seminarians" in Basel. He was at different times suspected of theft, an "unacceptably favorable attitude" toward Catholicism, and accused of "not participating fully in the Christian fellowship that should prevail" in the BMTI.¹²⁸ His expulsion was seriously considered, but because of the lack of workers he was assigned to the Guinea team.

---

125. Barker, "Missionary Frontier," 92.

126. Debrunner, *Christianity in Ghana*, 97.

127. Miller, *Missionary Zeal*, 154–59. Citations in this section are from these pages.

128. Miller cites BMA, KP 10, 74–76 from September 13 and 20, 1826 and Henke's Personnel File (PF 55). The minutes of teacher conferences confirm these considerations. For example BMA, QS-7-1a "Lehrerkonferenz Protokolle" from April 14 and May 6, 1826 report discussions about Henke's dismissal and his Catholic tendencies.

Commenting on the letters from Henke's colleagues, Miller observes that the questions raised about his character, spirituality, and competency "show that mutual surveillance was as active and as divisive outside the seminary as it had been in Basel." This extension of their practice was to be expected from a group with such a strong sense of belonging and common vision. While fellowship between individuals broke down, the practice reflected behaviors instilled by the "community of practice" in Basel.

Minutes of teacher conferences from 1825 to 1827 confirm the misgivings. There are references to "quite a few scruples" about Henke, and further specifics include his weak performance in English and on preaching tours.[129] However, they also provide evidence that Henke's main opponent, Schmid, was the object of equally serious concerns. Compunctions about him included "sectarian tendencies" and "judgmental pride" accompanied by a "cocky and harsh nature" and questions about his moral behavior, although his "honesty and humility, and very fervent missionary zeal" weighed in his favor.[130] In April 1826 he was also considered for dismissal.[131]

Miller emphasizes that in spite of the problems mutual supervision caused and expressed concerns from CMS leaders, Basel Mission leaders were not prepared to revise it. In order to demonstrate "organizational contradictions," he argues that they "expected and absorbed" the "deep seated hostilities tied to the policy of mutual surveillance . . . in the interest of some higher value" which indicates "the strength of the organization's investment in its core values and policies."[132] Throughout, Miller implies that the dynamic was intentionally pursued by the leaders to ensure submission and aimed at "institutional control of missionary zeal." To strengthen this argument, he misquotes Director Blumhardt at one point—putting words of the critic Beck into his mouth.[133] Possibly this

129. For example, BMA, QS-7-1a "Lehrerkonferenz Protokolle" from August 26, 1825.

130. Ibid., August 26, September 2, and December 2, 1825.

131. Ibid., April 14, 1826.

132. Miller, *Missionary Zeal*, 163–68.

133. After reading the letters from Henke, Holzwarth, Salbach, and Schmid, Miller claims that Blumhardt "described their quarreling to the Committee as 'divisive arrogance, patronizing self-aggrandizement, masochistic severity, and childish gossiping.'" Ibid., 155. He references Vogelsanger, who in that context actually cites Beck's speech as cited by Schlatter. Schlatter, *Basler Mission in Afrika*, 127–28; Vogelsanger, *Pietismus und Afrikanische Kultur*, 57. Miller continues to quote Vogelsanger's comment

only indicates limited proficiency in German, but it shows that lack of historical perspective causes the argument to fall short of truly grasping the mutuality of religious-cultural convictions between leaders and missionaries. Moreover, it does not make the important distinction between this earlier period and the later suppression of negative effects of mutual surveillance by tighter institutional control.

Scharfe also disapproves of hierarchy, but accurately describes Württemberg Pietist religious-ethical ideas that created the social behavior of mutual surveillance.[134] The BMTI not only upheld the practice, it added a confidence the students did not have before. The consequence was an unhealthy alliance of individual convictions assumed to be universal and the felt responsibility "to be my brother's keeper."[135] This resulted in incapacity to accept different perspectives and practices, which created tensions as soon as they lacked controlling patriarchal oversight. The BMTI greatly amplified this dynamic by making it part of a hierarchical reporting structure and requiring mutual correction and confession.[136] Thus, both, their context of origin and the BMTI "trained" the missionaries for this incapacity.

---

as "perceptive" in which she states: "The fact that complaining and arguing with colleagues, suspicions, criticisms, and gossip were reported faithfully over the ocean to the Inspector shines a light not only on the pitiful isolation and loneliness of the missionaries in the tropics, but also on the powerful position which the Inspector claimed in their existence." The comment reveals Vogelsanger's critical stance towards the power relationships in the Basel Mission which Miller shares. However, citing the Beck speech as Blumhardt's words is putting a more negative tone in his mouth than he would have ever employed and Vogelsanger's comment overemphasizes power dynamics in a way that dismisses the close relationships years together in the BMTI created.

134. Scharfe, *Religion des Volkes*.

135. This is a reference to Genesis 4:9. After Cain had murdered his brother, God asked him where his brother was. Cain's response, "I do not know; am I my brother's keeper?" has come to symbolize unwillingness to accept responsibility for others, our "brothers" in the extended sense of the term. As we saw above, German Pietists strongly believed in accepting such responsibility as Christian community.

136. A "lack of joyful willingness to freely share among the brothers" is observed frequently in teacher or Board meetings. See for example BMA, QS-7-1a "Lehrerkonferenz Protokolle" from January 14, 1825. In the same meeting one student is said to be "touchy" because "the brothers hardly dare to correct him on anything."

"Brotherhood" Required Mutuality Never Experienced

Mission instructions presumed a weekly "conference" for fellowship, prayer and sharing, and as a "fellowship of brothers," their unity was to strengthen them and become a testimony to the people around.[137] In one way this was a continuation of the community in Basel, but the implied mutuality in decision making and working out strategies was at variance with everything they had experienced thus far. At the BMTI and during their upbringing the missionaries had never lived in a truly mutual context that would resemble this expectation to engage in a "brotherly" team. Instead, what had been emphasized all their lives were hierarchical relationships and mutual supervision with reporting to patriarchs. Those were the dynamics in Pietist fellowships and the BMTI intensified them. Consequently, they always fell back on this practice when they faced the inevitable challenges of unaccustomed circumstances of intercultural life—beginning with their stay in Denmark. The egalitarian brotherhood of mutual support their instructions expected of missionaries did not work because nothing in their preparatory processes had prepared them for it.

The Difficulty to Merge Different Contexts of Origin

Furthermore, the conflicts also reveal unrealistic expectations that the ideal of "brotherhood" would easily merge different contexts of origin. A closer look at what the disagreements were about reveals the difficulty of bringing together people from diverse backgrounds in this international and interdenominational venture. Debrunner hints at this, when he describes Henke as "a harsh Prussian" and Schmid as "sensitive . . . though well-meaning Swiss," but he does not explore the cultural differences.[138] The first four men sent to Ghana originated from different parts of German speaking Europe. Henke was from Hessen-Nassau, Salbach from Köpenick near Berlin, the Prussian capital but also a traditional Moravian center, Schmid from pious Swiss circles, and Holzwarth from Württemberg. The tensions that arose were along cultural and religious lines. Henke was the only one less inclined towards the emotional moralist outlook of the majority in the Basel Mission. Consequently, the

---

137. BMA, D-10.3,3a1. Instructions 1828, 9 (II). See also MM 1830, 473, 477–79.
138. Debrunner, *Christianity in Ghana*, 97.

falling-out was about the "enthusiasm" and "emotionalism" of the others versus Henke's "lack of penitence and humility."[139]

Henke dismissed the "feelings of being estranged from him" the other three expressed without being able to point to specific incidents. Already on the journey to Denmark he felt judged unfairly by Holzwarth. In the latter's words, Henke told him, "You have to know that I will not allow you to rule over me, I will not allow your emotional judgments to condemn or guide me."[140] Salbach, Schmid, and Holzwarth, on the other hand, referenced the previous issues in Basel and refused to refer the matter to the committee in Copenhagen, whom Henke considered more neutral than the Basel Board. All three had initially voiced their reluctance to be sent with Henke and only accepted this Board decision after Blumhardt's strong exhortation to "think it over in prayer." The leadership expected the ideal of brotherhood to overcome the differences in this intercultural team. The fact that they reconciled seemed to justify this confidence.

Wurm, himself clearly critical of Henke's stance, reports of contrary evaluations of the team by pious Basel Mission supporters and the Danish Lutheran Bishop Münter.[141] The former found "Henke's Christian character ... questionable" and felt "he lacked Christian love and humility," while Münter and the Danish king "favored" Henke for "his sincere, Christian inclination, free from all enthusiasm." These recurring differences between Lutheran theologians and Pietist subgroups prevalent in the Basel Mission were behind many tensions and also affected the mission in Ghana.

Despite their differences, the way they worked them out shows that all four Basel missionaries had adopted the BMTI practice that combined individual spirituality with conviction of biblical universality and group pressure. This led to strong feelings of their moral right to speak to each other about failures to conform to what they regarded as Christian behavior or attitudes. In the process diverging backgrounds of theology and practical spirituality were not erased, but contributed to emotionally charged frictions. Disagreements and discomfort with each other found expression in the summary accusations of "judgmental pride

---

139. BMA, D-10.3,2 "Briefe der Brüder Cappeler, Henke, Holzwarth, Salbach, J.G. Schmidt," letter from Salbach, Schmid, Holzwarth February 23, 1828. The letters and report of their conference give clear evidence of these differences.

140. Ibid., Holzwarth's letter.

141. Wurm, "Anfänge," 147–49.

and enthusiasm" by one side, and "insubordination and lack of humility" by the other. Furthermore, they reported to their superiors in detailed descriptions, almost transcripts of their conversations, and explicit accounts of their feelings. These also represented practices encouraged in Basel.

In the final analysis what affected the incapacity to get along was a combination of mutual supervision, emotional individual religion, and strong convictions fostered in the BMTI. The organizational control mechanism sanctioned students' use of their personal convictions as criteria to judge their "brothers." It fostered a conviction that when two differed in opinion, by definition one of them failed to conform to biblical universal truth. Such unorthodoxy then, had to be uprooted, repented from, and confessed publically to receive forgiveness. Not surprisingly, this was accompanied by strong emotions and led to harsh conflicts and some students leaving the institute. This dynamic functioned to standardize behaviors, procedures, attitudes, and evaluations. However, conflicts inevitably rose because of the international and interdenominational character of the organization. Standardization was not as complete as typically suggested because the BMTI attracted applicants from a greater variety of contexts of origin as other missions. This created internal tensions between the value of embracing the wider brotherhood of the pious and the necessity to hold together and smooth out differences that surfaced in the institute and overseas.

Reasserting the Patriarchal Hierarchy as Solution

Eventually, reasserting patriarchal hierarchy subdued the destructive tensions. Blumhardt's strong admonition to the Ghana group to reconcile or return to Basel effected temporary reconciliation. But over time, the leaders established organizational structures that extended the hierarchical supervision from Basel to the overseas fields.

The 1842 instructions still stated that the "missionaries as brothers are equal to each other and none of them is to be regarded as head of the mission," with the caveat that in the case of different opinions the Board in Basel would decide.[142] This is repeated in 1844 with the caution to new missionaries to "consider the experience of the older brothers in the country and the work."[143] The same year "General Rules" were introduced

---

142. BMA, Q-3-3,26 Instructionen 1842 §§ 32–33.
143. BMA, Q-3-3,26 Instructionen 1844 (Sebald Schied, HN Riis) §8.

that stipulated a list of cases which were "reserved to the decision of the Committee."[144] It required prior permission for establishing new stations, building projects, buying land, and missionaries committing to different ministries or stations than those assigned originally. It also regulated what had been general practice; that engagement or marriage needed Board permission and could not be requested before missionaries had proven their abilities for at least two years.[145]

In 1850, with the new leadership in Basel, the egalitarian ideal overseas was abandoned. Additions to the General Rules introduced "station conferences" with a "president" who was responsible to the Board for the performance of the team.[146] The other missionaries were commanded "willing and complete obedience" to the president and novices had no vote. Thus, in effect the same supervisory and decision making structures that existed in Basel were introduced in missionary teams. The organizational streamlining of all Basel Mission ministries in India, China, and Africa implemented by Director Josenhans was aided by the arrival of more reliable and regular communication. It restored the practice the missionaries knew, thereby effectively subduing their disagreements to familiar authority structures and control mechanisms. However, it also increased organizational intervention based on leaders' evaluations in Europe and their assumption that appropriate measures in one place could be applied in another.[147]

Challenges of Survival Aggravated By Lack of Collaboration

For all Europeans in West Africa at the time "the most important problem . . . was simply that of keeping alive."[148] Basel Mission instructions regarding survival reveal the lack of genuine knowledge in Europe. The Board confessed their unfamiliarity with "the conditions on this distant coast" and inability to advise.[149] They promised prayer support and ex-

---

144. BMA, Q-3-3,26 Allgemeine Regeln §§ 3–6. See also KP 17 from November 20 and 27, 1844.

145. BMA, Q-3-3,26 Allgemeine Regeln §§ 7–8.

146. BMA, Q-3-3,26 Instructionen Steimle und Süß (November 1850) §§ 9–14. They also demanded prior permission for returning to Europe, stipulating a minimum six year term.

147. An illustration for this assumption is the introduction in Ghana of the church order used in India.

148. Curtin, *Image of Africa*, 177.

149. BMA, D-10.3,3 Instructions 1828 (II).

horted the missionaries to entrust themselves to God in fervent prayer and "strengthen daily the bond of love and unity among themselves." During the assumed acclimatization period, the missionaries were urged "to acquire the local way of life gradually" and use the advice and experience of others.[150] Generally, they should not be "fearful and despondent" but use "wise caution without faithless anxiety."[151]

Ideas of "healthy tropical life" covered "a somewhat diverse set of rules" and—similar to British perceptions—reveal a "half-conscious belief in a connection between morality and disease as well as the usual "medical topography" that regarded certain locations as more healthy than others.[152] For example, Salbach speculates about the effect of diet and clothing on tropical sickness and later judges "the air filled with unhealthy vapor" from the river in Ningo as "not quite as healthy as Osu.[153] Henke also suggests seven "precautions against the climate" along similar lines of behavior, diet, and clothing.[154] Such speculations had little medical value as general experience demonstrated.

However, in its first years in Ghana the Basel Mission suffered even higher death rates than others. Curtin collected statistics of European mortality in West Africa.[155] In "costal posts in the early nineteenth century" the percentages of European deaths range from 33 percent among soldiers to 46 percent among merchants and 60.5 percent in the CMS. But of the nine missionaries and one woman the Basel Mission sent to Guinea until 1840, only Andreas Riis and his wife survived, a death toll of 80 percent.[156] Apparently, the advice to balance wise caution with bold faith proved too vague and impractical. As we saw, the "bond of love

150. Instructions 1827 in MM 1830, 457.

151. BMA, D-10.3,3 Instructions 1828 (II); Q-3-3,26 Instructionen 1842 §7.

152. Curtin, *Image of Africa*, 71–83, 177–97, 353–62. Curtin discusses in detail the developments of various European perceptions and prescriptions, as well as medical research until the breakthrough with quinine in the mid nineteenth century.

153. BMA, D-1,1 Christiansborg 1829 #5 and #7 Salbach March 20 and June 20, 1829. See also Wurm, "Anfänge," 200–1.

154. BMA, D-1,1 Christiansborg 1830 #2 Henke May 20, 1830.

155. Curtin, *Image of Africa*, 483–87.

156. Basel Mission statistics typically omit Anna Riis and claim that eight of the nine missionaries died, which would represent a death rate of 89 percent. The Riis also had two children before 1840; the firstborn girl died just over a year old, the secondborn boy returned with them to Europe. If the children are counted, nine out of twelve died, a death rate of 75 percent. However the statistics are calculated, the fact remains that the Basel Mission death toll was even higher than others.'

and unity" had serious cracks, and the argument can be made that their attitudes often discouraged supportive relationships.

The Strain of Missing Mutual Support

Their interpersonal conflicts eroded emotional and physical support. Schmid's diary reveals the pain and drain on their energies which this lack of practical and spiritual fellowship inflicted on the missionaries. Shortly after they moved to a house in Osu the tensions flared up again. Schmid's repeated confessions of hatred towards Henke and detailed accounts of conflicts include his religious reflections. They show troubling mental and emotional turmoil that also affected his health. He interprets anger, mistrust, hatred, and desperation about his own feelings as temptations, and—mixed with physical exhaustion—this led to days when he felt "so disturbed in his heart that [he] could not work anything all day and slept for hours."[157] Schmid did not feel able to reinstitute the daily devotions which they had abandoned in Copenhagen and refused to pray with Henke. At the same time such breach of Christian fellowship deeply perturbed him.

Not less disturbing are Henke's self-justifying comments in the margins, next to Schmid's confessions of "honest hatred." Underlining the statement, Henke defends himself: "I was always aware of Schmid's hostile attitudes toward me, as well as his hypocritical and dishonest nature. What do you think, dear Director, about this admission? Are you still inclined to see in me the cause for our alienated existence?"[158] He confesses his own aversions and affliction by the strained relationships: "For this reason I could never stand much of [Schmid] and I needed to call his attention to this [hypocrisy] and his lack of self-discipline."

Henke's statement also illustrates the continuing practice of mutual correction which was at the root of their animosity. Miller aptly highlights that the leadership never publicly acknowledged its detrimental effects.[159] Evidence is offered in the accounts of Basel Mission authors

---

157. BMA, PF 64, Gottlob Schmid, "Fortsetzung meines Tagebuchs von meiner Ankunft zu Cap Coast u. Besuch in Ellomina in Afrika von 12ten Dezember bis 9ten August 1829." (Diary from December 12 to August 9, 1829), 36–43. This is the culmination of an incident on January 13, 1829 that Schmid found particular disturbing which involved Henke refusing to give him the key for their storage so he could get what he needed to take a bath.

158. BMA, PF 64 Gottlob Schmid, Diary, 43, 120.

159. Miller, *Missionary Zeal*, 156. He comments on this "protective insularity"

Wurm, Schlatter, and Debrunner, who all omit the problems.[160] Wurm alone gives a hint when he cites Henke's description of Schmid as "more difficult to treat when he was sick," but he explicitly claims that "there was no trace of their disunity anymore" in Africa.[161] Contrarily, the ongoing tensions contributed to a sense of alienation and isolation that added to weaken the missionaries' constitution. Sadly, they reflected a pattern instilled in their upbringing and education, therefore a *trained* incapacity to fully support each other.

While they had differences among themselves, when they arrived in Africa the missionaries were united in their condemnation of others. They found what they expected on the coast, "depraved Europeans" and African "heathen." This judgment tended to prevent collaboration which could have enhanced their chances of survival and success.

Depraved Europeans Who Did Not Support Mission

Their observations confirmed Monrad's descriptions and reflected similar repulsion at the polygamy of Europeans, their possession and ill-treatment of African slaves, debauchery, and greed, and their disinterest in Christian mission among native Africans. Henke comments that "it seems more advantageous to the greedy merchants' minds to keep the Africans in ignorance, moreover, this way they can indulge their fleshly lust undisturbed," and concludes, "we do not fit to the merchants in the fort."[162] Initially they accepted the hospitality of the Danish Governor Heinrich Gerhard Lind (1797–1833; governor August 1828 to January 1831), but they rented a house from a mixed-race merchant in Osu town within a week.[163] Henke and Holzwarth quickly began baptism class and a Bible study, but created strained relationships by their evaluations of

---

that, despite the extensive discussions about the letters in the Board meetings, "little of the turmoil that engulfed Henke and his coworkers was revealed to the seminarians in Basel or to the Missions supporters in Europe."

160. Debrunner, *Christianity in Ghana*, 97–98; Schlatter, *Basler Mission in Afrika*, 23–26; Wurm, "Anfänge," 195–208.

161. BMA, D-1,1 Christiansborg 1830, #2; Henke May 20, 1830; Wurm, "Anfänge," 205, 199.

162. BMA, D-1,1 Christiansborg 1829 #1 Henke Diary December 15, 1828; MM 1829, 515; Debrunner, *Christianity in Ghana*, 94; Wurm, "Anfänge," 195–96.

163. BMA, D-1,1 Christiansborg 1829 #1 Henke Diary December 20–27, 1828; MM 1829, 518–20; Wurm, "Anfänge," 198. They rented the house on December 26, 1828 and their luggage arrived with a ship from Cape Coast the next day.

the attendees. They refused baptism to anyone above twelve, insisting on prior instruction, and refused communion to "those who live careless and impenitent lives and do not marry one wife in the Christian way."[164] The observation that Henke proved "by no means more lenient towards bad Europeans and Mulattos than his brothers" confirms that he was no less shaped by BMTI practice.[165]

The despicable conduct of Europeans remains a theme in the letters. The missionaries reported with dismay of slave trade still going on, despite Danish abolition in 1803.[166] According to Hernæs there were about eighty fort-slaves in Christiansborg in the 1830s and by their final emancipation (March 16, 1848) there were still about seventy.[167] Even though they were referred to in cosmetic ways as "serfs" or "villeins" and some had a pawn status, they shared living and working conditions and the same rough treatment, and "pawns" were rarely redeemed.[168] The missionaries were appalled at European treatment of Africans including the travel in carts pulled by serfs.[169] Their descriptions confirm that Europeans (and some mulatto traders) considered African workers more like slaves, both, in the town and on the plantations. With such men they did not want to associate, even when their advice could have helped them.

There were exceptions, like the "pious Dr. Trentepohl," a scientist, who sometimes assisted medically and had a plantation outside Christiansborg where Henke repeatedly recuperated.[170] But, like Isert and Monrad before him, Henke experienced that the quality of fort life depended on the governor. He had tensions with Lind, especially over the

164. BMA, D-1,1 Christiansborg 1829 #1 Henke Diary January 3–20; MM 1829, 520–21.

165. Wurm, "Anfänge," 199.

166. BMA, D-1,1 Christiansborg 1829 #1 Henke January 21, 1829; MM 1829, 522.

167. Hernæs, "Fort Slaves," 202–3.

168. Carstensen, *Closing the Books*, 189–92; Hernæs, "Fort Slaves," 201. In his letter from January 22, 1846 Carstensen argues—mostly on economic grounds—for their release. He adds that, although he has shown that to keep them was considerably more expensive than to free them and rely on hired labor, the fact "should not be ignored that, even though these people are called villeins, they are actually slaves . . . and subject to the same conditions. But in these days when everything speaks of emancipation of the slaves, this would probably not be tune in with the wishes of the government–the possibility of being described in public as slave owners" (191).

169. BMA, D-1,1 Christiansborg 1829 #1 Henke Diary December 13 and 20, 1828; MM 1829, 515, 519.

170. BMA, D-1,1 Christiansborg 1830 #2 Henke May 20, 1830.

teaching of the fort slaves' children. Lind objected to them being taught to read and write, but wanted them to learn only Danish and "Christian morals."[171] However, on the whole Lind had assisted the missionaries, contrary to his successor. Ludwig Vincent von Hein (1799–1831) managed to "make life a vestibule of hell" for Henke with his "pride, suspicion, greed, and sensuality."[172] While there was truth in their descriptions of rough European behavior in Africa, the missionaries' wholesale condemnation and refusal to associate alienated them from other Europeans in Christiansborg and precluded benefiting from their experience and practical support.

Henke's final letter complained of the "thousand difficulties, especially from the depraved nominal Christians" and—feeling increasingly weaker—anticipated his impending death. A month later he died. In three years he had not revised the moral dismissal of other Europeans in Africa and consistently refused any closer association. Consequently, he was opposed in many ways and felt lonely and unsupported, reflecting similar sentiments as Monrad earlier, who described his whole stay in Guinea as "a terrible inner struggle; a string of bitter insults," and blessed God who brought him back home.[173] However, returning home was not an option for Basel missionaries. Death in a twisted way became the only honorable way out of an almost completely unsupported situation in which, at least in part, their preconceptions had landed them. Nevertheless, while their attitudes did not help, much in the colonial context was beyond their control, and many Europeans died with or without supportive friends.

Presuming Ulterior Motives of African "Heathen"

BMTI teaching had instilled the general European moral and theological dismissal of all things African. Consequently, the missionaries stereotypically judged Africans and African customs they encountered by these prejudices. Shortly after their arrival they observed "idol images," traditional music, and dancing which pierced their eyes as "terrible sight" that "could hardly be worse in a madhouse."[174] BMTI instilled sensitivities

---

171. BMA, D-1,1 Christiansborg 1831 #5 Henke January 30, 1831.

172. BMA, D-1,1 Christiansborg 1831 #6 Henke October 31, 1831. Hein was governor from January 29, 1831 to 21 October 21, 1831. Helmut von Ahrenstorff (1807–1831), governor October 21, 1831 to December 4, 1831, had just been governor for ten days when Henke wrote this last letter, but received no better evaluation.

173. Monrad, *Description*, 265–66. Monrad 1824: 374–75, Danish 367.

174. BMA, D-1,1 Christiansborg 1829 #1 Henke Diary December 13, 1828; MM

perceived African ceremonies, music, and dancing as "great raucous din" and "drunken binge," the noise "almost unbearable," that ignited their desire to "teach them how they could truly be happy."[175] How missionaries' preconceptions influenced their communication of Christianity will be discussed below. At this point, it is important to note that they prevented any expectation that Africans could assist their survival and help them discern how to live in Africa, even though African leaders welcomed them and offered the help of their physicians.[176]

In fact, they received assistance from Africans in a number of ways. The son of a Ga ruler, Frederik Davunnah, accompanied them from Denmark to Africa and became an important source of support.[177] According to Debrunner, Davunnah assisted the eminent linguist Rasmus Rask to compile a Ga grammar published in 1828.[178] In Denmark the missionaries began learning Ga from him as well as a former Danish governor.[179] In Guinea Davunnah's father helped the missionaries to find the house they rented in Osu, Davunnah continued as language helper and became an indispensable translator in the school.[180] Employed by the governor as teacher, Davunnah must have taken over the task during the missionaries' frequent bouts of sickness and after Henke's death. Even when he

---

1829, 515.

175. BMA, D-1,1 Christiansborg 1829 #7 Salbach June 30, 1829. In this section Salbach reported in detail on a funeral celebration he observed in Ningo.

176. Ibid.; Wurm, "Anfänge," 201.

177. Information about Davunnah is very scarce. His name appears in different spellings including *Davuna* and *Dowuonah*. Debrunner informs us that his original name was *Noi* and he "later became Osu Mantse, a Chief at Christiansborg." See Debrunner, *Christianity in Ghana*, 92. Wurm—without mentioning his name—claims that his father asked Richelieu to educate him in European sciences and religion, but Richelieu treated him like a slave and the Danish king had him taken to the garrison school. See Wurm, "Anfänge," 146–47.

178. Debrunner, "Notable Danish Chaplains," 29, Note 173; Debrunner, *Christianity in Ghana*, 92. Rasmus Christian Rask (1787–1832) was a Danish philologist and professor of Oriental Languages and Icelandic at the University of Copenhagen who studied Northern and Eastern languages. He is said to have mastered no less than twenty-five languages and dialects, and to have studied twice as many. See "Rask, Rasmus Christian."

179. Wurm, "Anfänge," 146–47. The governor was Johan Peter David Wrisberg (1771–1819) who translated the Sermon on the Mount and part of Luther's Catechism into Ga. See Debrunner, *Christianity in Ghana*, 92; Blumhardt, "Die Dänischen Besitzungen," 529.

180. BMA, D-1,1 Christiansborg 1829 #1 Henke Diary December 20, 1828, printed in MM 1829, 518; #5 Salbach March 20 and #10 Henke August 10, 1829.

translated, it is more than likely that he also interpreted the European concepts for the students in their native tongue Ga, despite the missionary's judgment that the interpreter "himself knows but little Danish and translates somehow."[181]

Others also offered hospitality and welcome, including the king of Winneba, two "fetish priests" in Osu, and the rulers of various coastal towns between Ningo and Christiansborg. But, in spite of the welcome and support by Africans, the missionaries' evaluations did not improve. One of the striking common features is the presumption of ulterior motives. In Winneba they commented on the generosity of the king that "receiving presents is the main motivation of African hospitality towards Europeans."[182] Later Salbach concludes his detailed report of the trip to Ningo and the friendly reception from town elders everywhere by observing that their desire for Christian religious teachers was probably "merely in expectation of worldly gain . . . and in hope of payment for the children who attend school."[183] He precludes genuine interest in Christianity but hopes that exposure to "the word of truth . . . would dispel all impurity in their hearts."

Any request for brandy was interpreted as indulgence in drunkenness, even when they recognized its religious purpose. Two examples are the canoe crossing of the Sakumu Lagoon and their encounters with the Osu priests. On the first occasion Henke described the lagoon as "a primary fetish of the Accra people" and the missionaries refused to supply the requested brandy.[184] With the priests they felt compelled by the "evil custom of the land" to supply the drink as a matter of politeness, but often they also refused.[185] By August they had recognized the purpose of libation but still articulated the suspicion that the priest's interest was more for drink than religious conversation.[186] Contrary to contemporary European perceptions of African insobriety, Rattray has shown the im-

---

181. BMA, D-1,1 Christiansborg 1829 #3 Holzwarth January 31, 1829.

182. BMA, D-1,1 Christiansborg 1829 #1 Henke Diary December 17, 1828; MM 1829, 516.

183. BMA, D-1,1 Christiansborg 1829 #7 Salbach June 30, 1829; Wurm, "Anfänge," 203.

184. BMA, D-1,1 Christiansborg 1829 #1 Henke Diary December 18, 1828; MM 1829, 517.

185. BMA, D-1,1 Christiansborg 1829 #1 Henke Diary December 20 and 27, 1828; MM 1829, 518, 520;

186. BMA, D-1,1 Christiansborg 1829 #10 Henke August 10, 1829.

portance in African religion to "propitiate the spirit owners of the land" with libations.[187] He convincingly argues Africans were very "cognizant of the evils of alcoholic excess" and only celebrated with drink after the conclusion of important business. However, as the "important business" was typically conducted in secret, Europeans made uninformed judgments from the concluding celebrations.

While Basel Missionaries were not teetotalers—they had brought wine in their luggage—they still shared European condemnations which had become accepted truth in the BMTI and did not overcome this trained incapacity to perceive honest intentions in the Africans they encountered.

Inklings of Trained Incapacity Overcome

There are some indications for modifications over time. Henke shows signs of a pattern that can be observed with several Basel missionaries who spent extended time in Africa; eventually some revised their perceptions of African abilities. After teaching the baptism class for eighteen months, Henke reported in October 1830 that "learning is not as difficult for mulattos and Negros . . . as Europeans typically imagine: On the contrary, I find it comes very easy to them."[188] He observed that most of his students "are little or not at all inferior in Christian knowledge to the typical confirmand in rural Europe." His exposure to Africans and the relationships he built with the students effected this change of mind over time. This indicates that extended exposure and close relationships are ways trained incapacity can be overcome.

However, regarding African religion and character Henke's judgment remained unaltered. He corrected Salbach's earlier excited report of the openness of African communities to receive Christian teachers. Henke discerned "absolutely no desire for the Gospel" and described Africans as "extremely shrewd and extremely corrupted" and "always out for gifts and brandy."[189] This persistent assessment prevented him and his colleagues to grow deeper relationships with people that would have opened more meaningful conversations about beliefs, both African and Christian.

---

187. Rattray, *Ashanti*, 135, 137.

188. BMA, D-1,1 Christiansborg 1830 #4 Henke to the Frankfurt Support Society October 2, 1830; Wurm, "Anfänge," 206.

189. BMA, D-1,1 Christiansborg 1831 #5 Henke January 30, 1831.

Another promising area was the Basel Mission stance on vernacular languages. Even though it led to no tangible results for many years, it is significant that Basel missionaries adopted a different approach than most Danish agents before. A school commission at Christiansborg was perplexed by discrepancies in the spelling of Ga in the translations of Protten, Wrisberg, and Schøning and "wrongly concluded ... that the Ga language was far too inarticulate and poor to be suitable as a medium of instruction and as a literary language."[190] The missionaries questioned this conclusion that even their instructions had referred to. Strongly exhorted throughout their training of the importance for people to hear and read God's word in their own language, they resolved to "learn the Accra-language with all seriousness and diligence" to decide whether the school in Osu should be established in "Accra" or Danish.[191] Repeatedly they expressed the desire to be able to speak to people in their language and they soon discovered that Ga "is difficult to speak for Europeans, but not as poor as its reputation."[192] They also defended its use against the recommendation that a language should have "at least 100,000 people to merit the effort" with reference to Greenlandic which the Moravians wrote down, "even though there were five times fewer people."[193] However, their untimely deaths ended this effort. The remaining survivor was compelled to engage in a ministry they had not envisioned and were not prepared for: chaplaincy.

Village Ideal Preventing Them to See Chaplaincy as Mission

The 1828 instructions clearly reveal a subliminal tension between the Basel Mission ideal of missionary work and the compromise of interests that enabled them to send missionaries to Ghana under Danish auspices.[194] According to their arrangement, one of the missionaries was to take care of the church and school for Europeans and Mulattos who were by name Christians. The Board mentioned the Danish establishments consistently with reverence, but emphasized the particular task of the missionaries to

---

190. Debrunner, *Christianity in Ghana*, 92. Christian Schiønning (1764–1817), governor April 15, 1807 to March 1, 1817, translated the Ten Commandments, Lord's Prayer, and Apostles Creed.

191. BMA, D-1,1 Christiansborg 1829 #1 Henke January 21, 1829; MM 1829, 522.

192. BMA, D-1,1 Christiansborg 1829 #3 Holzwarth January 31, 1829.

193. BMA, D-10.3,3 Instructions 1828 (III); D-1,1 Christiansborg 1829 #3 Holzwarth January 31, 1829.

194. BMA, D-10.3,3 Instructions 1828 (I and III).

work among Africans and evinced contempt for coastal settlements. For example, the existing fort school was a "charitable preparatory work on this coast" which they should build on to "expand the spread of Christian culture and religion among the Negros." But they were to "guard carefully against getting involved in political affairs, trade, or other merely temporary things which do not … directly further your missionary work among the African Negros." They were not "traders, public servants, preachers of an existing church, government employed teachers, but … messengers of Jesus Christ in the heathen world." This was "the true meaning of the holy profession for which your Christian brothers in Europe sent you to Africa."

Thus injected with a sense of caution, the Basel missionaries arrived with preconceived negative evaluations of the people they would encounter on the African coast and with the hope to move quickly to a ministry solely directed to native Africans beyond coastal settlements. Their directives had referred them back to the Liberia instructions for an outline of the "nature of the missionary profession."[195] Its foundations were choosing a mission station, building "huts" for themselves, and establishing gardens and farms to provide the necessities of life with the expectation that they would become self-sufficient eventually.[196] However, the reality they experienced for many years was that circumstances forced a sole survivor to fill the chaplaincy position in Christiansborg.

Official Agreements, Unrealistic Expectations, and Economic Need

Initially, Henke and Holzwarth shared the chaplain responsibilities in the fort, preaching and teaching baptism candidates and children without official employment or remuneration.[197] Frequent sickness meant that all of them spent most of their time and energy on these tasks. Chaplaincy was not "mission work" as they defined it, but the envisioned ministry directed to "pure" Africans in supposedly untouched areas proved unrealistic. Not only did such imagined "untouched areas" not exist, even among Africans, in the coastal settlement agriculture for self-support

195. BMA, D-10.3,3 Instructions 1828, 1–2.

196. Instructions 1827 in MM 1830, 458–62. They were to establish gardens and farms in order to "win the necessities of life for the missionary family from their own soil."

197. BMA, D-1,1 Christiansborg 1829 #10 Henke Diary, December 25, 1828 to January 20, 1829.

was out of the question. They had to rent a house, rather than build one, and purchase food.

Moreover, communication and support from Basel were perpetually delayed. By August 1829 Henke intended to apply to the Danish king for the post of the fort preacher.[198] He received the affirmative response from the Board only after economic dire straits, Trentepohl's encouragement, and a letter from Denmark offering him the position had caused him to accept the employment.[199] The material need that contributed to the decision to become a government employee against explicit instructions can only be deducted "between the lines." It is hidden in requests for regular shipment of food stuffs and accounts of barrels, mattresses, blankets, shoes, and other equipment destroyed by rust, termites, and cockroaches.[200] Left alone, Henke also moved to a rented room and eventually back to the fort.[201] For the remainder of his time interactions with local Africans were very limited.

The Basel Board eventually had to revise its parsimonious missionary support. The last Basel missionary in Liberia sharply criticized this policy.[202] Kißling highlighted the unhelpfulness of the Board's prohibition to build a second room for the school and the "untenable notion" of a self-supporting mission in Africa. In 1833 the Board finally decided to offer Andreas Riis the necessary finances, whether he decided to return home or stay, and even Schlatter, who is typically uncritical of Board policies, comments that they "had to learn to accept the necessity and value of friendly provision," if they wanted their missionaries to survive in Africa.[203]

The official explanation for accepting the chaplaincy, still upheld by later Basel Mission authors, was to prevent someone else taking the post, especially a "rationalist."[204] As recent as 1967 Debrunner defends

198. BMA, D-1,1 Christiansborg 1829 #10 Henke August 10, 1829.

199. BMA, KP December 9, 1829; D-1,1 Christiansborg 1829 #1 Henke March 11, 1830; Wurm, "Anfänge," 205. At this point the Board was still unaware that the other three had died.

200. For example: BMA, D-1,1 Christiansborg 1829 #3 Holzwarth January 31, 1829.

201. BMA, D-1,1 Christiansborg 1830 #2 Henke May 20, 1830.

202. Cited in Schlatter, *Basler Mission in Afrika*, 16.

203. Ibid., 27; Wurm, "Anfänge," 245–46. The decision is recorded in BMA, KP January 9, 1833.

204. BMA, KP December 9, 1829; Wurm "Anfänge," 205.

the Basel missionaries against "sophisticated rationalists" criticizing their simplicity, humble artisan background, and "crude orthodoxy, lacking . . . manners and . . . the simplest erudition" by commending their "straightforward and wholehearted" faith that "preserved them from the temptation to while away their time in conversation with their countrymen."[205]

No Vision and Not Prepared for Urban Ministry

Debrunner's comments illustrate the abiding priorities in the Basel Mission that evince no vision for the decadent Europeans or multi-cultural urban context of the coastal communities. The Basel Mission village ideal was in stark contrast with disdained city life. The perception of cities as evil they brought from their Pietist context acted to reinforce the general European Protestant disapproval of African coast towns.

Consequently, not only did the missionaries not have a vision for chaplaincy, nothing in their training had prepared them for the challenges urban ministry involved. The mixed-race, multi-cultural, and multi-lingual community did not fit the expectations their instructions built on. Apart from the impossibility to live on subsistence farming, the mixed character of the community presented a problem in identifying which language to learn. Their directive that Danish would be most useful proved challenging as few people knew Danish beyond what they needed for daily use.[206] Fante and Twi, recommended by the Board (because of their prevalence in British areas), were considered, but the missionaries eventually decided on Ga, even though it was spoken by fewer people. However, Henke was so occupied with teaching and preaching that little time remained for language learning. Furthermore, he found what Fage observes later, that in spite of limited proficiency, the European language was what this mixed community as a whole had in common.[207] The African language they shared was Ga. As a result Henke mostly worked bilingual with a translator.

Their incapacity and unwillingness to engage the multicultural, multiracial coastal community in Christian mission left the missionaries struggling to define the work and persistently longing to progress to the "real mission." Almost every letter testifies to their keen awareness of

---

205. Debrunner, *Christianity in Ghana*, 97.

206. BMA, D-10.3,3 Instructions 1828 (III); D-1,1 Christiansborg 1829 #5 Salbach March 20, 1829.

207. Fage, *Ghana*, 51.

home expectations and their desire and attempts towards work with Africans "unspoiled by the bad influence of Europeans." The main advance in that direction was Salbach's exploratory trip to Ningo and his plan to move there with Schmid.[208] These plans, however, came to nothing because of their untimely deaths.

Much is made of this option in the 1830 Annual Report in Basel.[209] It is a telling testimony to the tensions within the Board about the realities missionaries reported from Africa and the ambivalence the situation created towards their supporters. The report defends chaplaincy as worthwhile "preparatory ministry" and cites unidentified "further advantages for the missionary task" in the European settlements. But it is clear about the priority to "bring the light of divine knowledge to still completely ignorant and raw heathen tribes" and the conviction that mission work is "less obstructed ... in areas outside general European movements."[210] Salbach's letter is cited in detail culminating in a striking image of the "great field of work ... inland poor and dark Africa." So far the report was already written when the news of Salbach, Schmid, and Holzwarth's deaths finally reached Basel. It is an appendix to the report. Significantly, the earlier Liberian instructions from 1826 that outline the idealized rural vision of African mission work were published in the same edition of the *Missions-Magazin*.[211] During the period of this study the Basel Mission never revised their ideal of ground-breaking work in untouched African villages and their dismissal of coastal settlements.

PASTORING A DESPISED FLOCK

Consequently, the missionaries became pastors to a flock they despised. Not surprisingly, they had little success among them while constantly attempting to reach out to the "true heathen" whose life and religion they—ironically—despised as well. Their reports identify similar issues to Monrad earlier, complaining like him about Europeans' decadent and polygamous life style, their possession and ill-treatment of African slaves as well as the immorality, debauchery, and deceptiveness of mulattos. The

---

208. BMA, D-1,1 Christiansborg 1829 #5 and #7 Salbach March 20 and June 30, 1829. His report is cited extensively in HB 1830, 25–27; Wurm, "Anfänge," 200–3.

209. MM 1830, 406–9.

210. MM 1830, 407. The German word "roh" can be translated *raw, crude, barbarous* or *virgin, untouched*.

211. MM 1830, 451–82.

chaplaincy work consisted of preaching on Sundays to a small church of mostly nominal Christian Europeans, teaching the mixed-race children (about hundred in 1830) Danish, reading, and writing, and catechizing baptismal candidates.[212] Nobody on the coast had much interest in their role expanding to the native African population. The Board speculated that the mixed-race population could provide an inroad to Africans, but Henke's conclusions were unaltered: Mulattos were "altogether an extremely depraved class of people . . . who combine in them the evil of Europeans and Negros."[213] In the end he was so disturbed that he asked for advice whether he should even give the Lord's Supper to his unrepentant church.[214]

Obviously, the Basel missionaries were not alone in their evaluation of Europeans and their mixed-race descendants. Previous chaplains, other observers, and many more recent writers share their evaluation.[215] For example, Tufuoh cites Monrad and Henke to make his point that at Christiansborg "the climate was far from favorable to missionary enterprise," and the Europeans there "were certainly not the best advertisement for a civilization with which the Africans generally identified Christianity."[216] As we saw above, Europeans who came to Africa at the time were indeed of a questionable character, and the mixed race towns around forts had serious social and economic problems. However, the missionaries never seemed to perceive these perturbed, uprooted communities as a field for purposeful missionary engagement, but persisted in the vision of untouched "ignorant heathen tribes" that had guided their preparation. This inability to engage what was right in front of their eyes is a strong indication for the inflexibility to adjust to circumstances different from expectations which indicates trained incapacity. Henke died, alone left of the initial attempt to establish the Basel Mission in Ghana. Shortly, Andreas Riis picked up right where he left.

---

212. BMA, D-1,1 Christiansborg 1830 #1 Henke March 11, 1830. In this letter Henke gives a detailed account of his daily schedule which shows that most of his day was filled with teaching.

213. MM 1830, 407; BMA, D-1,1 Christiansborg 1830 #4 Henke October 2, 1830.

214. BMA, D-1,1 Christiansborg 1831 #6 Henke October 31, 1831.

215. As cited above: Cruickshank, *Eighteen Years, Vol. 1*; Debrunner, "Notable Danish Chaplains"; Isert, *Letters*; Monrad, *Description*.

216. Tufuoh, "Relations," 37–38.

CONCLUSIONS FROM THE FIRST BEGINNING OF THE BASEL MISSION IN AFRICA

This chapter outlined the historical context the Basel Missionaries entered in early nineteenth century Ghana and assessed the first group's missionary efforts. It identified many indications that the religious convictions and practical emphases the BMTI community of practice had established impeded the missionaries' adjustment to different situations, the realization of organizational goals, and positive African responses.

The most significant observation during this period is that the Basel Mission ideal of the missionaries' harmonious, loving brotherhood as attractive model of the Christian life broke down because of the practice of mutual supervision and reporting to superiors. This eroded relationships of mutual trust and caused perpetual conflicts between the missionaries. Furthermore, the supervisory, hierarchical dynamics of previous experience had not prepared them for the mutual, egalitarian leadership of the venture envisioned by the Board and became a factor in undermining the collaboration needed for emotional and physical survival. While there are some indications for rivalry with other missionary groups and disagreements over specific strategies in the unfamiliar context (major issues in other contemporary endeavors), the social relationships instilled by Basel missionaries' preparation processes were their most significant debilitating factor. Thus, they constitute a major case of trained incapacity.

Their different cultural origins and varying religious emphases contributed to the conflicts among the missionaries. Towards other Europeans and Africans in Guinea, however, it was BMTI instilled evaluations and practice that eroded supportive relationships and openness to the missionaries' message. The European image of Africa guided the missionaries' assessment of Africans they encountered and led them to conclude ulterior motives of financial gain and presume alcohol abuse as motivation, where, generally, genuine hospitality and religious traditions were the real driving factors. Preoccupation with the evils of slavery and Pietist morality caused rifts with the European and mixed-race population as well. Thus, the BMTI community had ensured confidence and criteria to judge others which proved destructive to relationships with everybody and hampered the missionaries' ability to attract people to Christianity.

Nevertheless, there are small indications that the missionary who persevered the longest made some revisions to the initial presumptions, especially regarding African intellectual ability and languages. Henke observed the equal intelligence of his African and mixed-race pupils to European children and the complexity of the Ga language. But he made no revisions of the moral disapproval of everyone he engaged with, from the children in the school to the Danish governor.

Finally, the Basel Mission rural ideals of "mission work" were confounded by colonial circumstances that forced missionaries to be chaplains. For this urban ministry to a mixed and uprooted community they had no vision and no strategy. Nothing in their training and experience had prepared them for this context. Consequently, they continued to offer negative evaluations that echoed Pietist disapproval of urban life but failed to elicit positive responses from their congregation. Instead of revising their goals to reach out to the needy people around them, the missionaries continued to nurture visions of a rural "Christian" settlement. But the Basel Mission goals of establishing a mission station among and reaching "pure" Africans remained elusive during this period.

5

Andreas Riis's Pioneering (1832–1840)

WITH RIIS THE MAN arrived in 1832 who is hailed as the pioneer and founder of the Basel Mission in Ghana.[1] After four months he also was a lone survivor. Like Henke, he had to be chaplain in Christiansborg until a permanent replacement arrived in December 1834. Riis made the crucial decision to move to Akuropon, the capital of Akuapem. Not only was this finally the kind of mission among Africans outside European influence they had envisioned, it included the important discovery that—contrary to previous perceptions—Akuapem provided a healthier climate than the coastal settlements.[2] King Addo Dankwa (Okuapemhene 1816–1836) welcomed the missionary, a house was built, Riis began learning Twi and set out on reconnaissance trips of the area. In October 1835 he requested the permission to marry and asked for reinforcements who would find a large house and a wide field of ministry.[3] Notified of this improved situation, the Board decided to send Andreas Stanger (1811–1837), Johannes Mürdter (1809–1838), and—as a bride for Riis—the first Basel Mission woman, Anna Margaretha Wolters (1816–1845). They arrived in November 1836. However, in the meantime, political disturbances had forced Riis to spend several months in Christiansborg, and the repercus-

---

1. For example, Debrunner, "Moses"; Steiner, "Andreas Riis."

2. Both, the 1827 and 1828 instructions advised the missionaries to stay at the coast until they were acclimatized to the tropical climate. See BMA, D-10.3,3a1) Instructions 1828, 8–9 (II); MM 1830, 455.

3. BMA, D-1,1 Christiansborg 1835 #9 Riis October 10, 1835; printed in MM 1836, 564.

sions were to affect the mission's engagement in Africa for some time to come.

A revised biography of Andreas Riis would be highly desirable because of the prevailing hagiographic accounts of his pioneering role.[4] However, I will focus on specific aspects of his experience that illustrate trained incapacity or its overcoming.

Figure 5
Andreas Riis in 1831[5]

RIIS'S PIOUS UPBRINGING AND MISSIONARY TRAINING

Andreas Riis was born on January 12, 1804 in Løgumcloster, Schleswig, and grew up speaking German and Danish. The original official entry in Basel omitted that Schleswig, culturally a German region, was under Danish governance.[6] Both parents died early, and after the father's death Riis finished a glazier apprenticeship with his older brother and

---

4. Examples are Oelschner, *Landung in Osu*; Opoku, *Riis, the Builder*.

5. BMA, QS-30.001.0082.01: "Riis, Andreas." Creator unknown, 1831, *BMArchives*, http://www.bmarchives.org/items/show/100206874.

6. BMA, BV 124 Riis, Andreas, "Dänemark" (Denmark) is obviously added later. Peter Jäger and Hans Nicolai Riis also came from Schleswig (BV 106, BV 247). Another student from this region was Christian Gottlieb Forchhammer (BV 178). In his record the remark that this was in Denmark is missing.

continued to work for him. His biographical account from 1827 reveals a rather timid young man who articulated a thoroughly Pietist faith.[7] He described his religious upbringing and "falling into sin" rather vaguely as if there were no specific transgressions to be accounted.[8] From an early age "thinking seriously about his eternal salvation . . . , reading the Word of God, and . . . spiritual conversations" shaped him. His pastor's reference letter confirms that Riis "unmistakably tends to think little of himself" and was "thoroughly revived, strong, and healthy, a lively but sober nature, without scientific education, only speaking Danish and German without knowing grammar, but showing mental facilities and talents."[9] Thus, while Riis did not originate from the South-West German region prominent in the BMTI, he grew up in a similar socio-economic and religious environment, marked by rural subsistence through agriculture and practical trades, Pietist fellowships, and traditional patriarchal relationships.

Exposure to Pietist Missions

Riis attests to "frequent talk about missions." There are at least two confirmed exposures to Pietist foreign mission efforts. Oelschner opens his narrative biography of Riis describing a close friendship with the famed missionary Hans Nicolajsen (1803–1856) when he visited Løgumcloster in 1825 between his training by Jänecke in Berlin and departure for Jerusalem.[10] Given their close age and origin in the same village, it is certain they knew each other and probable they went to school and the local fellowship together. Riis would have witnessed Nicolajsen's decision to

---

7. BMA, PF 124 Andreas Riis, *Lebenslauf* (autobiographical account).

8. The German word he uses frequently to describe his sinful ways is "Leichtsinn" which could be translated carelessness or foolishness.

9. BMA, PF 124 Andreas Riis, Matthiesen in his first letter on Riis from July 22, 1827.

10. Oelschner, *Landung in Osu*, 7–16. Nicolajsen (John Nicolayson) became well known as one of the first Protestant missionaries to Jews in Jerusalem with the London Society for Promoting Christianity amongst the Jews. This society had its roots in the LMS and was founded in 1809 by the Messianic Christian Joseph Samuel C.F. Frey (1771–1850). Its name was later shortened to London Jews Society (LJS) and it is today the Church's Ministry among Jewish People (CMJ). In fact, Nicolajsen was at Jänicke's missionary college in Berlin only from 1821 to 1823 and attended LJS's newly established seminary at Stanstead Park from 1823 to 1825 before he departed from London on August 25, 1825. A visit home that summer for final farewells is probable. See Kjær-Hansen, "John Nicolayson"; "CMJ'S History."

become a missionary which makes Oelschner's imagined challenge by the friend to volunteer himself quite believable. Oelschner also describes relationships with the Moravian village Christiansfeld about thirty-five miles north-east of Løgumcloster. Given that later Riis requested a wife from this village and Anna did originate from there, this too seems plausible.[11] In Christiansfeld the ten missionaries who lost their lives in Guinea in the first Moravian attempt (1737–1770) would have still been remembered.[12] The church declined the request for a second attempt in 1773, but at least one member, Anna's brother H. Wolters, was a Moravian missionary in Antigua.[13]

Consequently, Riis's biography shows great awareness of the possibility of martyrdom and is permeated by a somberness that alternates between the conviction of personal calling and feelings of inadequacy and apprehension. However, impressed by what he learned about missionaries who had "left everything out of love for their savior to win souls for him," Riis felt an increasing "desire to offer himself for the ministry of the Lord in the cause of mission" and applied in Basel in September 1827.[14]

Shaping Experiences in Basel

In Basel Riis was exposed to the intense curriculum, emphasis on order, punctuality, diligence, humility, and personal spirituality of the BMTI, and the strong, fatherly personality of Blumhardt. He did not attract much attention—negative or positive. The traits of deep religious conviction and Pietist ethics obvious in his autobiography were encouraged and strengthened. For Riis the most significant impact of the BMTI was increased confidence and clear definition of the missionary task by the

---

11. BMA, D-1,1 Christiansborg 1835 #9 Riis October 10, 1835; BV 124, PF 124 "Riis, Andreas," and Familien Register FRI:1a.

12. Oelschner cites eight graves in 1768. In fact, ten Moravians went to work with Christian Protten 1737, 1768, and 1769; all of them and Protten died by 1770. A second attempt requested by the Danish Trading Company in 1773 (the founding year of the Christiansfeld Moravian Church) was refused in light of the previous sacrifices. See Beck, *Brüder in vielen Völkern*, 110–12.

13. Anna visited her brother in Antigua on route to the West Indies in 1842. See *Periodical Accounts, Vol. 16*, 156 "Miscellaneous Intelligence" June 1842 Report. His name is misspelled "Wotiler" in this report.

14. BMA, PF 124 Riis, Andreas. His autobiographic account is dated September 16, 1827.

shared vision. This is illustrated throughout his correspondence from Africa.

During his time students followed with excitement and trepidation the beginnings and difficulties of the Basel Mission ventures in Liberia and Ghana. Again, Oelschner describes imaginatively how the news in June 1830 of the deaths in Guinea almost a year earlier must have impressed on the BMTI community.[15] It confirmed the seriousness of their venture and strengthened their passionate resolve. When Riis was designated for Guinea with his fellow Dane Jäger and the Saxon Heinze (who had studied medicine at Basel University) in April 1831, they brazed for the possibility to lay down their lives for this calling.[16]

In 1830 Switzerland erupted in civil unrest in the wake of the French July revolution.[17] This beginning of the Regeneration Movement's fight against traditional structures which led to the 1848 Swiss constitution was experienced by BMTI students with mixed feelings. As most were foreigners and the leadership strongly emphasized political neutrality, they saw their primary involvement in tending to the wounded on both sides. Later Riis attempted to emulate this response in a similar situation in Africa.

Indications for Strained Danish Relationships

Henke's reports of enforced chaplaincy and "rationalist" opposition contributed to the protracted considerations by the Board about continuing the African mission. Beyond the death toll, they felt hindered by Bishop Münter who insisted on a lengthy stay in Denmark and opposed German ordination. However, with two of the designated being Danish and unwilling to delay, the Basel Mission eventually ordained them in Lörrach on July 15, 1831. Jäger and Riis still had to visit Denmark to obtain permissions from the Danish king and connect with their Support-Societies. They report "almost everywhere joyful support" for their mission, and their audience with King Frederick VI (1768–1839, reign 1808–1839) brought the desired permissions to work and authorization for Heinze to practice medicine in Guinea. Wurm and Schlatter indicate a probability

---

15. Oelschner, *Landung in Osu*, 21–22.

16. This first attempt at sending a medical doctor is significant and reflects their recognition of the health challenges. However, Heinze quickly died and the Basel Mission did not engage in medical work in Africa until the 1860s.

17. "Regeneration 1830–48"; "History of Switzerland."

that the king also coerced the bishop to confirm their ordination a few days later.[18]

The progress of events indicates that Basel Mission relationships with Danish Church authorities were uneasy. Later articles by German mission circles on Danish foreign mission engagement confirm this analysis.[19] Pietist groups always were in the minority and often opposed and ridiculed by church officials, both in Denmark and in Germany. Bahl rightly asserts that Danish protestant missionary involvement depended on initiatives from Germany, the fact that Denmark had colonies early on, and the support of piously minded kings. Predictably, the reluctant acceptance of the Basel Mission by Danish ecclesiastical authorities later created difficulties for its agents.

REVISED PERSPECTIVES OF SOME AFRICANS AND EUROPEANS

Initially, Riis faced similar challenges as Henke. After the death of his colleagues and a Danish minister he was compelled to stand in as chaplain, even though he refused to officially take on the position.[20] His general evaluations parallel Henke's, describing Europeans' immorality and mistreatment of Africans and Africans' deceptiveness.[21] However, he revised some of these views in the face of African realities.

Reliance on an African Healer

His training predisposed Riis to a negative evaluation of everything African, and many references in his letters testify to this attitude. He attributed European cruelty to African tendencies to lie and steal, complained about the "deafening noise" and drunkenness of African celebrations, and summarily described Africans as "a poor and ignorant generation, deeply entangled in sin."[22] He also shared the earlier missionaries' presumption of ulterior motives that assumed expectations of gifts behind

---

18. Schlatter, *Basler Mission in Afrika*, 26; Wurm, "Anfänge," 240. See also Oelschner, *Landung in Osu*, 25–30.

19. Bahl, "Die dänische Missionsthätigkeit"; Stocks, "Die Mission in Dänemark."

20. BMA, D-1,1 Christiansborg 1833 #4 Riis September, 22, 1833.

21. For example: BMA, D-1,1 Christiansborg 1832 #12 Riis June 6, 1832.

22. BMA, D-1,1 Christiansborg 1832 # 12 Riis June 6, 1832; Christiansborg 1835 #11 Riis diary March 26, April 4 and 26, 1835 (printed in MM 1836, 510–64).

every African assistance.²³ Their Instructions went as far as to suggest learning "from the abhorrent slave traders... who managed to stay alive and healthy on this coast," but never implied that native Africans might be able to help them survive.²⁴ However, in this respect Riis revised his negative predisposition drastically.

Within a few weeks all three fell sick and Heinze died six weeks after their arrival. Feeling somewhat better, Jäger and Riis went to the plantations. On this trip—against their humility value and aversion to such "slave labor"—they gave in to European custom and allowed themselves to be carried in hammocks half of the way.²⁵ This was based on the assumption that physical exertion caused European illness. It proved in vain for Jäger who died in July, leaving Riis alone. He was also sick for weeks before he could return to Christiansborg—in a hammock.

Up to this point they had sought help with other Europeans and the fort physician Tietz. But in August Riis fell seriously ill again and when he did not recover for weeks, he became desperate enough to compromise his assumptions and Basel Mission instructions. Following the advice of seasoned Europeans, he allowed a "Negro doctor" to treat him. Later he reported:

> Under the treatment of Dr. Tietz, I became weaker and the sickness worse each day.... Some old Europeans, who visited me and recognized my ailment from experience... pleaded that I refrain from taking that medicine, but rather I should contact a Negro-doctor.... [He] washed me every time with soap and lemon and then with plain cold water all over my body and that was the whole cure: The cold baths were not only very pleasant and invigorating, but also worked upon the illness extremely quickly.²⁶

Riis continued to trust this African herbalist and claimed in 1834 that "the present European physician is useless. Nobody trusts him nowadays..., those he recently treated all died, while no European who was

---

23. BMA, D-1,1 Christiansborg 1835 #11 Riis diary March 23; MM 1836, 516.

24. Instructions 1827 in MM 1830, 461. See also BMA, D-10.3,3a1) Instructions 1828, 8. Here "other inhabitants" whose advice and experience they were to consult were obviously other *Europeans* in contrast to the consistent depiction of Africans as "Negros" in these instructions.

25. BMA, D-1,1 Christiansborg 1832 #14 Riis August 10, 1832.

26. BMA, D-1,1 Christiansborg 1832 #15 Riis December 2, 1832.

242   PART II: Indications for Trained Incapacity

treated by the Negro has died."[27] This was a major paradigm shift from the view of African medicine as inferior superstition and from the prevailing perception that Africans had nothing significant to offer. It also contradicted the stereotyping descriptions of traditional practices as dark and in need of salvation that Riis's gave otherwise. The main reason for this change of mind was probably his desperation, caused by the deaths of his colleagues and his own prolonged and recurring sicknesses.

Various authors' comments are interesting. Wurm gives a brief account of Riis's healing by the "negro-doctor" treatment, but his main remarks concentrate on the need for more generous financial support (which Basel finally granted its Africa missionary in 1833) and a lengthy defense of hammock travel as a necessity "for protection of their health" in a land "where there are no horses or carts."[28] Schlatter treats the African healer even more curtly and cites Wurm adding that "grave experience" taught the missionaries "the inner freedom . . . to be grateful for the hammock and leave the proud ideal of needlessness in Africa."[29] Even these later Basel Mission representatives had not revised the European evaluation of African abilities. But they felt the necessity to defend Riis's means of transportation to the European supporters of the organization. The "proud ideal of needlessness" continued to influence the missionaries' actions in other aspects, as we will see. By contrast, the African author Opoku, emphasizes the contribution of the African herbalist to Riis's survival and mentions explicitly that he healed him on several separate instances.[30]

For this study it is significant that Riis became what Miller calls a "strategic deviant" who went against instructions and engrained BMTI practice, in order to further the goals of the mission.[31] Miller emphasizes the organizational dynamic that such men were praised in public, while their creative initiative triggered internal tensions. In this context he uses the concept of *trained incapacity* to explain that the majority of Basel missionaries did not dare to break out of established patterns; they rather waited for the slow communication lines to reach them with instructions than taking independent action. His observation confirms that inability

27. BMA, D-1,1 Christiansborg 1834 #6a Riis June 10, 1834.
28. Wurm, "Anfänge," 244–46.
29. Schlatter, *Basler Mission in Afrika*, 27.
30. Opoku, *Riis, the Builder*, 9–14.
31. Miller, *Missionary Zeal*, 124–31.

to alter engrained patters was the rule. Riis managed to overcome this trained incapacity in some aspects. In part, this was also true for his decision to move to Akuropon. Relationships with some other Europeans became important in discerning this location.

Friendship and Support from some Europeans

By and large Riis concurred with the negative preconception of Europeans on the coast as degraded, immoral, and cruel, but he showed some independent evaluation from the beginning. His first letter commented that "apart from living in illicit liaisons with Mulatto and Negro women, the whites here are perhaps not worse than in many European towns."[32] Riis's exceptions began with President Maclean in Cape Coast whose support of Christian missions impressed the missionaries. Had Henke found "neither clergy nor teacher and not the least desire for them" in 1828, Riis and his colleagues met a church service conducted by Maclean and a well-attended school.[33] Debrunner asserts that "Maclean ... developed a real and lasting friendship with the Basel missionary ... and repeatedly urged and invited Riis to move from the Danish territories to the English sphere of influence on Cape Coast."[34] It is hard to determine how close this relationship actually was, but there were certainly mutual appreciation, repeated invitations, and practical support that later created problems for Riis with the Danish governor Mørck. This contact also provided an alternative supply route for goods and communication with Basel to the often infrequent and unreliable Danish ships.[35]

In Christiansborg Riis met the Danish trader Georg Lutterodt early on and by June reported that they ate their main meal with him and acquired from him what they needed advantageously.[36] Lutterodt's experience and positive stance towards their mission proved an invaluable asset. Not only were the missionaries able to get supplies from him,

32. BMA, D-1,1 Christiansborg 1832, #12 Riis from June 6, 1832.

33. BMA, D-1,1 Christiansborg 1829 #1 Henke diary December 10, 1828; MM 1829, 513; Christiansborg 1832 #8 Heinze April 2, 1832; Metcalfe, *Maclean*, 118-19.

34. Debrunner, *Christianity in Ghana*, 96. See BMA, D-1,1 Christiansborg 1832 #12b Riis June 6, 1832; Akropong 1836 #1 Riis February 10, 1836; Akropong 1837 # 9 Mürdter October 25, 1837.

35. Mentioned, for example, in BMA, D-1,1 Christiansborg 1837 #5 Riis, Mürdter, and Stanger April 30, 1837.

36. BMA, D-1,1 Christiansborg 1832 #12 Heinze (a), Riis (b), Jäger (c) June 6-20, 1832.

he invited them to his plantation for recuperation and was most likely behind their ideas to start a school on the plantations.[37] After the death of his colleagues Riis stayed in Lutterrodt's Osu house. It was also the trader who introduced him to Akuapem already in November 1832. Riis reported excitedly the beauty and fruitfulness of the land and the friendly reception by the people and envisaged living among these Africans, learning their language, and teaching the youth.[38] Opoku rightly suggests that Lutterrodt's trade connection with Akuapem gave the impetus, and Isert's previous glowing accounts and plans for the region inspired Riis's vision to move to Akuropon.[39]

Thus, Riis aligned himself with a European trader who like others had an African wife and almost certainly had "serfs" working for him. As we saw above, serfs were not that different from slaves in the treatment they received. Consequently, the missionary's friendship implied compromises with important Basel Mission values and practices like the opposition to any form of slavery and European immorality in Africa. It indicates that he overcame some aspects of the trained incapacity to build relationships with others on the coast who could offer assistance.

Reluctant Chaplain with Familiar Tensions

However, Riis's attitude to the chaplaincy was similar, if not less favorable than Henke's. He too, had no vision for this urban ministry as valid Christian missionary work. Opoku comments that impatiently "Riis awaited the arrival of a chaplain from Europe to relieve him of the undesired job" because he "considered the time as a chaplain wasted" and a "real burden to lead an idle life," in spite of the busy work in school and congregation.[40] From his recovery in December 1832 Riis functioned as chaplain. In summer 1833 a new Danish chaplain arrived but soon fell sick and died. Riis had investigated the possibility of establishing a mission in Ningo, but again felt obliged to take care of the Christiansborg

---

37. BMA, D-1,1 Christiansborg 1832 #13 Jäger and Riis June 20, 1832. Governor Lind supported such a school on the royal Danish plantation Frederiksgave in 1833, but the plan was thwarted by his death on July 21, 1833, less than five months after his return to Africa. See BMA, D-1,1 Christiansborg 1833 #1, #3, and #4 Riis June 6, August 19, September 22, 1833.

38. BMA, D-1,1 Christiansborg 1832 #15 Riis December 2, 1832; Wurm, "Anfänge," 244–45.

39. Opoku, *Riis, the Builder*, 15–16. See also Isert, *Letters*.

40. Opoku, *Riis, the Builder*, 14.

congregation.[41] Like Henke before, he gave up on living in the town and moved to a room in the fort in early 1834.

Riis's descriptions of the work parallel his predecessor's.[42] The mulatto school dominated. Even though now teachers were employed for the boys and the girls, he felt the need to supervise them "to maintain discipline." His evaluations emphasize the immoral and pagan context of the children's families, and he suggests a boarding school to remedy its influence. This idea was already articulated in Basel instructions and later implemented in Akuropon and Osu.[43] It expressed the same principles of training up young people in an intense community of practice, which undergirded the BMTI.

Riis's strong Pietist bias earned him ridicule and opposition from other Europeans. Like Henke, he was pastor to a flock he despised and, not surprisingly, reaped little and often negative response. Riis testifies to difficulties with the Europeans whose friendliness towards him had disappeared "because of his ... love of the truth when speaking about sin."[44] For a time, he even found his friendship with Lutterodt disturbed which was part of the reason why he moved to the fort and was eating his main meal with the War Commissioner Richter by then. Thus, Riis also displayed the trained incapacity to engage the multi-cultural urban context as Christian mission. In Basel attitudes remained unrevised too. The detailed publication of Riis's account of the Ningo trip shows continuing embarrassment about chaplaincy.[45] Like before, Ningo was held up as prospect for "true mission work" towards the supporters, in spite of the resistance Riis reported.[46]

It is not surprising that Basel Mission related authors like Schlatter and Smith dismiss the coastal community in favor of ministry "among a truly indigenous people as yet largely unaffected by the demoralizing influence of Europeans on the coast."[47] More significantly, some African

---

41. BMA, D-1,1 Christiansborg 1833 #1 and 4, Riis letters from June 6 and September 22, 1833.

42. BMA, D-1,1 Christiansborg 1833 #5 and 6, Riis letters from April 1 and June 10, 1834.

43. Instructions 1827 §7 in MM 1830, 466.

44. BMA, D-1,1 Christiansborg 1834 #5 Riis April 1, 1834.

45. BMA, D-1,1 Christiansborg 1833 #1 Riis June 6, 1833; HB 1833, 79–81.

46. BMA, D-1,1 Christiansborg 1834 #6a Riis June 10, 1834. His report highlights the resistance of the Ningo elders against establishing a European school in their town.

47. Smith, *Presbyterian Church*, 30; Schlatter, *Basler Mission in Afrika*, 27–28.

scholars like Opoku and Antwi also cite this view uncritically.[48] This indicates that they too consider urban ministry at the time futile.

"OSIADAN" THE HOUSE-BUILDER—AFRICAN AND EUROPEAN PERCEPTIONS

The desire to work among indigenous people and the drier, cooler mountain climate were among the reasons Riis moved to Akuropon when he was relieved from chaplaincy in 1835.[49] The "duke," as Riis usually referred to the ruler, Okuapemhene Addo Dankwa, welcomed the missionary presence for his own hopes of political advantages in the ongoing internal strife and "rivalry between the Danish and the English trading companies . . . for commercial supremacy."[50] Riis rejoiced to finally being able to begin "real mission work," enjoyed the hospitality and support of the Okuapemhene, and set about establishing a station. However, he faced numerous unforeseen obstacles. Riis struggled with the physical work of building a house and breaking ground for European type agriculture, the unfamiliar African culture, and building deeper relationships. In this context of unexpected challenges Riis's actions have drawn contradictory evaluations.

Was Riis "An African to Africans"?

Antwi claims that Riis was a "strategist and facilitator in horizontal mission" because he developed a "methodology of 'becoming an African to Africans'" which from the perspective of nineteenth century Eurocentric mission was "probably an aberration."[51] He builds mostly on Opoku's biography that presents a similar strongly positive assessment of Riis's relationships with Africans.[52] Certainly, Riis's diaries report that he lived in the simple accommodation Addo Dankwa provided, staying in one room

---

48. Antwi, "African Factor," 59; Opoku, *Riis, the Builder*, 15.

49. BMA, D-1,1 Christiansborg 1835 #7 Riis February 27, 1835 describes his exploratory visit in January 1835. MM 1836, 510–564 are published extensive excerpts of BMA, D-1,1 Christiansborg 1835 #9 and #11 Riis's letter from October 10 and diary from March 19 to October 7, 1835 in which he described his move to Akuropon, convivial reception by the Okuapemhene, and settling there.

50. Kwamena-Poh, *Akuapem State*, 95.

51. Antwi, "African Factor," 58–60.

52. Opoku, *Riis, the Builder*, iii, 79–86.

with several people and various animals.⁵³ He slept, ate, and worked with Africans. He had become used to African food, even snail soup and "half rotten fish," not only because it was burdensome to carry food along, but also because he wanted to "get as close to the Africans as was possible and conducive to introducing Christianity."

He attests to numerous conversations with Addo Dankwa that touched various subjects of interest to the king and explanations of African customs and thought as well as Riis's biblical message.⁵⁴ The African ruler appreciated and sought out these interactions. Every evening Riis shared with "his people" (his employees) and anybody gathering around. Opoku concludes that these descriptions show someone who "was able to befriend the Africans and win their respect" and did his "evangelistic work not so much by street preaching as by conversations with people who came to see him."⁵⁵ Furthermore, Riis did not take a "fanatic and over zealously destructive" attitude to the "fetish service" but even observed local taboos.⁵⁶

It seems Riis managed to adjust well, thereby overcoming much of the trained incapacity that prevented his predecessors from associating closely with African "heathen." Then again, many of Riis's behaviors were in line with Basel Mission instructions that charged him to win the trust of Africans by showing kindness, "patiently forgiving their weaknesses, and serving them in love."⁵⁷ Missionaries' lives were to convince by quiet confidence, unselfish love, simple honesty, and eager service for African's well-being, not through hostile opposition or ridicule even of fetish priests.⁵⁸ Those aspects suggest that there were areas of BMTI training that did not incapacitate the missionaries for intercultural engagement, but prepare them for it.

However, even though the Basel Mission instructions encouraged relationships and learning African ways, their rationale reveals European perceptions of Africa. Simplicity, love, and patience was required of missionaries because Africans were ignorant, and "resembled immature children" who needed caring fatherly guidance to overcome the mistrust

53. MM 1836, 526. Riis diary April 16, 1835.
54. For example MM 1836, 526 and 536–37, Riis diary April 16 and May 18, 1835.
55. Opoku, *Riis, the Builder*, 80.
56. Ibid., 79, viii–ix.
57. BMA, Instructions 1827 in MM 1830, 470–72.
58. BMA, D-10.3,3a1) Instructions 1828 (III) "Euer Missionsgeschäft auf jener Küste."

European mistreatment and greed had caused.[59] Consequently, they proudly published the comment by an African, that Riis treated Africans differently, not like other whites.[60] Indeed, in comparison to European traders and soldiers, his interest in living among them and learning African culture was unusual. However, such relationships for the most part did not mean a revision of European judgments of Africa. While it is true that Riis lived closer to Africans than any Basel missionary before (or after), there is also ample evidence that he shared dominant European views. They included assumptions of notorious alcohol abuse, laziness, and immorality as "prevalent vice" among Africans.[61]

Riis's attitude to African religious traditions is illustrated by his description and assessment of the "Yam Festival" in September 1835.[62] Its proper name is *Odwira* and it was introduced in 1826 by Addo Dankwa after the defeat of the Asante as an annual festival when "all Akuapem pay homage to the ... paramount chief" in Akuropon "to unite the various communities by sentiments of solidarity and nationhood."[63] Its purposes also included purification of the King and his insignia, the royal stools, mourning for the dead, and harvest thanksgiving. Rattray describes the *Odwira* in the context of death and funerals because he identifies it as "essentially a rite in connexion with the dead" that was held "in honour and propitiation of the Ashanti kings who 'had gone elsewhere' and for the cleansing of the whole nation from defilement."[64]

Riis's comments reveal both, his pioneering observations of African traditions and his shortcomings. While Rattray focuses on detailed description of ceremonies by religious professionals, Riis provides a perspective closer to the common people. He recounts the giving of presents of "firewood, yam, meat, and chicken" to friends and neighbors—a custom still practiced today. The actual ceremony is brief in Riis's account

---

59. Instructions from 1827 in MM 1830, 471–72.

60. MM 1836, 525; Riis diary April 14, 1835.

61. For example MM 1836, 524, Riis diary April 7–8, 1835 (requests for brandy and drunkenness); MM 1836, 550–51, Riis diary August 17, 1835 (the laziness and unfaithfulness of Africans in building his house); MM 1836, 563, Riis diary October 7, 1835 (immorality as "prevalent vice" among Africans).

62. MM 1836, 560–62, Riis diary September 27, 1835.

63. Kwamena-Poh, *Akuapem State*, 11–12, 49, 59, 135, 149–50.

64. Rattray, *Religion and Art*, 122–43. Rattray cites extensively from Bowdich, *Mission from Cape Coast Castle*, 226–30, but emphasizes that the impression of a drunken orgy given by previous authors was "most unfair in judging these customs by these outward signs."

and seeps of his contempt for the "great din" of drumming and dancing, the drunkenness of commoners, and the "commotion late into the night." Riis presents one major part of the ceremony only from the description of his "nosy translator" because he had "withdrawn" and it "happened behind a curtain." A possible explanation is that as a foreigner he was excluded from proceedings, but his account implies that his Pietist sensitivities were hurt by watching the pagan rituals. Most revealing is the final commentary on his "feelings of discomfort as a poor messenger of Christ among such hordes."

Even though Riis moved from a more confrontational approach with "fetish priests" early on to quietly listening to their explanations—accepting that arguing brought no results and only caused anger—and generally kept local taboos to avoid causing offense, he consistently offered his rational explanations of sickness and misfortunes.[65] While he had many conversations with African priests, he clearly stated that he found their visits a nuisance, and consistently dismissed them as lying, greedy deceivers of people.[66] This contradicts Oelschner's claim that Riis realized he "could not confront pagan officers with arrogant Western superiority" or regard their questions "as a mixture of nonsense and trickery."[67] Conversely, Riis's descriptions evince negative stereotypes throughout, in spite of his adjustments to African food and housing, and good relationships with some Africans. This indicates that he suffered from similar trained incapacity to overcome the European "image of Africa" as his colleagues. In fact, his letters evince a hardening of attitudes as I demonstrate below.

Furthermore, like other missionaries in pre-colonial times, alone as a foreigner in Akuropon, Riis's survival largely depended on "carefully cultivating alliances with local leaders," and as guest of an African ruler he relied heavily on his protection and provision of basic material needs.[68] Nevertheless, he could not resist offering advice whenever the opportunity arose. He consistently dismissed the king's beliefs to promote his

65. MM 1836, 554–55, Riis diary August 30 to September 16, 1835. The example for his keeping taboos in this section is that he did not eat yam before the festival like everybody else. But he offered his ideas about the weather and old age as reasons for sicknesses the king and others suffered.

66. An example for a lengthy discussion on the deceptiveness of "fetish priests" is MM 1836, 556–60, Riis diary September 20, 1835.

67. Oelschner, *Landung in Osu*, 90.

68. Barker, "Missionary Frontier," 86–87.

own, and acted according to his convictions even when it displeased the ruler. One example for the latter is his insistence to work alongside house slaves in order to "give an example of diligence worthy of imitation to the lazy Negros."[69]

Finally, the fact that Riis's letters and diaries are the only sources available for any assessment needs to be considered. One wonders what the perceptions of contemporary Africans of their relationship with the missionary truly were. However, Riis's accounts are sufficiently detailed and honest that they enable various perspectives on what happened. Opoku points out that Riis lived in the dichotomy of "recording both christian and non-christian [sic] history in one diary" as "a perfect stranger in a most incongenial [sic] society."[70] He and Antwi present Riis as someone who befriended Africans, avoided fanatic attitudes, and overcame Eurocentric mission. To the degree this is accurate, Riis either overcame the trained incapacity or Basel Mission practice did not actually incapacitate him. However, Quartey and Jenkins use the same accounts to come to quite different conclusions. Quartey identifies "colonial fantasies" and Jenkins highlights cultural insensitivity around the house building project.

Did Riis live out "Colonial Fantasies"?

From the outset it is important to notice that both, Seth Quartey and the scholar his section on Riis primarily builds on, Susanne Zantop, are primarily scholars of German literature, not historians.[71] Furthermore, the texts Zantop examines relate to Latin America and the Caribbean.[72] Nevertheless, hers is a fascinating analysis of "the emergence of 'latent colonialism,' as an unspecific drive for colonial possession" in German pre-colonial literature.[73] It articulated itself "not so much in statements of intent as in 'colonial fantasies': stories of sexual conquest and surrender,

---

69. MM 1836, 535–36, Riis diary May 13, 1835.

70. Opoku, *Riis, the Builder*, vii.

71. At the time his book was published Quartey was Assistant Professor of German at Washington and Jefferson College. See http://www.cambriapress.com/cambriapress.cfm?template=6&bid=83. Susanne Zantop (1945–2001) was tragically murdered with her husband in 2001. Both taught at Dartmouth College and the crime made considerable headlines at the time as the "Dartmouth College murders." For an obituary see Lennox et al., "In Memoriam: Susanne Zantop 1945–2001."

72. Zantop, *Colonial Fantasies*, 9.

73. Ibid., 3.

love and blissful domestic relations between colonizer and colonized, set in colonial territory." Quartey combines Zantop's framework with a random reference from the Comaroffs to a mission station as "place in which the seed might fall on fertile earth" to claim that Riis's "practices relegated the landscape to a feminine object over which he had power."[74] The primary incident Quartey uses to posit this thesis happened in March 1835 when Riis moved to Akuropon.[75]

From the outset there was disagreement between Riis and the African carriers he had employed. They opposed his choice of route—via Teshie which he possibly (and erroneously) supposed to be shorter. The following day Riis's insistence on starting out at one in the night (to avoid the heat of the day) made the carriers more disgruntled because they stumbled in the dark on the rugged path. Riis, however, attributed the true reason for their discontent to the lack of palm wine in which "they desired to swim." Eventually, he relented and let the Africans lead the way. That evening (after they had climbed the steep ascent of the Akuapem ridge) new quarrel arose about the weight of the luggage. Exasperated, Riis refused to negotiate and commanded that either they take the luggage to Akuropon without further complaints or else take it immediately back to Osu. He reports, "now their insolence left them as if the terror of God had fallen on them and the heavy burden of such stubbornness was lifted off my shoulders for the rest of the journey."

Ignoring the two days of ongoing negotiations and omitting Riis's compromise about the route, Quartey claims that he entered the scene "not ready for any discussion" and—his words resembling the "tone of a slave driver"—suggested "that the people are posited as inferior from the start, for it is the missionary who determines the rules of the game."[76] Quartey alleges that Riis refused requests for a rest, even though the incident happened in the evening and was followed by spending the night in Mampong. Requests for a rest were granted by Riis the following day

---

74. Quartey, *Missionary Practices*, 44, 48–49. He cites Comaroff and Comaroff, *Of Revelation and Revolution*, 181. The allegory of the landscape as feminine Quartey implies is not in Comaroff beyond the agricultural metaphor.

75. MM 1836, 510–13, Riis diary March 19–22, 1835. All citations in the following are my translations. Quartey and most Anglophone authors use a faulty English translation of this diary by Hans Debrunner from 1983 in BMA, D-10.27,8. This is surprising in Quartey's case, as his field is *German* literature.

76. Quartey, *Missionary Practices*, 51.

in Mamfe. Quartey creates the impression that all this happened in one incident.

From Riis's contemplations during the break in Mamfe Quartey posits that Riis, "drunk in his god and zealous to the brim" perceived "his actions as 'the will of my Lord.'... Assertiveness in his voice, [he] 'entered Akropong,' ready to take possession of land, body and mind.... Africa must be converted at all cost; cost in his life or those of his carriers." Quartey continues to argue—contrarily to Opoku and Antwi—Riis's "inability to grasp other people's thoughts, to understand and pursue genuine human relations," and perception of "the colonized as inferior beings ... to be dispossessed of those ideal landscapes in their possession."[77] However, Riis's sentiments contemplating his future in Akuropon were considerably more ambiguous than Quartey alleges. Riis writes:

> My thoughts went to Akropong ... where the dark future with its sorrows and sufferings was to reveal itself.... A strange mixture of dark thoughts made me fear this future and the sad feeling of my inadequacy to establish the great work I serve lay like a millstone on my soul. I felt wistfully how much I missed a faithful companion. There was nobody whom I could have entrusted with some of my burden except the invisible friend of my soul. He ... took my sin on himself and strengthened my soul through the grace of a glimpse of his mercy before I stepped on the ground which the guide of my life had assigned as my working place. Calmly and fully submitted to the blessed will of my savior, and in expectation of the fulfillment of his wise and gracious council ... I was able to enter Akropong.[78]

Apart from the fact that Quartey gravely misquotes Riis, these reflections reveal the inner struggle of a missionary who had been alone for almost three years, had seen many Europeans die, and struggled himself with repeated close death experiences. He was now about to embark on a totally new venture the outcome of which was unsure. His thoughts show someone who is torn between the challenges he anticipates and feelings of loneliness and inadequacy at the greatness of the task he feels called to. He finds comfort in his faith in God's presence, calling, and enabling grace.

Riis's long-winded pious language reflects the parlance of all Basel Mission publications and was well rehearsed during his training.

77. Ibid., 51–52.
78. MM 1836, 512–13, Riis diary March 22, 1835.

Regarding the thesis of this book, it provides evidence against trained incapacity of Basel missionaries. Much can be said about their stubborn persistence in the ways they internalized in Basel, often to the detriment of their declared objectives. But their deep-seated pious faith in God's grace through all challenges and their commitment to God's calling—as they understood it—at whatever cost enabled the remarkable endurance of BMTI graduates. Evidence for this attitude is common throughout the missionaries' letters and it is a major factor in Riis's perseverance.

Quartey's presentation is problematic for a variety of reasons. Not only does the way he skews Riis's words to serve his thesis lack scholarly integrity, he repeats similar suggestive selective citations throughout the book which contains many factual mistakes and faulty English translations of the German sources. He also ignores Riis's Danish citizenship—which should at least occasioned a justification of assigning *German* "colonial fantasies" to him. Furthermore, most of the literature Zantop analyzed would have been on the banned reading list in Basel and could therefore hardly influence the students. Most significantly, Quartey does not engage with the historical scholars who offer different evaluations of Riis. This makes his study an illustration of scholars from other fields that "dabble" in history to advance their theses without appreciation for historiographical issues, historical perspective, and engagement with historians.

Nonetheless, Quartey chimes into an often made accusation against missionaries. He does not discuss John and Jean Comaroff, but it is obvious that his thesis is informed by their claim of missionary collaboration with the colonial enterprise.[79] They posited European missionaries as "vehicles of a hegemonic worldview [who] purveyed its axioms in everything they said and did" and whose "prime object was to engage the Africans in a web of symbolic and material transactions that would bind them ever more securely to the colonizing culture." Earlier "postcolonial" authors voiced similar critique of missionaries.[80] A Ghanaian example is the poet and politician Kofi Nyidevu Awoonor who claimed missionaries

79. Comaroff and Comaroff, *Of Revelation and Revolution*.

80. "Postcolonial" authors analyze and respond to the legacies of European colonialism and imperialism in Africa and elsewhere. In particular, they critique the intellectual and social discourse of European colonization and address the problems and consequences of political and cultural independence. In Africa they often choose fiction, like Chinua Achebe who arguably contributed the most widely read novel: Chinua Achebe, *Things Fall Apart*.

"came because they were part of the large imperial scheme of things. They came to 'soften' us up so that the traders and their political masters could take over our resources."[81]

Such direct conclusions have been critiqued in various ways. Landau and Elbourne criticize the Comaroffs from an understanding of their specific South African context for oversimplifying complicated situations, overemphasizing missionary agency, and underestimating African agency, interests, and ability to selectively engage foreign agents and adapt their message.[82] Furthermore, "even before the advent of European missionaries the region was already affected by colonialism" which was also true in Ghana when the Basel Mission arrived. Lamin Sanneh represents African historians who also sharply critique the dismissal of African independent motivations, thinking, and actions. He posits that "Christianity has been a religion of dynamic responsiveness and not a device simply of mind manipulation."[83] Hanciles adds that "an acute sense of guilt about missionary complicity in the Western colonial movement . . . ironically . . . only serves to underscore the enduring tendency to assess the history and development of non-Western peoples merely in terms of Western activity."[84] Another level of irony is highlighted by Kalu, "while condemning missionaries, the authors fail to see that their own people, the Africans, were the real agents who spread Christianity."[85]

Furthermore, the indiscriminate application of conditions during the imperial period of colonialism to the context of German missionaries who worked in pre-colonial times in regions controlled by African rulers in conflict with the Danish and British governments is highly questionable. Even when national thinking intensified in the late nineteenth century, studies of Basel missionaries reveal intense reservations against colonial governments and show many areas of contention and opposition to colonial policies and practice, even in a German colony.[86] Pugach outlines several cases of German missionaries who left German societies to join British ones and concludes, "German missionaries were not harbingers of German Empire and maintained an ambivalent relationship

81. Awoonor, *Ghana*, 78.
82. Elbourne, "Word Made Flesh"; Landau, "Hegemony and History."
83. Sanneh, *Disciples of All Nations*, 131–61.
84. Hanciles, *Euthanasia*, 2.
85. Kalu, *African Christianity*, 17.
86. Halldén showed this, for example, for the Basel Mission in Cameroon where they actually worked in a German colonial context. Halldén, *Culture Policy*.

to imperialism."[87] Nevertheless, Walter Rodney is probably correct that "missionaries were agents of colonialism in the practical sense, whether or not they saw themselves in that light," and European colonial interests certainly impacted the mission of Andreas Riis.[88]

However, before an assessment of his entanglement with European and African politics a more helpful explanation for his apparently contradictory engagement with Africans is needed. The fact that narratives of collaboration and heroism both marginalize the African actors and context provides the key. It points to the "continuing intercultural blindness in mission historiography" Paul Jenkins highlighted.[89]

Illustrations of Cultural Maladjustment

Most all evaluations of Riis are informed by political perspectives. "Nationalist historiography" (as Kalu terms it) like Awoonor's is highly sensitive to colonial links of missionaries in the nineteenth and twentieth century and often assumes more collaboration and concurrence than actually existed.[90] By contrast, organizational political interests drive the heroic assessment of Riis's contribution by authors related to the Basel Mission or its successor church in Ghana.[91] Reindorf's focus is on African politics, but he tellingly limits his account of Riis to a bare minimum, thereby avoiding the critical assessment he might have had.[92] The shortcoming of all these accounts is their omission of cultural perspectives.

In three articles Jenkins has put forward a different interpretation of the nickname Riis was given in Akuropon for his building efforts, *Osiadan*, the house-builder or architect.[93] Jenkins identifies "most flagrant discrepancies between rhetoric and performance" in the events. Traditional Basel Mission narrative declares the title was "honorific"

---

87. Pugach, *Africa in Translation*, 28. Many of her cases are from the German colonial period; thus her emphasis that this was true "even after 1871."

88. Rodney, *How Europe Underdeveloped Africa*, 252.

89. Jenkins, *Scandal*.

90. Kalu, "African Church Historiography," 17–18; Awoonor, *Ghana*.

91. Examples are Oelschner, *Landung in Osu*; Opoku, *Riis, the Builder*; Schlatter, *Basler Mission in Afrika*; Smith, *Presbyterian Church of Ghana*; Steiner, "Andreas Riis"; Wurm, "Anfänge."

92. Reindorf, *History*, 218–19, 308–17.

93. Antwi and Jenkins, "The Moravians"; Jenkins, *Scandal*; Jenkins, "A Letter to Adu."

and expressed the Africans' amazement at Riis's diligence and skill.[94] It conjures up images of the acclaimed pioneer and the later characteristic two-story houses Basel Missionaries built in Ghana. However, Jenkins rightly criticizes this rhetoric because it assigns Africans to "the role of receptors who became active only in dependence on the missionary's skills and initiative."[95] By contrast, if we look for it in Riis's diary, it is clear that actually both, the initiative to build the house and the bulk of the workforce came from local Africans. Jenkins goes as far as to suggest that the decision to invest "much political capital in getting a missionary resident in his capital" backfired for King Addo Dankwa who lost the ability to hold his multi-ethnic state together because Riis "turned out to have the political and social sensibility of a sledge-hammer."[96] His alternative interpretation of *Osiadan* concurs with my own observations of Ghanaian witty handling of European arrogant ignorance. He offers that "even a fleeting knowledge of Ghanaian humor" suggests that African workers "who suffered from Riis's stubborn use of European models of co-operation" more likely told the story of what had happened with quite another accentuation: "Boy, did *he* build that house!"[97] This is also supported by Riis's own words—conceding that Akuapem people called him "stubborn" and "impatient" because he refused to respect their perceptions.[98] Jenkins's evaluation highlights the intercultural incapacity Riis displayed in abundance in the house building project. They may in part be assigned to his personality, but closer analysis reveals the roots of this maladjustment in the BMTI practice, thus indicating trained incapacity.

Riis Violated a Patron-Client Relationship

It is obvious that King Addo Dankwa perceived the relationship with the missionary as clientage. Chinchen studied the patron-client concept in order to apply it to teachers and African Bible School students, but he provides a useful summary of the literature.[99] Anthropologists define a patron-client relationship as "a relationship of personal dependency,

---

94. Opoku, *Riis, the Builder,* 20–34; Debrunner, *Christianity in Ghana,* 99.

95. Jenkins, *Scandal,* 69.

96. Ibid., 72; Jenkins, *Ghana in Africa and the World,* 45.

97. Jenkins, *Scandal,* 71–72; Jenkins, *Ghana in Africa and the World,* 44–45. Emphasis in original.

98. MM 1836, 540, Riis diary May 27, 1835.

99. Chinchen, "Patron-Client Relationship Concept," 51–57, 260–62.

excluding kinship ties, maintained by reciprocal exchanges of favors, between two persons... who control unequal resources."[100] The relationship assumes dependency relationships, reciprocity, fictive kinship, and is central to politics and power in Sub-Saharan Africa. Protection, material assistance, and social mobility are motivations for clients. For leaders, attracting and holding on to (valuable and/or many) followers signifies wealth, status, and security. Both sides accept obligations. Patrons visit, counsel, protect, and mediate for clients, they show concern and offer hospitality. Clients in return are expected to show respect by giving gifts and returning favors, prove loyalty by supporting and defending their patron, and give leadership to the patron acknowledging his/her superiority.[101] Both parties maintain harmony and cooperation by helping or not hindering the other's interests. Chinchen's application to expectations African students have of missionaries as patrons is insightful, but more challenging to Western minds is imagining the missionary as client of an African patron which applies in Riis's context.

Even Riis's slanted account of events gives many indications that Addo Dankwa acted as patron towards him by offering generous hospitality and protection.[102] On the day of Riis's arrival after representatives from the Danish governor, Labadi, and Osu officially declared their agreement to his settling in Akuropon, the King promised the requested protection and assistance. That evening he visited Riis to inform him that his whole kingdom had agreed "to build him a better and more comfortable house." Daily he sent provisions and visited Riis. Three days later the complete Akuapem council gathered and confirmed the permission for Riis to settle in Akuropon and the promise to build a house. Addo Dankwa publically declared his protection of Riis and commanded his sub-chiefs to do likewise. Throughout, the King was indisputably holding the power in this relationship; he was the patron, Riis the client.

Riis's lack of expected response, misinterpretation of the relationship and cultural practices quickly became apparent and an embarrassment for the king. Almost daily Riis received gifts of foodstuffs and people began to honor the promise of building a house by cutting the necessary sticks. As beneficiary of this communal support Riis was under social obligation to support his benefactor, especially as it turned out with

100. See also Clapham, *Private Patronage and Public Power*, 5–14, 166.
101. Barnes, *Patrons and Power*, 117.
102. MM 1836, 512–18, Riis diary March 22–25, 1835.

the brandy for religious ceremonies.[103] Rattray details the obligations of "tenants" towards supporting the religious responsibilities of their "overlords."[104] As a European foreigner Riis's position would have been special and it is not likely to have included expectations of military service or fealty, but "aids" (*etuo*) were obviously anticipated. They included contributions to royal expenses and religious customs.

Riis, however, instead of returning the favors complained about Africans always expecting presents, in spite of the numerous gifts he was receiving. Because of his preoccupation with African alcoholism, he was unable to see the ritual significance of brandy or perceive its role as exchange currency. He misinterpreted these requests with a long discourse on the evil of drunkenness among Africans.[105] Later his own account clearly identified brandy as a means of payment, together with gold-dust and cowries, confirming Kimble's observation that those commodities were used as "something approaching monetary use."[106] Imported brandy—in contrast to locally brewed palm-wine—had taken on a function resembling currency, and on the occasion of negotiating payment Riis could not refuse to give it.[107] But the European prejudice of African alcohol addiction consistently prevented him from making the distinction or identifying its importance for traditional rituals.

While Riis returned the visits of his benefactor often, there is no indication that he acknowledged an inferior position to the King. On the contrary, he comments on the primitive stage of the ruler's education, assumes the right to advise him on many occasions, and makes disapproving remarks about Addo Dankwa's religious functions as "fetish service."[108] Riis welcomed attempts by the king to introduce him to African manners and customs but typically diverted them to an opportunity to "cor-

---

103. Kuada and Chachah explain how this dynamic of social obligations of beneficiaries of communal support is still functioning in relation to education: "Many of the younger generation of African managers excel to the heights of their academic achievements through the collective financial contribution of their extended families and, in some cases, from the whole clan. Since these contributions are seen as investments to yield dividends in folds, it imposes huge social obligations on the beneficiary." Kuada and Chachah, *Ghana*, 73. Riis's repeated complaints about requests for brandy are recorded in MM 1836, 518, 523–24, Riis diary March 26 and April 7–10, 1835.

104. Rattray, *Ashanti*, 224–27.

105. MM 1836, 516 and 518, Riis diary March 23 and 25, 1835.

106. Kimble, *Political History*, 3.

107. MM 1836, 534, Riis diary May 6, 1835.

108. For example MM 1836, 516–17, 532, Riis diary March 25 and May 4, 1835.

rect things" with his perspectives.[109] The stereotypes of African limited intellectual ability and ignorance and their beliefs as mere superstitions continued to shape Riis's responses.

He also presents the choice of land for the building as his selection, while it was most certainly granted by Addo Dankwa and the elders who viewed the plot with him.[110] This doubtless constituted the "witnessing by the proper persons in authority" and "fixing of the boundaries" required.[111] Rattray demonstrated that there was "no such thing as the individual ownership of land" and outlined the complicated traditions related to a stranger settling on granted land.[112] Often payment was involved and certainly "services" were expected of the settler as indicated above, and he was regarded as attached to the clan which granted the land, thereby increasing that ruler's status. This answers to an extent Jenkins's question of historical precedents and Akan rationale for the offer to build a house.[113] Rattray's findings confirm Jenkin's speculation that "it was an attempt to bind the guest to the existing cultural and political structures."

Riis accepted no such bond and saw himself above any obligations. He made clear on several occasions that as long as he felt the Africans' wishes and orders "went against God's laws I cannot fulfill them."[114] In May 1835 the smoldering tensions became a breach when Riis enforced a contract regarding the building work.[115] This in itself was an offensive request that Addo Dankwa repeatedly had tried to dissuade him from, but the timing aggravated the insult.[116] Riis forced the negotiations the day after the people had erected a house in concerted community effort. The work was given voluntarily by family heads of the town out of loyalty to the King, while Riis consistently pushed for a European labor contract. However, the way Riis conducted the negotiations and their outcome prove the utter offensiveness of this to both, the King—who apparently

---

109. MM 1836, 526, Riis diary April 16 reports that Addo Dankwa suggested that he also taught Riis African customs because he had been telling him so much about European' customs and beliefs. Riis welcomed it but responded to the king's explanation of specific evil days immediately with a Bible quotation about all days being evil.

110. MM 1836, 518–19, Riis diary March 26, 1835.

111. Rattray, *Ashanti*, 236.

112. Ibid., 213–41.

113. Jenkins, *Scandal*, 70; Jenkins, *Ghana in Africa and the World*, 44.

114. MM 1836, 536, Riis diary May 13, 1835.

115. MM 1836, 533–36, Riis diary May 6–13, 1835.

116. For example MM 1836, 524, Riis diary April 9, 1835.

was not involved in the proceedings—and the Akuropon family heads. The clearest sign is that anybody of standing in the town deserted Riis that afternoon. His insistence to continue working alongside the remaining serfs seriously embarrassed and angered Addo Dankwa. His patron had asked him repeatedly to halt this work but Riis—convinced to provide a shining model of Christian diligence—ignored him. Above all, the ongoing conflicts around the building project violated the patron-client relationship thereby undermining the King's authority. They reveal numerous intercultural maladjustments and, as Jenkins posits, "can be seen as a cause of the major political crisis which developed . . . in 1836."[117]

Riis's Work Values Clashed with African Realities

When Riis first arrived in Akuropon the Akuapem Royal Council promised to build him a dwelling "as quickly as possible."[118] Riis's language is often inaccurate when it comes to this building, even though initially he correctly described the typical African compound consisting of several one-room buildings around a courtyard.[119] Actually, several "houses" were built towards such a compound, a fact Jenkins also does not clarify. When Addo Dankwa encouraged Riis early on to take advantage of the people's willingness and "expand the house," he meant a compound.[120] Later Mürdter details at least four buildings, the missionaries' house, a "boys-quarter" for their workers, a carpenter shop, and a stable.[121] But in 1835 Riis consistently creates the impression of one building.

More important than how many houses, however, is Jenkins's question, "Who built that house really?"[122] Oelschner's false claim that "Riis had erected for himself a provisional hut on the building site" illustrates the persistent bias of Basel Mission representatives.[123] With his depiction of Riis's disdain for this first house he is, however, correct. Over the following months, Riis increasingly described it as primitive and flawed, a "wet, small, and dark hut" in contrast to the "house" he was

---

117. Jenkins, *Scandal*, 72.

118. MM 1836, 518, Riis diary March 25, 1835.

119. MM 1836, 513–514, Riis diary March 22, 1835. This is a detailed description of the Royal Palace in Akuropon as he saw it during his welcome ceremony.

120. MM 1836, 520, Riis diary March 30, 1835.

121. BMA, D-1,1 Akropong 1837, #9.Mürdter from October 25, 1837.

122. Jenkins, *Ghana in Africa and the World*, 43–46.

123. Oelschner, *Landung in Osu*, 86.

building.[124] The Akuapem people built this first dwelling which was a traditional building of straight sticks tied closely together from both sides and plastered with clay. Just four days after the site was inspected the first Africans began to clear the land.[125] During the following weeks people brought the building materials.[126] In the first week of May they cleared grass, trees, and brush, and on May 4 about hundred men from the entire Akuapem-District erected the building. Riis overstates his contribution to clearing the land but reports the building process in detail and with some admiration.[127] More seriously, his insistence the following day on negotiating above mentioned contract with agreed payment for the labor people had offered liberally cost him much of their goodwill. The free family heads of Akuropon were not servants or "workers" the foreigner could employ, and they were not going to be treated as such. It is hard to imagine the consternation they must have felt at Riis's accusations of broken promises and insolence.[128] They left with the house not completely finished which is the most likely reason for the shortcomings Riis reports later when the roof leaked under the first heavy rains of the season.[129]

These are the "circumstances" which forced Riis from May onwards "to lay on hand myself."[130] But he blamed "the inability of local Africans to deliver one useful board for the house" and regularly spent days in the forest with "his people" to cut wood and make "proper planks" for door and window frames.[131] This group he refers to as "his people" were two young men who had been with him from Christiansborg, a third employee from Akuropon, his translator, and two carpenters from Osu he had hired in early April.[132] Apart from ongoing occasional conversations with Addo Dankwa, these six people, mostly foreigners, were the audience of his evening devotions.

124. MM 1836, 547–48, Riis diary July 12, 1835.
125. MM 1836, 520, Riis diary March 30, 1835.
126. For example: MM 1836, 523–24, Riis diary April 6 and 10.
127. MM 1836, 532–33, Riis diary May 4, 1835.
128. MM 1836, 533–35, Riis diary May 6, 1835.
129. MM 1836, 541, Riis diary June 6, 1835.
130. MM 1836, 539, Riis diary May 26, 1835.
131. MM 1836, 538 and 542, Riis diary May 19 and June 21, 1835.
132. MM 1836, 544 and 538–39, Riis diary, June 23 and May 19–21, 1835.

In spite of Riis's emphasis on having to do all the work, his diary testifies to the fact that Akuropong people continued to build his compound.[133] Riis kept interfering with their efforts. Despising the quality of work, he felt the need to "bring everything into its [proper] order." This proper order included straight walls, doors and windows which the local houses did not have, as well as regular daily work. Beyond misrepresenting his contribution, Riis's expectations and judgments show his insensitivity to the African culture and context. Jenkins rightly asserts that the building of this house raised all sorts of issues of inter-cultural relations and misunderstanding."[134] Curiously, he and Antwi do not reconcile the tension between his strong criticism and Antwi's highly positive evaluation of Riis in their shared article.[135] Jenkins claims Riis demanded payment "in *Akkord*, [i.e.] piece-work, or daily payment for the work actually done." This interpretation of Riis's use of this word as "Akkordarbeit" as it is understood today is probably incorrect. All indications are that Riis merely meant a labor-contract. But he certainly expected workers—according to European patterns—"to appear every day at what he regarded was the proper time" and intended to pay "the individuals who did the work . . . instead of the family head being given an occasional gift to cover the services offered by family members."[136] This communal perception of the work was not the only cultural reality Riis did not understand.

Jenkins points to the timing of the work in relation to other economic activities of Akuapem and the seasons.[137] Local people's repeated observations of the futility of Riis's work and his stubborn impatience that "cannot wait for more favorable conditions" confirm this.[138] Riis arrived at the peak season of palm-oil production and its transportation to the coastal trading-points.[139] Building the first house was a sacrifice for Akuapem men when their primary trading commodity needed to be harvested and processed. With a first room built, they focused on what

---

133. MM 1836, 538–39, Riis diary May 19–21, 1835.
134. Jenkins, *Scandal*, 71.
135. Antwi and Jenkins, *Moravians*.
136. Jenkins, *Ghana in Africa and the World*, 44.
137. Jenkins, *Scandal*, 71.
138. MM 1836, 540, Riis diary May 27, 1835.
139. Kyei-Baffour and Manu identify January to June as the "peak season for harvesting palm fruits in Ghana," followed by July to October which are "regarded as the mid-season." Kyei-Baffour and Manu, "Smallscale Palm Oil Process Improvement."

was more important. Riis's observation that nobody was in town to cook food for him because everybody was on their plantations supports this.[140]

Furthermore, building was—and in my observation still is—done towards the end of the rainy season when water is plentiful for the necessary wet clay. Riis—judging by his diary entries—is oblivious to these factors and complains from June to August about the broken promises to build his house and African indolence.[141] In the meantime Riis and "his people" cut wood in the forest, made boards, door and window frames, and continued building. The diary gives several indications that others helped them at least occasionally, but Riis creates the impression that he alone was working hard, while lazy Africans watched and scoffed. Even if nobody from Akuropon had helped, it would have still been Riis's employees who did the bulk of the work. In late September the "more favorable conditions" finally were met and (in another large community effort) men, women and children worked from three in the morning carrying water, pounding clay, and plastering Riis's second building.[142] Indicative of the missionary's deteriorating attitudes towards Africans is his comment that evening that "the building progresses so slowly ... because Negros are slow and take their time with every kind of work." Yet more disconcerting is Oelschner's bias in depicting the traditional Ghanaian clay as Riis's invention and the large community effort as the work of one of Riis's employees.[143]

Even earlier, notwithstanding the previous offenses, the Africans brought roofing grass when the rainy season arrived and Riis's first house leaked.[144] Apparently, the King had convinced them to help Riis once more. But the missionary again refused his obligation to give brandy and himself reports the King's anger and exclamation: "The white man disgraces me!" This is the most direct utterance Riis records scolding his violations of the clientage. Nonetheless, he continued to be convinced of his righteous cause. The interpreter falls from Riis's grace for "lying and deception" and only the intervention of Addo Dankwa and his elders stop Riis from dismissing him.[145] He also continually quarreled with the

140. MM 1836, 548–49, Riis diary August 2, 1835.

141. MM 1836, 540–41 and 547–551, Riis diary June 1, July 12, August 2 and 17, 1835.

142. MM 1836, 562, Riis diary September 28, 1835.

143. Oelschner, *Landung in Osu*, 87.

144. MM 1836, 541 and 545, Riis diary June 6 and 25, 1835.

145. MM 1836, 543–44 and 546–547, Riis diary June 23 and July 5, 1835.

hired carpenters over their lack of enthusiasm for his ideas of the work until he eventually hired two others.[146] Shortly similar issues arose with them too.[147] They only stayed because they feared Riis reporting them to the Danish authorities in Christiansborg.

These repeated struggles of Africans to work with Riis were not so much due to their incapability and laziness as the missionary alleges, but to Riis's inability to compromise. The standards he had internalized as "proper work with his own hands" constituted following Jesus' example, were his duty, and would please God.[148] This mindset disabled him to perceive how his behaviors alienated the very people he wanted to win. The BMTI humility value pushed him to engage in work that exposed him to unnecessary physical hardship and offended his position as honored guest of the King. However, he displayed cultural arrogance in his ignorant misinterpretations of African behaviors and by insisting on building a house after rural European patterns using Pietist measurements of diligence and European labor contracts. This incongruity of humility and cultural arrogance apparent in Riis's behavior characterized the entire mission in Akuropon and caused many tensions. Thus, the BMTI instilled values caused serious trained incapacity that continuously threatened the mission's success.

When in November 1836 two colleagues and his wife joined Riis, they continued to be preoccupied with building work.[149] Consequently, they had little time and energy left for the "real mission work" of language learning and preaching—a fact the missionaries repeatedly bemoaned. The Board acknowledged the problem when they reviewed the mission in 1839 and Wurm also lists the necessary practical work among reasons they "did not manage to begin any lasting work."[150] Another obstacle both emphasize were "the increasingly confused [political] conditions in Akropong" and Riis's problems with the Danish Governor Mørck.

---

146. MM 1836, 540, Riis diary June 1, 1835.

147. MM 1836, 550 and 553, Riis diary August 2 and 23, 1835.

148. References to this pious self-understanding of his work are numerous in the diary. For example: MM 1836, 528, 535, 540, Riis diary April 22, May 13 and 27, 1835.

149. BMA, D-1,1 Akropong 1837 #9 Mürdter October 25, 1837.

150. BMA, KP February 27, 1839; Wurm, "Anfänge," 266.

THE FUTILITY OF THE PRINCIPLE OF POLITICAL NEUTRALITY

In October 1835 a new chapter opened in Riis's missionary experience when governor Mørck ordered him to Christiansborg and subsequently travelled with him to Akuropon for an inaugural visit "to introduce himself as the new governor of the Gold Coast."[151] Abun-Nasr rightly interprets this visit as "demonstration of power that was addressed both, to the native rulers in Akuapem and Krobo, and the British."[152] Riis was inevitably drawn into the ensuing political crisis and became "a pawn in a political intrigue between the Danish governor and the chiefs and people of Akuapem."[153] This was in spite of his explicit instructions to "guard carefully against getting involved in any political affairs ... and other merely temporary things which do not befit you and do not agree with your missionary profession."[154] The principle of political neutrality was a prime Basel Mission value that reflected German Pietist preferences and supported the organizations' international interdenominational stance. Riis no doubt shared this value as he was at pains to assert in his reports over the following years.[155]

However, for a number of reasons, political neutrality proved elusive and even at variance with other BMTI values. Danish colonial aspirations and economic interests coincided with grievances of Akuapem factions over Addo Dankwa's rule. Consequently, Riis's Danish citizenship, location in Akuropon, and affiliation with the Okuapemhene resulted in inevitable entanglements in politics. Moreover, his BMTI inspired evaluations of Africans and Europeans added to complicate relationships.

The Events and their Presentations

When Mørck visited Akuropon Addo Dankwa used the opportunity to present his grievances with Krobo—a conflict over Krobo dependence on Akuapem land for palm-oil farming, Akuapem extortions, and the king's recent capture of Krobos to pay off a debt to Asante—and succeeded in

---

151. Reindorf, *History*, 309. BMA, D-1,1 Akropong 1836 #1 Riis February 10, 1836.

152. Abun-Nasr, *David Asante*, 43.

153. Antwi, "African Factor," 60.

154. BMA, D-10.3,3a1) Instructions 1828 (I.4).

155. For example MM 1837, 540; BMA, D-1,1 Akropong 1836 #6 Riis July 27, 1836.

convincing the ambitious governor.[156] Mørck ordered the rulers of Shai and Krobo to pay their homage to him in Akuropon, probably not realizing that this also implied their submission to the Okuapemhene.[157] Shai complied but Krobo requested the Governor came to them. This enraged Mørck and he marched against Krobo with Addo Dankwa, reinforced by Danish soldiers and armory and various coastal groups. Riis was obliged to accompany him. While Mørck was still negotiating, Addo Dankwa attacked, but not receiving Danish support withdrew.[158] Eventually, Mørck forced Krobo to surrender imposing a heavy fine to be paid in palm-oil. This diverted the trade temporarily almost completely to the Danish traders, which Metcalfe suggests was the purpose of the whole venture.[159] In any case, it enraged the British merchants and Maclean complained about Danish unjustified intervention in the affairs of African states. The matter was referred to the home governments who eventually (in April 1838) warned Mørck "to exercise caution and maintenance of good understanding between neighboring colonies" ordering him "to give up his personal ideas in favor of superior political considerations."[160] Kwamena-Poh declares that subsequently Mørck "became addicted to alcohol and died."

Meanwhile, Akuropon rulers were angry at Mørcks failure of support and the wing-chiefs "offered the ill-disposed advice that 'the Danish government was deceitful, weak, and unreliable; and that they preferred throwing off their allegiance and declaring in favour of the English.'"[161] Mørck was "hooted at in every town" on his return but back in Christiansborg summoned the Akuapems "to justify their leaving him on the

---

156. Reindorf, *History*, 307–8. Reindorf describes the details of the recent capture of Krobo women and consequent Krobo renunciation of their allegiance to Addo Dankwa. He also recounts several grievances over hunting incidents and Addo Dankwa's inability to strike against Krobo because of tensions within Akuapem between him and his subjects.

157. Abun-Nasr, *David Asante*, 43; Metcalfe, *Maclean*, 200; Reindorf, *History*, 309.

158. Metcalfe, *Maclean*, 200; Reindorf, *History*, 310. Reindorf suggests that Addo Dankwa suffered heavy loss and great discontent of his subjects because Mørck refused to supply fire arms. But they also did a lot of damage to the Krobo and their plantations.

159. Metcalfe, *Maclean*, 200, 227. Metcalfe suggests that "British merchants did not fail to conclude that such a diversion of trade had been Morch's aim from the beginning."

160. Abun-Nasr, *David Asante*, 43–44; Kwamena-Poh, *Akuapem State*, 102–7.

161. Kwamena-Poh, *Akuapem State*, 63; Reindorf, *History*, 311.

field of battle." In early March 1836 Addo Dankwa pretended to comply but defected to British Accra. Maclean, who happened to visit Accra at the time, arranged a meeting with Mørck that ended with deferring the decision to Europe. However, the disgruntled Akuapem sub-chiefs had come to a secret arrangement with Mørck "aimed at the overthrow of Ado Dankwa and his replacement by his nephew Adum."[162] Consequently, Mørck "publicly proclaimed Adum king of Akuapem, but Ado an outlaw, and had a salute fired upon it."[163] British soldiers escorted Addo Dankwa to Kwabenyan, where he and his loyalists stayed with relatives. Mørck suspected Riis to be behind Addo Dankwa's defection and ordered him to the coast. Only in June he allowed Riis to return to Akuropon.[164] Metcalf emphasizes the fact that Mørck made his next move against Addo Dankwa the week Maclean embarked for Europe in June 1836.[165] Danish soldiers were sent to arrest the old Okuapemhene and bring him to Christiansborg, but he escaped to British Jamestown where he stayed until his suicide in 1839.[166]

However, this was not the end of the "serious political and social crisis" in Akuapem. Part of Akuropon and some other towns still supported Addo Dankwa. They did not recognize Adum's enstoolment by foreign authorities, while Addo Dankwa held on to the royal stool and was exercising his rule from the distance.[167] In September 1836 the Akuapem council attempted to prevent Danish influence with a decree against anybody going to Osu, but in the long run Mørck's support decided in favor of Adum.[168] The division of the kingdom continued between Addo

162. Metcalfe, *Maclean*, 202.

163. Reindorf, *History*, 313.

164. BMA, D-1,1 Akropong und Ussu 1836 #2, 4, 6, Riis from April 1, June 14, July 27, 1836.

165. Metcalfe, *Maclean*, 202.

166. MM 1837, 540 Riis letter #6 from July 27, 1836; Kwamena-Poh, *Akuapem State*, 63–64.

167. Abun-Nasr, *David Asante*, 50–52; Kwamena-Poh, *Akuapem State*, 64–65; Reindorf, *History*, 315. In Akan, specially treated low chairs, so-called "stools," function in similar ways crowns in Europe did, albeit with much deeper spiritual significance. The "enstoolment" of a king is his inauguration ceremony.

168. Abun-Nasr, *David Asante*, 51–52. This is Abun-Nasr's interpretation. Riis interprets the prohibition as part of Adum's schemes. But, as Abun-Nasr rightly contents, it was the Akuropon party that had an interest in cutting off Danish interventions in favor of Adum. BMA, D-1,1 Akropong 1836 #9 Riis diary September 12, 1836. The publication of this section in MM 1838, 554–55 has significant omissions.

Dankwa's chosen successor, Owusu Akyem, and Adum as "a conflict about royal succession."[169] Akuapem remained politically divided for almost a decade, many left for their home villages, and in the town "prevailed a climate of enmity, fear, and violence."[170] Only in 1844–1845 the conflict was resolved, after the murder of Owusu Akyem in Accra and Adum's subsequent imprisonment and deportation by Governor Carstensen.[171]

These events—that illustrate the complicated interactions of European colonial interests with African political intricacies—are presented in significantly different ways by various authors. Basel Mission writers attempt to minimize reporting and limit the effect to "the hostile Governor Mörck" who opposed the missionary's brave efforts.[172] Contemporary published accounts omit many details and generally ignore the African maneuvering in the disputes, even though Riis reports them meticulously, at least to his limited understanding.[173] By contrast, his frequent reconnaissance trips were printed in detail.[174] Oelschner takes much literary freedom and focuses on contrasting Riis positively with other Europeans' attitudes to native Africans.[175]

Reindorf is the earliest to divert from this pattern. Even though he wrote under the tutelage of a Basel Missionary during the height of colonial imperialism, his emphasis on the African actors and oral traditions in Akuapem fifty years after the events makes him the source everybody cites who followed.[176] Opoku is clearly literature of tutelage. While he includes the African actors, he is highly hagiographic of Riis's motivations,

---

169. Ibid., 50.

170. Ibid., 53.

171. Kwamena-Poh, *Akuapem State*, 66–68. Carstensen's reports from January 13, February 26, November 1 and 20, 1845 in Carstensen, *Closing the Books*, 88–90, 95–99, 154–55, 161–75. Carstensen describes it as part of the Adum conflict. However, the trigger in Akuropon was that Adum captured some people to be sacrificed as part of the funeral rites for Addo Dankwa.

172. Schlatter, *Basler Mission in Afrika*, 29–31; Wurm, "Anfänge," 261–64.

173. For example MM 1837, 535–61; MM 1839, 382–88.

174. For example MM1839, 455–76 *Missionsreise der Brüder Riis und Mürdter von Akropong in das Aquambuland* (Mission-trip of the Brothers Riis and Mürdter from Akropong into the Aquambu Land) which presents extensive excerpts of BMA, D-1,1 Akropong 1838 #10 Riis December 6, 1838.

175. Oelschner, *Landung in Osu*, 94–122, 138–44. He again has a number of factual inaccuracies.

176. Reindorf, *History*, 307–22.

skills, and actions.[177] Metcalfe favors British viewpoints, mostly uncritical of Maclean, while Per Hernæs presents the Danish perspective of events, as do governor Carstensen's reports.[178] African realities feature prominent in Kwamena-Poh's thorough analysis which builds on all previous studies as well as oral traditions and attempts to relate the complicated Akuapem politics of the period from the African, European, and missionaries' perspectives in separate chapters.[179] He attributes the "revolts by the divisional chiefs against the center" besides "interference by outside powers" to the prevailing ethnic, linguistic, and cultural differences and the weak financial position of the Okuapemhene.[180] Finally, most recently Abun-Nasr describes in detail the intricacies of Akuapem politics, showing how Danish interventions aggravated and prolonged the conflict, in her thorough study of David Asante's background, the son of Owusu Akyem and one of the first Christian converts in Akuropon.[181]

Riis was inevitably drawn into these events on account of his location in Akuropon and his Danish citizenship. While he struggled to maintain political neutrality, European and African politics affected his mission in various ways. In the following, I cannot provide a comprehensive analysis but will focus on specific issues related to how values and practices instilled in Riis's preparation processes shaped his engagement in Africa.

African Political Realities Affected the Mission

As we saw above, Akuapem was not a homogeneous state. Up to today it divides into two main groups, the Twi speaking matrilineal Akan, who form the majority in Akuropon and four other towns, and the "indigenous patrilineal Guan, some of whom have become Twi speaking."[182] These differences created constant subversive tensions. However, the missionaries' reports evince no awareness of these subtleties. Throughout

---

177. Opoku, *Riis, the Builder*, 34–61. His Basel Mission related "tutor" was Hans Debrunner who at the time taught at the Akuropong Seminary.

178. Carstensen, *Closing the Books*; Hernæs, "Introduction"; Metcalfe, *Maclean*, 196–203, 227–29.

179. Kwamena-Poh, *Akuapem State*.

180. Ibid., 68.

181. Abun-Nasr, *David Asante*, 31–68.

182. Gilbert, *Christian Executioner*.

they dispute the "true foundational and root language" of the land.[183] They recognized "several different dialects spoken" but did not identify the two distinct languages. Mürdter, for example, suspected in 1837 that Asante is "the Ur-language out of which the remaining dialects emerged." Such misconceptions were probably in part due to the limited time they spent learning language, but they also illustrate the assumption instilled by their training that such a "root language" exited in Guinea. This prevented them from identifying the distinct cultural groups and gaining deeper insights into Akuapem political realities. Furthermore, the missionaries evaluated African leaders by European criteria. Their subsequent partiality affected the mission, while they continued to claim political neutrality. As Barker shows for early missionaries elsewhere, by attaching themselves to "worthy" rulers by their standards they "implicated themselves in long-running political contests they could scarcely comprehend and over which they had little control."[184]

BMTI Inspired Partiality towards African Rulers

Basel Mission instructions exhorted missionaries to acknowledge local rulers as "God-instituted government" that they should support and assist in "ruling ... after God's holy laws."[185] Beyond these general ideas, attitudes and values instilled in Basel guided missionary engagement. Consequently, their evaluations had less affinity with African realities than with German Pietist concepts of a good and wise ruler. Addo Dankwa was an "old man but still very strong, effective, alert, chatty, and friendly; at the same time a man with a sharp mind that he knows how to use in his position, therefore loved and respected by many and feared by all."[186] Riis portrayed Addo Dankwa as undisputed wise ruler with sovereign powers, but the king was neither undisputed nor did he exert limitless power. Rather, his authority depended on carefully negotiated alliances.

Addo Dankwa's leadership was weakened by several factors. Above we saw that Riis's insensitive behavior contributed to discrediting him. This added to his longstanding antagonism with the *Adontehene* Kwafum, his primary rival among the sub-chiefs, who represented the Guan

---

183. MM 1838, 384–85; Mürdter letter #9 October 25, 1837.
184. Barker, "Missionary Frontier," 88.
185. BMA, Instructions 1827 in MM 1830, 480–81.
186. MM 1836, 525, Riis diary April 12, 1835.

majority of Akuapem. According to Reindorf's credible account Kwafum had played a central role in forcing Addo Dankwa to join the coalition against the Asante invasion in 1823.[187] Addo Dankwa's reluctance was understandable because "he owed his stool to Asante."[188] However, in 1826 he was credited with significantly contributing to the decisive victory over Asante that restored independence for Akuapem.[189] This enabled him in the following years to repeatedly violate the expectation of African rulers "to do little or nothing without having previously consulted [their] counselors."[190] By virtue of this military achievement and through shrewd nepotism Addo Dankwa was able to act independently of his sub-chiefs who in turn resented him. Incidents of the King breaching traditional custom added to his unpopularity.[191] Thus, after the unsuccessful Krobo excursion in 1836 conditions were ripe for Kwadum's clever maneuvering of the Danish governor into deposing Addo Dankwa and installing Adum in his place.

Riis—oblivious to these dynamics—admired Addo Dankwa's strong leadership, even though he also reported his heavy-handedness and subsequent disobediences to his rulings.[192] This was due to Addo Dankwa meeting a second condition for missionary approval, support for the mission. Abun-Nasr argues convincingly that the Basel missionaries consistently were "quite partial" by "the decisive criterion . . . whether and how far the . . . aspirant to kingship supported their work."[193] Consequently, even in the 1840s Addo Dankwa had a good reputation with

187. Reindorf, *History*, 175–77.

188. Abun-Nasr, *David Asante*, 39–40; Kwamena-Poh, *Akuapem State*, 92–93. Kwamena-Poh and Abun-Nasr outline the details of Addo Dankwa's controversial ascension to Okuapemhene at the price of delivering his predecessor to Asante.

189. Kwamena-Poh, *Akuapem State*, 93–94.

190. Rattray, *Ashanti Law*, 87.

191. For example, Reindorf accounts an incident when Addo Dankwa refused to execute the man who had been identified by 'custom' as responsible for another man's death. See Reindorf, *History*, 311–12.

192. BMA, D-1,1 Akropong 1836 #9 Riis October 27, 1836, diary entry September 7, 1836; MM 1837, 553 and 558. Riis also claimed at one point that the Akuapem dispute was over "whether the state would belong to Danish or British government protection." See BMA, D-1,1 Akropong 1837 # 10 Riis November 14, 1837; MM 1838, 387.

193. Abun-Nasr, *David Asante*, 51–59.

the missionaries and his favored successor Owusu Akyem "continued the pro-missionary stance and expanded it for his own interests."[194]

Backing Addo Dankwa and Owusu Akyem put the missionaries firmly "on the wrong side" of Akuapem politics, because—outside intervention or not—Adum Tokori was the rightful Okuapemhene after his enstoolment in January 1837 and enjoyed the support of the majority of Akuapem.[195] Even Riis conceded to this and reported attempts by the Akuapem court to prevent Danish interventions through prohibiting people going to Osu.[196] Nevertheless, the missionaries continued in the 1840s to "play the game of uniting internal and external opposition against the Okuapemhene" in favor of their plans.[197] Akuapem people, logically, integrated the missionaries in local African politics as opponents of Adum Tokori. Abun-Nasr contends that the presence of the Basel missionaries prolonged the African conflict because their political positioning forced Adum out of Akuropon and effectively installed an alternative authority in part of the kingdom.[198]

Beyond support for the mission, moral judgments caused missionary partiality, official political neutrality notwithstanding. Riis and his successors strongly emphasized moral evaluations by virtues of BMTI practice. Consequently, alcohol abuse and sexual offenses became primary issues. Adum fared badly by these criteria, while Addu Dankwa and Owusu Akyem found favor. Riis claims that Adum was "hated . . . because of his behavior" and later Widmann comments that "Adum . . . is spoiling his game with all the drinking; it is no wonder that he is not well respected."[199] Later, Riis defends his stance by emphasizing that he had opposed Adum "for moral and Christian reasons."[200] Kwamena-Poh

194. Ibid., 55. For example, Widmann claims in 1844 that "the lovable Abodankva [sic] was a better ruler than the drunkard Adum." BMA, D-1,2 Akropong 1844 #8 Widmann May 28, 1844.

195. Hernæs, "Introduction," xvi.

196. BMA, D-1,1 Akropong 1836 #9 Riis October 27, 1836, diary September 12, 1836. The publication of this section in MM 1838, 554–55 has significant omissions that downplay the support for Adum in Akuapem. See also Abun-Nasr, *David Asante*, 51–52.

197. Ibid., 56–57.

198. Ibid., 56–61.She concludes this in her analysis of the collaboration of Owusu Akyem with the missionaries in favor of the mission's interests, in order to strengthen his political position in 1843–44.

199. JB 1844, 189–90. Widmann diary 1 October 1843.

200. BMA, D-1,2 Akropong and Ussu 1845 #11 Riis April 14, 1845.

concurs: "Adum was not a good choice as a ruler. Throughout his reign the missionaries never ceased to report of his acts of debauchery, cruelty, and quarrels."[201] For an African author this is a surprisingly uncritical stance of the Basel missionaries which Kwamena-Poh maintains in his chapter on "the missionary factor in Akuapem."[202]

All this shows that the Basel missionaries were not as politically neutral as they claimed. The instruction to support "rule . . . after God's holy laws" implied a judgment of local authorities by BMTI values and missionary intervention towards what they were taught to regard as good and godly government. The resulting definite favors for some rulers significantly influenced how they were perceived by Africans and affected their mission. In effect, they were only able to communicate their message to the small section of the Akuapem population that shared the missionaries' political position.

AFRICAN ECCLESIASTICAL POLICY

The missionaries' experience in Akuropon illustrates Warren's observations of Church-State relationships in nineteenth century colonial Africa.[203] He highlights "the ambivalence of the Church in its relations to the State, whether African or British." Like the Basel Mission, the CMS feared "being too much mixed up with secular affairs" but was "quite inevitably involved in local politics" and colonial interests. Warren's most striking example is the appointment of Dr. Edward Irving in 1853 as "lay agent of the CMS" with the expressed instruction to advise African rulers "respecting the principles of law and sound policy" and to function as liaison between African and British colonial authorities, "so as wholly to relieve the missionaries of this employment."[204] This implies that missionaries had been fulfilling these functions previously.

In Ghana, Riis and his successors also attempted to advise African rulers in order to influence them towards European values, if needed backed by colonial force. Early on this met with little success, mostly because of Riis's strained relationship with the Danish governor, but in

201. Kwamena-Poh, *Akuapem State*, 65.
202. Ibid., 111–23.
203. Warren, *Social History*, 24–35.
204. Ibid., 27–28. See also Adeuyan, *Contributions of Yoruba People*, 60–61. This Nigerian author is very critical and posits Irving's African assistants as collaborators with the "civilization in Africa" after European models and to the disadvantage of African independent economic development.

the 1840s they succeeded to gain permission to establish schools and were instrumental in the prohibition of human sacrifices against Adum's opposition.[205] Gilbert explains the highly complex understanding and practice of "human sacrifice" in Akuapem which had a number of social functions including capital punishment, and Abun-Nasr shows that the Danish legislation was "solely justified by European norms."[206] Not surprisingly, Warren's observation that African rulers "viewed the arrival of missionaries with very grave suspicion" is confirmed in this context.[207]

Those who welcomed the foreigners came to regret it. Jenkins suggests that Addo Dankwa's relationship with Riis illustrates the beginnings of "an Akan kingdom's ecclesiastical policy" that also involved "mechanisms ... to bend churches and missions to their will."[208] His analysis results in his conviction that the Okuapemhene suffered "because he had sunk so much political capital in getting a missionary resident in his capital" who lacked cultural and political sensitivity. Investigating the relationship of the Akuropon church with changing local society, Middleton posits that until the 1860s it was characterized by "opposition of interests, if not antagonism, and frequent hostility."[209] Primarily, he argues this on the basis of missionary opposition to practices like slavery, human sacrifice, and "coffin-carrying" that Africans interpreted as "attacks on local 'custom' and the kingship itself" because of the synergy between these practices and Akuapem kingship.[210] Furthermore, the prospect of converts no longer accepting the king's religious position threatened the stability of the entire society.

Thus, the Basel missionaries' evaluations of African political realities by German Pietist values and practices they had internalized during their preparation processes significantly affected their intercultural mission. It

---

205. Abun-Nasr, *David Asante*, 58–60. See also the Danish governor Carstensen's perspective on the negotiations in his report from October 20, 1843 that recounts his visit to Akuropon, 27–29 September 1843, in Carstensen, *Closing the Books*, 58–60.

206. Gilbert, *Christian Executioner*: 252–56.

207. Warren, *Social History*, 25–26.

208. Jenkins, *Ghana in Africa and the World*, 45.

209. Middleton, "One Hundred and Fifty Years," 3–6.

210. Middleton explains the practice of "coffin-carrying." When a person was "suspected of having been killed by witchcraft" their coffin was carried "through the streets of the town: the lurching of the coffin on the shoulders of the bearers indicated the house of the guilty witch." Ibid., 17. See also Reindorf, *History*, 311–12. Addo Dankwa refused to execute a man who had been identified by this "custom" as responsible for another man's death.

prevented them from identifying African legal and religious dynamics and made them a threat to the stability of the Akuapem state. This started off church-state relations on a very negative note. The subsequent decade of strife robbed the missionaries of their audience, but also brought unexpected ministry opportunities.

No Audience in a Deserted Town

Kwamena-Poh recounts the history of Akuropon as relatively recently built capital town for the Opuapemhene after the arrival of the Akyem rulers.[211] Even hundred years later it consisted of a "conglomeration of peoples" and many returned to their "home-towns" during the prolonged tensions in 1835–1845. Middleton explains the significance of home-towns in Ghana as "focus of clan and family life" in a "region marked by continuous movement of population."[212] Consequently, when Akuropon became riddled with constant conflicts and a "climate of enmity, fear, and violence" prevailed, many returned to their villages.[213]

The missionaries testify to a depopulated town throughout these years.[214] Not only was by 1843 more than half of Akuropon "deserted ... and therefore fallen into ruins," already in the 1830s Riis felt they could have little close contact with the population because of the frictions.[215] The missionaries carefully evaded such implications, but quite possibly people avoided them because of their partiality in the conflict. Furthermore, if the missionaries managed to have conversations, they found the people "too preoccupied with their political disputes to be able to guide their thoughts towards higher matters."[216] Consequently, the ministry remained limited to their "own people," the employees living with them, by July 1838 comprising of laborers, two carpenters, a tailor,

---

211. Kwamena-Poh, *Akuapem State*, 49. See also Reindorf, *History*, 89–90.

212. Middleton, "Home-Town." The complex meanings of "home-town" (Twi: *kurom*) in Ghana as a center of people's roots and identity they will always return and refer back to go are still important. In this article Middleton identifies the roles of Akuropon as "home-town" in the late twentieth century.

213. Abun-Nasr, *David Asante*, 63.

214. For example: BMA, D-1,1 Akropong 1838 #6 Riis July 6, 1838; BMA, D-1,2 Akropong 1843 #5 Widmann July 20, 1843.

215. BMA, D-1,1 Akropong 1837 #10 Riis November 14, 1837; MM 1838, 386.

216. BMA, D-1,1 Akropong 1836 #9 Riis diary August 17, 1836; MM 1837, 552.

an interpreter, and a cook, sixteen people altogether.[217] With them they sought conversations and held daily devotions.

This way, whatever the missionaries' role in it, the political conflict affected their ability to accomplish their mission. Akuropon became a location with no audience and the few there were had more pressing issues on their minds than the foreigners' strange message. This only changed after 1845 with peace restored under a new King.

Neutrality That Attracted: Medical Assistance

The Basel Mission idea of political neutrality made Riis's situation difficult in a number of ways, but in time his commitment to staying in Akuropon and especially the medical assistance he rendered irrespective of parties attracted some.

Already in the Krobo campaign Riis's desire for political neutrality and honest care for people had led him to help the wounded from both sides as best as he could.[218] He continued this practice throughout the various skirmishes he witnessed and by 1837 testified to the effect on the people of all factions who trusted him and brought their wounded.[219] Opoku emphasizes Riis's "witness by his life" as most important: "his opposition to drink, his hard working, fair and just treatment of his servants . . . and first aid given . . . to the wounded and the sick."[220] While Opoku is generally too uncritical of Riis, there was an attraction in this medical help.

However, this was not part of the "mission work" the Basel Mission instructions had outlined, and Riis was little prepared for it. The short basic medical course at the BMTI was not geared at ministry to Africans but at the survival of the missionaries. Yet, Riis's experience in the short civil unrest in Switzerland during his training had modeled this response to war and suffering. Like then in Basel, he now felt pity for the injured of both sides of the struggle and attempted to help them. The Africans in turn appreciated the physical aid but—as Riis himself testifies—were not so receptive to his spiritual message.[221] While Riis's descriptions of

---

217. BMA, D-1,1 Akropong 1838 #6 Riis July 6, 1838; Opoku, *Riis, the Builder*, 65.
218. Ibid., 38–39. BMA, D-1,1 Akropong 1836 #1 Riis February 10, 1836.
219. BMA, D-1,1 Akropong 1837 #10 Riis November 14, 1837; MM 1838, 386–87.
220. Opoku, *Riis, the Builder*, 84–85.
221. BMA, D-1,1 Akropong 1836 #9 Riis diary August 12, 1836; MM 1837, 551–52.

Africans are no compliment, his mission was to them and he cared for their wellbeing as he understood it.

Akuapem people too, were curious about this different kind of European in their midst. This is probably the best way to interpret the statement Riis records, that he was not like other Europeans. His message and much of his behavior made little sense to the Africans but they testified that "we know you have good intentions for us" and asked him to stay and bring others.[222] In some ways Riis developed more patience with their response. Beyond the typical stereotypes of African indolence, drunkenness, deceptiveness, and indifference, he makes the significant observation that it will take time for Africans to accept "a thing that so far is completely foreign to them."[223] His hope was that the suffering and need they experienced would draw people to God.

In these various ways African political realities affected the mission. Danish colonial interests, however, created the greatest tensions and earned the missionaries serious reprimand from the Basel leadership.

Danish Colonial Interests Affected the Mission

Warren posits "three quite distinct angles" from which church-state relationships in the period must be viewed.[224] Beyond the missionaries' representation of the church to African states, he highlights the relationships between British parliament and cabinet and missionary societies, and between the British Colonial Government and the local Church. This close association of British missionaries with British authorities cannot be paralleled in the Basel Mission. As an international organization they highly valued political neutrality and had no specific national alliance in Europe. This made their political relationships considerably more complicated. While situated in a Swiss city, the majority of Basel Mission members were German. There were long-standing relationships in Britain through the German Lutheran community and key leaders like Steinkopf, as well as the cooperation with the CMS. However, only collaboration with Danish authorities enabled them to send missionaries to Guinea. Instructions to the missionaries, therefore, explicitly admonished

---

222. BMA, D-1,1 Akropong 1837 #9 Riis diary September 29, 1837; MM 1837, 555.

223. BMA, D-1,1 Akropong 1836 #9 Riis October 27, 1836; MM 1837, 549, 558–59.

224. Warren, *Social History*, 24–35.

them to avoid political or commercial involvement. Yet, entanglements with colonial interests were inevitable and greatly complicated missionary engagement.

Riis settled in Akuropon shortly after governor Mørck's arrival. During 1835 he was preoccupied with building work and Mørck struggled with sickness. Towards the end of the year the governor began to pursue his policy of consolidating Danish power. Visiting Akuropon to recover his health was only a pretext; subsequent events confirm Kwamena-Poh's observation that he "was more obsessed with the other aim of the visit, that is 'to examine whether colonization is possible.'"[225] Mørck self-evidently assumed residence in Riis's house and the missionary tried his best to make him comfortable.[226] Later Mørck accused him of building "a snug dwelling place for his personal comfort, not really for the purpose of evangelizing."[227]

Mørck obviously expected Riis as loyal Danish citizen to fully support his aspirations. However, the missionary only reluctantly accompanied him to Krobo and restricted his involvement to caring for the wounded of all sides.[228] When shortly afterwards Addo Dankwa defected to British Accra, Mørck suspected Riis's influence and ordered him to the coast. Not given a choice, Riis complied and was held up in Osu for four months. He grew increasingly impatient to return, feeling "no consolation in the company of [his] landsmen since their moral life is so bad."[229] Finally permitted to leave in June 1836, Riis met the entourage of the arrested Addo Dankwa in Aburi, just before the king escaped the Danish soldiers.[230] Riis's report emphasizes that he met Addo Dankwa only very briefly and ensured everybody of his political neutrality. For the Okuapemhene this was apparently good news, while the Danish Governor sent an order recalling Riis to Christiansborg. This time the missionary

---

225. Kwamena-Poh, *Akuapem State*, 104. Kwamena-Poh cites a letter by Mørch to Copenhagen from February 12, 1836.

226. BMA, D-1,1 Akropong 1836 # 1 Riis February 10, 1836; Akropong 1837 #5 Riis April 30, 1837.

227. Opoku, *Riis, the Builder*, 32. Opoku cites BMA, D-1,1 Akropong 1838 #6 Riis July 6, 1838.

228. BMA, D-1,1 Akropong 1836 #1 Riis February 10, 1836.

229. BMA, D-1,1 Akropong 1836 #2 Riis April 1, 1836.

230. BMA, D-1,1 Akropong 1836 #6 Riis July 27, 1836; MM 1837, 540–43.

refused.²³¹ An earlier letter expressed his fear that the governor would hold him indefinitely, possibly arrest him or even have him deported.²³²

Both men's reports triggered conversations and communications in Europe. The Danish king commended Riis and two traders (Lutterodt and Svanekjaer) for their "free willingness in the part they took in the expedition" against Krobo.²³³ In Basel the Board discussed the implications of Riis's forced stay in Osu and Mørck's threats, and sent enquiries to their contacts in Copenhagen.²³⁴ The Danish king, in turn, asked Mørck for a detailed investigation. This instruction arrived in November 1836 on the same ship as Riis's new colleagues and bride.

Riis was called before the Danish Colonial Council in Christiansborg.²³⁵ Both Oelschner and Opoku present this as a major court hearing during which Riis had to respond to a list of accusations which he described in a letter from April 1837.²³⁶ He was charged with persuading Addo Dankwa to defect and exchanging secret messages with him, speaking against the Danish in Akuropon telling people not to fear Mørck, selling gunpowder, promoting English language schooling, buying goods from the British, and generally behaving "curiously" towards Mørck. Riis's letter detailed his defense: He maintained that he had met Addo Dankwa only very briefly and asserted his neutrality. According to Riis, there were no secret messages, but his diary did report repeated communications with Addo Dankwa.²³⁷ He had only bought from British traders because some things were not available in Christiansborg. He admitted that he had been given a small amount of gunpowder by a Danish officer to buy food, but emphasized that this was unavoidable common exchange economy practice. Finally, English language teaching would be more useful for Africans in trade, but he would much rather teach in vernacular. Anyway, Riis emphasized, Mørck would end all disputes with

---

231. Ibid., 544–45.

232. BMA, D-1,1 Akropong 1836 #3 Riis May 28, 1836.

233. Kwamena-Poh, *Akuapem State*, 107. Kwamen-Poh suggests this campaign contributed to Mørck's promotion from acting to full governor in 1837.

234. BMA, KP July 18, 1836; Copybook 26. Januar 1836—1. April 1837, Inspector's letter to Riis from July 19, 1836. cited in BMA, D-12.1 *Ghana. Auszüge aus den Akten* (Excerpts from the Files) 1828-1851 by Hans Debrunner, 1856, 20.

235. BMA, D-1,1 Akropong 1836 #12 Riis November 24, 1836.

236. BMA, D-1,1 Akropong 1837 #5 Riis April 30, 1837; Oelschner, *Landung in Osu*, 138–44; Opoku, *Riis, the Builder*, 50–55.

237. MM 1837 552 and 555, Riis diary April 2 and September 6, 1836.

stating a "moral conviction" of his guilt which was proof of the governor's bias against him.

Again the reports were discussed in Europe. The Basel Mission enquired in Denmark and Britain, and even wrote to Lutterrodt for his opinion.[238] Riis, Mürdter, and Stanger were told to "keep out of politics, but try to maintain good relations with the Government, if possible."[239] Mørck's reports led to a "royal decree permitting him to remove Riis to Copenhagen, if he thinks it advisable," which the Basel Mission Director communicated to Riis in October 1837.[240] In the same letter Blumhardt ordered the missionaries to "continue work quietly" and if Mørck used force, they "should yield." Meanwhile, their enquiries in Britain had opened "the possibility to remove to English territory, where they would be welcome." Thus, political entanglements in Africa also forced the mission leaders into more political engagement than anticipated or desired. They reminded the missionaries to remain neutral, even though it was, at least in part, BMTI instilled judgments that prevented this. The international mindset of the Basel Mission meant they had no apprehensions to move to another colonial sphere of influence. However, this added to making the missionaries' position suspicious to the Danish officials.

While the conversations continued in Europe, in Guinea the situation during 1837 and 1838 was a stalemate that enabled the missionaries to establish their station in Akuropon and take various reconnaissance trips to regions beyond. Later Riis claimed that he saw Mørck the last time in April 1837.[241] The latter's death in March 1839 ended the personal hostilities, if not the unease between Danish officials and Basel missionaries.

The "Bitter Palaver" Between Mørck and Riis

Debrunner describes the "long and bitter palaver" between Riis and Mørck as "an early example of the clash between colonial and missionary

---

238. BMA, Copybook June 1837—July 12, 1838, cited in BMA, D-12.1 *Ghana Auszüge*, 23. Inspector's letter "to Lutterrodt in Danish Accra" from April 26, 1837.

239. Ibid., Inspector's letter "to the Brethren in Africa" from April 26, 1837.

240. Ibid., Inspector's letter from October 19, 1837; Kwamena-Poh, *Akuapem State*, 116. Kwamena-Poh cites Guineiske Journaler, Royal Resolution, 5 September, 1837. He sets this in the wrong historical context (referring to Riis's return in 1843). This resolution was issued in September 1837 at the height of the palaver and before Mørck fell into disrepute in Copenhagen.

241. BMA, D-1,1 Akropong 1839 #3 Riis February 20, 1839.

interests" and by emphasizing the Danish governor's hostility to Christian mission follows the traditional Basel Mission narrative.[242] Tellingly, beyond this assertion published reports omit much of the conflict. The political entanglements of the missionaries were an embarrassment for the leaders and hard to explain to their supporters who valued political non-engagement. The BMTI training had not envisioned such complications. Riis admits this gap in his preparation stating that in Basel they could "hardly imagine the difficulties of our position under these conditions." Abun-Nasr interprets this correctly as "a partial confession ... that theoretical maxims of political neutrality sound more convincing at home, far away from the daily mission-work at the Gold Coast."[243] Colonial realities and Riis's Danish citizenship meant he was inevitably drawn into Mørck's Danish colonial aspirations.

Furthermore, there were significant personal differences between the two men. Oelschner's imagined conversations—while fraud with many inaccuracies—illustrate well the variances of intent towards Africans between Riis and other Europeans in Guinea who cared only "to take what we can and leave before we die."[244] The missionary had developed relationships with Akuapem people well beyond the general European ignorance, disregard, and maltreatment of Africans. He desired to teach and help Africans and did not share other European's primary focus on material gain. However, BMTI inspired evaluations led to his partiality, not only in the African conflict but also against the Danish governor.

Riis's evaluations of Governor Mørck are never positive, but worsen over time. In 1836 he described him as "a man who wants to rule absolutely over everybody" but was "otherwise a good man."[245] Later he claims that Mørck "lives like a pagan out here" and rumor has it that "excess of drink is undermining the poor man's health."[246] Riis evinces the persistent missionary condemnation of European immorality on the coast, and Mørck added in his view reprehensible political ambitions and ungodly leadership. Consistently, Riis judged Europeans, including the governor, by the same BMTI instilled values and practice which guided his

---

242. Debrunner, *Christianity in Ghana*, 100.
243. Abun-Nasr, *David Asante*, 67.
244. Oelschner, *Landung in Osu*, 98–102.
245. BMA, D-1,1 Akropong 1836 #3 Riis May 28, 1836.
246. BMA, D-1,1 Akropong 1838 #4 Riis May 28 1838; Akropong 1839 #3 Riis February 20, 1839.

evaluation of Africans: their morals and "godly" leadership, and whether they supported Christian mission.

Riis can hardly be called an unbiased observer, but others also portray Mørck in a less than flattering way. Kwamena-Poh describes him as "an energetic and ambitious naval officer who ... was obsessed with establishing a European 'colony' in Akuapem" and Metcalfe as a "young man in a hurry" who "hastened not only his own end, but the end of Danish rule."[247] Both recount the headlong clash with British interests of trade and political control Mørck's actions involved. In this clash Riis was caught up, not least because he was Danish.

Riis's Danish Citizenship and Perceptions of Neutrality

Initially, Riis's Danish citizenship was regarded as asset because he knew the language and did not have to spend extended time in Denmark before his departure like the preceding Germans. His relationships to the Danish support societies ensured their assistance, strengthened the connections with the pious circles in Denmark, and contributed to the king's backing of the venture. However, in Guinea Riis's Danish citizenship became a mixed blessing.

As Debrunner comments, Mørck "hoped that Andreas Riis ... would promote the Danish colonial interests in Akwapim, especially since Riis was himself Danish."[248] Opoku adds Mørck "had hoped that Riis would use his influence in favour of the Danes ... that he would move Adow Dankwa to return to the Danes, and that he would keep him informed of all political maneuvers going on in Akwapim."[249] Mørck imposed on Riis, saw in him an informant, and expected Danish loyalty. Riis was not prepared to offer either because of his self-understanding as neutral agent of an international Christian mission. This dynamic lay beneath the tensions between the two men.

Missionary neutrality is maintained as the primary cause of the conflict by most authors. Debrunner claims that in conformity with Basel Mission policy, Riis "remained neutral, attending to the ... wounded in the civil strife and trying to pacify the political opponents within Akwapim," and this attitude was considered by Mørck "to be high treason

---

247. Kwamena-Poh, *Akuapem State*, 102–7; Metcalfe, *Maclean*, 196–202.
248. Debrunner, *Christianity in Ghana*, 100.
249. Opoku, *Riis, the Builder*, 52.

against Denmark."[250] Commenting in an unpublished document on Riis's descriptions, Debrunner's position is even clearer. He suggests that the palaver "seems to originate in the fact that the governor cannot understand the christian [sic] neutrality in the political matters concerned and that he was offended at the moral strictness of Riis."[251] This comment by a Basel Mission representative almost hundred-thirty years later not only illustrates the prevailing interpretation of the events in the organization, it also shows that Riis's stance was seen as "Christian" and his morality approved of. Many Ghanaian authors agree. Kwamena-Poh posits that "Riis's neutrality . . . had been misunderstood in the Danish circles," and Opoku asserts Mørck "could not understand this attitude of a missionary and therefore accused Riis of high treason."[252] Quartey, conversely, sees in Riis's behavior evidence for "colonial fantasies" and completely ignores the counterargument to his thesis that Riis's tensions with the Danish governor and attempts at neutrality entail.[253]

Riis's conflict with the Danish Governor is the clearest indication that it was not national or colonial interests that motivated the missionary but the values and virtues he had acquired through his preparation processes. In spite of his Danish nationality, Riis was opposed to Mørck's crude efforts to expand Danish influence in Akuapem. He expressed clearly his refusal to be an informant for the Danish governor.[254] In the same letter Riis condemned Mørck morally and religiously as one who "uses Christian language but in Africa lives like a pagan and despises the word of God." Most authors follow Riis's own account that consistently pleaded his innocence and the governor's unjust accusations of treason while he followed Basel Mission policy of neutrality.

However, the point of contention was not so much his neutrality as he claimed—and practiced as far as medical aid was concerned—it was his actual partiality which infuriated the governor. As Tufuoh rightly observes, Riis's stand was "influenced by two things: his disgust with the Danish community at Christiansborg and his great regard for Ado

250. Debrunner, *Christianity in Ghana*, 100.

251. BMA D-12,1 *Ghana Auszüge*, 25. This comment follows Debrunner's summary of Riis's letter from April 30, 1837 which details Mørck's accusations and Riis's responses.

252. Kwamena-Poh, *Akuapem State*, 115–16; Opoku, *Riis, the Builder*, 52.

253. Quartey, *Missionary Practices*, 52–54. He devotes only a very brief and superficial section to the protracted conflict.

254. BMA, D-1,1 Akropong 1838 #4 Riis May 28, 1838.

Dankwa."²⁵⁵ Riis's BMTI training had persuaded him of distinct judgments which he applied in both. As a result, he was anything but a neutral participant in African and colonial politics. Riis's identification with Addo Dankwa and Owusu Akyem made him suspect, not only to the factions on the other side of the Akuapem conflict, but also to Mørck. His contempt for Mørck's moral life and refusal to follow orders added to the governor's consternation with his defiant subject. Furthermore, sympathies for the British de-facto governor Maclean because of his support for Christian mission are obvious. Riis regularly communicated with the British missionaries in Cape Coast and Maclean who invited him repeatedly to relocate.²⁵⁶ British sympathies were also evinced by the Basel Board when they considered the option to transfer the mission to the British area and had already taken steps to ensure support.²⁵⁷ It was Riis's Danish citizenship that almost certainly saved him from imprisonment or expulsion during this period, in spite of his contempt of the governor and obvious British sympathies.

The Need for a Supportive Colonial Government

The British sympathies in the Basel Mission during the 1830s reflected the conviction that for the success of their mission a supportive government was essential. Mørck's lacking support was perceived and communicated to the supporters as major reason for the failure to achieve organizational goals.²⁵⁸ Tufuo's comparison with early Methodist missionaries on the British Gold Coast arrives at a similar conclusion: While in Cape Coast missionary Freeman acted as advisor to Maclean and there was a "sense of involvement and unity of purpose between various sections of the expatriate community . . . , the Basel mission . . . was never really in accord with the [Danish] administration."²⁵⁹ Riis's confession that they did not dare to visit the Africans too much, for fear the governor would suspect them of political agitation, raised great concern and was

---

255. Tufuoh, "Relations," 54.

256. BMA, D-1,1 Akropong 1836 #1 Riis February 10, 1836; Akropong 1837 #9 Mürdter October 25 and #13 Riis December 2, 1837.

257. BMA, Copybook June 1837—July 12, 1838, Inspector's letters to Riis from April 26 and October 19, 1837; cited in BMA, D-12.1 *Ghana Auszüge*, 23.

258. BMA, KP February 27, 1839; Wurm, "Anfänge," 266. See also Blumhardt's comments preceding excerpts from Mürdter and Riis's letters in MM 1838, 383.

259. Tufuoh, "Relations," 52.

quoted repeatedly.²⁶⁰ The Board discussed this predicament and decided to write to the Danish king again in 1838 requesting "a decisive statement whether the brothers can work freely and unhindered; if not, they would leave the Danish area and move to the capital of Asante."²⁶¹

In 1840, when Riis was in Europe and the Basel Mission rethought its engagement in Africa, a noteworthy article reported both, Riis's sobering account at the annual festival and the former Liberia missionary Sessing's ideas about the African mission.²⁶² Riis's admission that all he could think of was trusting God is juxtaposed with Sessing's concrete admonition that reliance on African protection was unwise and, as long as the slave trade continued on the coast, only a supportive colonial government promised success to the mission. The example he cited to support this conviction was "the mission-colony in Sierra Leone which owes its existence besides God only to the protection and support of the English government." Sessing's suggestion was the contemporary practical solution. The conviction was widely spread that missionaries needed European government protection. Especially in Britain, there was a close association between Evangelical mission supporters and government interventions in Africa. It was what most European missionaries in time chose, which renders legitimacy to common claims of missionary collaboration with the European colonial enterprise.

By the time of the third beginning in the 1840s the Basel Mission in Ghana enjoyed a supportive Danish governor too. Carstensen, according to Hernæs in many respects "pursued the same policy as Mørck, although more diplomatically."²⁶³ He visited Akuropon in September 1843 to pursue "two important issues: namely to enforce a peaceful relationship among the Akuapem people themselves and the expansion of the Basel Mission's activities in the Akuapem country."²⁶⁴ On this visit Carstensen dealt forcefully with the Akuapem council. Under threats of military intervention and withdrawal of the palm-oil trade they surrendered to his demands. They included a settlement between the conflicting fac-

260. BMA, D-1,1 Akropong 1838 #2 Riis February 3, 1838; cited, for example by Schlatter, *Basler Mission in Afrika*, 30. See also earlier statements to the same effect, i.e. that they have to keep more distance from the Africans than they would like, in BMA, D-1,1 Akropong 1837 #10 Riis November 14, 1837, cited in MM 1838, 386.

261. BMA, KP June 13 1838.

262. HB 1840, 71–72.

263. Hernæs, "Introduction," xvii.

264. Carstensen letter October 20, 1843 in Carstensen, *Closing the Books*, 58–60.

tions (at least to Carstensen's satisfaction, subsequent events show that this was not the end of conflicts), allowing the Basel Mission to establish schools in the state, and Adum's concession to live in Akuropon (which he had avoided because of the opposition by both, the missionaries and a section of the population). In 1844 Carstensen articulated his vision for the missionaries along familiar lines. He posited that "the goal was "the introduction of culture and civilization among the Negroes," and Denmark could make its contribution "through the well-aimed efforts of the [Basel] missionaries." Therefore, "Danish officials should establish close contact with the Basel Mission, support its enterprises, and protect its members."[265]

In this way the Basel Mission—despite their preference for political neutrality—eventually also bought into general European perceptions and practice that regarded European military and economic support of Christian mission in Africa as indispensable. The "image of Africa" was too pervasive and prevented the alternative approach that Riis's initial relationships had suggested. Reliance on the hospitality and friendship of local people would have actually been a more "biblical" approach.[266] Given more cultural sensitivity and less European arrogance, who knows what the response in Akuapem would have been. Alas, the early missionaries' condemnation of African culture and misconceptions of African rulers prevented them and those who followed to ever consider this alternative approach. Consequently, they were occupied with "station building" and for years did not have the time and energy to learn the vernacular sufficiently to truly understand what was going on around them.

Dependence on Traders Affected the Mission

In the absence of government support Riis relied all the more heavily on individual traders to acquire provisions and gain assistance. Foremost among them was Lutterodt. Debrunner also mentions the "Mulatto trader H. Richter" who was later entrusted with collecting the palm oil payments of the fine imposed on Krobo in 1836.[267] In 1834 Riis had food

---

265. Carstensen "Remarks," June 30, 1844 and letter July 25, 1844 in ibid., 78, 84.

266. At least, Jesus seems to suggest this in Matthew 10:11 when he instructed disciples he sent on mission to find someone who offered hospitality and "stay at their house" until they left the town.

267. Metcalfe, *Maclean*, 200; Debrunner, *Christianity in Ghana*, 99.

and lodgings with Richter in exchange for teaching his children.[268] Collaboration between missionaries and merchants was not unique. Kobia, for example, identifies close connections between CMS missionaries and the British East Africa Company.[269] He concludes that "there were either the chartered companies or individual white businessmen to help Christian mission with finance and some other assistance" and until the 1850s across Africa "every missionary depended for passage, freight, and correspondence on the trading vessel."[270] In the British Gold Coast Maclean's long period of supportive rule was a major factor for the establishment of the Methodists.[271] This is Tufuoh's main argument in his comparison with the relative animosity of the Danish against Riis during the same time.[272] Significantly, Maclean was "President of Merchants" in a period when British government had conceded rule of the Gold Coast to the Company of Merchants. More importantly, as Tufuoh shows, Maclean represented a different kind of merchant of the post-abolition period with ideas of "legitimate commerce." He was aided by "pressures generated by humanitarians in Britain" (affecting closer scrutiny on traders' activities in Africa) and "transformed . . . the local administration from a mere agent of British trading interests into an instrument of social reform." In this process, merchant administration and missionaries shared "a common interest in providing . . . a foundation for the spread of Christianity and Western culture" in Africa, which led to very close collaboration between them—at least until the Gold Coast became "protected territory" and British governors proved less sensitive to local conditions and interests.[273]

In the Danish region early Basel missionaries could not count on government support. Consequently, they established close relationships with individual merchants. Henke already relied on some traders' generosity.[274] For Riis, Lutterrodt and Richter became key providers of needed assistance. Curiously, Tufuoh discusses the lack of Danish official support but, in spite of his argument of merchant-missionary collaboration, he leaves the traders unmentioned who enabled Riis to persevere. This eco-

268. BMA, D-1,1 Christiansborg 1834 #5 Riis April 1 and #6 June 10, 1834 Riis to Büchelen.
269. Kobia, "The Christian Mission and the African Peoples," 158–59.
270. Tufuoh, "Relations," 49.
271. Metcalfe, *Maclean*, 117–23, 235–42.
272. Tufuoh, "Relations," 38–55.
273. Ibid., 47–51.
274. BMA, D-1,1 Christiansborg 1830 #2 Henke May 20, 1830.

nomic reliance, however, not only entailed some compromise with moral judgments of coastal Europeans, it affected the missionaries' ability to remain politically neutral.

British Support Aggravated Danish Suspicions

Already Henke and his colleagues failed to find voyage in Denmark and ended up traveling from London.[275] Subsequently, all Basel missionaries used British ships, landed first at Cape Coast, and maintained contact and cordial relationships with the British governor and missionaries there.[276] Arrangements for correspondence and financial support from Basel were made via London too. In 1828 they were instructed to send letters to contacts in London, checks were to be made out to Rönne via Copenhagen, but Coates of the CMS in London was already proposed as alternative "we hear should be easy."[277] After 1840 all proceedings were conducted through London.[278]

Riis's experience confirmed the infrequency and unreliability of Danish ships and traders. Consequently, he suggested to the Basel Mission treasurer that it would be "good if the missionaries were not so dependent on the Danish royal stores in Christiansborg and the moods of the officers there."[279] Another indication is his report in March 1837 that he had bought two years' worth provisions from a Danish ship, presumably stocking up while he had the (rare) opportunity.[280] Later that year his Danish credit was overdrawn and only a "kind store administrator" and an "English merchant" gave him "secretly" what he needed.[281] Almost two years later a large consignment Riis ordered finally arrived—alas, by

---

275. BMA, D-10.3,2 "Briefe der Brüder Cappeler, Henke, Holzwarth, Salbach, J.G. Schmidt."

276. BMA, D-1,1 Christiansborg 1832 #8 and #11 Heinze April 2 and Jäger May 16, 1832; Akropong 1836 #11 Mürdter November 14, 1836. For regular relationships and communications, see BMA, D-1,1 Akropong 1835 #6 Riis July 27, 1835; Akropong 1837 #9 Mürdter October 25, 1837.

277. BMA, D-10.3,3 Instructions 1828 (IV.2 and 3).

278. BMA Q-3-3,26 Instructionen 1842 §1; June 1846 (Meischel, Dieterle, Stanger, Mohr) §2. The latter includes instructions to travel via London and obtain all equipment there, anticipating assistance from Basel Mission contacts in the city.

279. BMA, D-1,1 Akropong und Ussu 1836 #10 Riis to Büchelen October 30, 1836

280. BMA, D-1,1 Akropong 1837 #2 Riis to Büchelen March 14, 1837.

281. BMA, D-1,1 Akropong 1837 #10 Riis November 14, 1837.

then his colleagues had died and, left alone with his wife and child, he asked for advice whether to keep it.[282]

Thus, conditions in Guinea repeatedly forced the missionaries to obtain provisions from English traders. This contributed to their British sympathies and aggravated Danish government suspicions against them. Not surprisingly, trade dealings with British agents were among the accusations Mørck levied against Riis.[283] His defense expressed their dilemma: true, he had bought goods in English Accra, but "only because they were unobtainable at Christiansborg."

Compelled to Engage in Politics with Lutterodt

The close relationship with the merchant Lutterodt on whose plantation the missionaries regularly recuperated, in whose house Riis stayed in Osu, and who generally provided the Basel missionaries with necessities into the 1850s, can be argued as a major factor facilitating their survival in Guinea. Even the Basel leadership acknowledged this trader's contribution and asked his advice in the protracted conflict with Mørck.[284] Lutterodt's response in March 1838 confirmed Riis's presentation of events, stating that "the unfortunate palaver ... originates in hostile feelings of the governor, [and] Riis is innocent."[285] He also promised to "continue to show kindness to the missionaries."

However, this relationship caused Riis eventually to be drawn into political involvement much beyond what he or his superiors appreciated. In 1844 Lutterodt was acting governor in Carstensen's absence. When he had to deal with a complicated local dispute in Akuapem, he recruited Riis's assistance which the missionary could not refuse. Consequently, he took part in a rather unfortunate intervention that involved marching with twenty soldiers against Adum's supporters in Tutu and Mampong.[286] Carstensen's report indicates that Riis's partiality in the African royal conflict influenced Lutterodt's actions.[287] Later he went so far as

282. BMA, D-1,1 Akropong 1839 #1 Riis to Büchelen January 9, 1839.

283. BMA, D-1,1 Akropong 1837 # 5 Riis April 30, 1837.

284. BMA, Copybook June 1837—July 12, 1838, Inspector's letter "to Lutterodt in Danish Accra" from April 26, 1837, cited in D-12.1 *Ghana Auszüge*, 23.

285. BMA, D-1,1 Akropong 1838 #2a Merchant Lutterodt from Ussu to Inspector, March 1, 1838, cited in D-12.1 *Ghana Auszüge*, 29.

286. Kwamena-Poh, *Akuapem State*, 67.

287. Carstensen letter November 20, 1845 in Carstensen, *Closing the Books*, 165–66.

to implicate Riis to have instigated the whole expedition.[288] Even to this missionary-friendly governor Riis became discredited.

Thus, the friendship with the merchant Lutterodt eventually pulled Riis into political matters so deeply that it earned him rebuke, not only from the mission leaders in Basel, but also the Danish establishment. It caused Riis to be suspected again in Copenhagen, and Carstensen would not recommend a redeployment of Riis in Guinea. Kwamena-Poh sums it up: "Riis ... became discredited as a result of his involvement with Lutterodt in Akuapem politics" in 1844 and "had to depart from the Gold Coast in 1845."[289] However, Carstensen continued to strongly support the Basel Mission and refused a full-scale inquiry because a "public investigation of the conduct of Missionary Riis will prove harmful to the mission."[290]

In the 1850s the Basel Mission "developed a vigorous trade section as integral part of its work" which, as Tufuoh rightly observes, afforded them independence from the banking services of the "mercantile establishments."[291] He does not pursue the argument, but an obvious incentive for developing this independent trading company seemed to have been the lack and unreliability of material support early Basel missionaries had experienced in the Danish region.

CONCLUSIONS FROM ANDREAS RIIS'S PIONEERING

This chapter explored indications for trained incapacity in Andreas Riis's pioneering. It focused on specific aspects of his life and ministry, to identify correlations between his background and preparation and his engagement in Africa. The findings are mixed. There are indications for helpful revisions to BMTI instilled values but also for trained incapacity hindering Riis's adjustment, the achievement of organizational goals, and a positive African response.

For the sake of survival Riis compromised with BMTI ideas. His trust in the treatment of an African healer marked a significant departure from European perceptions of African ignorance and savagery. Later, moving to Akuropon established this mountainous region as healthier

---

288. Carstensen letter September 14, 1846 in ibid., 254–58.

289. Kwamena-Poh, *Akuapem State*, 116–117.

290. Carstensen letter September 14, 1846 in Carstensen, *Closing the Books*, 254–58.

291. Tufuoh, "Relations," 48.

for Europeans than the coast. The move itself reflected the vision to engage native Africans beyond the influence of European officials and traders. But the assertion of this region as healthier was in contrast to initial Basel Mission perceptions of the coast as the best place to acclimatize to the tropical climate. Furthermore, Riis compromised the "proud ideal of needlessness in Africa" by occasionally using hammock travel and eventually employing many African workers. There are indications that Riis established relationships of open exchange with some Africans, and he clearly received generous support and hospitality from African rulers. He also adjusted to African food and accommodations, especially when he travelled.

Notwithstanding these adjustments, the European perceptions of Africa and Basel Mission priority of "cultivating the wild land" alienated Riis from Africans as soon as he began to implement the mission. BMTI values regarding humility, independent self-sufficiency, and diligence, as well as European ideas of workmanship and labor remuneration shaped his actions and created tensions. This became particularly obvious around the building project in Akuropon. In the process, the missionary's incapacity to adapt to a different set of work values and the general circumstances in Akuapem upset the African leadership of the state, caused serious frictions, and alienated the people he wanted to reach, thereby reducing his ability to communicate the Christian message to a few laborers who were mostly foreign to Akuapem.

While Riis and his colleagues were not intentional or conscious agents of colonialism or living out any "colonial fantasies," they found it impossible to maintain the political neutrality they valued. Neutrality proved elusive because it was at variance with other BMTI values which caused them to evaluate African rulers and European officials by German Pietist concepts of benign authority and morality and by their support of the mission. The resultant partiality meant missionaries took sides in the African conflict without understanding its intricacies. It also lay at the root of the protracted tensions with the Danish governor. Mørck added in the missionaries' evaluation to general European misbehavior reprehensible political ambitions, ungodly leadership, and hostility towards mission. The frictions with both, African and colonial authorities contributed to the difficulties the missionaries faced to implement their goals and attract African converts. One aspect of their practice of neutrality, however, was appealing, their medical aid to injured people from all parties of the ongoing conflict.

Danish obstructions of their goals caused the Basel Mission and its agents in Africa to sympathize with more supportive colonial powers which resulted in greater suspicions towards them. Furthermore, economic need compelled the missionaries to associate with some of the morally despised Europeans and traders. Riis even developed friendships with individuals. However, these relationships also affected the ability to remain politically neutral and contributed to impediments of the mission. In Riis's case, they eventually expedited his dismissal from Africa.

Overall, the compromises with Basel Mission values Riis made were minor in comparison to the ways in which attitudes and priorities acquired from preparation processes affected the ministry negatively. Thus, in the pioneering ministry of Andreas Riis and his colleagues trained incapacity became a major factor preventing the realization of organizational goals, adjustment to African conditions, and positive African responses to the Christian gospel. This is further seen in the failures at "mission work" in the late 1830s.

6

Early Failures at Mission Work (1836–1840)

EVALUATIONS OF EARLY PROTESTANT missions in Africa are unanimous. Rüther summarizes, "mission initiatives along the so-called West African slave coast almost always resulted in failure between 1450 and 1850."[1] She adds that "individual missionary expeditions were divided by long interruptions, and they hardly impacted on the way African societies conceived of themselves, their immediate surroundings, and of the wider world." So far we saw that in the Basel Mission too, individual survivors made little impact in the early years. But the failure to achieve missionary goals continued and there are indications that trained incapacity was a contributing factor.

When the reinforcements joined Riis in November 1836, for a period there was a small missionary team in Akuropon. Andreas Stanger and Johannes Mürdter hailed from Württemberg, the Basel Mission heartland. The minutes of the Board meeting describe them as "unpretentious, simple, and proven brothers, yielded to the Lord."[2] Though Stanger did not have a particular gift for languages, he had "excellent abilities" and a "clear comprehension of Christianity." Mürdter's assets were his skillfulness as carpenter and that he was "serious, simple-minded, and punctual." The descriptions show that these BMTI graduates had internalized the practice of this community and passed the leaders' evaluation of their proficiency in it. All were considerably younger than Riis, Mürdter five,

---

1. Rüther, "Conversion to Christianity," 253.

2. BMA, KP April 20, 1836; Schlatter, *Basler Mission in Afrika*, 29; Wurm, "Anfänge," 261.

Stanger seven, Anna twelve years.³ The age difference probably contributed to Riis's undisputed leadership, in addition to his experience in Africa.

Very little is known of Anna Riis, nee Wolters, beyond the report of her pastor as it is recorded in the Board minutes.⁴ She is praised for her "simple, childlike inclinations, devotion to the savior, humility, unpretentiousness," and "nice talents." Furthermore, she was a penniless orphan and her brothers were friends of her husband. The missionaries' letters contain almost no records of her life in Africa beyond various bouts of illness and the births and deaths of her children. As there is also no other information on her, Sill concludes that "her presence does not appear to have had any noticeable effect in Akuapem."⁵ Sill analyzed the role of women in the Basel mission very incisively, but my study focuses on the men who trained in the BMTI, in order to identify effects of this preparation on their intercultural engagement.

The missionary team embarked on efforts towards articulated Basel Mission goals. Primarily, they were occupied with expanding, improving, and repairing the buildings and establishing agricultural projects in Akuropon.⁶ They attempted to learn language and proclaim their message, and went on various trips into the adjacent regions. But they also experienced continued tensions with local authorities, this time especially the Danish chaplain. Eventually, death struck again. After just over one year Stanger died and Mürdter after exactly two years, leaving Andreas and Anna Riis. Riis went on a number of reconnaissance trips culminating with the journey into Asante from November 1839 to January 1840. He

---

3. In fact, Riis commented on the youth of his bride, but submitted to the Board decision as the will of God, stating his conviction that "the Lord sends her to him." BMA, D-1,1 Akropong und Ussu 1836 #9 Riis October, 27, 1836. In 1836 Riis was thirty-two and Anna was twenty years old.

4. BMA, KP April 20, 1836; Wurm, "Anfänge," 260.

5. Ulrike Sill, *Encounters in Quest of Christian Womanhood: The Basel Mission in Pre- and Early Colonial Ghana* (Leiden: Brill, 2010), 200.

6 BMA, D-1,1 Akropong 1837 #7 Riis June 19, 1837 reports of a collapsed wall, #9 Mürdter October 25, 1837 describes how termites had destroyed buildings and they had to erect two new buildings, an animal stable and quarters for their employees; # 11 Riis to Büchelen November 15, 1837 reports the garden now in order with plantings of various citrus trees and coconuts. BMA, D-1,1 Akropong 1838 #2 Riis February 3, 1838 reports that they spent most of their time at home, repairing and strengthening the houses; #6 Riis July 6, 1838 describes in detail the role of their sixteen employees, the house and the garden; #8 Mürdter September 25, 1838 mentions that the fence around their compound was finished and expressed the hope to now have more time for learning the language.

reached the capital Kumasi but was stalled for weeks, returned without meeting the king, and concluded that the time was not yet ripe for a mission to Asante. This he reported before the Board when they returned to Basel in July 1840.[7]

ECCLESIASTICAL TENSIONS AND MISUNDERSTANDINGS

One would have hoped that in the challenging conditions of early nineteenth century Guinea at least those who were there for Christian ministry supported each other. However, difficulties arose with Danish ecclesiastical representatives on the coast. Instructions on relationships with Danish clergy were ambivalent.[8] The missionaries were to obey Danish authorities, incorporate any converts into the Danish church, and not refuse reports to Demark. Then again, their independent position as missionaries to native Africans and primary accountability to Basel had been emphasized.[9] As we saw above, indications for strained relationships were already present before they arrived. Bishop Münter in Copenhagen accepted Riis and Jäger's ordination in Germany only under pressure from the king. In Africa the differences surfaced, for example, when Henke felt the need to accept the chaplaincy position, in order to prevent the appointment of a "rationalist." Riis later reported difficulties with the Europeans because as chaplain he "loved the truth when speaking of sin."[10] But the tensions became outright conflict when chaplain Tørsleff arrived and the diverging approaches of Danish clergy and Basel missionaries collided.

Repercussions from their Evaluation of Chaplain Tørsleff

The incident that exposed their differences was the conflict over Riis and Anna's wedding in November 1836. The Basel Mission narrative is that

---

7. BMA, KP July 7, 1840. These Board minutes record Riis's report to the leadership.

8. BMA, D-10.3,3a1) Instructions 1828, 3–8 (I).

9. The instructions emphasized that the Danish church "is a Protestant church . . . that also builds solely on the cornerstone of the Christian revelations in scriptures and the creeds." The missionaries were reminded that the Basel Mission did not intend to plant independent churches, that they "worked not for any specific church but for the blessed Kingdom of Christ at large." They should respond to Danish requests for reports, but they were also advised of their "special position in regards to our particular work and calling" and that the Basel Mission Board was the only authority to issue instructions for their work.

10. BMA, D-1,1 Christiansborg 1834 #5, Riis April 1, 1834.

Tørsleff refused to conduct the ceremony; evinced for example in Debrunner's digest of Riis's report: "Palaver with the local chaplain who does not want to celebrate the marriage of Riis."[11] However, from the details it can be deducted that Tørsleff merely asked for necessary papers and the traditional banns three weeks prior to a wedding.[12] The missionaries were less concerned with such official procedural details than the appearance of immorality, if Anna lived any length of time with the men, or even with the Lutterodts. This is Oelschner's interpretation. Even though he embellishes the story, the concern he presents is in line with BMTI sentiments. It is also confirmed by the missionaries' actions. Upon arrival in Akuropon they decided, based on the ordination of the new arrivals, to conduct the wedding themselves, performed by Mürdter on December 6, 1836.[13]

Prior to the introduction of civil marriage in the mid nineteenth century European state churches had the prerogative to conduct legal marriages.[14] Ihli's study of church legislation confirms Oelschner's insinuation that Tørsleff as Danish Lutheran pastor would have regarded the marriage illegal because it was not conducted by him and required legal documents were not presented.[15] Consequently, the missionaries' independent action was perceived as contempt for ecclesiastical legislation and had repercussions. In September 1838 they received a letter from Christiansborg "prohibiting missionaries to bless marriages" or officiate other church functions, "otherwise to be sent back."[16] This threat also indicates a concord between the Danish governor and Tørsleff. Both threaten to implement the royal decree from 1837 that authorized Mørck

---

11. BMA D-12, 1 *Ghana Auszüge*, 21. This is Debrunner's summary of D-1,1 Akropong und Ussu 1836 #12 Riis November 24, 1836.

12. The "banns of marriage" were—and often still are—in the central European state churches a notice read out on three successive Sundays in the parish church, announcing an intended marriage and giving the opportunity for objections. See for example: http://dictionary.reference.com/browse/banns?s=t.

13. BMA, D-1,1 Akropong 1837 #5 Riis April 30, 1837.

14. Stefan Ihli, *Kirchliche Gerichtsbarkeit in der Diözese Rottenburg im 19. Jahrhundert ein Exempel der Beziehungen zwischen Kirche und monarchischem Staat* (Münster: LIT Verlag, 2008). Ihli's "example" for church-state relationships is the introduction of civil marriage in central Europe (with focus on Württemberg and Baden) in the nineteenth century.

15. Oelschner, *Landung in Osu*, 139–40.

16. BMA, D-1,1 Akropong 1838 #8 Mürdter September 25, 1828; D-12,1 *Ghana Auszüge*, 30.

to deport Riis. Thus, the missionaries' nationalist non-conformity probably contributed to the ecclesiastical tensions. Tørsleff had arrived with Mørck and apparently remained close to the governor and shared to a degree his Danish nationalist interests.

Later Riis's suspicions confirm that his condemning evaluations of the Danish on the coast generally and Tørsleff in particular caused this strong action against the missionaries. Riis suggests that "Tørsleff must be behind the resolution that we cannot celebrate any marriages or even have the Lord's Supper" because in his letters he "had counted him among those who were enemies of the mission."[17] Then again, the chaplain also maintained that "from Henke and Riis the children in the Mulatto school had learned less than under him." His letter reveals the mutual disdain between Riis and Tørsleff and their petty bickering resulting from the deeper theological differences they held.

As we saw above, BMTI teachers opposed "rationalist" critical theology and emphasized "supernaturalism" and pious practical Christianity. These theological positions, Pietist morality, and support of the missionary effort became in Africa the primary criteria for evaluating state church clergy, notwithstanding the instructions to collaborate. In the 1830s they lay at the root of the tensions with Tørsleff. Thus, their training had disabled them to cooperate with Christians from other traditions. Pietist convictions made true collaboration with state clergy difficult because Pietists assessed everybody by their values and virtues. BMTI training had instilled this confidence in the missionaries that exalted them to critics over everybody else's religion. Furthermore, conviction of the import of their missionary task caused them to regard anybody who did not share their passion as "an enemy of the mission." On the other hand, Danish Lutheran officers saw the activities of Basel missionaries with suspicions of sectarianism and questioned the legitimacy of their ordination. This is obvious in Münter's objections in 1827 and 1831, and Tørsleff evinced the same attitude.

The reporting of these tensions is also revealing. Basel Mission reporters Wurm and Schlatter omit this episode altogether. It can be speculated that they did not want to offend supporters who, while Pietists, were also members of Protestant state churches. Oelschner, a sympathetic supporter, and Opoku, an African pastor in the Basel Mission, recount the incident with a negative assessment of "the haughty

---

17. BMA, D-1,1 Akropong 1839 #3 Riis February 20, 1839; D-12,1 *Ghana Auszüge*, 32.

chaplain."[18] For Opoku it is another proof of Riis's perseverance against all odds. Oelschner represents Pietist circles in Denmark who shared the Basel Mission's critical stance towards state church officials, rationalist theology, and too much formality in church life. Two articles on "Mission in Denmark," published by the Evangelical Mission-Society in Berlin and the Basel Mission respectively, show the disagreements between Pietist groups and Danish Lutheran theologians, especially over foreign mission and missionary training.[19] While theologians could see only "clerically trained men" as missionaries and "anyway felt the time for mission has not yet come," Pietists felt misjudged and accused the state churches of passivity. The general dismissive treatment of clergy in both articles demonstrates that Basel missionaries' perceptions of the chaplain in Guinea were shaped by the European context of Pietist believers within regional state churches. Furthermore, there was some confusion over the organs of Danish foreign mission engagement which caused misunderstandings.

Mistaken for a "Danish Missionary Society"

Denmark was the first Protestant European nation to engage in foreign mission—initially in collaboration with the Pietist Halle University—in India, the West-Indies, and Greenland. For the purpose of training and support the "Danish Missionary College" was founded in 1714.[20] It was allocated funds from Danish state coffers but "financial support and men came mostly from Germany." A century later, in 1821, Pietist groups with relationships to Jänicke in Berlin and the Basel Mission, led by Rev. Bone Falck Rönne (1764–1833), founded a "Danish Missionary Society" to support missionary efforts of Danes anywhere.[21] In typical Pietist fashion they disregarded customary divisions and published information about all European societies, aided Danish pastors in Greenland, published vernacular translations for the West Indies, and sent young Danes to train in Berlin and Basel. They also mediated Basel Mission arrangements with the Danish government to establish the work in Guinea.

18. Oelschner, *Landung in Osu*, 136–37; Opoku, *Riis, the Builder*, 51. Opoku also wrongly states that Mürdter conducted the wedding at Christiansborg.

19. Bahl, "Die dänische Missionsthätigkeit"; Stocks, "Die Mission in Dänemark."

20. Stocks, *Die Mission in Dänemark*, 84. The proper title of this Danish Missionary College was "Collegium de Cursu Evangelii Promovendo" (College for the Promotion of Course of the Gospel).

21. Bahl, "Die dänische Missionsthätigkeit," 202; Stocks, "Die Mission in Dänemark," 86.

The two Danish mission related organizations are often not clearly distinguished. Both had strong links with German mission minded circles, and the Danish Mission Society supported efforts of the older royal mission as well as the newer work of Berlin and Basel trained Danes. Thus, it is not surprising that the Basel Mission's request in 1827—relayed by the director of the Danish Mission Society—was mistaken by the king as an effort of the Danish Missionary College and Rönne had to clarify the facts.[22] The renewal of cooperation between willing German activists and Danish ecclesiastical needs and logistical means led to the Basel Mission being frequently mistaken as a "Danish Missionary Society," notwithstanding its expressed self-perception as *German* Mission, its international character, its base in Switzerland, and most of its missionaries being German.[23]

An indication that the Basel Mission was identified as Danish mission in Denmark is the fact that the money and goods left by the first four Basel missionaries was mistakenly put into "a fund for Danish missionaries."[24] The letter that informed the missionaries of this fact cautioned them to avoid political engagement and advised that "care is to be taken that such mission property is not lost in the future." Kwamena-Poh points out that until 1845 the Basel missionaries were regarded as officials of the Danish government in Africa for their names appear on the list of Danish officials sent out to the Guinea coast between 1820 and 1850.[25] Governor Carstensen promoted in 1843 the work of "the Danish mission in Akropong" among African leaders.[26] While he also referred to the "Basel Mission," his vision of Denmark's contribution to African civilization counseled that "no measures are to be taken for the direct spreading of culture and civilization in Africa, but indirectly by drawing

22. On June 3, 1827 the royal approval was given, but it was issued in the name of the Danish Missionary College. The leaders of the Danish Missionary Society had to explain until the permission was changed to the name of the Basel Mission and extended to several missionaries from only one originally. See Schlatter, *Basler Mission in Afrika*, 21; Wurm, "Anfänge," 141–42.

23. Instructions 1827 in MM 1830, 454. These instructions request the missionaries to investigate the viability of a "German mission" on the African coast.

24. BMA, Copybook June 1837–12. July 1838, Inspector's letter "to the Brethren in Africa" from April 26, 1837, cited in D-12.1 *Ghana Auszüge*, 23.

25. Kwamena-Poh, *Akuapem State*, 111–12. He cites from: Guineiske Journaler, 1852, Oversigt over Dødelighede blandt de siden September 1820 til Guinea udsendte Embedsmænd.

26. Carstensen letter October 20, 1843 in Carstensen, *Closing the Books*, 60.

a plan for the work of the Danish missionaries in West Africa."[27] This perception continues into the twentieth century, as Metcalfe's reference to "the Danish missionary Andreas Riis" indicates.[28]

There are several facts which communicated to onlookers a Danish affiliation. Kwamena-Poh suggests two, the original initiative by the Danish governor Richelieu "to re-start the work of the eighteenth century" and "the international character of the Basel Missionary Society."[29] Another possible reason was that three of the early missionaries were actually Danish: Besides Andreas Riis and Peter Jäger who arrived in Christiansborg together in 1832, a nephew of Andreas, Hans Nicolai Riis, came in 1845. However, of these only Andreas Riis had an extended ministry. Jäger died within four months and H. N. Riis struggled with various illnesses and effectively only worked in Africa about two and a half years.[30]

It is still curious that the Basel Mission should be mistaken as a Danish organization. It reflects growing nationalist sentiments in Europe. Most people did not share the idealistic international, interdenominational outlook of the German and Swiss Pietists who organized the Basel Mission. The brotherhood of Pietists, expressed in the global networks of communication and cooperation, broke down in many places. The tensions we saw above in the CMS collaboration were only one example.

The primary effect of these misunderstandings on the missionaries in Guinea was that it increased pressures to comply with Danish sentiments in Africa. When they did not fulfill Danish expectations and, furthermore, acted and spoke very independently and even judgmental of Danish church officials, opposition to their efforts grew. Eventually, the frictions with other Europeans in Guinea created a situation where the missionaries in Akuropon felt they had to "keep a distance from their African neighbors" and "could not visit African villages" for fear of being suspected of treason.[31] This defeated their purpose of communicat-

27. Carstensen letter July 25, 1844 in ibid., 84. See also Carstensen's "Remarks concerning the Danish-Guinean possessions" from June 30, 1844.

28. Metcalfe, *Maclean*, 196.

29. Kwamena-Poh, *Akuapem State*, 111–12.

30. BMA, PF "BV 241 Riis, Hans Nicolai" and various letters from H.N. Riis in D-1,2 indicate that he was only in Africa from January 1845 to July 1846 and from March 1849 to March 1850. Incidentally, this also invites caution about the importance often attached to his linguistic work in Twi.

31. BMA, D-1,1 Akropong 1837 #10 Riis November 14, 1837, published in MM

ing the Christian message to Africans. While the Basel Mission blamed the "hostile governor" for this state of affairs, it was, in fact, the disconnect between Danish political and ecclesiastical expectations and BMTI fostered values of neutrality and Pietist spirituality that ended them in this plight. Organizational embarrassment is palatable in contemporary publications. For example, Blumhardt's comments on the latest letters in 1838 claim civil unrest in the land and infrequent naval connections among the reasons for lack of progress in "real missionary work."[32] With the primary objective, Christian converts, nowhere near in sight, their main achievement was that they were still alive. However, this too was frequently threatened by another Basel Mission practice.

THE WANDERING NATURE OF THE MISSIONARY PROFESSION

As we saw above, Missionary reporting contributed to establishing the image of the "dark continent" and gained disproportionate influence in Europe by its pioneering character.[33] Basel Missionaries' instructions explicitly cautioned that they were not explorers for scientific information. Nevertheless, their reports, descriptions, and collections of artifacts contributed new insights in geography, anthropology, and various sciences.[34] This was a side product of the numerous trips they took to investigate possibilities and conditions for expanding the mission. These journeys were also based on the view that missionary work was of a "wandering nature."[35] However, the experience of the early years shows that they impeded the mission in Africa.

1838, 386; Akropong 1838 #2 Riis February 3, 1838.

32. MM 1838, 383.

33. Curtin, *Image of Africa*, 413.

34. This was true for most of the early missionaries as Etherington observes and Harries expands in the same volume, "missionaries were often in the vanguard of what became known as the discipline of anthropology" See Etherington, *Missions and Empire*, 10, 238–60. For example, Riis mentions a collection of insects and a number of stuffed birds he was sending to Europe in 1839. BMA, D-1,1 Akropong 1839 #1 Riis to Büchelen January 9, 1839. The Basel Mission House became well known for its extensive collections of non-European artifacts.

35. BMA, D-10.3,3a1. Instructions 1828, 10–11 (III).

302   PART II: Indications for Trained Incapacity

Missionary Trips and their Negative Consequences

In search for a location away from the coast Jäger and Heinze visited the inland plantations within a couple of weeks of their arrival. Afterwards all three fell sick and Heinze died.[36] On another reconnaissance trip three months later Jäger died and Riis became seriously sick.[37] In 1835 and 1836 Riis took several trips from Akuropon to other Akuapem villages, Larteh, Shai, and Krobo.[38] When his colleagues joined him, much of the next two years they were occupied with building and farming, but they also continued to go on trips. With Mürdter Riis visited Shai and Krobo again in April 1838 and Akwamu in October.[39] Returning from the second trip, they found Riis's wife and children not well, and Mürdter, too, was sick. Anna Riis recovered, but their firstborn girl died October 21 and Mürdter died November 4, 1838.[40]

When the Board in Basel discussed the Africa mission in February 1839, the news of these fatalities had not arrived yet.[41] Opinions were divided about the validity of Akuropon as mission station and the suggestion prevailed that the missionaries should "investigate further inland for a fitting station and report ... the findings." Wurm cites the descriptions of these journeys and fatalities in detail and comments, "victory did not fail to materialize. Thirty years later ... in 1868 the Jubilee-Church opened [and] filled with Aquapim Christians [who] now number 900 in Akropong alone."[42] Steiner offers a similar evaluation when he claims "the significance of Riis's ministry was not in his successes but ... in his perseverance on his post" which prevented the Basel Mission from abandoning this mission.[43] They exemplify the Basel Mission attitude to sacrifices and problems that focused on successes in hindsight. While it is

---

36. BMA, D-1,1 Christiansborg 1832 #12, Riis June 6, 1832.

37. BMA, D-1,1 Christiansborg 1832 #14 Riis August 10, 1832.

38. BMA, D-1,1 Akropong 1835 #11 Riis diary April 1 (Larteh), April 16 (Davu, Aikuga, Adukrong, Aprette), August 17, (Mamso), 1835, in MM 1836, 521, 525, 550; BMA, D-1,1 Akropong 1836 #9 Riis diary August 12 (Larteh) and September 11 (Mamfö and Amanna), 1836, in MM 1837, 551, 554.

39. BMA, D-1,1 Akropong 1838 #6 Riis July 6, 1838, published in HB 1839, 63–56 (Krobo and Shai); #10 Riis December 6, 1838, published in MM 1839, 455–76 (Akwamu).

40. BMA, D-1,1 Akropong 1838 #9 Riis November 18, 1838.

41. BMA, KP February 27, 1839.

42. Wurm, "Anfänge," 267–70.

43. Steiner, "Andreas Riis," 8.

true that later the church was established, the early missionaries not only suffered, their frequent absences prevented the consistency required to accomplish the goals of their mission sooner.

Riis—blessed with an exceptional physical constitution—followed his leaders' instructions and undertook two more major trips in 1839. In April and May he explored Akyem for three weeks and November to January 1840 he visited Fante and Asante.[44] The latter had been on the mission's mind all along because of the general fascination in Europe with this mighty African nation.[45] An indication for this underlying motivation is the fact that Riis's reports were titled in publications as letters from "Akropong in Ashantiland."[46] Contrary to this depiction, Akuapem was outside the Asante state and only part of its population were Akan. Upon Riis's sobering account from Kumasi, the Basel Mission finally settled on Akuropon as most promising initial station. However, Wurm cites Riis's reports extensively in 1874 when Asante still was an unrealized vision for the Basel Mission.[47]

Trips Threatened Survival

From this summary of their trips the first conclusion Riis drew is obvious: journeys in Africa threatened Europeans' lives. After reporting about Akwamu and Mürdter's subsequent death, he posited that "it is not advisable . . . to take exhausting trips" because humidity, heat, and lack of good food and water were detrimental to (especially newly arrived) Europeans' health.[48] However, the Board in Basel was reluctant to agree. Up to their last letter, which included the instruction to return to Europe for recuperation, they asked Riis to explore other options for mission stations. Only after Riis reported in person in July 1840 and emphasized that "generally, traveling is the worst one can do in Africa" the Board relented somewhat.[49] The instructions for the new venture in 1842 were

44. BMA, D-1,1 Akropong 1839 #4 Riis June 16, 1839, published in MM 1840, 93–112 (Journey to Akyem). Riis's description of the Kumasi trip from 10 November 1839 to 13 January 1840 in BMA, D-1,1 Akropong 1839 #8 "Journey to Ashanti" was published in MM 1840, 174–238.

45. Curtin, *Image of Africa*, 226, 255.

46. See for example MM 1837, 535.

47. Wurm, "Anfänge," 306–18.

48. BMA, D-1,1 Akropong 1838 #10 Riis December 6, 1838; MM 1839, 476.

49. Riis's report was summarized in detail in the Board minutes in BMA, KP July 7, 1840.

to not undertake journeys "before the health of the brothers allows for it safely and only if the work in Akropong is not hindered."[50] However, they still were to establish schools in neighboring villages.

Trips Hindered Language Learning and Relationships

There were other negative effects on the mission which are neither acknowledged in the missionaries' letters nor in Board meetings. Both identify practical work, African upheavals, and hostile Danish officials as causes for not achieving organizational goals, but not the frequent trips. Riis blamed the political situation. Because of it they could not do much beyond the evening meetings with their employees, he had lost his language teacher, and nobody would listen.[51] The Board summarized "dissensions among the Negros, physical needs that require much practical work, [and] the discord with the governor" as "continuous interrupting influences" preventing the preaching of the gospel.[52] While these circumstances certainly contributed to their struggles, the numerous trips also thwarted important Basel Mission objectives.

First, they affected their ability to learn language. Wurm acknowledges that the missionaries acquired only just enough to get by.[53] Opoku for all his admiration of Riis admits that he never learned enough to communicate his message without an interpreter.[54] This is in contrast to Kwamena-Poh's erroneous claim that Riis "found time to learn the Twi language, thus laying a foundation for the great work of Christaller," revealing again his pro-missionary bias.[55] Below I will discuss other reasons for their failure to acquire the vernacular, but the frequent absences from Akuropon contributed to it. They prevented the consistent presence and practice necessary for language learning. The journeys also exposed them to different dialects and languages which made it harder to study any one of them. Consequently, they struggled to identify suitable language assistants, often used men who were not native speakers, and continued to

---

50. BMA, Q-3-3,26 Instructionen 1842 §31.

51. BMA, D-1,1 Akropong 1838 #6 Riis July 6, 1838 and Akropong 1839 #4 Riis June 16, 1839.

52. BMA, KP February 27, 1839.

53. Wurm, "Anfänge," 266–67.

54. Opoku, *Riis, the Builder*, 87–90.

55. Kwamena-Poh, *Akuapem State*, 114.

discuss which would be the most useful language to learn.[56] Furthermore, the linguistic and ethnic divisions of Akuapem for the most part evaded their notice, as they dismissed distinct languages as "dialects" and continued to search for a "national" and "root" language. Riis's struggles to keep up language study "as strength, circumstances, and other business allow" and repeated requests for someone with the explicit commission to analyze the language and produce translations might also indicate that he was not particularly gifted in this area.[57]

Second, the frequent trips affected the missionaries' ability to build relationships that could have facilitated communication, understanding, and possible acceptance of the message. There was no time and energy for this, not only because of the general conditions caused by African and European strife over the region, but also because of the lack of consistent presence of the missionaries in Akuropon and the strain on their health the journeys caused. Such serious negative consequences raise the question why the organization would be reluctant to give up a practice that so obviously proved damaging to the missionaries' survival and ministry?

The Need for Reconnaissance and Support

Early on, the primary motivation to uphold this detrimental activity was the great need in Europe for more information on Africa. The Basel missionaries were not the first Europeans to visit Akuapem, but they were the first to settle for extended time and investigate adjacent areas.[58] More specifically, the Board wanted facts about peoples and conditions in Africa to facilitate more informed decision making.[59] For years the leaders questioned the location Riis had chosen and requested investigations of the wider area. Fascination in Europe with the large and powerful Asante kingdom contributed to this reluctance to settle in Akuropon, as did the political disturbances Riis reported.

56. The most explicit discussion of these issues are in BMA, D-1,1 Akropong 1837 #9 and #10 Mürdter October 25 and Riis November 14, 1837.

57. See previous note and also: BMA, D-1,1 Akropong and Ussu 1836 #9 Riis October 27, 1836. After Mürdter's death Riis determined to return to language study "as strength, circumstances, and other business allow." See BMA, D-1,1 Akropong 1839 #4 Riis June 16, 1839. Opoku also suggests that "Riis seems not to have had a great gift for languages" in Opoku, *Riis, the Builder*, 87.

58. Isert was the first European to make an attempt to settle in Akuapem. See Isert, *Letters*, 16–17, 293–319; Kwamena-Poh, *Akuapem State*, 97–101.

59. MM 1830, 472–73, 476–77; BMA, D-10.3,3a1. Instructions 1828, 10–11 (III).

Given the lack of "real mission work" in Akuapem, reports of various African regions and people were also better publishing material to raise missionary passion and monetary contributions of supporters and inspire new missionaries. This is very obvious in what was printed from Riis's letters. Publications concentrated for the most part on long excerpts from the travel reports and omitted many of the more challenging issues.[60] They also confirm the observation that missionary reporting upheld the image of African need, savagery, and spiritual darkness, in contrast to the missionaries' perseverance and faith to validate their labor and sacrifice.[61] Riis exemplified such "descriptions of the 'hardhearted, sinful, slothful heathen' [that] helped European missionaries account for their slow progress in winning converts."[62] For example, in 1836 he identified the "natural slothfulness and carelessness" of Africans as "significant obstacle to the reception of the gospel" and characterized the people as "sluggish and especially devoted to the vices of fornication and drunkenness, ... lying and deception."[63]

The shortage of eye-witness information of the period is also exposed by the fact that Riis's letters and diaries are a primary source of information for most researchers. Consequently, it is obvious in their evaluations of contemporary conditions and political dissensions that they rely on this biased observer. Apart from Metcalfe—who adds a pro-British bias—this includes Opoku, and Antwi, as well as the Basel Mission authors Schlatter, Smith, Wurm, and Debrunner. Reindorf and Kwamena-Poh include African oral traditions and focus on African motivations and actions, but their evaluation of the Basel missionaries remains fundamentally uncritical.

While longer trips were later discouraged, shorter journeys for exploration and outreach remained consistently part of Basel engagement despite missionaries' repeated warnings of the health hazard.[64] However,

60. See for example HB 1839, 63–56 (Journey to Krobo and Shai); MM 1839, 455–76 (Journey to Akwamu); MM 1840, 93–112 (Journey to Akyem); MM 1840 III, 174–238 (Journey to Ashanti).

61. Curtin, *Image of Africa*, 326.

62. Etherington, *Missions and Empire*, 7.

63. BMA, D-1,1 Akropong 1836 #9 Riis October 27, 1836, published in MM 1837, 558–59.

64. For example Schiedt's trip to Labadi and Teshie in 1846 (JB 1847, 150) and Zimmermann's extensive report on a trip with Stanger East as far as the Volta river on the way to a conference in Akropong and then to various villages on the return trip (D-1,3 Ussu 1851 Berichte #13). After his trip to "Krobo, Akomu, und Krepe" in 1848

evidence that missionaries also upheld "the ideal of the independent missionary who traveled freely from town to town ... to preach the gospel" comes from Zimmermann in 1850.[65] Reconnaissance and evangelism were the stated reasons for continued expectation and practice of trips. Underlying was a missiological principle they had acquired in Europe.

The Ideal of the Wandering Evangelist

The rationale for the instruction that at least one of the missionaries should always be traveling is highly significant. It posits that "the business of mission is of wandering nature and the church settles on the land" thereby proposing itinerant preaching as ideal of missionary work in contrast to the "settled" nature of the church.[66]

This idea did not originate with the Basel Mission. In Anglophone contexts the generally more well-known version of this pattern are open-air preaching and Methodist Circuits traced back to George Whitefield (1714–1770) and John Wesley (1703–1791). Eayrs describes their beginnings in eighteenth century Britain.[67] He demonstrates that "open-air or field-preaching was one of the chief means by which the people were gathered," and it was required from preachers every Sunday. Methodist preachers in a "system of itineration" moved from place to place in their circuits to evangelize and meet regional group leaders. More significantly, Eayrs shows Methodism's "indebtedness to the Moravians." Among other features, Wesley had "witnessed open-air preaching, preaching by laymen, [and] itinerant preachers" in Herrnhut. Stoeffler explains that from 1727 Moravians were "undertaking evangelistic tours to many parts of Europe" and "settlements in places other than Herrnhut [came] out of such evangelistic activity."[68]

The Basel Mission practice was more than likely influenced directly by existing Pietist relationships and some of the earliest Moravian churches in the region. Moreover, for the students it resonated with the

---

Widmann again highlighted that travelling in the sun was a challenge to missionaries' health (MM 1849, 126 citing D-1,3 Akropong 1848 #27 Annual Report December 1848).

65. BMA, D-1,3 Zimmermann October 7, 1850. However, he also acknowledged that "reality is different" and promoted missionary families who have people live with them as alternative strategy.

66. BMA, D-10.3,3a1. Instructions 1828, 10–11 (III).

67. Eayrs, "Developments, Institutions, Helpers, Opposition."

68. Stoeffler, *German Pietism*, 140.

traditional artisan journeymanship. Many biographies testify to missionaries' experience of travelling after their apprenticeship, working with different masters and visiting various fellowships.[69] For rural lay believers itinerant preaching was a Christian version of "Wanderschaft." BMTI teachers often had also followed the practice of theologians to undertake post-graduation journeys. Since the early Pietist leaders this was a common means of communication between the fellowships Europe-wide. During BMTI vacations students and teachers went on visitation and evangelistic trips. This was judged good missionary preparation.

However, the transfer of this practice to Africa was problematic, not only because of its effects on missionaries' health and ability to build relationships. In Europe the evangelists addressed a "Christian society" where the population confessed Christianity, albeit not Pietism. Walls makes the same observation for Evangelicals in Britain.[70] Like Pietists on the continent, they emphasized "inward religion as distinct from formal, real Christianity as distinct from nominal" and took their identity from protest. Consequently, "Evangelical religion presupposes Christendom, Christian civil society." The lack of morality and personal spirituality they identified caused Pietists to travel the land and preach repentance, renewal, and a new kind of Christian community. But they shared language, culture, and basic worldview with their audience.

In Africa they faced communication problems posed by language and cultural barriers, and "the assumptions that had shaped their religion did not apply." Nominal Christianity "as the reference group—indeed as the target group—of preaching" had still worked partially in the chaplaincy position, so far as they addressed relapsed Europeans, but among Africans there was no Christian society to address. Not surprisingly, the missionaries lamented Africans' lack of response. But nowhere they or the Basel Board recognized the frequent absences from Akuropon and short visits elsewhere as factors that prevented language learning and deeper understanding of local people and worldviews which would have facilitated a more relevant message. Thus, the mindset and methodology that had served them well in Europe proved quite unhelpful in Africa. This illustrates the definition of trained incapacity in that it represented attitudes, behaviors, and ways of thinking instilled by previous experience

69. For example the Ghana missionary Dieterle spent the five years between graduating from his apprenticeship and acceptance in Basel "in foreign parts" (BMA, BV 248 "Lebenslauf").

70. Walls, *Missionary Movement*, 81–84.

and education that "served well in the past" but led to "serious maladjustments" under new and changed conditions and to actions which ultimately defeated their own interests.[71]

Finally, the distinction between the "wandering nature of mission" and the "settled nature of the church" expressed a conceptual difference between the church and Christian mission that is highly problematic. It has prevailed in the Protestant missionary movement into the present, as the continuing popularity of Ralph Winter's "two structures of God's redemptive mission" shows.[72] He postulated the necessity of both, local churches (modalities) and mobile mission structures (sodalities) for the Christian movement. While he advocated better collaboration, in practice, sodalities are almost always independent organizations and rarely cooperate well with churches. Skreslet more recently outlined the variety of such "extracongregational" structures from medieval "missionary monks" to modern NGOs (Non-Governmental Organizations) and suggested they will be more "niche oriented," better networked, and "technologically adept" in the twenty-first century.[73] However, he highlights the "persistent inclination of many mission practitioners to favor parachurch structures over the local church as frameworks for their labor" and the danger that this "obscures the fact that groups of believers ... are, in truth, the most basic means of mission at the disposal of the Gospel." Skreslet concludes that while they are useful, "mission structures ... cannot replace witnessing communities that worship together and, in fact, must assume them as the primary means by which the Good News of Jesus Christ is made known to the world." Yet, in practice, most Western missionary endeavors are still informed by this unhealthy division of church and mission.

---

71. Burke, *Permanence and Change*, 7–11, 38–49; Merton, *Social Theory*, 197–200.

72. Winter, "Two Structures." Winter presented the concepts of this article first to the First International Congress on World Evangelization in Lausanne 1974. It has been printed and reprinted numerous times. This version was published online in 2006 by the Presbyterian Center for Mission Studies and can be found on the websites of a number of other prominent Protestant mission organizations like Frontiers (http://frontiermissionfellowship.org/uploads/documents/two-structures.pdf) and Campus Crusade for Christ (http://resources.campusforchrist.org/images/4/48/The_Parachruch.pdf).

73. Skreslet, "Impending Transformation."

310   PART II: Indications for Trained Incapacity

STRUGGLES TO DO "REAL MISSION WORK"

Both leaders and missionaries frequently expressed frustrations with how little "real missionary work" they were able to accomplish.[74] As we saw above, the Basel Mission defined "real mission" as preaching to Africans, winning converts, and teaching them.[75] Beyond the political unrest, two major reasons contemporary and later Basel Mission writers cite were the necessity to establish a station and their inability to speak the vernacular yet. For example, in 1838 Blumhardt commented that civil unrest in the land, infrequent naval connections, "the nature of a first settlement in wild heathen lands," and "the difficulty of learning a language that is divided into many dialects" hindered progress in "real missionary work."[76] Wurm lists the missionaries' lack of language proficiency, the confused state of affairs in Akuropon, Danish-British rivalry, the amount of "necessary physical work" to maintain the buildings, and the lack of available (African) workers.[77] We saw that frequent trips contributed to the frustration of organizational goals. Their preoccupation with practical work revealed obstructive presumptions, and the difficulties to learn African vernaculars show their unpreparedness for unwritten languages. Furthermore, African scholars highlight the inappropriateness of their message.

"Station Building" Took Energy and Alienated Africans

Mission stations as European missionary strategy in Africa have amply been critiqued for alienating African Christians from their communities and culture.[78] Agbeti, for example, posits that "new converts were completely uprooted from among their own people and resettled on the Mis-

---

74. BMA, D-1,1 Akropong 1837 #4 Stanger, March 25, #9 Mürdter October 25 and #10 Riis November 14, 1837; Akropong 1838 #2 Riis February 3 and #6 Riis July 6, 1838.

75. For example, BMA, D-10.3,3a1. Instructions 1828, 9 (III) stated that they were "above all messengers of Christ to spread his saving knowledge among the pagan inhabitants of those coast lands and their youth according to the full content of the Word of God."

76. MM 1838, 383.

77. Wurm, "Anfänge," 266–67.

78. See, for example, Addo-Fenning, "Christian Missions," 205–6; Ajayi, *Nigeria*, 126–66; Baëta, *Christianity in Tropical Africa*, 15–17; Busia, "Christianity and Ashanti." For an incisive discussion of the enormous diversity of mission villages across Africa, see Hastings, *Church in Africa*, 209–15.

sion area in order to preserve them from falling back to non-Christian practices."⁷⁹ However, during the period this study is concerned with there were no African believers yet. Rather, there are indications that the assumption that European "civilization"—or, as the Basel Mission articulated it, "cultivation of the pagan wilderness"—is necessary for the survival of missionaries and a prerequisite of Christian mission alienated potentially interested Africans. This was already revealed above in the early building efforts of Riis.

The small team continued to be preoccupied with "station building" along previously established patterns. Gone were the days of African community efforts to provide for the foreigners in town. The missionaries worked themselves and employed Africans from the coast and a few local serfs. Against the odds of termites, rain, and sickness more houses, a garden, and a fence around the compound were erected with the help of sixteen employees.⁸⁰ This number renders Wurm's comment that there were not sufficient helpers somewhat unreasonable as it represented four times as many African workers. But the missionaries permanently stressed the importance of laying on hands themselves and the need to oversee the Africans to achieve the quality of work their European artisanship desired.⁸¹ In Basel the leadership agreed that this was "necessary practical work," even though they lamented the time and energy it took.

This shows that they maintained the conviction that such "station building" was foundational prerequisite to establishing a mission. The organization acknowledged with regret that this practical work took time and energy from language learning and communicating the Christian message, but they did not revise their goals. We saw above how their perceptions of "proper" building and agricultural work deprived the missionaries of voluntary contributions by local African families and led to estrangement from them. In the later 1830s the ongoing conflict that preoccupied locals certainly contributed to their lack of interest in the foreigners, but the missionaries' persistence in European artisanship, which their BMTI training had reinforced as biblical universal standard of good work and "cultivation" of the land, cannot be ignored as a factor

79. Agbeti, *West African Church History,* 67.

80. BMA, D-1,1 Akropong 1837 #7 Riis June 19, #9 Riis November 15, and #11 Mürdter October 25, 1837; Akropong 1838 # 6 Riis July 6, and #8 Mürdter September 25, 1838.

81. For example in BMA, D-1,1 Akropong 1838 #6 Riis July 6, 1838.

causing the reality that their employees were the only audience for their message.

Unprepared to Learn Unwritten Languages

Basel Mission training and instructions for missionaries placed great emphasis on vernacular languages. They were told to make language study and analysis a priority, teach "Aschantee," and eventually conduct schools in vernaculars.[82] Consequently, it is not surprising that eventually BMTI graduates became famous for their work in African languages. Hastings observes that "Basel . . . missionaries were excellent linguists" and lists their achievements.[83] In contrast to the "vast majority of missionaries [who] knew none other than English," the fact that the BMTI taught several languages set its graduates apart. Walls adds that the "CMS often looked to Germany for its linguists. . . . Henry Venn, its ever busy secretary, got his commercial advice from Manchester, but his linguistic counsel from Germany."[84] However, as we saw above and Eichholzer confirms, "acquisition of the local languages by the Basel missionaries was slow and imperfect in the period prior to [H.N.] Riis and Christaller's arrival" (1845 and 1853 respectively).[85] Andreas Riis and his colleagues bemoan their limited progress in this task.[86] Opoku, in spite of his otherwise overly positive evaluation of Riis, admits that his efforts at gathering vocabulary and "learning . . . the unwritten Asante language" were "largely futile endeavours" and he only "could stammer a few words in Twi."[87] Opoku's remark identifies a core issue without discussing it further, the fact that African vernaculars were *unwritten* languages.

Above I identified the frequent trips as an unacknowledged factor that kept them from being involved in Akuropon consistently enough to acquire much of the local language. Another reason was that "the missionaries found it difficult to locate appropriate 'language assistants'

---

82. Instructions 1827 in MM 1830, 462–64; BMA, D-10.3,3a1) Instructions 1828, 12 (III) and BMA, Q-3-3,26 Instructionen 1842 §§20, 23–24, 28.

83. Hastings, *Church in Africa*, 242–43, 279–80, 341.

84. Walls, *Cross-Cultural Process*, 209.

85. Eichholzer, "Missionary Linguists on the Gold Coast," 73–75.

86. BMA, D-1,1 Akropong 1837 #4 Stanger, March 25, #9 Mürdter October 25, and #10 Riis November 14, 1837.

87. Opoku, *Riis, the Builder*, 87–90.

(*Sprachgehilfen*), let alone to assess their linguistic proficiency."[88] Their assistants reflected the "high degree of linguistic diversification" of southern Ghana that also caused doubts as to which language should be learned. Abun-Nasr confirms that most African assistants were "not really native speakers" of Twi but spoke several languages to varying degrees of fluency.[89] In 1838 the missionaries worked with an "old mulatto from Ussu" who knew "Accra, Crepee, Aschantee, und Danish," an interpreter from Cape Coast who probably was Fante, and a young man who spoke "Danish, Accra, Aschantee, ... Adampe, and Crepee" and probably was Ga.[90] The latter was Riis's favorite companion on trips because of his "decent oral translations" and general helpfulness.

Even when they were able to obtain the assistance of native Twi speakers, the missionaries struggled with learning a language without written tools. Riis complained that "without any language aid, learning such a foreign language as Aschantee causes many difficulties."[91] With the help of an apparently rather unreliable Asante man they had compiled "a word list of 1200 words whose correctness we do not doubt." Later this list and the primer Riis compiled in 1840 were used in the school but their usefulness was limited.[92] Abun-Nasr highlights the "practical difficulties of an arduous learning process," but Eichholzer addresses the core issue: In spite of the many languages they studied at the BMTI, "they had not learned how to describe purely oral languages that had first to be reduced to writing and that, moreover, ... were typologically very distinct from the Indo-European languages with which the missionaries were familiar."[93] She relates two detailed examples of missionaries using

88. Eichholzer, *Missionary Linguists*, 75. Riis expressed the conviction that Twi was the "country's language" already in 1832 when he still lived in Osu which is Ga area (BMA, D-1,1 Ussu 1832 #13 Riis June 20, 1832). Later Mürdter described in detail their difficulties with the various "dialects" and their struggle to identify a "root language" (BMA, D-1,1 Akropong 1837 #9 Mürdter October 25, 1837). On the linguistic diversity see also Eichholzer, *Missionary Linguists*, 73.

89. Abun-Nasr, "Von der 'Umbildung,'" 189–90.

90. BMA, D-1,1 Akropong 1838 #6 Riis July 6, 1838.

91. Ibid.

92. See MM 1846, 136. Eichholzer comments: "From a linguistic and also didactic point of view ... that booklet was not useful for language learning, neither for the missionaries themselves nor for the future pupils in Akropong, as Twi words were listed under every corresponding letter of the Latin alphabet with no indication of their meaning in English or German. See Eichholzer, *Missionary Linguists*, 76.

93. Abun-Nasr, "Von der 'Umbildung,'" 196; Eichholzer, *Missionary Linguists*, 78.

faulty Twi that "illustrate the fundamental problems in language learning with which Basel missionaries were confronted; for they could not assess the proficiency of their assistants, and found it difficult to learn a language, without the aid of books that anchored (oral) languages in time and space."[94]

Her analysis highlights the primary difficulty Basel missionaries faced in learning African languages. Despite their awareness of the absence of writing in Africa, their training had not prepared them for unwritten vernaculars. All their previous studies had relied heavily on dictionaries, grammars, and written texts. In fact, three of the languages on the BMTI curriculum were unspoken "dead" languages, biblical Hebrew, Greek, and Latin. Thus, their preparation fostered an incapacity to learn languages without written aids, which was a major factor that their efforts "yielded few results." Interestingly, Director Hoffmann later acknowledged the challenge. His plea to send better trained people to Africa primarily argued the need to prepare missionaries for the difficult tasks of analyzing oral languages and developing written materials.[95] It was under his watch that the famous linguist Christaller was prepared for Ghana with the explicit purpose to analyze Twi. His appointment also indicates that, by then, there was some recognition of the fact that African languages were not nearly as poor and primitive as expected.

Sanneh is the prominent scholar among those who have shown the importance of the language studies and translations missionaries produced later for African appropriations of the faith.[96] But in this early period other priorities instilled in their training, the expectation that African languages would be "simple and poor in expressions," and the exclusively written methodology of language learning prevented a speedy acquisition of African vernaculars.

Their Message "Made No Sense"

While the missionaries and subsequent Basel Mission writers openly lamented the lack of language acquisition, there are no signs they recognized the primary reason African authors identify for the failure of early missions in Africa; the incongruity of their message. For example, Njoku

---

94. Eichholzer, *Missionary Linguists*, 81–83.

95. Hoffmann, *Eilf Jahre*, 96–97.

96. Sanneh, *Translating the Message*. See also Andrew Walls on "The Translation Principle in Christian History" in Walls, *Missionary Movement*, 26–42.

maintains that "preaching by European missionaries, with the intention to persuade the people rationally to abandon the faith of their ancestors and embrace the Christian faith . . . in general failed to convince the adult population" because much of the message was in the eyes of Africans, "simply illogical and even nonsensical."[97] Evidence for puzzled African reactions is abundant. Missionaries' letters frequently expressed frustrations with people's apparent inability to comprehend or unwillingness to listen to the message.[98] Riis concludes that Africans will take time to be convinced and laments his inability to communicate well in their language. But there is no recognition of the inappropriateness of the Pietist message.

Kobia explains that to Africans, "the 'good news' did not make sense" because "it is impossible for a people who have a very strong view of the world to suddenly respond favourably to strange ideas about the world."[99] Moreover, "what prompted Africans to hate the 'good news' is that the preachers condemned the African ways of life and their gods." Above I discussed the "amazing degree of confidence" European missionaries had in the supremacy of Christianity and European culture which caused them to assume that Africans would quickly abandon their "superstitions" and "savage" way of life to embrace Christianity.[100] Unexpectedly, Africans proved hesitant to respond to the missionary message.

The Pietist notion of individual conversion as an event and a "clean break from the past" has been amply critiqued. In a recent articulate contribution Hanciles emphasizes that conversion is a process and "often involves a reconstitution and reinterpretation of previous beliefs, symbols, and ritual to form a new dynamic which enables the convert to meet new challenges."[101] He agrees with other scholars who highlight that "some form of 'crisis,' be it religious, cultural, psychological, or political usually precedes conversion."[102] Such "crisis" developed in Africa in the era of co-

97. Njoku, "Missionary Factor," 204.

98. For example, in BMA, D-1,1 Akropong 1836 #9 Riis October 27, 1836; MM 1837, 544–49.

99. Kobia, "Christian Mission and the African Peoples," 159–60.

100. Kalu, "Church Presence in Africa," 18; Gunson, *Messengers of Grace*, 268–69.

101. Hanciles, "Conversion and Social Change," 160.

102. Hanciles discusses in particular Rambo and, in regards to the African experience, Horton, Fisher, and Hefner. See Fisher, "Conversion Reconsidered"; Hefner, *Conversion to Christianity*; Horton, "African Conversion"; Rambo, *Understanding Religious Conversion*.

lonialism which portended massive social and political changes.[103] Consequently, "for many Africans conversion to Christianity became a way of coping with innumerable crises and dilemmas, a means of adapting to rapid change."[104] However, prior to imperial colonialism, missionaries relied predominantly on their powers of persuasion. To their mission's detriment they ignored the fact that "new ideas and concepts can be absorbed only via the categories of the old."[105]

Furthermore, European condemnation of African religion and way of life, which resulted from cultural and religious convictions of superiority, did not constitute "good news" and was for the most part rejected during this early period. This is obvious in the missionaries' records of conversations that typically include African responses. For example, Riis was eager to direct the attention of his African workers "towards their sinful and lost condition, as well as the great sacrifice that God brought in Christ for our salvation," and complained about their relapses into "old excesses" and their unwillingness to recognize and confess their sins.[106] He concluded that "generally Negros stubbornly deny every mistake" and expressed his exasperation at Africans' unwillingness to accept their sinful condition. The missionary regularly used dismissive language of African religious practices, like declaring someone's "fetish stuff" a "useless thing" he should dismiss, and describing the Odwira festival as "eleven uproarious days" of one pagan ritual after another that "caused a highly unpleasant frenzy among the inhabitants."[107] Another time listeners objected strongly to the missionary's repeated claim that "all humans are evil" and a priest interrupted him to communicate African ideas of the supernatural until Riis felt "entirely weary."[108] In many encounters the missionary felt that he "often found no opportunity to speak a word with these people about that which alone is necessary."

It can be deducted from those accounts that the willingness of Africans to listen was limited. They disagreed with the often negative message,

---

103. For a general summary of crucial changes in Africa, see Hastings, *Church in Africa*, 400–5. Specifically for Ghana, one of the most detailed studies is Kimble, *Political History*.

104. Hanciles, "Conversion and Social Change," 162–64.

105. Ibid., 167.

106. BMA, D-1,1 Akropong 1836 #6 Riis July 27, 1836; MM 1837, 536–39.

107. BMA, D-1,1 Akropong 1836 # 9 Riis diary September 11–21, 1836; MM 1837, 554–55.

108. Ibid., 446–47.

and responses ranged from incredulity and objections to walking away and laughter. The latter was sometimes interpreted by the missionaries as recognition of the uselessness of African idols, but more likely it was a sign that Africans thought the message strange or ridiculous.[109] By 1838 the missionaries did not expect a positive response any more to their insistent emphasis on "the sinful perdition of humans," as their surprise about some African's willingness to hear more in Akwamu indicates.[110]

African assessment of the failure of the European missionary movement during this early period hones in on the fact that their message produced "jarring notes in the ears and religious sensibilities of the custodians of the traditional religious heritage."[111] Only when missionaries were aided by the crisis colonialism caused, the introduction of "extra-doctrinal" methods of education and medical work, and recruitment of "local hands in the missionary project," Africans began to convert. However, eventually, in response to the European dismissal of African traditions and life, African theologians emphasized the pre-Christian religions tradition of their people. Bediako states their aim was "to achieve some integration between the African pre-Christian religious experience and African Christian commitment in ways that would ensure the integrity of African Christian identity and selfhood."[112]

Growing up, Basel missionaries were exposed to Pietist Christianity and had read some reports from Africa, but in the BMTI they received a strong biblical validation of their Pietist values as universal and the image of Africa was consolidated. This added to the normal human tendency to favor one's own culture and undervalue that of others, the conviction that "their own way of life represented values of universal application."[113] The Basel Mission version of this characteristic of contemporary Europeans emphasized the sinfulness and lost condition of humans and devalued

109. In all the above cited conversations Riis interpreted laughter as agreement to his statements. See also BMA, D-1,1 Akropong 1838 # 6 Riis July 6, 1838.

110. BMA, D-1,1 Akropong 1838 #10 Riis diary October 14, 1838; MM 1839, 469–70.

111. Njoku, "Missionary Factor," 204.

112. Bediako, "Types of African Theology," 56. Bediako explores various approaches, ranging from radical "Indigenisers" who stressed the continuity between African religious traditions and Christianity, to "Biblicists" who posited a radical discontinuity, and "Translators" between these two extremes. He identifies Bolajo Idowu as "indigeniser" and Byang Kato as "Biblicist." See also his examination of these, John Mbiti, and Mulago gwa Cikala Musharhamina in Bediako, *Theology and Identity*.

113. Curtin, *Image of Africa*, 259.

the material aspects of life. The latter led the missionaries to conclude that African religious practices were solely directed towards physical desires and Africans did not know God or care about the eternal life of their soul.[114] The perspectives their preparation had instilled made them unable to take African religious traditions seriously, or even identify the basic reality that religiosity permeates all of African life.[115] Not surprisingly, Africans did not accept their message.

RIIS'S RESPONSE TO HIS APPARENT FAILURE

The one surviving Basel missionary responded to his apparent failure in achieving the mission's goals in two contrasting ways. There are definite depressive tendencies in Riis's letters, and there is evidence for a deterioration of his attitudes to Africans. From these he deduced missiological ideas that influenced further Basel ministry in Africa.

Depressive Tendencies and Pious Religiosity

Both, Riis's admirers and critics tend to portray him as a strong-willed confident man. Hagiographic examples are his obituary (praising the "strong faith it took to persist"), Steiner, who credits the continuation of the mission to Riis's courage and "patient perseverance," and Wurm's emphasis that Riis "remained on his post as faithful guard," even when the Board gave him the option to return.[116] By contrast, Miller criticizes these attempts to hold Riis up in public view "as an example of Pietist strength" by positing his "stamina and imagination" and "willful insubordination" which made him a "strategic deviant" from Basel Mission accountability structures and policies.[117]

---

114. For example: BMA, D-1,1 Akropong 1836 #9 Riis October 27, 1836; MM 1837, 560–61 and #6 Riis July 27, 1836; MM 1837, 551–52, diary from August 8 and 12, 1836.

115. The eminent analyst of Asante traditions, Rattray, put it this way: "This religious element among a people such as the Ashanti can never properly be ignored in a critical survey of any of their customs, their laws, or even perhaps of their unpremeditated actions. In Ashanti the divorce of religion from any of these is wellnigh impossible, and it is hardly an exaggeration to say that any such estrangement would tend to result in an illegality." Rattray, *Ashanti*, 214.

116. HB 1854, no. 10 (October), 80–81; Steiner, "Andreas Riis," 8; Wurm, "Anfänge," 305–6. Wurm refers to the Board's decision to give Riis the choice to stay or return and finance him for either after his colleagues' deaths in 1832 (KP January 9, 1833).

117. Miller, *Missionary Zeal*, 131–32. He continues to compare Riis to the

Contrary to these assessments, it is obvious in the missionary's letters that he struggled with feelings of inadequacy and depressive tendencies. Repeatedly he refers to tears he shed, sometimes to sleepless nights, and often to the burdens that "filled his heart with sadness."[118] That such emotions persisted is illustrated from statements on the Akwamu trip with Mürdter. When both had health problems, Riis confesses that their "spirit was deeply depressed and hopeless" and his mind filled with "sundry heavy thoughts about my unfaithfulness, and I could only sigh: Lord have mercy on me!"[119] It also comes through in his final reflections (after his wife's death) on the ship that brought him back to Europe. Recounting their last months in Africa he wrote, "our situation was highly discouraging," and lists "so many sicknesses, fears, worries, needs, troubles, sorrows, and frustrations."[120]

Riis described various strategies he employed to overcome his dark feelings. Among them were prayer, retreats alone into nature, physical exercise, hunting, and visits to neighboring villages.[121] One day after "some time of walking around deeply depressed and hardly finding enough comfort ... to not be completely overcome by discouragement" illustrates the way Pietist spirituality helped him find encouragement.[122] Riis felt "driven into solitude" by "an unusual spiritual drive" to pray fervently "for the salvation of this poor negro people" and found encouragement and new hope in the scripture verse of the day. Thus, while there are definite depressive tendencies, Riis also found renewed courage in the pious faith and spiritual practices Basel missionaries developed throughout their preparation. In this way, the BMTI practice became a source of strength that explains the missionaries' extraordinary resilience in the face of seemingly insurmountable challenges.

Furthermore, there are indications that the Pietist dualistic worldview provided Riis with a rationale for his depressive emotions and lack of success. He refers on several occasions to the "poisoned atmosphere that surrounds the lonely wanderer, when he often walks about deeply depressed without being able to say why" and once describes the inability

---

"charismatic but contrary and contradictory personality" of Livingstone.

118. BMA, D-1,1 Akropong 1836 #6 Riis July 27, 1836; MM 1837, 537, 539–42.

119. BMA, D-1,1 Akropong 1838 #10 Riis diary October 10, 1838; MM1839, 458.

120. BMA, PF 124 "Riis, Andreas," Letter from the "Ship Robert Heddle" dated September 27, 1845; cited in Wurm, "Anfänge," 328–29.

121. BMA, D-1,1 Akropong 1836 #6 Riis July 27, 1836; MM 1837, 539.

122. BMA, D-1,1 Akropong 1836 #9 Riis diary August 28, 1836; MM1837, 553.

to communicate his message "as if an iron lock was put on mouth and tongue so that I cannot speak."[123] Jäger had expressed similar sentiments in 1832, comparing the happy atmosphere in the BMTI with the "spiritually unhealthy as if it was poisoned" atmosphere he felt in Africa.[124] Thus, the demonization of popular religion that Pietists practiced in Europe was transferred to African religious traditions.[125] Meyer's study demonstrates how African Christians appropriated this. She identifies not only the common European notion "that the devil was behind the power of African religions" but shows that for African converts Pietist dualism provided a way of integrating their religious traditions into Christian discourse "by emphasizing the image of the Devil and transforming gods and ghosts into 'Christian' demons."[126] For Riis and his colleagues this dualism became an important coping strategy. The hindrances and challenges they experienced were interpreted as demonic opposition to their "holy task" which could be counteracted with more intense Pietist spiritual practices.

Deteriorating Attitude towards Africans

Sickness, physical strain, and the death of colleagues were valid reasons for the missionaries to feel down at times. But their lack of success also caused another, contrary, feeling to rise. Riis became increasingly impatient and struggled with anger about Africans' lack of responsiveness and—as he perceived it—misdeeds towards him. He described repeated confrontations with his workers, whom he accused of "lying and deceiving attitudes," and concluded that the "stubbornness of some Negros is great," declaring the example of the carpenters he reported that day was "only one of many he could recount."[127] On several occasions he admitted struggles to control his temper towards such offenders and eventually generalized that there is no shortage of situations that exercised his pa-

---

123. For example: BMA, D-1,1 Akropong 1836 #6 Riis July 27, 1836; MM 1837, 539, 547–48.

124. BMA, D-1,1 Christiansborg 1832 #12 Jäger June 20, 1832.

125. Meyer, *Translating the Devil*, 49–51.

126. Ibid., 108–11. Meyer's context is the work of the North German Mission in the Ewe area in Southwest Ghana. The fact that NGM missionaries were trained in the BMTI for a good part of the period she covers makes her study pertinent to the Basel Mission as well.

127. For example in BMA, D-1,1 Akropong 1835 Riis diary June 23, August 3 and 23, 1835; MM 1836, 543–44, 550, 553.

Early Failures at Mission Work (1836–1840)   321

tience and faithfulness because "one deals here with people who often tire the heart and who not infrequently provoke irritation."[128] Thus, there is evidence that his evaluations of Africans went from the early compromises with African medical abilities and appreciation of some individuals he considered of higher moral standing to an increasingly clear condemnation of African behaviors, beliefs, and culture. This is obvious in the way he treated his employees and in his assessment of unresponsiveness to the message.

In growing exasperation with the behavior of African workers he frequently reminded them of "their sinful and lost state" and felt the need to adopt "stern measures" and to "punish in love."[129] His measures caused some workers to run away, others stayed upon being threatened with the Danish authorities.[130] Riis claimed that other Europeans felt he treated Africans "too mild and too friendly," but the "friendly condescension" he suggested did not mean that misdeeds should go unpunished.[131] Later controversies in the 1840s between Riis, the West-Indian Christians, and other missionaries have their roots in this earlier struggle with anger. When he found the African Christians and even fellow missionaries not living up to the standards of morality, hard work, and exceptional stamina that he applied, he "snapped" emotionally and became quarrelsome, demanding, and hard to live with. The resulting conflicts eventually led to his recall to Europe in 1845.[132] Miller's claim of Riis's insubordination predominantly focuses on these last two years and his argument of Riis's "troublesome relations with Africans" gains much of its substantiation from the angry letters of his colleagues in this period.[133] This ignores by and large the background to Riis's reactions in the earlier years. However,

---

128. BMA, D-1,1 Akropong 1836 #6 Riis July 27, 1836; MM 1837, 549.

129. BMA, D-1,1 Akropong 1836 #6 Riis July 27, 1836; MM 1837, 536–38.

130. An example for the latter happened in August 1835. Two of the workers were packed and ready to leave. Riis tells them "do not go because on this way you will only meet misfortune" and they decided to stay, afraid "the thing would become known in Christiansborg." (BMA, D-1,1 Akropong 1835 Riis diary August 23, 1835; MM 1836, 553).

131. BMA, D-1,1 Akropong 1836 #6 Riis July 27, 1836; MM 1837, 537–38.

132. BMA, D-1,2 Akropong und Ussu 1842–1848, various letters from May 1845, especially #13 Sebald May 16, 1845 and Widmann May 26, 1845. Discussions of the Board are recorded in KP from October 23 and November 13, 1844; KP from May 14 and 28, September 24, October 15 and 22, 1845.

133. Miller, *Missionary Zeal*, 129–36.

even a scholar as positive of Riis as Opoku has to admit that he was "no diplomat and, unfortunately, given violent temper as pioneers often are."[134]

Illustrations of blaming African ignorance and religious ideas for the unsuccessful communication of the missionaries' message also abound. One example happened on the Akwamu trip. Speaking to people in a village where they spent the night, Riis commented that African "great ignorance coupled with the falsest ideas of all transcendent things makes it very difficult for the missionary to talk about divine things understandably."[135] In other words, it was the African's fault that the message was so incomprehensible to them. This conclusion, which built on the presumptions of "African character" and primitive stage of development that their training had established, affected Riis's ideas of mission in Africa which in turn influenced Basel Mission policy decisions.

Riis's Ideas Informed Further Basel Mission Engagement

In 1836 Riis reflected on his experience and offered ideas about Christian mission in Africa.[136] He gave detailed descriptions of Akuapem geography, agriculture, and political structures, and stereotype portrayals of the people. While he acknowledged African hospitality, he observed that they rather talked with his employees than him; only when he told "short lively stories" they listened "without objections" but occasionally asking questions. From this he concluded that African "natural indolence and carelessness which made them indifferent about the future" were a "significant obstacle for the acceptance of Christianity." He also made the significant observations that African culture and world view was resilient, and change of beliefs required a crisis of some kind and would take time and sustained engagement of missionaries.[137] As we saw above, scholars examining African conversions confirm the tenacity of African culture and beliefs and identify the onslaught of colonial rule as the crisis event that caused many to embrace Christianity later.

While Riis had these missiological insights, the conclusions he and the organization drew reflected contemporary European cultural arrogance. Reporting in Basel in 1840, Riis expressed optimism about the

---

134. Opoku, *Riis, the Builder*, 60.
135. BMA, D-1,1 Akropong 1838 #10 Riis diary October 11, 1838; MM 1839, 461.
136. BMA, D-1,1 Akropong 1836 #9 Riis October 27, 1836; MM 1837, 556–61.
137. Ibid.; MM 1837, 549, Riis diary July 25, 1836.

continuation and establishment of a mission in Akuapem.[138] In contrast to Asante, there was no slave trade and the people were more open to European influence; they welcomed missionaries, and had asked him to return with colleagues. It was also a healthier location, easier to travel to than Kumasi, and some of the obstacles were now removed, in particular the hostile governor had died—circumstances Riis saw as "divine providence." His report entailed the (not so) subtle suggestion that a more enduring and intentional approach was needed with more missionaries, less travelling, and concentration on the promising location he had identified. Riis's reasoning reveals well established presumptions: Long-term sustained work was necessary because Africans were "children of the moment, forgetful, easily sidetracked and excited." Riis's experience and especially how he interpreted it amplified what he had been taught about Africa in Basel, and his reports in turn contributed to cementing the image in Europe. Furthermore, his evaluations contributed to the organizational decision to modify the approach in Africa, if not their missionary training.

THE BASEL MISSION ORGANIZATIONAL RESPONSE TO ITS FAILURE

The Basel Mission identified goals for their work in Africa included "cultivation" activities like building houses, clearing and planting land, as well as learning vernaculars, translating the Bible, establishing schools, and the "fruitful spread of the knowledge of God."[139] Africans were expected to be "ashamed of the wild life, desire instruction," and settle in a new community of Christians. The preceding analysis of the early Basel missionaries' engagement in Africa demonstrated that very little of this was achieved in the first twelve years. Apart from some progress towards building a station with houses and gardens, the missionaries had not learned any language well enough to communicate their message effectively nor convinced any Africans to accept it and drastically change their lives. Towards a school the only development was that Riis taught four

---

138. BMA, KP July 7, 1840.

139. MM 1829, 353–56. See also Instructions 1827 in MM 1830, 451–82; BMA, D-10.3,3a1) Instructions 1828.

boys for a brief period in 1839.[140] Even the buildings and plantings the missionaries had established were in ruins when they returned in 1843.[141]

When the Board discussed this failure, they identified "divisions among the Negros, physical needs that needed much handiwork, and the conflict with the Danish governor" as obstructions to "the proclamation of the Gospel."[142] Even internally, the organization blamed solely the circumstances in Africa for its disappointment. The issues of trained incapacity this study highlighted remained unacknowledged. But they did realize that all that had transpired so far, the sacrifices and lack of any tangible success called for serious rethinking. Taking into account Riis's evaluations and British precedents, the Board responded with a "new approach." It entailed a larger group which included West Indian African Christians and a more intentional effort to establish a model community that replicated European models. It also illustrates the general development that lack of responsiveness led to more deliberate implementation of indirect methods.

Intentional Replication with the Help of African Christians

Miller claims that recruiting African Christians from the West Indies was Riis's proposal.[143] Schlatter ascribes it to the fresh energetic leadership of Director Hoffmann and most others follow Schlatter.[144] Hoffmann does become the public voice advocating this "new approach" in official publications, but it is clear from his report of the 1840 summer trip to the Board that the impetus came from Britain.[145] In Frankfurt he had met Robert Pinkerton (1780–1859), since 1830 the "Principal Agent of the British and Foreign Bible Society in the Kingdoms of Germany," who promised any necessary British support for the Basel Mission to continue its African mission.[146] According to Hoffmann, Pinkerton suggested trying with "transferred West Indian African Christians like at

---

140. BMA, D-1,1 Akropong 1839 #5 Riis July 29, 1839.

141. MM 1844, 179 citing BMA D-1,2 Gold Coast 1843 #3 Riis July 19, 1843.

142. BMA, KP February 27, 1839.

143. Miller, *Missionary Zeal*, 130.

144. Schlatter, *Basler Mission in Afrika*, 32. For one example of other scholars that adopt Schlatter's perspective, see Groves, *Planting of Christianity, Vol. 2*, 24.

145. BMA, KP September 2, 1840.

146. For Pinkerton's important role in linking Continental and British efforts, both in Europe and "overseas" missions, see Detzler, "Robert Pinkerton."

Early Failures at Mission Work (1836–1840) 325

the beginning in Sierra Leone" as a basis for the mission. "One would have immediately a small church of immigrated and settled Christian Negros [and] through cultivation the climate would become healthier." The Board consulted Riis, who found this plan "doable and useful," and decided to proceed.[147] The British Civilization Society turned down their request.[148] However, by then the idea had taken root, and in February 1841 the Board made the basic decision to continue the African mission and to approach the Moravian Conference for a few West Indian families to migrate to Africa.[149]

The establishment of the British colony Sierra Leone as a settlement of liberated Africans, initially from London, then from America, but in rising numbers, quickly overtaking all others, "recaptives" from the British naval blockade of the slave trade, was well known in the Basel Mission.[150] Many BMTI graduates worked with the CMS in Sierra Leone and reports of this mission regularly featured in the *Missions-Magazin*. From the responsiveness of displaced Africans in Sierra Leone the Basel Mission had (falsely) concluded its earlier optimistic expectations for Guinea. Consequently, the strategy adopted in 1841 was not particularly new. However, there were several distinct features to the Basel approach in Ghana. Most significantly, only a small number of West Indians moved with the new missionary team to Guinea, six families and a few singles, twenty-five persons altogether. Contrary to Sierra Leone, no new settlers followed and they were soon overtaken in numbers by native African Christians. Furthermore, throughout the nineteenth century the European missionary contingent remained large enough to dominate the mission. A closer comparison of the British and Basel approaches, as well as other projects that included West Indian missionaries, would be highly desirable as parochial scholarship has prevented this so far, but it is beyond the scope of this study.[151] Within the Basel Mission, only Vallenga's

147. BMA, KP September 9, 1840.

148. The British negative response was reported in BMA, KP January 6, 1841.

149. BMA, KP February 10, 1841 reports the decision to continue and approach the Moravians.

150. On Sierra Leone see: Avery, *Christianity in Sierra Leone*; Fyfe, *History of Sierra Leone*; Hanciles, *Euthanasia*, 5–14; Walls, "Christian Experiment"; Walls, *Missionary Movement*, 102–10.

151. An exception is Vassady, "Role of the Black West Indian Missionary." This dated thesis is the only study to date that compares the nineteenth century missionary projects in Africa which included the participation of West Indian Christians. Vassady's section on the Basel Mission project (108–27) is quite brief and unsatisfactory,

article addresses some of the issues that arose when Moravian Africans from the West Indies and BMTI trained German missionaries attempted to establish a mission together.[152]

Most significant for the present research are the arguments for the new strategy Hoffmann listed on various occasions.[153] They reveal a number of European assumptions as well as their specific Basel Mission expression, and clearly Riis's ideas were given much weight. Hoffmann reiterates as "signs of divine providence indicating a continuation" the deaths of the Danish king and governor who were opposed to mission, the end of the civil war with the suicide of one of the opponents (Owusu Akyem in 1839), and the Africans' openness reported by Riis. Furthermore, Riis's willingness to return, his conviction that Akuropon was preferable to Kumasi, and the support of the current Danish king were encouragements to continue in Akuropon. Hoffmann suggested to counteract the challenges of "the climate and the difficulty of the language" by avoiding too much physical work and too early mission trips and by sending people with "decisive gifts for languages." While the latter did not happen until the 1850s, the West-Indian immigrants were expected to relieve physical challenges. The roles assigned to them were to be exemplar and nucleus of an African church and to help to improve the physical conditions. The expectation that they would be more resistant to the climate reflected European presumptions regarding African immunity.

The Basel Mission plan also was, as Groves confirms, "a more limited form of Christian witness by native agency than others intended by their use of the term."[154] He cites Buxton's and earlier proposals by Moravians that Africans in the West Indies should be considered "the best means of Christianizing Africa."[155] It is obvious from their speeches at the valedictory service that the West Indians eventually recruited perceived themselves as missionaries to Africa[156] Predictably, this contributed to the later tensions and would invite a more detailed study than is possible here.

---

offering simplistic evaluations based solely on secondary sources.

152. Vellenga, "Racial and Ethnic Conflict."

153. BMA, KP February 10, 1841; Hoffmann, *Missionsgesellschaft*, 51–61, 103; Hoffmann, *Eilf Jahre*, 56–70.

154. Groves, *Planting of Christianity*, Vol. 2, 24.

155. Buxton, *African Slave Trade*, 491–97; Hutton, *Moravian Missions*, 217–19.

156. Zorn's letter from January 5, 1843 reports in detail the valedictory service and speeches of the West Indians in "Periodical Accounts" Relating to the Missions of the Church of the United Brethren Established Among the Heathen. *Periodical Accounts,*

Defending the continuation in an official "Proclamation to all evangelical Christians," Hoffmann adds the sacrifices already made, the misery of West African peoples, and counteracting the horrors of the slave trade through preaching the Gospel and introducing Christian morals as further motivations.[157] These arguments restated general European ideas about Christian mission in Africa. More significantly, the revisions based on the early failures were limited to recruiting African assistants for an otherwise unchanged program. Thus, while this "new approach" was a recognition that "something needed to change" and—very significantly—brought in African actors, it did not constitute a revision of the organization's visions, goals, and strategies for mission in Africa. Most importantly for the argument of this study, it did not entail a change in the BMTI preparatory processes and trained incapacity remained unconscious.

Instructions for the new mission team were considerably more comprehensive than before.[158] They cover the kind of African Christians to be selected in the West Indies and arrangements with them, first steps in Africa including buildings and agriculture, "Rules for the Christian Negro-village," missionary work in the church and "among the heathen," and the "internal order of the mission." It was regarded as essential "that the Christian Negros live together and close enough to the mission-house to clearly represent a church before the heathen and assist each other easily." They were to hold daily devotions and Sunday services, establish a school for the children, and train African catechists. Local Africans were welcome to settle in the Christian village, but only if they built their own huts and farms, renounced idolatry, cursing and swearing, and the possession or trade of slaves, wore "proper clothes," gave up drinking, regularly sent their children to school, attended church and celebrated the Christian holidays, no unmarried people of both genders slept in one room, and they lived in "regular marriage." All this clearly indicates that the Basel Mission envisaged the replication of a Pietist German rural settlement. Furthermore, the BMTI served as model for the church, from pious dress codes, diligent work and study to morality and daily spiritual disciplines.

The practical implementation of this plan is accounted in great detail in letters, publications, and subsequent accounts of the Basel Mission in

Vol. 16, 244–47.

157. Hoffmann, *Missionsgesellschaft*, 57–61.
158. BMA Q-3-3,26 Instruktionen 1842.

Ghana.[159] Andreas and Anna Riis travelled with the new graduates Georg Widmann (1814–1876) and George Peter Thompson (1819–1889) to the West Indies.[160] They were able to recruit twenty-five African Christians assisted by the Moravian Superintendant, Jakob Zorn (c.1803–1843), who was an important voice in Jamaica fanning missionary vision for Africa among liberated Africans.[161] Zorn had established a small missionary training school hoping "that Africa must and will be evangelized by blacks from the West Indies."[162] Despite their disparate views of the extent to which the West Indians would contribute to the mission, he generously supported the Basel missionaries. When the group arrived in Akuropon in 1843, they were a sufficiently large party and the general historical developments increasingly in favor to implement the envisioned model to a great extent.

It can be categorized under the four headings often used in communications, "culture work," "school work," "church work," and "language work." *Culture work* involved establishing mission stations—separate from African villages—with European style buildings and agriculture, workshops, school, and church. *School work* referred to the comprehensive effort in (Western) education and *church work* to evangelism and care for Christians. *Language work*, finally, reflected the emphasis on learning vernacular languages and translating Christian materials. There were Basel Mission specific aspects to each one of these areas of engagement, but the most significant observation is that what ensued was an illustration of the dominant model of mission into the twentieth century, "replication."

---

159. BMA, D-1,2 "Die Übersiedlung der Neger betreffend 1842–1843" (Concerning the Migration of the Negros); MM 1842, 131–38, 258–66; MM 1843, 180–87, 231–42. See also Schlatter, *Basler Mission in Afrika*, 32–36; Smith, *The Presbyterian Church of Ghana*, 35–39; Wurm, "Anfänge," 318–28.

160. George Thompson was a Liberian Sessing had brought to Europe in 1829. He had attended school in Beuggen and then studied at the BMTI (1837–1842). See BMA, PF 223 Thompson, Georg Peter.

161. Jakob Zorn, superintendent of the Moravian mission in Jamaica 1834–1843, had begun training young men as teachers and catechists for Africa in 1837. See for example his letter from October 9, 1837 in *Periodical Accounts, Vol.* 14, 299–300. He also reports frequently on the recruitment process of the Basel Mission. See for example his letters from August 17–24, 1841; November 8 and December 26, 1842, and January 5, 1843 in *Periodical Accounts, Vol.* 16, 42, 302–4, 244–47.

162. Zorn's letter from March 29, 1843 in ibid., 348.

The Inherent Trained Incapacity of the Replication Model

Wilbert Shenk highlighted that "various conceptions of the task have guided missionaries" through the history of Christian missions.[163] He identifies three models of mission, based on different conceptions of culture: replication, indigenization, and contextualization. In the "replication model" missionaries as primary agents—charged with responsibility for the successful outcome—seek to reproduce a faithful replica of the church in their homeland, based on a pre-critical, ethnocentric view of culture. Foundational to replication is the conviction "that there is such a thing as a Christian culture" which is "definitive ecclesiastically and culturally." Both, Roman Catholics and Protestants were firmly committed to the "historical synthesis of the Christian religion and European culture, as the standard by which they measured their results." Mission was about "civilization" of uncivilized peoples. As we saw above, the main point of debate among those whose idea of mission was replication "was whether civilization was prerequisite to Christianization or not." But they agreed that Christianization can only be achieved by civilizing and that the task of mission was to reproduce what was perceived as a Christian existence—European patterns of life, economy, and church.

It is obvious that the Basel Mission in Ghana was an exemplar of replication. Figure 6 clearly illustrates the parallels between the Mission-House in Basel and the Secondary School eventually built in Akuropon.[164] Both depict the ideal of tranquility, order, diligent work, and agricultural landscaping that was upheld in the BMTI Community and attempted to replicate in Africa.

---

163. Shenk, *Changing Frontiers*, 48–58. Shenk articulated a variation of this chapter with the same three phases of missionary thinking about culture in Shenk, "Missionary Encounter with Culture."

164. BMA, QS-30.018.0006: "Mission house in Basel." Max Beck, Schaffhausen, Switzerland (publisher/distributor), *BMArchives*, http://www.bmarchives.org/items/show/81915, accessed May 21, 2015; BMA, D-30.11.030: "Secondary School Akropong." Ramseyer, Friedrich August Louis (Mr), *BMArchives*, http://www.bmarchives.org/items/show/56476. The picture in Akuropon was taken between 1888 and 1895 by the Basel Missionary Ramseyer.

330   PART II: Indications for Trained Incapacity

Figure 6
Illustrating Replication: The Mission House in Basel and the
"Secondary School Akropong"

Shenk's second model, *indigenization*, refers to the well-known and widely discussed "three-selfs" principle, generally associated with Henry Venn (1796–1873) and Rufus Anderson (1796–1880), mission administrators of the CMS (1841–1872) and the American Board of Commissioners for Foreign Missions (1832–1866) respectively.[165] Similar ideas had been around previously, but Venn and Anderson synthesized them into a coherent formula. The goal of an "indigenous church" was reached when the church was "self-financing, self-governing, and self-propagating." Shenk dates this model from 1850 to 1970. While these ideals and the evolutionary view of culture that underlay them were applied during this period, indigenization was actually only a variation of the replication model. Indigenous Christians were promoted to

165. See also Shenk, "Origins and Evolution of the Three-Selfs."

lead, finance, and expand their churches themselves, but European and American missionaries still assumed Western models as goal. Shenk also observes that this ideal, while attempting adjustments to the new culture, "essentially did this by changing the cast of players without rewriting the script" and eventually failed. Furthermore, Hanciles incisively examined African responses, the eventual failure of the native pastorate experiment which indigenization fostered, and African independent developments it inspired.[166] He confirms that the type of Christianity in Sierra Leone "was essentially a carbon copy of English versions."[167]

In other words, replication remained the dominant model during the modern Christian missionary movement. But even today, as Shenk rightly asserts, "elements of the replication model can readily be found in contemporary missionary practice" in spite of the promotion of *contextualization* since the 1970s. This third model is based on a "dynamic and evolving" view of culture, expects the process to emerge from within the context, and aims at "the formation of a faith community, which is culturally authentic and authentically Christian."

In the Basel Mission replication included building and farming techniques from rural Europe, German Pietist ethical virtues, patriarchal social relationships, and contemplative spirituality. Everything about the endeavor sought to replicate home models which were idealized in missionary preparation. A detailed examination of the Basel Mission version of this general European approach to Christian mission would be desirable, but it goes beyond the scope of this study. It suffices here to emphasize that the response of the Basel Mission to its early failures included no recognition of the issues of trained incapacity. Rather, they embarked on a long-term strategy to establish alternative Christian communities in Africa, patterned after European cultural expressions that were presumed to be "civilization," in contrast to and intended to replace African traditions and beliefs. In other words, the organization decided that their "new approach" would not be more engagement with African culture, in order to facilitate an appropriation of the gospel in that context, but a more intentional imposition of the European cultural patterns which the BMTI practice reinforced in its graduates.

---

166. Hanciles, *Euthanasia*.

167. Ibid., 8. He adds that "European missionaries [were] determined that it should be so and the African inhabitants [showed] a particular proclivity for imitating the white man's ways."

The approach raises numerous missiological issues that characterized in variations most of the modern missionary movement. They have been discussed and critiqued by a large body of literature. Most pertinent for the Ghanaian context is Mobley's study of dominant African critics.[168] Educated Ghanaians of the early twentieth century criticized the missionaries' residential segregation, "color prejudice, racial discrimination, and social distance" that were driven by "cultural superiority, religious pride, and vocational dominance." They point to the "blanket condemnation" and "failure to relate Christianity to indigenous beliefs," but also to the "discriminating acceptance of the missionary's interpretation" by Africans who made a difference between "Christianity in Europe and Christianity according to Jesus Christ." Furthermore, Ghanaians criticize the missionaries' "inadequate understanding of either the social or ritual activities" which led them "to introduce the 'extra-religious morality' of the West into a society in which already existed a 'moral plenum.'" In particular, they highlight European forms of church organization, education, marriage customs, political and economic association, the use of schools as "recruiting ground" for denominations, and "the missionaries' identification with commercial and governmental concerns [which] caused their mission to become suspect."

These critiques have been voiced for the better part of a century and much has been written on the gospel, mission, and culture.[169] This raises the question, why the replication model still often prevails. This case study of the Basel Mission illustrates important reasons for the elusiveness of the ideal of contextualization and the struggle of missionaries to facilitate truly indigenous appropriations of Christianity in new cultural contexts. Homogeneous religious groups like the BMTI community of practice are prone to endorse a "pre-critical" view of culture that assumes their particular expression as universal. Missionaries who pass the preparation processes of such communities embrace these normative values and practices and, consequently, develop trained incapacity to flexibly adjust

---

168. Mobley, *Ghanaian's Image*. He examined a wide range of Ghanaian literature including works from men related to the Basel Mission founded church like Joseph Kwame Boakye Danquah (1895–1964) and Joseph Hanson Kwabena Nketia (b. 1921), and prominent politicians and scholars like Kofi Abrefa Busia (1913–1978) and Christian Goncalves Kwami Baeta (1908–1994).

169. For example, the seminal works: Hiebert, *Anthropological Insights for Missionaries*; Kraft, *Christianity in Culture*; Loewen, *Culture and Human Values*; Luzbetak, *The Church and Cultures*; Mayers, *Christianity Confronts Culture*; Nida, *Customs and Cultures*.

to and embrace other values and practices. Thus, trained incapacity is inherent to the replication model. Flexible adjustment to other contexts is not desired, but perceived as aberration and heresy. As a result, the intercultural incapacity this study critiques becomes exalted as ideal of Christian missionary engagement.

CONCLUSIONS FROM EARLY FAILURES TO ACHIEVE THE MISSION'S GOALS

This chapter examined various ways the small missionary team attempted what they regarded as mission work. It identified a number of indications for trained incapacity in these efforts. Furthermore, the lack of success in the first twelve years of the Basel Mission involvement in Ghana triggered responses, individually and organizationally, which show additional indications of incapacity to make changes that would have fostered an African appropriation of Christianity.

Missionaries' evaluations of Danish clergy by BMTI criteria of "true Christianity" and resulting insolence towards ecclesiastical authority led to tensions and difficulties with the chaplain. However, historical relationships with Danish mission interests also contributed to misunderstandings and disappointed expectations that created obstacles for the missionaries. Because Danish political and ecclesiastical ideas of engagement in Africa clashed with BMTI fostered values of neutrality and Pietist spirituality the mission continued to lack much needed support.

The perceived need for reconnaissance and the view of missionary work as of "wandering nature" sent Basel missionaries on numerous trips that jeopardized their health and hindered language learning and relationships. They had acquired this pattern of evangelism in the "Christianized" European context but in Africa it made little sense. Here was no audience to call back to "true Christianity," but a people who had never heard of the missionaries' message and shared none of their intellectual assumptions. An African appropriation of Christianity would have needed long-term commitment to developing mutual understanding. In some ways the trips resembled today's so-called "short-term missions." Like them, they lacked the deeper engagement necessary for true intercultural communication. Relationships with people they met on trips remained superficial and in Akuropon the frequent absences also hindered the establishment of deeper friendships.

When they were not traveling, BMTI instilled ideas of a "Christian" settlement caused the missionaries to be preoccupied with building and agricultural work. This also impeded progress in language learning and building relationships to communicate the Christian message. Basel missionaries' German Pietist standards of work continued to strain relationships and left their employees as primary audience. Moreover, their efforts at learning vernacular in this early period revealed that the predominance of written language aids in BMTI training had not prepared them for the acquisition of unwritten African vernaculars. It made their progress in this highly prioritized task slow, prevented their understanding of the linguistic and ethnic diversity in Akuapem, and impeded their ability to communicate meaningfully.

Finally, African scholars highlight the inappropriateness of their message. Pietist emphasis on human depravity combined with the European image of Africa caused the missionaries to preach a message which was not "good news" to people. Their condemnation of African ways of life and religious traditions offended rather than attracted. Assumptions about African preoccupation with the material that ignored the foundational religiosity of African traditions rendered much missionary preaching incomprehensive. Not surprisingly, responses ranged from ridicule to objection and rejection.

Rather than revising their ideas, mostly the missionaries felt confirmed in their preconceptions of African character and primitive culture. The last survivor, Andreas Riis, articulated this forcefully despite maintaining some good relationships in Akuropon. The latter made him hopeful for a positive response in time, but definite depressive tendencies and hardening attitudes towards Africans can be observed in Riis. The way Pietist spirituality offered encouragement is a sign that not their entire preparation incapacitated the Basel missionaries for the intercultural encounter. Personally, the BMTI practice had prepared them to persevere through many truly challenging circumstances.

A number of those circumstances were also beyond the missionaries' control. As the general failure of Protestant missions in the early nineteenth century indicates, while missionaries were relatively few and powerless and African states and traditional life remained relatively intact, the incentives for the major social change Christian conversion required remained small. The social and economic upheaval caused by developments towards stronger colonial control by European powers also stimulated greater openness to missionary efforts as the nineteenth century progressed.

These historical developments aided the more intentional replication mission effort which became the organizational response of the Basel Mission to its initial failures in Africa. This approach, that presumes an uncritical view of culture, continued to foster trained incapacity because it made the inflexible application of European patterns of evangelism, church organization, and Christian life official mission policy.

Conclusion

Pitfalls of Trained Incapacity in Integral Missionary Training

GERMAN MISSIONS CONTRIBUTED SIGNIFICANTLY to the protestant missionary movement in the nineteenth century—an under-researched and often neglected fact. This study explored the preparation processes of the largest continental mission organization of the period. It investigated the thesis that the Basel Mission Training Institute constituted a community of practice which had the propensity to establish trained incapacity for intercultural engagement in its missionaries. The analysis focused on the work of Basel missionaries in their early years in the region of the former Danish Guinea (1828–1840).

By this focus it highlighted German missions prior to and outside German colonial involvement. Examining the pre-colonial venture of the largest and most influential German mission in Africa revealed tensions and difficulties in Christian mission which are not typically paid attention to. The intercultural, interdenominational character of the Basel Mission and its strong preference for political neutrality created situations of divided loyalties and suspicions by those in power which at times greatly hindered the ministry of its workers. This became particularly evident in the case of the missionary of Danish nationality who refused to be a Danish agent. Thus, the missionary engagement examined here is not consistent with the often assumed colonial collaboration. However, because so many BMTI graduates worked in dominant Anglophone societies, the effects of their preparatory processes in that context and a comparison with British missionaries would be a highly desirable study. Unfortunately, this was beyond the scope of this project.

The BMTI Community of Practice and Trained Incapacity

The detailed analysis of the BMTI through the lens of the *communities of practice* framework showed the development and impact of foreign missionary training in the nineteenth century. It revealed an approach to missionary preparation which intentionally employed social dynamics of mutual shaping to foster the specific religious convictions, socio-ethical priorities, and practical emphases of a particular, essentially homogeneous group of participants. The findings confirm the powerful effectiveness—from an educational perspective—of communities of practice.

Basel missionaries embraced the vision of foreign mission privileged in the BMTI which in many ways reflected the general European image of Africa and ideas of Protestant mission in the non-European world. Yet, Basel Mission specific emphases, like the strong preference for political neutrality and rural German ideals of agriculture and artisanship, also became evident. The students' strong Pietist religious convictions and their rural German socio-economic values were reinforced and streamlined by BMTI emphases. This demonstrated that the community was generally successful in "training" missionaries to embrace the shared vision and practice.

Crucial for the analysis presented here is that both, proficiency in the practice of *communities of practice* and "trained" in the *trained incapacity* framework do not necessarily or exclusively refer to intentional, systematic, formal educational intervention towards the acquisition of specific skills. Rather, they refer to the combination of social influences in experience and education that shape mental frameworks, attitudes, behaviors, and ways of thinking which in turn act as guides and limitations of a person's engagement with unfamiliar contexts. This makes *community of practice* a pertinent framework to analyze preparatory processes of foreign missionaries, which in turn serves to identify indications for *trained incapacity* in the cross-cultural environment.

However, I do not suggest that the Basel Mission could or should have known better. It lies in the character of trained incapacity that it typically occurs unintentionally and unconsciously. Nobody trains intentionally for incapacity. Incidentally, this also means that the BMTI preparation did not constitute lack of training (even though there were gaps they were not aware of in the considerable curriculum they covered), inadequate, or inappropriate training. All these adjectives would assume they could have known what was adequate or appropriate. But in this early period of the Protestant missionary movement everybody was in an experimental phase. By contrast, this study describes a dynamic that offers an explanation for early failures beyond those previously suggested. Its relatively short time span and limited sample of missionaries invites further examination of the continuing work of the Basel Mission and of other missionary efforts. This would extend the discoveries and insights and provide a comparative basis to suggest causality beyond the correlations and propensities this investigation was able to establish.

TRAINED INCAPACITY IN THE EARLY BASEL MISSION

The findings demonstrate that attitudes, virtues, and emphases established in BMTI graduates contributed to the missionaries' challenges when they engaged in Christian mission in an environment different from their own cultural and religious background. Such "inadequate flexibility" in the application of learned judgments and behaviors which resulted in the changed circumstances "in more or less serious maladjustments" illustrates trained incapacity. I assessed this by examining the missionaries' adjustment to different contexts, the realization of organizational goals, and African responses to the endeavor. All these areas indicated inflexible applications of BMTI instilled practice—theological assumptions, religious convictions, social ideals, practical emphases—with negative consequences for themselves and others.

Inadequate Adjustment to Unaccustomed Contexts

For the first group the BMTI practice already created challenges in Denmark. Separated from organizational oversight, the missionaries displayed a surprising inability to collaborate. When fellowship broke down, it was shared BMTI "practice"—the social dynamics of mutual supervision and reporting to superiors—which significantly contributed to the tensions. Differences of cultural and religious background also re-emerged, despite the Basel Mission's intercultural, interdenominational ideal. The analysis revealed that these relational patterns undermined mutual trust, caused frequent conflicts, and did not prepare them for the egalitarian leadership envisioned.

In Africa, the environment the Basel missionaries entered was characterized by a variety of colonial European and African circumstances. I demonstrated that BMTI instilled evaluations and practice contributed to many of the problems they encountered in this context. Their training had established confidence in Pietist religious convictions and criteria to judge African realities which continued to erode relationships of support among themselves, but also with other Europeans and Africans. Their moral evaluations furthermore undermined responsiveness to their message, both among Africans and the European and mixed-race church they led as chaplains. BMTI graduates used German Pietist virtues of frugality and rural work ethics as criteria to evaluate everyone. They also insisted on living them out, even when the tropical environment would have advised more rest and accepting advice and help from others.

However, especially Andreas Riis made some adjustments. He developed a few supportive relationships with traders (which gained him essential practical assistance) and African rulers who offered generous hospitality. He also made some compromises and adjustments, in order to survive, most significantly, trusting the treatments of an African healer. Riis, furthermore, identified the inland mountain kingdom of Akuapem as a healthier location. Nevertheless, many of these adjustments were superficial, limited to occasional hammock travel, simple living, eating and working alongside Africans, and accepting hospitality, at least initially. Riis's dismissive remarks about the "hut" Africans had built for him, and the missionaries' efforts to introduce European building and farming skills, which they always regarded as superior, attest to the temporary character of any adjustments. They were made more out of necessity than conviction of their pertinence.

It became also clear that Basel missionaries' high value of humility did not extend to their moral and theological judgment of others. This was seen in evaluations of political authorities, both European and African, as well as Danish clergy. These judgments by BMTI emphases contributed significantly to the troubles the missionaries faced. They led them to refuse association with other Europeans, thereby depriving them of much needed support systems. Moral judgments by BMTI standards also aggravated the condemnation of African life, traditions, and especially religion. Consequently, the missionaries did not revise the European image of Africa, despite adjustments to aspects of African life and even occasional adherence to African local taboos.

Failure to Realize Organizational Goals

The failure to achieve organizational goals was arguably the greatest frustration internally. As a rule, failure was the common experience of

European missions in Africa in this early period. However, this study highlighted indications that trained incapacity contributed significantly to the lack of success in the first twelve years of the Basel Mission.

Initially, Basel missionaries were compelled to engage in a ministry they were not prepared for, chaplaincy. The fixation of the organization on native Africans, "unspoiled by European influence," was not revised and prevented the missionaries from seeking out ways to truly engage the uprooted mixed-race urban community on the coast. The years they spent as pastors to this flock they despised were thereby lost as opportunity to establish a ministry of crucial importance.

When Riis moved to Akuropon in the seventh year of the mission's presence in Guinea and colleagues joined eight months later, they took some steps toward the first organizational goal of building a station. But BMTI values of "proper" work, diligence, and self-sufficiency created tensions with Africans and robbed the missionaries of the initial generous assistance. Consequently, the missionaries expressed increasing frustration with the amount of physical work and their lack of achievement of other, more important organizational goals, like language learning and evangelization. Furthermore, the ideal of itinerant preaching and ideas of mission as a "wandering profession" prevented the consistent presence and close relationships in one location that language acquisition and meaningful communication would have required. Thereby it contributed to the lack of success in the prioritized goals of making African converts and establishing an African church.

The missionaries revised some preconceptions of African limited intelligence and the simplicity of African languages. In fact, the difficulty of vernaculars became the privileged explanation for their failure to learn them. However, the prevalence of written language aids in the missionaries' training was as a major contributing factor to their difficulties in acquiring unwritten African languages.

Disappointing African Responses

In their relationships with Africans this study highlighted especially two issues which hindered positive African responses: the missionaries' message and the way they offended African cultural virtues. Riis in particular violated patron-client relationships with African rulers. BMTI work ethic and European traditions the missionary insisted on offended their hosts and eventually the missionaries were mostly left alone with their employees. Consequently, they lost the initial opportunities for open sharing of their message with the majority of the local population, and only a very limited, mostly marginal and foreign audience remained.

Furthermore, expectations raised at the BMTI that Africans would quickly repent from their "savage" ways and ideas to embrace superior Christianity were disappointed. Indeed, the message of Pietist Christianity, especially its emphasis on human sin, remorse, and repentance that entailed the condemnation of African ways of life and religious traditions, made no sense. Africans responded with incredulity, reluctance, sidelining the missionaries, and occasionally open objections. The missionaries observed the resilience of African culture and beliefs, but did not adjust their preconceptions. Furthermore, the assumption that Africans only cared for material advantages and had no concern for the supernatural revealed the ignorance and cultural blindness of the missionaries and their lack of engagement with African religious traditions. Consequently, it is not surprising that they did not attract any Africans to believe the Christian gospel. Some expressed interest but, by and large, the content and delivery of the message remained offensive or incomprehensible.

Some Strengths and Adjustments of BMTI Preparation

Nonetheless, there were some adjustments to BMTI practice and some ways it proved helpful. I already mentioned the physical adjustments for the sake of survival. Furthermore, the idea of "divine pity" entailed in the Basel Mission a strong emphasis on love and care for Africans, who were thought to suffer from the evil effects of European mistreatment in addition to their ignorance and depravity by nature. While it expressed itself in condescending ways, Basel missionaries' true care for people led to some genuine friendships, and—combined with the value of neutrality—to medical aid which held some attraction. Generally, it seems there was the perception—confirmed (and made much of) by the missionaries—that they were "a different kind of European" in comparison to military officers, governors, and traders.

Moreover, on a personal level the spiritual practices of the BMTI equipped the missionaries emotionally and mentally to cope and persevere. There are clear indications that times of prayer and retreat served to refresh Basel missionaries emotionally and physically, and spirituality sustained them through the difficulties of the intercultural encounter, including the self-induced challenges. Furthermore, the Pietist dualist worldview gave them a framework to interpret problems and opposition as demonic hostility to their "holy profession" which was to be expected and endured.

Personalities and Political Entanglements

The findings suggest that differing constitution and personalities of missionaries also played a role. During this period many Europeans died in the tropics before they could achieve much. Among those who survived longer, it seems Henke had less initiative and stamina than Riis. He remained chaplain in Christiansborg and there are no indications of attempts to reach out beyond this role in the latter part of his ministry. By contrast, Riis continued to seek opportunities to meet Africans outside the fort. He moved to Akuropon as soon as he could, without explicit instruction or permission from the Basel leadership, and his numerous journeys indicate exceptional physical resilience.

Riis developed some personal relationships with Africans, especially with Okuapemhene Addu Dankwa and his nephew Owusu Akyem. The latter helped him with language learning and both supported the settlement of the mission. However, these relationships also constituted partiality in ongoing political conflicts. They put Riis and his colleagues in opposition to the Danish governor and the rightful new Okuapemhene. This predicament also illustrates political dynamics of the time and context which were not under the missionaries' control and rendered their strongly held convictions of political neutrality unfeasible.

As Europeans and being sent under the auspices of the Danish government they became inevitably involved in colonial dynamics. Especially Riis, as Danish citizen struggled with political issues the BMTI training had not prepared them for. The instruction to "keep out of politics" was not sufficient guidance how to engage ambitious governors and contesting African kings. Consequently, they used the priorities instilled by their preparation to evaluate and take sides with political entities. These criteria included moral evaluations, Pietist perceptions of what constituted benign authorities, and, most importantly, whether a ruler supported the missionary effort. The resulting partiality created various difficulties with Danish authorities. It also contributed to the position Africans assigned the missionaries in their succession dispute. Nevertheless, the latter did evolve into a civil war that depopulated Akuropon for several years which robbed the missionaries of some of their audience independent of their actions.

Historical Conclusions

From this study it can be concluded that the European "image of Africa" instilled by the missionaries' preparatory processes was arguably the most disabling aspect of their training. It prevented true intercultural engagement with African life and ideas. It shaped their message to focus on negative assertions of human (African) sinfulness. It caused presuppositions of African social and religious traditions, life, and environment that were entirely unfavorable. The revisions the lauded pioneer Riis made were superficial and compelled by circumstances and the need to survive. Furthermore, the negative evaluation of Africa based on predispositions and superficial understanding was not revised in this period. In fact, there are indications that it was strengthened, for example, in Riis's deteriorating attitudes. Much of their frustration came from attempts to convince Africans to conform to BMTI ideals of diligence, order, punctuality, methods of building and agriculture derived from European farming and artisan communities. Thus, it is clear that trained incapacity to engage with and adjust to the African cultural context contributed significantly to the missionaries' struggles.

As soon as they were able, Basel missionaries replicated European models of building, farming, and daily organization of life. Eventually, the Basel Mission approach—adopted from 1843 onwards—recruited West Indian African assistants to employ a more intentional larger scale and longer term effort to replicate the ideal of Christian spirituality, church organization, ethics, education, and material development that reflected BMTI practice. This constituted an illustration of the replication model of mission that was widely spread throughout the modern missionary movement and has been amply critiqued. Replication inherently promoted trained incapacity to adjust to African culture.

It also became obvious that wider historical contexts, both in Europe and in Africa, contributed to the shaping of missionaries and their intercultural engagement. In Europe, the BMTI community of practice evinced many influences from general developments and the various networks its participants originated from. This became particularly obvious regarding the ideas that shaped perceptions of Africa and foreign Christian missionary work. Furthermore, in Ghana the Basel Mission engagement took place in the wider context of early colonialism, and subsequently many of the issues raised in this study were present across nineteenth-century European Protestant missionary engagement in Africa.

Clearly, changes of historical conditions in Africa led to greater numbers of Africans turning to Christianity after the middle of the century. How much this contributed to the growth of the Basel Mission church in Ghana is difficult to determine. What is evident from this analysis is the early missionaries' trained incapacity to adjust flexibly to the vastly different circumstances they faced in Africa. It greatly limited the implementation of organizational goals and hindered positive African responses, not to mention African appropriations of Christianity. Thus, this study demonstrated that trained incapacity provides an explanatory framework for many of the struggles, difficulties, and tensions encountered by Basel missionaries in Ghana.

IMPLICATIONS FOR MISSIONARY PREPARATION TODAY

Finally, the significance of these findings beyond the specific historical case study needs to be briefly considered. Looking at intercultural missionary engagement through the educational-sociological lens of this study reveals dynamics that are not unique to one historical situation. Similar correlations can be identified for most European missionaries then and are arguably repeated in many contexts, both historically and contemporary. The findings suggest inherent pitfalls of trained incapacity for intercultural engagement in communities of practice, especially when they comprise of fundamentally homogeneous groups of participants.

Today the "replication model" of mission is by and large discredited, which does not mean that there are no instances of it. Effective intercultural engagement requires the capacity to understand and appropriately behave with people of other cultures as well as the willingness to do so. There is much literature that addresses this for the context of Christian mission, typically by employing anthropological frameworks.[1] However, intercultural competency does not come naturally to most people because enculturation makes us naturally ethnocentric, convinced that our

---

1. Skreslet offers a good summary of the various texts and approaches to "questions about how faith convictions interact with cultural realities" since the culture question began to be addressed by Western missions in Skreslet, *Comprehending Mission*, 69–95.

own culture is superior and our ways are inherently better than others.[2] Silzer calls this our "Culture based Judging System."[3]

The question arises, how educational processes can help people develop attitudes and capacities that make them competent intercultural actors. In this area too, there is an abundance of suggestions in literature and on a mushrooming number of websites.[4] They typically address international business and service providers in multicultural urban contexts. Much of this literature raises concerns whether true intercultural engagement is sought, or merely a more effective way to convince others of our own ideas and priorities.

For preparation of Christian missionaries there are many models, but the call is unanimous for integral training. This typically emphasizes spiritual, character, practical, professional, and psychological preparation in addition to academic study, and champions community learning, interactive teaching, and field experience.[5] Educationally, such integrative approaches are regarded as very effective. They use behavioral theories, draw on insights about how individuals—in particular adults—learn and on experiential learning theory, and community designs utilize the social dimension of learning.[6] While their effectiveness is acknowledged and

---

2. Earley and Ang comment: "Competence in cross-cultural functioning means learning new patterns of behavior and effectively applying them in appropriate settings. This kind of sophisticated cultural competence does not come naturally and it requires a high level of professionalism and knowledge." See Earley and Ang, *Cultural Intelligence*, 263.

3. Silzer, *Biblical Multicultural Teams*. She shows how the Culture based Judging System (CbJS) is established in our childhood family and home, visiting, eating working, resting, and cleaning practices.

4. A Google search on "intercultural training" comes up with almost nine million hits! Most of these are concerned with the increasingly multicultural character of Western societies and multicultural international relations. They predominantly address the needs of people involved in business and social services. But "missionary training" also gets over four million hits which predominantly refer to options of preparation for intercultural (Christian) missionaries. Examples for literature on intercultural (missionary) training are: Brynjolfson and Lewis, *Integral Ministry Training*; Earley and Ang, *Cultural Intelligence*; Ferris, ed. *Establishing Ministry Training*; Harley, *Preparing to Serve* Kohls and Brussow, eds., *Training Know-How*; Taylor, ed. *Internationalizing Missionary Training*.

5. Beyond those cited in the previous note, see for example: Elliston, "Moving Forward from Where We Are"; McKinney, "New Directions in Missionary Education."

6. These educational insights are expounded, for example, in Fenwick, *Learning Through Experience*; Merriam and Caffarella, *Learning in Adulthood*; Illeris, *Three Dimensions of Learning*.

was confirmed by the Basel Mission study, potential concerns need to be critically examined.

Those who decide which outcomes of training are desirable typically constitute fairly homogeneous groups, churches, or organizations. Consequently, they are likely to promote emphases, theological tenets, and religions ideals and practices which reflect their particular subculture. Even where cross-cultural sensitivity and skills are among the defined outcomes, the character formation and spirituality which are encouraged typically reflect the community's common theological values and social practices. The fact that these are shaped by a particular culture and history tends to remain hidden to conscious reflection and therefore unacknowledged.

This creates potential for difficulties in intercultural encounters where flexibility, adjustment to another cultural framework, and a new appropriation of the gospel are paramount. Missionaries thus trained can be oblivious to how significantly their theological emphases and religious practices are shaped by their own context of origin. The Basel Mission case study revealed this dynamic by examining integral training through the lens of an educational theory that emphasizes the context and social character of learning, *communities of practice*. It exposed the potential pitfalls of informal learning in intentional community for character development and spiritual formation that fosters a shared practice for the sake of a shared domain of interest—in this case intercultural Christian mission.

This study suggests that when the community is composed of a group of people who share commonly agreed knowledge, behaviors, ideals, values, attitudes, and goals plus a common perception of what constitutes success in their particular domain of interest, they establish mental frameworks that are potentially detrimental to intercultural engagement. Communities of practice are limited by the composition of their participants. Homogeneous groups create a community which—typically unconscious—champions their culturally shaped beliefs and practices. This can even be the case in international, interdenominational communities like the Basel Mission when theological convictions and socio-ethical emphases are shared by members and supporters of an organization. The outcome of such missionary training has been shown here to have a high potential of trained incapacity.

Missionary training that aims to preserve and establish religious and socio-ethical values, emphases, and practices of a particular community potentially prevents the cultural competence that should be its aim. Educational processes conducted by homogeneous groups can lead to *trained incapacity* which inhibits the flexibility required in cross-cultural ministry contexts. The very educational strength of a *community of practice* is its potential weakness. It perfects members' participation in the commonly valued *practice* to further the shared *domain of interest* by engaging together in the development and improvement of the practice. Thus, education functions as the transmission of culture; the more successful the learning process the more completely the culture is transmitted and its continuation ensured. Consequently, when largely homogeneous groups embark on this communal education process, culturally shaped assumptions, theological perspectives, and socio-ethical practices are typically reinforced which results in *trained incapacity* in the very competencies intercultural training desires to develop in people.

Further Research Needs

There are many areas of further research that would advance these insights but were beyond the scope of this study. Regarding the potential of communities of practice to create trained incapacity, research into other contexts, past and present, should assess whether trained incapacity in missionary preparation is as widespread as this study suggests.

Historically, the delimitation to the early period begs for a more detailed investigation of the Basel Mission from 1843 onwards. There are indications of continuing trained incapacity as well as various ways it was overcome by individual missionaries, especially those who worked in Ghana for many years. Furthermore, the role of the West Indian Christians has only been researched in a cursory way and would merit thorough exploration and comparison with other contemporary ventures that transferred West Indian missionaries to Africa. During the period of this study there were no African converts, but when Africans became Christians, there are indications that missionary imposed practices were subverted by individuals. In any case, it is likely that Africans appropriated Christianity through perspectives of their traditions. However, especially in the way training for African agents was designed—replicating the BMTI community—it is likely that trained incapacity was perpetuated in some African leaders.

Another related area that needs further investigation is the high regard in which the Basel Mission is held in Ghana today.[7] What were the factors that caused Africans later to appreciate this mission's engagement over others? It is likely that the significant work in analyzing two major languages, translating the Bible into them, and encouraging native speakers to write down their stories, histories, proverbs, and wise sayings contributed greatly to this. This represents the main area in which the Basel Mission eventually made revisions to their approach in Africa by sending experts in specific areas, first of all in linguistics.

Furthermore, the parochial nature of most studies of nineteenth century missions so far prevented a detailed assessment of the involvement of BMTI graduates in other societies. Most prominently, this would provide important insights into the early ministry of the CMS. It is a well-known fact that many of the dominant linguists in this society were BMTI trained men. Important questions would be, in what ways the development of linguistics as a discipline aided German missionaries and whether there were other factors that made them exceptional in this area.

Overcoming Trained Incapacity

Most significantly, this study invites the question of solutions. How can trained incapacity be avoided? Suggestions are offered by literature on "cultural intelligence" and "cultural competence."[8] Awareness of the problem is foundational. If preparatory processes for intercultural missionaries do not intentionally attempt to counteract the human default to regard our own culture as standard for all others, they have a high propensity to create trained incapacity for intercultural engagement. Yet, research that

---

7. Kwamena-Poh, for example, offers an entirely positive evaluation of the impact of the Basel Mission in Akuapem. See Kwamena-Poh, *Akuapem State*, x-xi, 111–23. He repeatedly emphasizes the high level of literacy as "a direct result of the Basel missionary work" and points to the fact that the collection and publication of oral traditions as early as the second half of the nineteenth century "by some African scholars educated by the Basel Missionary Society" was encouraged by the missionary J. G. Christaller. He mentions in particular David Asante, Paul Keteku, and Isaac Ado. The resulting collections in the "Papers in Tshi" were one of the sources he used for his Akuapem history.

8. For example Ang and Van Dyne, *Handbook of Cultural Intelligence*; Bennett, "Becoming Interculturally Competent"; Earley, Ang, and Tan, *CQ: Developing Cultural Intelligence at Work*; Livermore, *Cultural Intelligence*; Earley and Ang, *Cultural Intelligence*; Lambert, Myers, and Simons, *50 Activities for Achieving Cultural Competence*; Peterson, *Cultural Intelligence*.

investigates the effectiveness of educational approaches towards increasing intercultural competence is still needed. This requires more detailed studies of historical and contemporary contexts. Especially, analysis of exceptions to this dynamic could identify factors that alleviate it.

The findings of this study suggest some recommendations. They include mixed learning communities, exposure to different cultural contexts built into preparation processes, in-ministry training as one way to integrate cultural exposure and reflection on arising issues in light of intercultural theories. In the Christian context, it seems of great importance to also gather people from different cultural expressions of Christianity and different religious and denominational traditions.

I began this study with reference to my own experience of cross-cultural ministry and appreciation for the missiological training I received. Maybe the most important personal insight is that intercultural competence takes time to develop. Consequently, Christian mission can never be short term. Developing self-awareness and understanding of others needs extended exposure, growing relationships, and generally a learning posture and nonjudgmental attitude to difference. I find, the more often and the closer I relate to people from various backgrounds, the more sensitive to different perspectives I become.

A critical aspect is language learning which inevitably involves culture learning. It is not a coincidence that the eminent scholars Lamin Sanneh and Andrew Walls used this metaphor to describe the movement of Christianity across cultural borders. They show that the spread of the Christian movement is inseparable from the translatable quality of the Christian message.[9] When the Gospel moves from one cultural context to another the Christian faith is periodically transformed as it is incarnated in new cultures. This assumes "a relativized status for the culture of the message bearer."[10] Thus, Christian mission involves a tension between the *indigenization principle* and the *pilgrim principle*.[11] Walls explains, that indigenization is the desire "to live as a Christian and yet as a member of one's own society." This makes all churches cultural churches, shaped by their context. On the other hand, the *pilgrim principle* implies that there will be "rubs and frictions" with our own culture, "not from the adoption of a new culture but from the transformation of the mind towards that of

9. Sanneh, *Translating the Message*; Walls, *Missionary Movement*; Walls, *Cross-Cultural Process*.

10. Sanneh, *Translating the Message*, 29.

11. Walls, *Missionary Movement*, 7–9.

Christ." The tension between these two principles presents the challenge for Christian missionaries as they attempt to facilitate the appropriation of the gospel in new cultural settings.

For the demonstration and proclamation of the gospel to truly reflect the love and reign of God to the people who observe the lives and hear the words of cross-cultural missionaries, it has to be good news to them. The message of God's saving grace in Jesus Christ can only be meaningful and accepted, if it makes sense in the mental frameworks of the recipients and addresses their felt needs. Consequently, new communities of believers will always translate the gospel into their language and cultural frameworks and express faith and worship in their cultural concepts and forms. These facts about the spread of the Christian movement continue to challenge its messengers to find ways to overcome trained incapacity and grow in intercultural competence.

Bibliography

Abun-Nasr, Sonia. *Afrikaner und Missionar. Die Lebensgeschichte von David Asante.* Basel: P. Schlettwein, 2003.

———. "Von der 'Umbildung heidnischer Landessprachen zu christlichen'—Die Anfänge von Schrift und Schriftlichkeit in Akuapem, Goldküste." In *Wege durch Babylon: Missionare, Sprachstudien und interkulturelle Kommunikation*, edited by Reinhard Wendt, 181–220. Tübingen: Narr, 1998.

Achebe, Chinua. *Things Fall Apart.* New York: McDowell, 1959.

Addo-Fenning, Robert. "Christian Missions and Nation-Building in Ghana: An Historical Evaluation." In *Uniquely African? African Christian Identity from Cultural and Historical Perspectives*, edited by James L. Cox and Gerrie ter Haar. Religion in Contemporary Africa, 193–212. Trenton, NJ: Africa World, 2003.

———. "From Traditionalist to Christian Evangelist and Teacher: The Religious Itinerary and Legacy of Emmanuel Yaw Boakye (1834–1914)." *Journal of African Christian Thought* 7.1 (2004) 3–13.

Adeuyan, Jacob Oluwatayo. *Contributions of Yoruba People in the Economic and Political Developments of Nigeria.* Bloomington, IN: Authorhouse, 2011.

Agbeti, J. Kofi. *West African Church History: Christian Missions and Church Foundations, 1842–1919.* 2 vols. Leiden: Brill, 1986.

Agbodeka, Francis. *African Politics and British Policy in the Gold Coast, 1868–1900: A Study in the Forms and Force of Protest.* Legon History Series. London: Longman, 1971.

Ajayi, J. F. Ade. *Christian Missions in Nigeria, 1841–1891: The Making of a New Elite.* Ibadan History Series. Evanston, IL: Northwestern University Press, 1965.

Ajayi, J. F. Ade, and E. A. Ayandele. "Writing African Church History." In *The Church Crossing Frontiers: Essays on the Nature of Mission, In Honor of Bengt Sundkler*, edited by Peter Beyerhaus and Carl F. Hallencreutz, 90–108. Lund: Gleerup, 1969.

Altena, Thorsten. *"Ein Häuflein Christen mitten in der Heidenwelt des dunklen Erdteils:" Zum Selbst- und Fremdverständnis protestantischer Missionare im kolonialen Afrika 1884–1918.* Münster: Waxmann, 2003.

Ang, Soon, and Linn Van Dyne. *Handbook of Cultural Intelligence: Theory, Measurement, and Applications.* Armonk, NY: Sharpe, 2008.

Antwi, Daniel J. "The African Factor in Christian Mission to Africa: A Study of Moravian and Basel Mission Initiatives in Ghana." *International Review of Mission* 87.344 (1998) 55–66.

Antwi, Daniel J., and Paul Jenkins. "The Moravians, the Basel Mission and the Akuapem State in the Early Nineteenth Century." In *Christian Missionaries and the State in the Third World*, edited by Holger Bernt Hansen and Michael Twaddle, 39–51. Athens, OH: Ohio University Press, 2002.

Appiah-Kubi, Kofi, and Sergio Torres. *African Theology en Route: Papers from the Pan African Conference of Third World Theologians, December 17-23, 1977, Accra, Ghana*. Maryknoll, NY: Orbis, 1979.

Arndt, Johann. *True Christianity*. Translated by Peter C. Erb. Classics of Western Spirituality. New York: Paulist, 1979.

Avery, W. L. "Christianity in Sierra Leone." In *History of Christianity in West Africa*, edited by Ogbu Kalu, 103–21. New York: Longman, 1980.

Awoonor, Kofi. *Ghana: A Political History from Pre-European to Modern Times*. Accra: Sedco and Woeli, 1990.

Ayandele, Emmanuel Ayankanmi. *The Missionary Impact on Modern Nigeria, 1842-1914: A Political and Social Analysis*. Ibadan History Series. London: Longmans, 1966.

Baëta, C. G. *Christianity in Tropical Africa: Studies Presented and Discussed at the Seventh International African Seminar, University of Ghana, April 1965*. London: Oxford University Press, 1968.

Bahl, J. "Die dänische Missionsthätigkeit seit der Reformation." *Evangelisches Missions-Magazin* 13 (1869) 194–211.

Barker, John. "Where the Missionary Frontier Ran Ahead of Empire." In *Missions and Empire*, edited by Norman Etherington, 86–106. Oxford: Oxford University Press, 2005.

Barnes, Sandra T. *Patrons and Power: Creating a Political Community in Metropolitan Lagos*. International African Library. Manchester: Manchester University Press, 1986.

Bartels, Francis Lodowic. *The Roots of Ghana Methodism*. Cambridge: Cambridge University Press, 1965.

Barth, Christian Gottlob. *Die allgemeine Weltgeschichte nach biblischen Grundsätzen bearbeitet für nachdenksame Leser*. Calw: Vereinsbuchhandlung, 1837.

———. *General History, Briefly Sketched, Upon Scriptural Principles*. Translated by Robert Francis Walker. London: Religious Tract Society, 1840.

———. *Geschichte von Württemberg*. Stuttgart: Steinkopf, 1842.

Baur, John. *2000 Years of Christianity in Africa: An African Church History*. Rev. ed. Nairobi, Kenya: Paulines, 1998.

Beck, Hartmut. *Brüder in vielen Völkern: 250 Jahre Mission der Brüdergemeine*. Erlanger Taschenbücher. Erlangen: Verlag der Ev.-Luth. Mission, 1981.

Becker, Bernhard. *Zinzendorf im Verhältnis zu Philosophie und Kirchentum seiner Zeit*. Geschichtliche Studien. Leipzig: Hinrichs'sche Buchhandlung, 1886.

Becker, Judith. "Basel Missionaries Cooperating with their English Brothers: A Reciprocal Perspective. Portrayals of the Cooperation of CMS and the Basel Mission in their Periodicals During the First Half of the Nineteenth Century." In *Consultation and Cooperation in the History of Missions*. Edinburgh: Yale-Edinburgh Group on the History of the Missionary Movement and Non-Western Christianity, unpublished paper, 2010.

Bediako, Kwame. *Christianity in Africa: The Renewal of Non-Western Religion*. Studies in World Christianity. Maryknoll, NY: Orbis, 1995.

———. *Theology and Identity: The Impact of Culture Upon Christian Thought in the Second Century and in Modern Africa*. Oxford: Regnum, 1992.

———. "Types of African Theology." In *Christianity in Africa in the 1990s*, edited by Christopher Fyfe and Andrew F. Walls, 56–69. Edinburgh: University of Edinburgh Press, 1996.

Beecham, John. *Ashantee and the Gold Coast: Being a Sketch of the History, Social State and Superstitions of the Inhabitants of Those Countries, with a Notice of the State and Prospects of Christianity among Them*. The Colonial History Series. 1st reprinted ed. London: Dawsons, 1968.

Bennett, Milton J. "Becoming Interculturally Competent." In *Toward Multiculturalism: A Reader in Multicultural Education*, edited by J. Wurzel, 67–77. Newton, MA: Intercultural Resource Corperation, 2004.

Benrath, Gustav Adolf. "Die Erweckung innerhalb der deutschen Landeskirchen 1815–1888. Ein Überblick." In *Der Pietismus im neunzehnten und zwanzigten Jahrhundert*, edited by Ulrich Gäbler, 150–271. Göttingen: Vandenhoeck and Ruprecht, 2000.

Beyerhaus, Peter. *Die Selbständigkeit der jungen Kirchen als missionarisches Problem*. Studia Missionalia Upsaliensia. Wuppertal-Barmen: Verlag der Rheinischen Missions-Gesellschaft, 1956.

Beyreuther, Erich. *Die Erweckungsbewegung*. Kirche in ihrer Geschichte; Bd. 4, Lf.R-1. Göttingen: Vandenhoeck and Ruprecht, 1963.

———. *Kirche in Bewegung: Geschichte der Evangelisation und Volksmission*. Studien für Evangelisation und Volksmission; Bd. 7. Berlin: Christlicher Zeitschriftenverlag, 1968.

Blumhardt, Christian Gottlieb. "Charakter eines Missionars." *Missions-Magazin* (1818) 5–11.

———. "Die Dänischen Besitzungen in Westafrika." *Missions-Magazin* (1827) 524–43.

———. "Geographischer Überblick über sämtliche evangelische Missionsstationen in außereuropäischen Ländern." *Missions-Magazin* (1818) 3–14.

———. "West-Afrika." *Missions-Magazin* (1839) 181–342.

Boahen, A. Adu. "Politics in Ghana, 1800–1874." In *History of West Africa*, edited by J. F. Ade Ajayi and Michael Crowder. New York: Columbia University Press, 1974.

Bowdich, T. Edward. *Mission der englisch-afrikanischen Compagnie von Cape Coast Castle nach Ashantee, mit statistischen, geographischen und andern Nachrichten über das Innere von Afrika*. Neue Bibliothek der wichtigsten Reisebeschreibungen zur Erweiterung der Erd-und Völkerkunde. Weimar: Im Verlage des Landes-Industrie-Comptoirs, 1820.

———. *Mission from Cape Coast Castle to Ashantee: with a Statistical Account of that Kingdom and Geographical Notices of Other Parts of the interior of Africa*. London: John Murray, 1873.

Brecht, Martin. "August Hermann Francke und der Hallische Pietismus." In *Geschichte des Pietismus: Der Pietismus vom siebzehnten bis zum frühen achtzehnten Jahrhundert*, edited by Martin Brecht, et al., 440–540. Göttingen: Vandenhoeck and Ruprecht, 1993.

———. "Einleitung." In *Geschichte des Pietismus: Der Pietismus vom siebzehnten bis zum frühen achtzehnten Jahrhundert*, edited by Martin Brecht, et al., 1–10. Göttingen: Vandenhoeck and Ruprecht, 1993.

———. "Zur Konzeption der Geschichte des Pietismus. Eine Entgegnung auf Johannes Wallmann." *Pietismus und Neuzeit* 22 (1996) 226–29.

Brecht, Martin, et al., eds. *Die Basler Christentumsgesellschaft.* Vol. 7. Pietismus und Neuzeit: Ein Jahrbuch zur Geschichte des neueren Pietismus. Göttingen: Vandenhoek and Ruprecht im Auftrag der Historischen Kommission zur Erforschung des Pietismus, 1981.

———, eds. *Pietismus und Neuzeit: Ein Jahrbuch zur Geschichte des neueren Pietismus.* Göttingen: Vandenhoek and Ruprecht im Auftrag der Historischen Kommission zur Erforschung des Pietismus, 1974.

Brecht, Martin, et al., eds. *Geschichte des Pietismus. Im Auftrag der historischen Kommission zur Erforschung des Pietismus.* 4 vols. Göttingen: Vandenhoeck and Ruprecht, 1993–2004.

Bredwa-Mensah, et al. *Frederiksgave Plantation and Common Heritage Site. A Historical Exhibition and Cultural Centre Covering a Chapter in the History of Ghana's and Denmark's Common Past and Cultural Heritage.* Copenhagen: National Museum of Denmark, 2008.

Brown, Dale W. *Understanding Pietism.* Grand Rapids: Eerdmans, 1978.

Brynjolfson, Robert, and Jonathan Lewis, eds. *Integral Ministry Training: Design and Evaluation.* Pasadena, CA: William Carey Library, 2006.

Bundy, David. "Blumhardt, Christian Gottlieb." In *The Blackwell Dictionary of Evangelical Biography 1730–1860*, edited by Donald M. Lewis, 110. Cambridge, MA: Blackwell Reference, 1995.

———. "Hoffmann, Ludwig Friedrich Wilhelm." In *The Blackwell Dictionary of Evangelical Biography 1730–1860*, edited by Donald M. Lewis, 564–65. Cambridge, MA: Blackwell Reference, 1995.

———. "Jänicke, Johannes." In *The Blackwell Dictionary of Evangelical Biography 1730–1860*, edited by Donald M. Lewis, 603–4. Cambridge, MA: Blackwell Reference, 1995.

Bunge, Marcia J. "Education and the Child in Eighteenth-Century German Pietism: Perspectives from the Work of A. H. Francke." In *The Child in Christian Thought*, edited by Marcia J. Bunge, 247–78. Grand Rapids: Eerdmans, 2001.

Burke, Kenneth. *Permanence and Change. An Anatomy of Purpose.* 2nd rev. ed. Los Altos, CA: Hermes, 1954.

Busia, K. A. "Christianity and Ashanti." In *Christianity in Africa as Seen by Africans*, edited by Ram Desai, 94–98. Denver, CO: A. Swallow, 1962.

———. "Introduction to the Second Edition." In *Eighteen Years on the Gold Coast of Africa: Including an Account of the Native Tribes, and their Intercourse with Europeans*, edited by Brodie Cruickshank, 9–23. London: Cass, 1966.

Buxton, Thomas Fowell. *The African Slave Trade and its Remedy.* London: John Murray, 1840.

Carey, William. *An Enquiry Into the Obligations of Christians to Use Means for the Conversion of the Heathens.* Edited by John L. Pretlove. With an Introduction by Keith E. Eitel. Dallas, TX: Criswell, 1988.

Carstensen, Edward. *Closing the Books: Governor Edward Carstensen on Danish Guinea, 1842–50.* Translated by Tove Storsveen. Accra, Ghana: Sub-Saharan, 2010.

Chinchen, Delbert. "The Patron-Client Relationship Concept: A Case Study from the African Bible Colleges in Liberia and Malawi." PhD diss., Biola University, 1994.

Christian Council of the Gold Coast. *Christianity and African Culture: The Proceedings of a Conference Held at Accra, Gold Coast, May 2nd-6th, 1955, under the Auspices of the Christian Council.* Accra, Gold Coast, 1955.

Clapham, Christopher S. *Private Patronage and Public Power: Political Clientelism in the Modern State.* New York: St. Martin's, 1982.

Clarke, William K. L. *A History of the S. P. C. K.* London: SPCK, 1959.

Coates, Dandeson, et al. *Christianity the Means of Civilization: Shown in the Evidence Given before a Committee of the House of Commons, on Aborigines.* London: R. B. Seeley and W. Burnside, 1837.

Comaroff, Jean, and John L. Comaroff. *Of Revelation and Revolution: Christianity, Colonialism, and Consciousness in South Africa.* 2 vols. Chicago: University of Chicago Press, 1991.

Cox, Jeffrey A. *The British Missionary Enterprise since 1700.* Christianity and Society in the Modern World. New York: Routledge, 2008.

Crooks, J. J. *Records Relating to the Gold Coast Settlements from 1750 to 1874.* 2nd ed. London: Cass, 1966.

Cruickshank, Brodie. *Eighteen Years on the Gold Coast of Africa: Including an Account of the Native Tribes, and their Intercourse with Europeans.* 2 vols. London: Hurst and Blackett, 1853.

Curtin, Philip D. *The Image of Africa: British Ideas and Action, 1780–1850.* Madison, WI: University of Wisconsin Press, 1964.

Cuvier, Georges, et al. *Cuvier's Animal Kingdom: Arranged According to its Organization: Forming the Basis for a Natural History of Animals, and an Introduction to Comparative Anatomy.* London: Wm. S. Orr, Baker and Darby, 1840.

Danquah, J. B. *The Akan Doctrine of God: A Fragment of Gold Coast Ethics and Religion.* Missionary Research Series. London and Redhill: Lutterworth, 1944.

———. *Gold Coast: Akan Laws and Customs and the Akim Abuakwa Constitution.* London: Routledge, 1928.

Debrunner, Hans Werner. *A History of Christianity in Ghana.* Accra, Ghana: Waterville, 1967.

———. "The Moses of the Ghana Presbyterian Church." *Ghana Bulletin of Theology* 1.4 (1958) 12–18.

———. "Notable Danish Chaplains on the Gold Coast." *Transactions of the Gold Coast and Togoland Historical Society* 2.1 (1956) 13–29.

Degen, Bernard, and Philipp Sarasin. "Basel (-Stadt)." *Historisches Lexikon der Schweiz* (2010). Online: http://www.hls-dhs-dss.ch/textes/d/D7478.php.

Detzler, Wayne. "Robert Pinkerton: Principal Agent of the BFBS in the Kingdoms of Germany." In *Sowing the Word: The Cultural Impact of the British and Foreign Bible Society, 1804–2004*, edited by Stephen K. Batalden, et al., 268–85. Sheffield: Sheffield Phoenix, 2004.

Dewey, John. "Understanding the Savage Mind." In *Philosophy and Civilization*, by John Dewey, 173–87. Gloucester, MA: Peter Smith, 1931.

Dieterle, Johann Christian. "30 Jahre Missionsarbeit auf der Goldküste." In *Ghana MSS Restkategorie.* Basel: Basel Mission Archive, c.1877.

Drescher, Seymour. *Econocide: British Slavery in the Era of Abolition.* 2nd ed. Chapel Hill, NC: University of North Carolina Press, 2010.

———. *The Mighty Experiment: Free Labor Versus Slavery in British Emancipation.* New York: Oxford University Press, 2002.

Dupuis, Joseph. *Journal of a Residence in Ashantee*. London: H. Colburn, 1824.

Earley, P. Christopher, and Soon Ang. *Cultural Intelligence: Individual Interactions across Cultures*. Stanford, California: Stanford University Press, 2003.

Earley, P. Christopher, Soon Ang, and Joo-Seng Tan. *CQ: Developing Cultural Intelligence at Work*. Stanford, California: Stanford Business Books, 2006.

Eayrs, George. "Developments, Institutions, Helpers, Opposition." In *A New History of Methodism*, edited by W. J. Townsend, et al., 277–331. London: Hodder and Stoughton, 1909.

Eichholzer, Erika. "Missionary Linguists on the Gold Coast: Wrestling with Language." In *The Spiritual in the Secular: Missionaries and Knowledge about Africa*, edited by Patrick Harries and David Maxwell. Studies in the History of Christian Missions, 72–99. Grand Rapids: Eerdmans, 2012.

Eiselen, Tobias. "'Zur Erziehung einer zuverlässigen, wohldisziplinierten Streiterschar für den Missionskrieg'. Basler Missionarsausbildung im 19. Jahrhundert." In *Mission im Kontext. Beiträge zur Sozialgeschichte der Norddeutschen Missionsgesellschaft im 19. Jahrhundert*, edited by Werner Ustorf, 47–120. Bremen: Übersee-Museum, 1986.

Ekechi, Felix K. *Missionary Enterprise and Rivalry in Igboland, 1857–1914*. Cass Library of African Studies. London: Cass, 1972.

Elbourne, Elizabeth. "Word Made Flesh: Christianity, Modernity, and the Cultural Colonialism in the Work of Jean and John Comaroff." *American Historical Review* 108.2 (2003) 435–59.

Elliston, Edgar J. "Moving Forward from Where We Are in Missiological Education." In *Missiological Education for the Twenty-First Century: The Book, the Circle, and the Sandals: Essays in Honor of Paul E Pierson*, edited by J. Dudley Woodberry, et al. American Society of Missiology Series, 232–56. Maryknoll, NY: Orbis, 1996.

Eppler, Paul. *Geschichte der Basler Mission, 1815–1899*. Basel: Verlag der Missionsbuchhandlung, 1900.

Etherington, Norman. *Missions and Empire*. The Oxford History of the British Empire Companion Series. Oxford: Oxford University Press, 2005.

Fage, John D. *Ghana: A Historical Interpretation*. Madison, WI: University of Wisconsin Press, 1959.

Fenwick, Tara J. *Learning Through Experience: Troubling Orthodoxies and Intersecting Questions*. Malabar, FL: Krieger, 2003.

Ferris, Robert W., ed. *Establishing Ministry Training. A Manual for Programme Developers*. Pasadena, CA: William Carey Library, 1995.

Fisher, Humphrey J. "Conversion Reconsidered: Some Historical Aspects of Religious Conversion in Black Africa." *Africa* 43.1 (1973) 27–40.

Foster, Philip J. *Education and Social Change in Ghana*. Chicago: University of Chicago Press, 1965.

Francke, August Hermann. "Idea Studiosi Theologiae, 1712." In *A. H. Francke's pädagogische Schriften: Nebst der Darstellung seines Lebens und seiner Stiftungen*, edited by Gustav Kramer, 369–435. Langensalza: H. Beyer and Söhne, 1885.

———. "Kurtzer und Einfältiger Unterricht: Wie die Kinder zur wahren Gottseliglkeit und Christlichen Klugheit anzuführen sind, 1702." In *August Hermann Francke: Werke in Auswahl*, edited by Erhard Peschke, 124–50. Berlin: Luther Verlag, 1969.

Freeman, Thomas Birch. *Journals of Various Visits to the Kingdoms of Ashanti, Aku, and Dahomi in Western Africa*. Cass Library of African Studies. Missionary Researches and Travels. 3rd ed. London: Cass, 1968.

Frohnmeyer, Karl. "Barth, Christian Gottlob." *Neue Deutsche Biographie* 1 (1953) 601. Online: http://www.deutsche-biographie.de/pnd118821210.html.

Fulbrook, Mary. *Piety and Politics: Religion and the Rise of Absolutism in England, Württemberg, and Prussia*. Cambridge: Cambridge University Press, 1983.

Fyfe, Christopher. *A History of Sierra Leone*. London: Oxford University Press, 1962.

Fyfe, Christopher, and Andrew F. Walls. *Christianity in Africa in the 1990s*. Edinburgh: Centre of African Studies University of Edinburgh, 1996.

Ghana Statistical Service. "2010 Population and Housing Census: Summary Results of Final Report." Accra, Ghana: Ghana Statistical Service, 2012. Online: http://www.statsghana.gov.gh/pop_stats.html.

Gilbert, Michelle. "Aesthetic Strategies: The Politics of a Royal Ritual." *Africa* 64.1 (1994) 99–126.

———. "The Christian Executioner: Christianity and Chieftaincy as Rivals." *Journal of Religion in Africa* 25.4 (1995) 347–86.

———. "'No Condition is Permanent': Ethnic Construction and the Use of History in Akuapem." *Africa* 67.4 (1997) 501–33.

Gossman, Lionel. "Basel." In *Geneva, Zurich, Basel: History, Culture and National Identity*, edited by Nicolas Bouvier, Gordon Alexander Craig and Lionel Gossman, 65–98. Princeton, NJ: Princeton University Press, 1994.

———. *Basel in the Age of Burckhardt: A Study in Unseasonable Ideas*. Chicago: University of Chicago Press, 2000.

Gross, Andreas, Y. Vincent Kumaradoss, and Heike Liebau. *Halle and the Beginning of Protestant Christianity in India*. 3 vols. Halle: Verlag der Franckesche Stiftungen, 2006.

Groves, Charles Pelham. *The Planting of Christianity in Africa: Volume One to 1840*. 4 vols. London: Lutterworth, 1948.

———. *The Planting of Christianity in Africa: Volume Two 1840–1878*. 4 vols. London: Lutterworth, 1948.

Gundani, Paul H. "Teaching the History of Christianity in Africa: Pedagogical Considerations for Young Practitioners." *Journal of African Christian Thought* 6.2 (2003) 39–43.

Gunson, Niel. *Messengers of Grace: Evangelical Missionaries in the South Seas 1797–1860*. New York: Oxford University Press, 1978.

Haenger, Peter. *Slaves and Slave Holders on the Gold Coast: Towards an Understanding of Social Bondage in West Africa*. Basel: Schlettwein, 2000.

Halldén, Erik. *The Culture Policy of the Basel Mission in the Cameroons 1886–1905*. Berlingska Boklryckeriet, Sweden: Lund, 1968.

Haller, J. "Das Leben im Missionshaus." *Evangelisches Missions-Magazin* 41.4 (1897) 154–66, 201–17, 233–49.

Hanciles, Jehu J. "Back to Africa: White Abolitionists and Black Missionaries." In *African Christianity: An African Story*, edited by Ogbu Kalu, 191–216. Pretoria: Dept. of Church History University of Pretoria, 2005.

———. "Conversion and Social Change: A Review of the "Unfinished Task" in West Africa." In *Christianity Reborn: The Global Expansion of Evangelicalism in the*

Twentieth Century, edited by Donald M. Lewis. Studies in the History of Christian Missions, 157–80. Grand Rapids: Eerdmans, 2004.

———. *Euthanasia of a Mission: African Church Autonomy in a Colonial Context.* Westport, CT: Praeger, 2002.

———. "Missionaries and Revolutionaries: Elements of Transformation in the Emergence of Modern African Christianity." *International Bulletin of Missionary Research* 28.4 (2004) 146–52.

———. "New Wine in Old Wineskins: Critical Reflections on Writing and Teaching a Global Christian History." *Missiology* 34.3 (2006) 361–82.

Hanst, Michael. "Hoffmann, Ludwig Friedrich Wilhelm, Theologe." In *Biographisch-Bibliographisches Kirchenlexikon,* edited by Traugott Bautz, 966–68. Vol. 2. Hamm: Traugott Bautz, 1990.

Harley, C. David. *Preparing to Serve. Training for Cross-Cultural Mission.* Pasadena, CA: William Carey Library, 1995.

Hastings, Adrian. *Church and Mission in Modern Africa.* London: Burns and Oates, 1967.

———. *The Church in Africa: 1450–1950.* The Oxford History of the Christian Church Series. Oxford: Clarendon, 1994.

Haug, Richard. *Reich Gottes im Schwabenland: Linien im württembergischen Pietismus.* Metzingen, Württemberg: Franz, 1981.

Hauser-Renner, Heinz. "'Obstinate' Pastor and Pioneer Historian: The Impact of Basel Mission Ideology on the Thought of Carl Christian Reindorf." *International Bulletin of Missionary Research* 33.2 (2009) 65–70.

Hauss, Gisela. "Die sozialpädagogische Arbeit in der Armenschullehrer-Anstalt in Beuggen (Basel). Ihr Profil im Vergleich zum Rauhen Haus in Hamburg." *Pietismus und Neuzeit* 23 (1997) 27–38.

Hayford, Casely. *Gold Coast Native Institutions with Thoughts upon a Healthy Imperial Policy for the Gold-Coast and Ashanti.* London: Sweet and Maxwell, 1903.

Hebeisen, Erika. *Leidenschaftlich fromm: Die pietistische Bewegung in Basel 1750–1830.* Köln: Böhlau, 2005.

Hefner, Robert W. *Conversion to Christianity: Historical and Anthropological Perspectives on a Great Transformation.* Berkeley, CA: University of California Press, 1993.

Hernæs, Per O. "Fort Slaves at Christansborg and the Gold Coast: Wage Labour in the Making." In *Slavery Across Time and Space: Studies in Slavery in Medieval Europe and Africa,* edited by Per O. Hernæs and Tore Iversen, 197–229. Trondheim: Dept. of History, 2002.

———. "Introduction. Governor Edward Carstensen on the Gold Coast: A Historical Background." In *Closing the Books: Governor Edward Carstensen on Danish Guinea, 1842–50,* edited by Tove Storsveen, ix-xxii. Accra, Ghana: Sub-Saharan, 2010.

Hiebert, Paul G. *Anthropological Insights for Missionaries.* Grand Rapids: Baker, 1985.

Hoffmann, Wilhelm. *Das Leben Jesu kritisch bearbeitet von Dr. D.F. Strauss. Geprüft für Theologen und Nichttheologen.* Stuttgart: Balz'sche Buchhandlung, 1836.

———. *Die Erziehung des weiblichen Geschlechts in Indien und anderen Heidenländern. Ein Aufruf an die christlichen Frauen Deutschlands und der Schweiz.* Basel: Basler Mission, 1841.

———. *Die evangelische Missionsgesellschaft zu Basel im Jahre 1842. Eine Bekanntmachung an alle evangelischen Christen. Geschrieben im Auftrag der evangelischen Missions-Committee Basel.* Basel: Basler Mission, 1842.

———. *Eilf Jahre in der Mission. Ein Abschiedswort an den Kreis der Evangelischen Missionsgesellschaft zu Basel.* Stuttgart: Steinkopf, 1853.

———. *Missions-Fragen.* Heidelberg: Universitäts-Buchhandlung K. Winter, 1847.

Holborn, Hajo. *A History of Modern Germany, 1648–1840.* 3 vols. Princeton, NJ: Princeton University Press, 1964.

Holtwick, Bernd. "Licht und Schatten. Begründungen und Zielsetzungen des protestantischen missionarischen Aufbruchs im frühen 19. Jahrhundert." In *Weltmission und religiöse Organisationen: Protestantische Missionsgesellschaften im 19. und 20. Jahrhundert,* edited by Artur Bogner, et al., 225–47. Religion in der Gesellschaft. Würzburg: Ergon, 2004.

Horton, James Africanus Beale. *West African Countries and People, British and Native with the Requirements Necessary for Establishing that Self Government Recommended by the Committee of the House of Commons, 1865 and a Vindication of the African Race.* African Heritage Books. London: W. J. Johnson, 1868.

Horton, Robin. "African Conversion." *Africa* 41.2 (1971) 85–108.

Howard, Thomas A. *Religion and the Rise of Historicism: W.M.L. de Wette, Jacob Burckhardt, and the Theological Origins of Nineteenth-Century Historical Consciousness.* Cambridge: Cambridge University Press, 2000.

Hutton, J. E. *A History of Moravian Missions.* London: Moravian Publication Office, 1923.

Ihli, Stefan. *Kirchliche Gerichtsbarkeit in der Diözese Rottenburg im 19. Jahrhundert ein Exempel der Beziehungen zwischen Kirche und monarchischem Staat.* Tübinger Kirchenrechtliche Studien. Münster: LIT Verlag, 2008.

Illeris, Knud. *The Three Dimensions of Learning.* Malabar, FL: Krieger, 2002.

Irvin, Dale T., and Scott Sunquist. *History of the World Christian Movement. Earliest Christianity to 1453.* Vol. 1. Maryknoll, NY: Orbis, 2001.

———. *History of the World Christian Movement. Modern Christianity from 1454–1900.* Vol. 2. Maryknoll, NY: Orbis, 2012.

Isert, Paul Erdmann. *Letters on West Africa and the Slave Trade: Paul Erdmann Isert's Journey to Guinea and the Caribbean Islands in Columbia (1788).* Translated by Selena Axelrod Winsnes. Accra, Ghana: Sub-Saharan, 2007.

Isichei, Elizabeth. *A History of Christianity in Africa: From Antiquity to the Present.* Grand Rapids: Eerdmans, 1995.

Ising, Dieter. *Johann Christoph Blumhardt (1805–1880) und seine Möttlinger Amtsvorgänger Gottlieb Friedrich Machtholf (1735–1800) und Christian Gottlob Barth (1799–1862).* Metzingen: Ernst Franz, 1992.

———. *Johann Christoph Blumhardt, Life and Work: A New Biography.* Translated by Monty Ledford. Eugene, OR: Cascade, 2009.

Jackson, E. M. "Jänicke, Joseph Daniel." In *The Blackwell Dictionary of Evangelical Biography 1730–1860,* edited by Donald M. Lewis, 604. Cambridge, MA: Blackwell Reference, 1995.

Jackson, Philip W. *Life in Classrooms.* New York: Holt, Rinehart and Winston, 1968.

Jacobs, Sylvia M. *Black Americans and the Missionary Movement in Africa.* Contributions in Afro-American and African Studies. Westport, CT: Greenwood, 1982.

Jakubowski-Tiessen, Manfred. "Eigenkultur und Traditionsbildung." In *Geschichte des Pietismus: Glaubenswelt und Lebenswelten*, edited by Hartmut Lehmann and Ruth Albrecht, 195–210. Göttingen: Vandenhoeck and Ruprecht, 2004.

Jenkins, Paul. "Basler Mission." *Historisches Lexikon der Schweiz*. April 4, 2009. Online: http://www.hls-dhs-dss.ch/textes/d/D45256.php?topdf=1.

———. "The Church Missionary Society and the Basel Mission: An Early Experiment in Inter-European Cooperation." In *Church Mission Society and world Christianity, 1799-1999*, edited by Kevin Ward and Brian Stanley, 43–65. Grand Rapids: Eerdmans, 2000.

———. "A Letter to Adu." In *Ghana in Africa and the World: Essays in Honor of Adu Boahen*, edited by Toyin Falola, 37–50. Trenton, NJ: Africa World, 2003.

———. "Mission History: A Manifesto." *Missiology* 10.2 (1982) 199–210.

———, ed. *The Recovery of the West African Past: African Pastors and African History in the Nineteenth Century: C.C. Reindorf and Samuel Johnson: Papers from an International Seminar Held in Basel, Switzerland, 25-28th October 1995 to Celebrate the Centenary of the Publication of C.C. Reindorf's History of the Gold Coast and Asante*. Basel: Basler Afrika Bibliographien, 1998.

———. "The Scandal of Continuing Intercultural Blindness in Mission Historiography: The Case of Andreas Riis in Akwapim." *International Review of Mission* 87.344 (1998) 67–76.

———. "Towards a Definition of the Pietism of Wurtemberg as a Missionary Movement." In *African Studies Association of the United Kingdom. Oxford Conference 1978: Whites in Africa—Whites as Missionaries*. Basel: Mission 21, unpublished manuscript 9074.31 Sch., 1978.

———. "Villagers as Missionaries: Wurtemberg Pietism as a 19th Century Missionary Movement." *Missiology* 8.4 (1980) 425–32.

Jensz, Felicity. *German Moravian Missionaries in the British Colony of Victoria, Australia, 1848–1908: Influential Strangers*. Studies in Christian Mission. Leiden: Brill, 2010.

Kalu, Ogbu. *African Christianity: An African Story*. Perspectives on Christianity. Pretoria, South Africa: Dept. of Church History, University of Pretoria, 2005.

———. "Church Presence in Africa: A Historical Analysis of the Evangelization Process." In *African Theology en Route: Papers from the Pan African Conference of Third World Theologians, December 17-23, 1977, Accra, Ghana*, edited by Kofi Appiah-Kubi and Sergio Torres, 13–22. Maryknoll, NY: Orbis, 1979.

———. "Introduction: The Shape and Flow of African Church Historiography." In *African Christianity: An African Story*, edited by Ogbu Kalu, 1–23. Perspectives on Christianity. Pretoria, South Africa: Dept. of Church History University of Pretoria, 2005.

Kemp, J. Alan. "The History and Development of a Universal Phonetic Alphabet in the 19th Century: From the Beginning to the Establishment of the IPA." In *History of the Language Sciences: An International Handbook on the Evolution of the Study of Language from the Beginnings to the Present*, edited by Sylvain Auroux, et al., 1572–86. Berlin: Walter de Gruyter, 2001.

Kimble, David. *A Political History of Ghana: The Rise of Gold Coast Nationalism, 1850-1928*. Oxford: Clarendon, 1963.

Kirchberger, Ulrike. "'Fellow-Labourers in the Same Vineyard.' Germans in British Missionary Societies in the First Half of the Nineteenth Century." In *Migration and Transfer from Germany to Britain, 1660–1914*, edited by Stefan Manz, et al., 81–92. München: Saur, 2007.

Kjær-Hansen, Kai. "John Nicolayson and the Beginning of the Jerusalem Mission in the 19th Century." *Lausanne Consultation on Jewish Evangelism Bulletin* 72 (2003). Online: http://www.lcje.net/bulletins/2003/72/72_02.html.

Kobia, Sam M. "The Christian Mission and the African Peoples in the 19th Century." In *Separation Without Hope? Essays on the Relation Between the Church and the Poor During the Industrial Revolution and the Western Colonial Expansion*, edited by Julio de Santa Ana, 155–70. Geneva: World Council of Churches Commission on the Churches' Participation in Development, 1978.

Köhle-Hezinger, Christel. "Die enge und die weite Welt: Ländlich-traditionelle Welt im Aufbruch des 19. Jahrhunderts." In *Der ferne Nächste. Bilder der Mission—Mission der Bilder 1860–1920: Katalog zur Ausstellung im Landeskirchlichen Museum Ludwigsburg vom 25.5. bis 10.11.1996*, edited by Eberhard Gutekunst and Werner Unseld, 45–50. Ludwigsburg: Landeskirchliches Museum, 1996.

Kohls, L. Robert, and Herbert L. Brussow, eds. *Training Know-How for Cross-Cultural and Diversity Trainers*. Duncanville, TX: Adult Learning Systems, 1995.

Kollman, Paul V. "After Church History? Writing the History of Christianity from a Global Perspective." *Horizons* 31.2 (2004) 322.

Konrad, Dagmar. *Missionsbräute: Pietistinnen des 19. Jahrhunderts in der Basler Mission*. 2nd ed. Münster: Waxmann, 2001.

Kpobi, David N.A. "African Chaplains in Seventeenth Century West Africa." In *African Christianity: An African Story*, edited by Ogbu Kalu, 140–70. Pretoria, South Africa: Dept. of Church History University of Pretoria, 2005.

Kraft, Charles H. *Christianity in Culture: A Study in Dynamic Biblical Theologizing in Cross-Cultural Perspective*. Maryknoll, NY: Orbis, 1979.

Kuada, John E., and Yao Chachah. *Ghana: Understanding the People and their Culture*. Accra, Ghana: Woeli, 1999.

Kuhn, Thomas K., and Martin Sallmann, eds. *Das "Fromme Basel": Religion in einer Stadt des 19. Jahrhunderts*. Basel: Schwabe, 2002.

Kwamena-Poh, M. A. *Government and Politics in the Akuapem State, 1730–1850*. Legon History Series. London: Longman, 1973.

Kyei-Baffour, N., and C. Manu. "Smallscale Palm Oil Process Improvement for Poverty Alleviation and National Development." *The 3rd International Conference on Appropriate Technology: Promoting Research and Practice in Appropriate Technology—Energy Solutions in the Era of Climate Change* (2008). Online: http://www.appropriatetech.net/files/SMALLSCALE_PALM_OIL_PROCESS_IMPROVEMENT_FOR.pdf.

Lambert, Jonamay, Selma Myers, and George Simons. *50 Activities for Achieving Cultural Competence*. Amherst, MA: HRD, 2009.

Landau, Paul S. "Hegemony and History in Jean and John L Comaroff's Of Revelation and Revolution." *Africa* 70.3 (2000) 501–19.

Langton, Edward. *History of the Moravian Church: The Story of the First International Protestant Church*. London: Allen and Unwin, 1956.

Latourette, Kenneth Scott. *A History of Christianity*. Rev. ed. 2 vols. New York: Harper and Row, 1975.

———. *A History of the Expansion of Christianity: The Great Century in the Americas, Australasia, and Africa, A.D. 1800—A.D. 1914*. Vol. 5. Grand Rapids: Zondervan, 1970.

———. *A History of the Expansion of Christianity: Three Centuries of Advance, A.D. 1500—A.D. 1800*. Vol. 3. Grand Rapids: Zondervan, 1970.

Lave, Jean, and Etienne Wenger. *Situated Learning: Legitimate Peripheral Participation*. Cambridge: Cambridge University Press, 1991.

Ledderhose, Karl Friedrich. *Johann Jänicke, der evangelisch-lutherische Prediger an der böhmischen- oder Bethlehems-Kirche zu Berlin, nach seinem Leben und Wirken dargestellt*. Berlin: G. Knak, 1863.

Lehmann, Arno. *It Began at Tranquebar: The Story of the Tranquebar Mission and the Beginnings of Protestant Christianity in India*. Madras: Christian Literature Society on behalf of the Federation of Evangelical Lutheran Churches in India, 1956.

Lehmann, Hartmut. "Aufgaben der Pietismusforschung im 21. Jahrhundert." In *Interdisziplinäre Pietismusforschungen: Beiträge zum Ersten Internationalen Kongress für Pietismusforschung 2001*, edited by Udo Sträter, 3–18. Halle; Tübingen: Verlag der Franckeschen Stiftungen; Niemeyer, 2005.

———. "'Community' and 'Work' as Concepts of Religious Thought in Eighteenth Century Württemberg Pietism." In *Protestant Evangelicalism: Britain, Ireland, Germany and America c. 1750–1950. Essays in Honor of W. R. Ward*, edited by Keith Robbins, 79–98. Studies in Church History. New York: Blackwell, 1990.

———. "The Cultural Importance of the Pious Middle Classes in Seventeenth-Century Protestant Society." In *Religion and Society in Early Modern Europe 1500–1800*, edited by Kaspar von Greyerz, 33–41. London: The German Historical Institute, George Allen and Unwin, 1984.

———. "Die neue Lage." In *Der Pietismus im neunzehnten und zwanzigten Jahrhundert*, edited by Ulrich Gäbler, 1–26. Geschichte des Pietismus. Göttingen: Vandenhoeck and Ruprecht, 2000.

———. "Einführung." In *Geschichte des Pietismus: Glaubenswelt und Lebenswelten*, edited by Hartmut Lehmann and Ruth Albrecht, 1–18. Göttingen: Vandenhoeck and Ruprecht, 2004.

———. "Grenzüberschreitungen und Grenzziehung im Pietismus." *Pietismus und Neuzeit* 27 (2001) 11–18.

———. "The Mobilization of God's Pious Children in the Era of the French Revolution and beyond." *Pietismus und Neuzeit* 34 (2008) 189–98.

———. "Pietism in the World of Transatlantic Religious Revivals." In *Pietism in Germany and North America 1680–1820*, edited by Jonathan Strom, Hartmut Lehmann and James Van Horn Melton, 13–21. Burlington, VT: Ashgate, 2009.

———. *Pietismus und weltliche Ordnung in Württemberg vom 17. bis zum 20. Jahrhundert*. Stuttgart: Kohlhammer, 1969.

Lempa, Heikki. "Moravian Education in the Eighteenth-Century Context." In *Self, Community, World: Moravian Education in a Transatlantic World*, edited by Scott Paul Gordon, 269–89. Studies in Eighteenth-Century America and the Atlantic World. Bethlehem, PA: Lehigh University Press, 2010.

Lempa, Heikki, and Paul M. Peucker. *Self, Community, World: Moravian Education in a Transatlantic World*. Edited by Scott Paul Gordon. Studies in Eighteenth-Century America and the Atlantic World. Bethlehem, PA: Lehigh University Press, 2010.

Lennox, Sara, et al. "In Memoriam: Susanne Zantop 1945–2001." *The German Quarterly* 74.2 (2001) 197–200.
Lepsius, Karl Richard. *Standard Alphabet for Reducing Unwritten Languages and Foreign Graphic Systems to a Uniform Orthography in European Letters*. 2nd ed. London: Williams and Norgate, 1863.
Liebau, Heike. *Die indischen Mitarbeiter der Tranquebarmission (1706—1845) Katecheten, Schulmeister, Übersetzer*. Hallesche Forschungen. Tübingen: Verlag der Franckeschen Stiftungen; Niemeyer, 2008.
Livermore, David A. *Cultural Intelligence: Improving Your CQ to Engage Our Multicultural World*. Edited by Chap Clark. Youth, Family, and Culture Series. Grand Rapids: Baker Academic, 2009.
Loewen, Jacob Abram. *Culture and Human Values: Christian Intervention in Anthropological Perspective*. William Carey Library Series on Applied Cultural Anthropology. Pasadena, CA: William Carey Library, 1975.
Lohmann, Hartmut. "Koelle, Sigismund Wilhelm, ev. Missionar und Sprachwissenschaftler." In *Biographisch-Bibliographisches Kirchenlexikon*, edited by Traugott Bautz, 259–61. Vol. 4. Hamm: Traugott Bautz, 1992.
Lovejoy, Arthur O. *The Great Chain of Being*. Cambridge, MA: Harvard University Press, 1936.
Lovett, Richard. *The History of the London Missionary Society, 1795–1895: With Portraits and Maps in Two Volumes*. Vol. 1. London: Henry Frowde, 1899.
Luzbetak, Louis J. *The Church and Cultures: An Applied Anthropology for the Religious Worker*. Techny, IL: Divine Word, 1963.
MacLachlan, Herbert. *English Education Under the Test Acts: Being the History of the Non-conformist Academies 1662-1820*. Publications of the University of Manchester. Manchester: University Press, 1931.
Marks, Johnathan. "Great Chain of Being." In *Encyclopedia of Race and Racism*, edited by John Hartwell Moore, 68–73. New York: Macmillan Reference, 2007.
Mason, John C. S. *The Moravian Church and the Missionary Awakening in England, 1760–1800*. Royal Historical Society Studies in History. Woodbridge: Boydell, 2001.
Mayers, Marvin Keene. *Christianity Confronts Culture: A Strategy for Cross-Cultural Evangelism*. Contemporary Evangelical Perspectives. Grand Rapids: Zondervan, 1974.
McKinney, Lois. "New Directions in Missionary Education." In *Internationalizing Missionary Training: A Global Perspective*, edited by William David Taylor, 241–50. Grand Rapids: Baker, 1991.
Mercer, Matthew. "Dissenting Academies and the Education of the Laity, 1750–1850." *History of Education* 30.1 (2001) 35–58.
Meredith, Henry. *An Account of the Gold Coast of Africa: With a Brief History of the African Company*. Edited by John Ralph Willis. Cass Library of African Studies. Travels and Narratives. London: Paternoster, 1812.
Merriam, Sharan B., and Rosemary S. Caffarella. *Learning in Adulthood: A Comprehensive Guide*. Jossey-Bass Higher and Adult Education Series. 2nd ed. San Francisco: Jossey-Bass, 1999.
Merton, Robert King. *Social Theory and Social Structure*. Rev. ed. Glencoe, IL: Free Press, 1957.

Mesthrie, Rajend. "Contact Linguistics and World Englishes." In *The Handbook of World Englishes*, edited by Braj B. Kachru, et al., 273–88. Malden, MA: Blackwell, 2009.
Metcalfe, G. E. *Maclean of the Gold Coast: The Life and Times of George Maclean, 1801–1847*. London: Oxford University Press, 1962.
Mettele, Gisela. *Weltbürgertum oder Gottesreich: Die Herrnhuter Brüdergemeine als globale Gemeinschaft, 1727–1857*. Bürgertum Neue Folge. Göttingen: Vandenhoeck and Ruprecht, 2009.
Meyer, Birgit. *Translating the Devil: Religion and Modernity Among the Ewe in Ghana*. Trenton, NJ: Africa World, 1999.
Meyer, Dietrich. "Zinzendorf und Herrnhut." In *Geschichte des Pietismus: Der Pietismus im achtzehnten Jahrhundert*, edited by Martin Brecht and Klaus Deppermann, 5–106. Göttingen: Vandenhoeck and Ruprecht, 1995.
Middleton, John. "Home-Town: A study of an Urban Center in Southern Ghana." *Africa* 49 (1979) 246–57.
———. "One Hundred and Fifty Years of Christianity in a Ghanaian Town." *Africa* 53.3 (1983) 2–19.
Miller, Jon. "Class Collaboration for the Sake of Religion." *Journal for the Scientific Study of Religion* 29.1 (1990) 35–53.
———. *Missionary Zeal and Institutional Control: Organizational Contradictions in the Basel Mission on the Gold Coast, 1828–1917*. Studies in the History of Christian Missions. Grand Rapids: Eerdmans, 2003.
Millward, Peter N. "The Broad and Narrow Way." 2003. Online: http://pictureswithamessage.com/78/cat78.htm?931.
Mobley, Harris W. *The Ghanaian's Image of the Missionary: An Analysis of the Published Critiques of Christian Missionaries by Ghanaians 1897–1965*. Studies on Religion in Africa. Leiden: Brill, 1970.
Mohr, Joseph. "Tagebuch von Joseph Mohr." In *Ghana MSS Restkategorie*. Basel: Basel Mission Archive, 1881.
Monrad, Hans Christian. *Gemälde der Küste von Guinea und der Einwohner derselben, wie auch der dänischen Kolonien auf dieser Küste; entworfen während meines Aufenthaltes in Afrika in den Jahren 1805 bis 1809*. Translated by Hans Eiler Wolf. Neue Bibliothek der wichtigsten Reisebeschreibungen zur Erweiterung der Erd- und Völkerkunde. Weimar: Verlag des Landes-Industrie-Comptoirs, 1824. Original in Danish in 1822.
———. *Two Views from Christiansborg Castle. A Description of the Guinea Coast and its Inhabitants*. Translated by Selena Axelrod Winsnes. 2 vols. Accra, Ghana: Sub-Saharan, 2009.
Morgenthaler, Felix. "Die Verfassung der Basler Mission im 19. Jahrhundert." Basel: Basel Mission Archive, no date.
Müller, Karl. *200 Jahre Brüdermission*. 2 vols. Herrnhut: Missionsbuchhandlung, 1931.
Nagtglas, Cornelis Johannes Marius. *Een Woord aangaande de Vraag: "Wat moet Nederland doen met zijne Bezittingen ter Kuste van Guinea?"* Gravenhage: H. C. Susan, C.Hz, 1863.
Nida, Eugene A. *Customs and Cultures. Anthropology for Christian Missions*. 1st ed. New York: Harper, 1954.

Njoku, Chukwudi A. "The Missionary Factor in African Christianity, 1884–1914." In *African Christianity: An African Story*, edited by Ogbu U. Kalu, 191–223. Perspectives on Christianity. Trenton, NJ: Africa World, 2007.

O'Brien, Susan. "A Transatlantic Community of Saints: The Great Awakening and the First Evangelical Network, 1735–1755." *American Historical Review* 91.4 (1986) 811–32.

Oelschner, Walter. *Landung in Osu: Das Leben des Andreas Riis für Westafrika*. ABCteam. 2nd ed. Stuttgart: Evangelischer Missionsverlag im Christlichen Verlagshaus, 1983.

Olabimtan, Kehinde. "Hinderer, David." In *Dictionary of African Christian Biography* Center for Global Christianity and Mission, Boston University School of Theology, 2011. Online: http://www.dacb.org/stories/nigeria/hinderer_david.html.

Oliver, Roland Anthony. *The Missionary Factor in East Africa*. New York: Longmans, 1952.

Opoku, A. A. *Riis, the Builder*. Legon: Institute for African Studies, University of Ghana, 1978.

Ostertag, Albert. *Entstehungsgeschichte der evangelischen Missionsgesellshaft zu Basel: Mit kurzen Lebensumrissen der Väter und Begründer der Gesellschaft*. Basel: Verlag des Missionshauses, 1865.

Owusu-Ansah, David. *Historical Dictionary of Ghana*. Historical Dictionaries of Africa. 3rd ed. Lanham, MD: Scarecrow, 2005.

Parker, Irene. *Dissenting Academies in England: Their Rise and Progress and their Place Among the Educational Systems of the Country*. Cambridge: University Press, 1914.

Periodical Accounts Relating to the Missions of the Church of the United Brethren Established Among the Heathen. Vol. 16. London: Brethren's Society for the Furtherance of the Gospel, December 1841—March 1844.

Periodical Accounts Relating to the Missions of the Church of the United Brethren Established Among the Heathen. 34 vols. Vol. 14, London: Brethren's Society for the Furtherance of the Gospel, December 1836—March 1839.

Peterson, Brooks. *Cultural Intelligence: A Guide to Working with People from Other Cultures*. Yarmouth, ME: Intercultural, 2004.

Piggin, Stuart. *Making Evangelical Missionaries 1789–1858: The Social Background, Motives and Training of the British Protestant Missionaries to India*. Oxfordshire: Sutton Courtenay, 1984.

Pinnington, John Ernest. "Church Principles in the Early Years of the Church Missionary Society: The Problem of the 'German' Missionaries." *Journal of Theological Studies* 20.2 (1969) 523–32.

Porter, A. N. *Religion versus Empire? British Protestant Missionaries and Overseas Expansion, 1700–1914*. Manchester: Manchester University Press, 2004.

Potter, Sarah C. "The Social Origins and Recruitment of English Protestant Missionaries in the Nineteenth Century." PhD diss., University of London, 1974.

Prodolliet, Simone. *Wider die Schamlosigkeit und das Elend der heidnischen Weiber: die Basler Frauenmission und der Export des europäischen Frauenideals in die Kolonien*. Eckenstein-Studien. Zürich: Limmat, 1987.

Pugach, Sara. *Africa in Translation: A History of Colonial Linguistics in Germany and Beyond, 1814–1945*. Ann Arbor, MI: University of Michigan Press, 2012.

Quartey, Seth. *Missionary Practices on the Gold Coast, 1832–1895; Discourse, Gaze, and Gender in the Basel Mission in Pre-Colonial West Africa.* Youngstown, NY: Cambria, 2007.

Raith, Michael, and Christoph Peter Baumann. "Christentum in der Nordwestschweiz: Vom "frommen Basel" zur multireligiösen Stadt." Information Religion. Online: www.inforel.ch/i10e1.

Rambo, Lewis R. *Understanding Religious Conversion.* New Haven, CT: Yale University Press, 1993.

Rattray, R. S. *Ashanti.* Oxford: Clarendon, 1923.

———. *Ashanti Law and Constitution.* Oxford: Clarendon, 1929.

———. *Religion and Art in Ashanti.* Oxford: Clarendon, 1927.

Raupp, Werner. "August Karl Friedrich Freiherr von Schirnding." In *Biographisch-Bibliographisches Kirchenlexikon,* edited by Traugott Bautz, 227–29. Vol. 9. Hamm: Traugott Bautz, 1995.

———. *Christian Gottlob Barth: Studien zu Leben und Werk.* Quellen und Forschungen zur württembergischen Kirchengeschichte. Stuttgart: Calw, 1998.

———. "'Ein vergnügter Herrnhuter'—Johann Martin Mack, Württembergs erster evangelischer Missionar." *Blätter für Württembergische Kirchengeschichte* 92 (1992) 97–119.

———. *Mission in Quellentexten: Geschichte der Deutschen Evangelischen Mission von der Reformation bis zur Weltmissionskonferenz Edinburgh 1910.* Erlangen: Verlag der Evang.-Luth. Mission, 1990.

———. "'Vorwärts für das Reich Gottes, und nur vorwärts.' Der württembergische Pietismus und die heimatliche Missionsbewegung in der ersten Hälfte des 19. Jahrhunderts." In *Der ferne Nächste. Bilder der Mission—Mission der Bilder 1860–1920: Katalog zur Ausstellung im Landeskirchlichen Museum Ludwigsburg vom 25.5. bis 10.11.1996,* edited by Eberhard Gutekunst and Werner Unseld, 25–36. Ludwigsburg: Landeskirchliches Museum, 1996.

"Regeneration 1830–48." Federal Department of Foreign Affairs, General Secretariat. Online: http://www.swissworld.org/en/history.

Reindorf, Carl Christian. *History of the Gold Coast and Asante. Based on Traditions and Historical Facts Comprising a Period of More Than Three Centuries from About 1500 to 1860.* Accra, Ghana: Ghana Universities Press, 1966.

Rennstich, Karl. "Mission—Geschichte der protestantischen Mission in Deutschland." In *Der Pietismus im neunzehnten und zwanzigten Jahrhundert,* edited by Ulrich Gäbler, 308–19. Göttingen: Vandenhoeck and Ruprecht, 2000.

Robert, Dana L. "Shifting Southward: Global Christianity Since 1945." *International Bulletin of Missionary Research* 24.2 (2000) 50–58.

Rodney, Walter. *How Europe Underdeveloped Africa.* Washington, DC: Howard University Press, 1981.

Rømer, Ludvig Ferdinand. *A Reliable Account of the Coast of Guinea (1760).* Translated by Selena Axelrod Winsnes. Fontes Historiae Africanae. Oxford: Oxford University Press, 2000.

Russell, Jeffrey Burton. *Mephistopheles: The Devil in the Modern World.* Ithaca, NY: Cornell University Press, 1986.

———. *The Prince of Darkness: Radical Evil and the Power of Good in History.* Ithaca, NY: Cornell University Press, 1988.

Rüther, Kirsten. "Conversion to Christianity in African History before Colonial Modernity: Power, Intermediaries and Texts." *The Medieval History Journal* 12.2 (2009) 249–73.

Sanneh, Lamin O. *Disciples of All Nations: Pillars of World Christianity*. Oxford Studies in World Christianity. Oxford: Oxford University Press, 2008.

———. *Translating the Message: The Missionary Impact on Culture*. American Society of Missiology Series. Maryknoll, NY: Orbis, 1989.

———. *West African Christianity: The Religious Impact*. London: Hurst, 1983.

Sattler, Gary R., and August Hermann Francke. *God's Glory, Neighbor's Good: A Brief Introduction to the Life and Writings of August Hermann Francke*. Chicago: Covenant, 1982.

Scharfe, Martin. *Die Religion des Volkes: Kleine Kultur- und Sozialgeschichte des Pietismus*. Gütersloh: Gütersloher Verlagshaus Mohn, 1980.

Schattschneider, Allen W. *Through Five Hundred Years. A Popular History of the Moravian Church*. Rev. ed. Bethlehem, PA: Department of Publications and Communications, Moravian Church, 1990.

Schattschneider, David A. "William Carey, Modern Missions, and the Moravian Influence." *International Bulletin of Missionary Research* 22.1 (1998) 8–10.

Scheffbruch, Rolf. "Carl Köllner (3.3.1790—22.3.1853). Weinhändler und Menschenfreund, einer, der den Mut nicht verlor." In *Nicht aus eigener Kraft. Aus den Anfängen Korntals*, edited by Rolf Scheffbruch, 73–89. Korntal-Münchingen: Ludwig Hofacker Vereinigung, 2003.

Schick, Erich. *Vorboten und Bahnbrecher: Grundzüge der Evangelischen Missionsgeschichte bis zu den Anfängen der Basler Mission*. Basel: Basler Missionsbuchhandlung, 1943.

Schlatter, Wilhelm. *Geschichte der Basler Mission 1815-1915: Mit besonderer Berücksichtigung der ungedruckten Quellen*. 5 vols. Basel: Verlag der Missionsbuchhandlung, 1916.

———. *1. Band: Die Heimatgeschichte der Basler Mission. Geschichte der Basler Mission 1815-1915: Mit besonderer Berücksichtigung der ungedruckten Quellen*. 5 vols. Vol. 1, Basel: Verlag der Missionsbuchhandlung, 1916.

———. *3. Band: Die Geschichte der Basler Mission in Afrika. Geschichte der Basler Mission 1815-1915: Mit besonderer Berücksichtigung der ungedruckten Quellen*. 5 vols. Vol. 3, Basel: Verlag der Missionsbuchhandlung, 1916.

Schmalenberg, Gerhard. *Pietismus, Schule, Religionsunterricht: Die christliche Unterweisung im Spiegel der vom Pietismus bestimmten Schulordnungen des 18. Jahrhunderts*. Theologie und Wirklichkeit; Bd. 2. Frankfurt: M. P. Lang, 1974.

Schneider, Hans. *German Radical Pietism*. Translated by Gerald T. MacDonald. Revitalization: Explorations in World Christian Movements. Lanham, MD: Scarecrow, 2007.

Schnurr, Jan Carsten. *Weltreiche und Wahrheitszeugen: Geschichtsbilder der protestantischen Erweckungsbewegung in Deutschland, 1815-1848*. Göttingen: Vandenhoeck and Ruprecht, 2011.

Schoen, Jacob Friedrich. *Dictionary of the Hausa language. Part I Hausa-English. Part II. English-Hausa. With appendices of Hausa literature*. 9 vols. London: Church Missionary House, 1876.

———. *Grammar of the Mende language*. London: Society for Promoting Christian Knowledge, 1882.

———. *Grammatical Elements of the Ibo Language*. London: W. M. Watts, 1861.
Schön, James Frederick, and Samuel Crowther. *Journals of the Rev. James Frederick Schön and Mr. Samuel Crowther who, with the Sanction of Her Majesty's Government, accompanied the Expedition up the Niger, in 1841, in behalf of the Church Missionary Society*. London: Hatchard and Son, 1842.
Shantz, Douglas H. *An Introduction to German Pietism: Protestant Renewal at the Dawn of Modern Europe*. Young Center Books in Anabaptist and Pietist Studies. Baltimore, Maryland: Johns Hopkins University Press, 2013.
Shaw, Mark. *The Kingdom of God in Africa: A Short History of African Christianity*. BGC Monograph. Grand Rapids: Baker, 1996.
Shenk, Wilbert R. *Changing Frontiers of Mission*. Maryknoll, New York: Orbis, 1999.
———. "Coates, Dandeson." In *Biographical Dictionary of Christian Missions*, edited by Gerald H. Anderson, 139–40. Grand Rapids: Eerdmans, 1999.
———. *Enlarging the Story: Perspectives on Writing World Christian History*. Maryknoll, NY: Orbis, 2002.
———. "A Global Church Requires a Global History." *Conrad Grebel Review* 15.1 (1997) 3–18.
———. "The Missionary Encounter with Culture since the Seventeenth Century." In *Appropriate Christianity*, edited by Charles H. Kraft and Dean S. Gilliland, 35–48. Pasadena, CA: William Carey Library, 2005.
———. "The Origins and Evolution of the Three-Selfs in Relation to China." *International Bulletin of Missionary Research* 14.1 (1990) 28–35.
———. "Toward a Global Church History." *International Bulletin of Missionary Research* 20.2 (1996) 50–57.
Sill, Ulrike. *Encounters in Quest of Christian Womanhood: The Basel Mission in Pre- and Early Colonial Ghana*. Leiden: Brill, 2010.
Silzer, Sheryl Takagi. *Biblical Multicultural Teams: Applying Biblical Truth to Cultural Differences*. Pasadena, CA: William Carey International University Press, 2011.
Skreslet, Stanley H. *Comprehending Mission: The Questions, Methods, Themes, Problems, and Prospects of Missiology*. American Society of Missiology Series. Maryknoll, NY: Orbis, 2012.
———. "Impending Transformation: Mission Structures for a New Century." *International Bulletin of Missionary Research* 23.1 (1999) 2–6.
Smith, Joe William Ashley. *The Birth of Modern Education: The Contribution of the Dissenting Academies, 1660–1800*. London: Independent, 1954.
Smith, Noel. *The Presbyterian Church of Ghana, 1835–1960: A Younger Church in a Changing Society*. Accra, Ghana: Ghana Universities Press, 1966.
Spener, Philip Jacob. *Pia Desideria or Heartfelt Desire for a God-pleasing Reform of the true Evangelical Church, Together with Several Simple Christian Proposals Looking Towards this End*. Translated by Theodore G. Tappert. Edited by Theodore G. Tappert. Philadelphia, PA: Fortress, 1964.
Staehelin, Ernst. *Die Christentumsgesellschaft in der Zeit der Aufklärung und der beginnenden Erweckung: Texte aus Briefen, Protokollen und Publikationen*. Theologische Zeitschrift. Vol. 1. Basel: Friedrich Reinhardt, 1970.
———. *Die Christentumsgesellschaft in der Zeit von der Erweckung bis zur Gegenwart: Texte aus Briefen, Protokollen und Publikationen*. Theologische Zeitschrift. Vol. 2. Basel: Friedrich Reinhardt, 1974.

Stanley, Brian. *The Bible and the Flag: Protestant Missions and British Imperialism in the Nineteenth and Twentieth Centuries*. Leicester: Apollos, 1990.

Steiner, Paul. "Andreas Riis, der Begründer der Basler Mission auf der Goldküste. Zum Gedächtnis seines Geburtstages am 12. Januar 1804." *Evangelisches Missions-Magazin* 48 (1904) 1–8.

Stock, Eugene. *The History of the Church Missionary Society: Its Environment, its Men and its Work*. London: Church Missionary Society, 1899.

Stocks, H. "Die Mission in Dänemark." *Zeitschrift für Missionskunde und Religionswissenschaft* 22 (1907) 84–92.

Stoeffler, F. Ernest. *German Pietism During the Eighteenth Century*. Leiden: Brill, 1973.

———. *The Rise of Evangelical Pietism*. Leiden: Brill, 1965.

Stoll, Mike. "Die Bedeutung des Basler Daigs." April 15, 2011. Online: http://www.baselinsider.ch/enzyklopaedie/aus-der-geschichte/aus-der-geschichte/basler-daig.html.

Strauss, David Friedrich. *The Life of Jesus, Critically Examined*. Translated by George Eliot. Philadelphia, PA: Fortress, 1973.

Strom, Jonathan. "Problems and Promises of Pietism Research." *Church History* 71.3 (Sep 2002) 536–54.

Sundkler, Bengt. *Bantu Prophets in South Africa*. 2nd ed. New York: Oxford University Press, 1961.

Sundkler, Bengt, and Christopher Reed. *A History of the Church in Africa*. Cambridge: Cambridge University Press, 1998.

Tasie, G. O. M. *Christian Missionary Enterprise in the Niger Delta 1864–1918*. Studies on Religion in Africa. Leiden: Brill, 1978.

Taylor, John Vernon. *The Growth of the Church in Buganda: An Attempt at Understanding*. World Mission Studies. London: SCM, 1958.

Taylor, William David, ed. *Internationalizing Missionary Training: A Global Perspective*. Grand Rapids: Baker, 1991.

Terpstra, Chester. "David Bogue, D.D., 1750–1825: Pioneer and Missionary Educator." PhD diss., University of Edinburgh, 1959.

Trautwein, Joachim. *Religiosität und Sozialstruktur: Untersucht anhand der Entwicklung des württembergischen Pietismus*. Calwer Hefte zur Förderung biblischen Glaubens und christlichen Lebens. Stuttgart: Calw, 1972.

Tufuoh, I. "Relations Between Christian Missions, European Administrators, and Traders in the Gold Coast, 1828–74." In *Christianity in Tropical Africa: Studies Presented and Discussed at the Seventh International African Seminar, University of Ghana, April 1965*, edited by C. G. Baëta, 34–60. London: Oxford University Press, 1968.

Vassady, Bela. "The Role of the Black West Indian Missionary in West Africa, 1840–1890." PhD diss., Temple University, 1972.

Veblen, Thorstein. *The Instinct of Workmanship and the State of the Industrial Arts. With an Introduction by Joseph Dorfman*. Reprints of Economic Classics. New York: A. M. Kelley, 1914.

Vellenga, Dorothy D. "Racial and Ethnic Conflict in a Christian Missionary Community: Jamaican and Swiss-German Missionaries in the Basel Mission in the Gold Coast in the Mid-Nineteenth Century." In *Missionaries and Anthropologists, Part 2*, edited by Frank A. Salamone, 201–45. Williamsburg, VA: College of William and Mary, 1985.

Vogelsanger, Cornelia M.R. *Pietismus und Afrikanische Kultur an der Goldküste: Die Einstellung der Basler Mission zur Haussklaverei*. Zürich: A. Wohlgemuth Druck, 1977.

Vogt, Peter. "Die Mission der Herrnhuter Brüdergemeine und ihre Bedeutung für den Neubeginn der protestantischen Missionen am Ende des 18. Jahrhunderts." *Pietismus und Neuzeit* 35 (2009) 204–36.

———. "'Headless and Un-Erudite": Anti-Intellectual Tendencies in Zinzendorf's Approach to Education." In *Self, Community, World: Moravian Education in a Transatlantic World*, edited by Heikki Lempa and Paul M. Peucker, 107–26. Studies in Eighteenth-Century America and the Atlantic World. Bethlehem, PA: Lehigh University Press, 2010.

Wais, Erin. "Trained Incapacity: Thorstein Veblen and Kenneth Burke." *K.B. Journal* 2.1 (2005). Online: http://www.kbjournal.org/node/103.

Wallmann, Johannes. *Der Pietismus*. Die Kirche in ihrer Geschichte: Ein Handbuch. Edited by Bernd Moeller. Vol. 4/O1. Göttingen: Vandenhoeck and Ruprecht, 1990.

———. "Fehlstart." *Pietismus und Neuzeit* 20 (1994) 218–35.

———. "Was ist Pietismus?". *Pietismus und Neuzeit* 20 (1994) 11–27.

Walls, Andrew F. " A Christian Experiment: The Early Sierra Leone Colony." In *The Mission of the Church and the Propagation of the Faith. Papers Read at the Seventh Summer Meeting and the Eighth Winter Meeting of the Ecclesiastical History Society*, edited by G. J. Cuming, 101–29. Cambridge: Cambridge University Press, 1970.

———. *The Cross-Cultural Process in Christian History: Studies in the Transmission and Appropriation of Faith*. Maryknoll, NY: Orbis, 2002.

———. "The Eighteenth Century Protestant Missionary Awakening in its European Context." In *Christian Missions and the Enlightenment*, edited by Brian Stanley, 22–44. Studies in the History of Christian Missions. Grand Rapids: Eerdmans, 2001.

———. "Eusebius Tries Again: Reconceiving the Study of Christian History." *International Bulletin of Missionary Research* 24.3 (2000) 105–11.

———. *The Missionary Movement in Christian History: Studies in the Transmission of Faith*. Maryknoll, New York: Orbis, 1996.

———. "Missionary Vocation and the Ministry. The First Generation." In *The Missionary Movement in Christian History. Studies in the Transmission of Faith*, edited by Andrew F. Walls, 160–72. Maryknoll, NY: Orbis, 1996.

Walvin, James. *Black Ivory: A History of British Slavery*. Washington, DC: Howard University Press, 1994.

Ward, W. E. F. *A History of Ghana*. 2nd ed. London: Allen and Unwin, 1958.

Ward, W. Reginald. *The Protestant Evangelical Awakening*. Cambridge: Cambridge University Press, 1992.

Warren, Max. *Social History and Christian Mission*. London: SCM, 1967.

Weigelt, Horst. "Der Pietismus im Übergang vom 18. zum 19. Jahrhundert." In *Der Pietismus im achtzehnten Jahrhundert*, edited by Martin Brecht and Klaus Deppermann. Geschichte des Pietismus. Im Auftrag der Historischen Kommission zur Erforschung des Pietismus, 700–54. Göttingen: Vandenhoeck and Ruprecht, 1995.

———. "Die Diasporaarbeit der Herrnhuter Brüdergemeine und die Wirksamkeit der Deutschen Christentumsgesellschaft im 19. Jahrhundert." In *Geschichte des*

Pietismus: Der Pietismus im neunzehnten und zwanzigsten Jahrhundert, edited by Ulrich Gäbler, 112–49. Göttingen: Vandenhoeck and Ruprecht, 2000.

Weimer, Hermann. *Concise History of Education from Solon to Pestalozzi*. Translated by I. Langnas. New York: Philosophical Library, 1962.

Weimer, Hermann, and Juliane Jacobi. *Geschichte der Pädagogik*. Sammlung Göschen. 19th rev. ed. Berlin: Walter de Gruyter, 1991.

Welbourn, Frederick Burkewood. *East African Rebels: A Study of Some Independent Churches*. World Mission Studies. London: SCM, 1961.

Wellenreuther, Hermann. "Pietismus und Mission. Vom 17. bis zum Begin des 20. Jahrhunderts." In *Geschichte des Pietismus: Glaubenswelt und Lebenswelten*, edited by Hartmut Lehmann and Ruth Albrecht, 166–93. Göttingen: Vandenhoeck and Ruprecht, 2004.

Wenger, Etienne. *Communities of Practice: Learning, Meaning, and Identity*. Learning in Doing. Cambridge: Cambridge University Press, 1998.

———. "Introduction to Communities of Practice: A Brief Overview of the Concept and Its Uses." Online: http://wenger-trayner.com/introduction-to-communities-of-practice/.

Wenger, Etienne, Richard McDermott, and William M. Snyder. *A Guide to Managing Knowledge: Cultivating Communities of Practice*. Boston: Harvard Business School Press, 2002.

Wernle, Paul. *Der schweizerische Protestantismus im XVIII. Jahrhundert. Erster Band: Das reformierte Staatskirchentum und seine Ausläufer (Pietismus und vernünftige Orthodoxie)*. Tübingen: Mohr, 1923.

Whiteman, Darrell L. "Integral Training for Cross-Cultural Mission." *Missiology* 36.1 (2008) 5–16.

Wilks, Ivor. *Akwamu 1640–1750: A Study of the Rise and Fall of a West African Empire*. Trondheim Studies in History. Trondheim: Dept. of History, Norwegian University of Science and Technology, 2001.

———. *Asante in the Nineteenth Century: The Structure and Evolution of a Political Order*. African Studies. London: Cambridge University Press, 1975.

———. "The Rise of the Akwamu Empire 1650–1710." *Transactions of the Historical Society of Ghana* 3.2 (1957) 25–62.

Williams, Cecil Peter. "'Not Quite Gentlemen': An Examination of 'Middling Class' Protestant Missionaries from Britain, c. 1850–1900." *The Journal of Ecclesiastical History* 31.3 (1980) 301–15.

———. "The Recruitment and Training of Overseas Missionaries in England Between 1850 and 1900 With Special Reference to the Records of the Church Missionary Society, the Wesleyan Methodist Missionary Society, the London Missionary Society, and the China Inland Mission." M.A. diss., University of Bristol, 1976.

Winsnes, Selena Axelrod. "An Eye-Witness, Hearsay, Hands-On Report from the Gold Coast: Ludewig F. Romer's Tilforladelig Efterretning om Kysten Guinea." In *Encounter Images in the Meetings between Africa and Europe, edited by Mai Palmberg*, edited by Mai Palmberg, 37–53. Uppsala: Nordiska Afrikainstitutet, 2001.

Winter, Ralph D. "The Two Structures of God's Redemptive Mission." 2006. Online: http://www.pcms-usa.org/articles/.

Winterbottom, Thomas Masterman. *An Account of the Native Africans in the Neighbourhood of Sierra Leone; to Which is Added, an Account of the Present State of Medicine Among Them.* 2 vols. London: C. Whittingham, 1803.

———. *Thomas Winterbottom's Nachrichten von der Sierra-Leona-Kueste und ihren Bewohnern, nebst einer Schilderung der dortigen brittischen Kolonie; aus dem Englischen.* Translated by Theophil Friedrich Ehrmann. Bibliothek der neuesten und wichtigsten Reisebeschreibungen zur Erweiterung der Erdkunde. Weimar: Verlag des Landes-Industrie-Comptoirs, 1805.

Wurm, Paul. "Anfänge der Basler Mission auf der Goldküste." *Evangelisches Missions-Magazin* (1874) 129–50, 195–208, 238–50, 256–70, 305–30.

Zantop, Susanne. *Colonial Fantasies: Conquest, Family, and Nation in Precolonial Germany, 1770–1870.* Post-Contemporary Interventions. Durham, NC: Duke University Press, 1997.

Zimmerling, Peter. *Pioniere der Mission im älteren Pietismus.* Theologie und Dienst. Giessen: Brunnen, 1985.

Zimmermann, Johannes. "Die Lichtseiten des Negerlebens." *Missions-Magazin* (1853) 81–90.

www.ingramcontent.com/pod-product-compliance
Lightning Source LLC
Chambersburg PA
CBHW071144300426
44113CB00009B/1078